#True Love and A Cookie Box

OrangeBooks Publication

Smriti Nagar, Bhilai, Chhattisgarh - 490020

Website: www.orangebooks.in

© Copyright, 2022, Author

All rights reserved. No part of this book may be reproduced, stored in a retrieval system, or transmitted, in any form by any means, electronic, mechanical, magnetic, optical, chemical, manual, photocopying, recording or otherwise, without the prior written consent of its writer.

First Edition, 2022

ISBN: 978-93-5621-199-5

Cover design by Himanshu B.

The opinions/ contents expressed in this book are solely of the authors and do not represent the opinions/ standings/ thoughts of OrangeBooks or the Editors .

#True Love and A Cookie Box

Aashima Arora

OrangeBooks Publication
www.orangebooks.in

#Truelove Trilogy By Aashima Arora
Book I- #TrueLove and A Cookie Box
Book II- #TrueLove and A Change of Heart
Book III- #TrueLove and No one Else

Dedicated to my Family and Friends, who showed faith in me and encouraged me to turn my dream into reality.

'#True Love and a Cookie Box' by the author Aashima Arora, is a book that one should judge by the cover. The cover promises romance and the story delivers it. The story is of a Bollywood script writer Avinash Shastri. He is rich, temperamental, and controversial. He meets Sanam, a penniless orphan, and they are forced to marry.

The romance is set in a one room apartment of a middle class suburb in Mumbai. The premise is the cliche 'contract marriage' but the treatment is fresh and engaging. As it progresses, the story unveils a lot of layers. There are some steamy, some cute, some naughty and some downright hilarious scenes, especially when the bad guys are being punished.

The novelty factor of this story is the cookie box that contains love letters for Avinash written by Sanam. Each letter contains a slice of life of the lead couple.

The characters are well-etched and the writing is lucid. Although the plot and characters are gripping, it is a tad too long than your average romance. However, if toe-curling romance is what you are looking for, then it is the perfect book for the upcoming holiday season.

'#True Love and a Cookie Box' is the first book in the #TrueLove Trilogy by the author Aashima Arora.

-Times of India(Gurgaon) 9th October 2022

PROLOGUE

The Wedding Night

It was almost one at night. Sanam had been waiting for her newly wedded husband to come home. Her heart was beating with concern. She did not know what to do. Just then, a key clicked in the main door of their one room apartment. Avinash barged in drunk and with a girl in his arms. Their mouths were locked in a deep and passionate kiss. His hands were exploring every curve of the girl's body, much to Sanam's distress. Sanam stepped back in shock, breaking a glass tumbler in the process. The sharp sound caused everyone in the room to pause.

"Shit!" Avinash muttered under his breath.

"Who is she?" the girl asked.

"My wife…I had forgotten about her!" he said.

"Get out...come when I call you!" he screamed at Sanam.

She quickly made way to the small balcony and shut the door behind her, leaving them to get on with their business. She shut her ears to shut off the loud moans that tore the air. As she sat there crying, she cursed her luck for never ever being worthy enough to be loved.

CHAPTER-1
FANTASY

One month before the wedding….
"Hayo rabba…marja moye! Bas ghar walon ne Bullet dila diya hai toh sab par keechad girana hai! (What the hell! These spoiled brats…the family spoils them by getting them expensive motorcycles and these brats go around driving through the mud puddles!)" Sanam muttered to herself as a bike rider rode through a puddle of muddy water with absolutely no respect for the pedestrians passing by.

Much to her surprise, the bike rider had entered her housing Society.

"I must teach brats like him a lesson!" Sanam thought of going there and giving him an earful. The guy was parking as she reached the building compound. She stood right behind his bike and waited for him to dismount.

Sanam was ready to verbally pounce on him when he took off his helmet and sent her into a shock.

"How can I forget this arresting face?" Sanam asked herself as she gasped in surprise. She had seen him for the first time in the third year of her college two years back.

Two years before the wedding….
Sophia College, where she studied, had a theatre on the premises of the college. The manager was an oldie who had taken a liking to Sanam. Sanam absolutely adored theatre. She loved to perform and watch; however, her financial condition did not allow her to buy tickets for the same. The theatre managers have a privilege-a few seats which are always kept for them even if the theatre is full. The manager would always ask her to attend great plays if he had a spare ticket.

Sanam still remembered how excited she had been. It was her favourite actor Naseerudaullah and Ramona Shah's play on Ismat Chugtai. A very women centric play. Sanam had taken extra pains to get ready for the evening. She was a twenty-year-old beautiful petite girl. Her raven-coloured hair was thick and long. She had a round face, sharp nose, big almond eyes and a million-dollar smile. Sanam had long harboured the dreams of being able to perform on stage but had given it up long back. Yet she was excited to derive vicarious pleasure watching such big artists from so close.

The play had already started when Sanam felt someone come and sit next to her. She was so engrossed in watching the play that she did not even bother looking at her neighbour. It was an emotional play and Sanam was not able to control herself. Tears fell down her eyes silently as she watched, feeling the pain of the character. Suddenly, she felt a gentle touch on her arm. Sanam turned around, she saw a handsome, chiselled face offering her a handkerchief. She took it, their fingers touching briefly. This seemingly innocuous action sent shivers down her spine.

In the interval, she saw him clearly. Standing at almost six feet, two inches the stranger had a muscular build. He had an angular face, regal nose, and a sharp jawline. Her eyes followed his fingers that tried to set his rebellious thick and wavy hair. Dressed in a plain blue kurta with undone buttons and acid-washed jeans, he fit in easily with the artistic vibe of the place.

One thing Sanam realised quickly was that he was tall and handsome…yes…but this guy had an aura that turned heads. In a matter of a few moments, she was mesmerised by him.

Unfortunately, he had not returned after the interval. She had hoped to see him again, but that hope was dashed as the play ended and actors took a bow. Sanam knew she would not see him again. However, the evening had not gone in-vain; she still had a sweet souvenir of the evening-his handkerchief.

Sanam was wrong. She saw him again the next day.

"Sana, we are late. There is a guest lecturer today for the writing class - someone from the industry," spoke her friend urging Sanam to catch the train that had just touched the platform.

An hour later they reached college, they could feel something different. The whole place was abuzz with excitement. A lot of girls had gathered outside their department. The girls were gushing and swooning over someone. Sanam could not understand the hullabaloo.

"What? They are swooning over the guest speaker. Yaar he is just a writer, not a film hero!" Sanam told her friend in exasperation. However, this had no impact on her friend, who had already been consumed by the over excited girls.

"Shudena! [Mad cows!]" she chuckled in her native tongue, as she gently pushed the girls of the other departments to enter the office. As a CR (class representative) she had to take care of all the guest faculty members. The guest was talking to the Head of the Department, Professor Aditi Sharma.

In two minutes flat, Sanam bit her tongue. The guest was an incredibly handsome man. He ticked all the boxes of what girls would want- at least in looks.

"Hayo Rabba!" Sanam exclaimed to herself. It was the same stranger she had met yesterday. Today he had worn a long white kurta with dark blue acid washed denims. The stranger looked back at her, openly checking her out.

"Sanam, get all the girls in the seminar room and take this pen drive. Keep it ready for us. We shall join you in a few minutes," Professor Aditi dismissed her curtly and got back to gushing over the guest.

"It seems the professor too, just like all the girls, has been swept away by the 'Love Tsunami' brought by the guest," Sanam chuckled to herself, but she was soon brought back to her senses when the Professor called her again.

"Going!" Sanam said and left.

"Why did I have to wear the same dress? What will he think?" Sanam cringed and mentally cursed herself for wearing the same dress as yesterday.

"He is such a celebrity; he won't even remember you!" her mind asserted.

"Oh!" her heart felt the prick.

"Babe chill! Your yellow chikan patiala salwar kameez is old but still classy...accessories are artistic too!" her mind pacified. She had worn small jhumkas that she had bought yesterday in the local train. Her yellow glass bangles jingled as she moved. A small yellow bindi adorned her forehead. Essentially, she had repeated yesterday's look.

"Dear students, it is a privilege to have today a guest who needs no introduction. He is a leading Bollywood scriptwriter working for the leading commercial filmmakers. The writer of seven consecutive 100Cr movies. The only son of the legendary writer Alok Shastri and the heir of the 'Shastri Empire'. Put your hands together for Avinash Shastri. He is…" Professor Aditi continued in her booming voice. She eulogised him till he got embarrassed and asked her to stop. Sanam who was sitting in the front row let out a chuckle earning a half smile from him.

"Avinash Shastri-He looks so cute when he smiles! With his share of good looks, why has he never tried modelling or acting? Or was he?" Sanam couldn't stop thinking about him.

"Fred Allen once said 'A human being is nothing but a story with skin around it'…" the guest started speaking.

"He speaks so much sense!" Sanam marvelled to herself once Avinash started speaking. Avinash shared his journey as a scriptwriter. He talked to them about the initial stages of a script and how to develop the plot and gave an in-class assignment.

"You need to write a short story weaving all these words in it," he said, writing some random words on the board.

"Oh!" sighed the whole class collectively. No one wanted to do an assignment even if the handsome Avinash Shastri gave it.

"We will try," said Sanam a little loudly, while looking at her classmates making a small joke.

"Trying does not count Ms… Ms?" Avinash said sharply, demonstrating the fact that he was going to be an arduous task master.

"Sanam Kaur Bedi," Sanam blushed as it felt that the speaker was asking her something else as well. She also earned a dirty look from Professor Aditi, which curbed all the enthusiasm Sanam had for the day.

"You are overthinking…concentrate on writing the story," Sanam chided herself.

In the next half an hour, the stories were written and submitted.

"All right ladies...it was lovely meeting you all," Avinash said addressing the entire class.

"Sir...are you on Instagram or Twitter?" one girl asked, and the entire class burst into laughter.

Avinash smiled too. "No... not yet on Social Media but I will try to be there in future," he quipped.

"Trying doesn't count!" Sanam blurted before she could stop herself, making Avinash chuckle.

The entire class broke into laughter again at her quick comeback.

The two-hour lecture ended with Sanam falling in love with 'The Avinash Shastri'. Not only she, other forty -five girls had fallen for him too-just like the rest of the female population of India, whoever had the good fortune to meet him.

An hour later, Sanam still could not stop herself from smiling as she ran through each and every moment of the interaction with the stranger.

She did not realise what a fetching picture she made as she waited for her bus at the Breach Candy bus stop. She had some work in the library and had missed returning home with her friends.

Suddenly, a Royal Enfield Thunderbird stopped right in front of her pulling her out of her fantasy land.

"Oye cute Punjaban!" the rider called her out as he took off his helmet to reveal himself.

"Shastri ji aap?" Sanam blushed and blurted out not realising how funny it sounded from her mouth.

Avinash broke into a huge grin.

"Where are you going? May I drop you?" he said with chivalry.

"No...it's ok. I will take the bus," she said, suddenly shy.

"It's your wish, but it is a great day for a ride and fortunately I don't bite!" he said softly, a smile playing on his lips.

"Umm...Ok," Sanam succumbed to his charm and told him the address.

She sat putting both her legs one way, a style which modesty demanded but was extremely uncomfortable.

"Cross your legs and sit," Avinash advised.

She sat as instructed but was confused where to hold.

"Well, you will have to hold me," he said boldly, making her blush.

"I swear he is enjoying my discomfort!" She thought to herself.

Sanam shifted closer to him and put her hand on his shoulder. The first few minutes were awkward; however, as the time passed, she started enjoying the ride. The breeze was playing with her dupatta and hair. She took her dupatta and rolled it in her bag. Over the course of the journey, she had put her hand around him and rested her head on his back, listening to his heartbeat.

"What are you thinking?" Avinash asked.

"I am wondering if I will fail the 'Film Appreciation' course!" Sanam spoke as always without thinking.

"As in?" Avinash asked intrigued.

"I mean if Professor Aditi gets to know that I took a lift from you...she will probably butcher me in her subject," Sanam said innocently, making Avinash shake with laughter.

"Aww Baby!" He said and patted her hand which was holding him around his chest.

Sanam felt an awareness rushing through her body. It seemed just a pat but felt like a very intimate gesture to her. Her body erupted in goosebumps in an instant. She felt frozen in the moment. She did not want to let this moment go. There was no chance of her meeting Avinash again.

"So, this is the sexual attraction that the novels talk about. This is the peace one would get hearing your lover's heartbeat!" Sanam thought to herself.

"Lover! Lover?" Sanam was shocked at her own flight of fantasy. She pictured Avinash kissing her lips, tracing the path of her jawline to her throat, cupping her breasts...The image sent shivers in her body pebbling her nipples with desire. Sanam was shocked at the hot, molten desire she felt for a man for the first time in her life. Her body automatically shivered at her thoughts. A shiver which he felt because she was stuck to his back.

"Baby, are you ok?" Avinash held her hand to ask out of concern, watching her in the rear-view mirror. Their eyes met in the rear-view mirror. She blushed, closed her eyes, and hugged him a tad tighter. He did not take his hand away. He kept holding hers. Sanam sighed as she rested her head and drifted in a small nap, feeling his heartbeat next to hers.

She had asked him to drop her near her society. They said their goodbyes. Sanam did not want him to leave, but every fantasy had to end. Avinash left as she stood rooted to the spot trying to take in his retreating figure as much as possible. After all, she was not going to meet him again.

"Or so I thought!" Sanam sighed and was brought back from her fantasy world by the horn of another bike that had entered the building. She realised that Avinash had moved on and she was still standing in the building compound beside Avinash Shastri's bike.

CHAPTER- 2
PASSION AND DESIRE

One week before the wedding….
"What in the hell do you think you are doing?" Sanam's Aunty (maternal) yelled at her as she entered the kitchen. Sanam had been daydreaming yet again and had burnt the masala for the vegetables. She had been goofing up since the time she had met Avinash in her society compound three weeks back. She was rewarded with a smack across her cheek by her aunt.

Sanam had been ten when her parents had passed away in a car accident. Her Uncle (mother's brother) and his wife brought her to Mumbai to stay with them after selling all that her parents owned. She was then subjected to mental and verbal abuse by her aunt and uncle and cousins…Bunty and Amrita twenty-four and nineteen, respectively. Her only support in the house and source of joy was the fifteen years old Deepu, who loved her as a sister.

Since the time she had come to this house, Sanam had been relegated to sleeping on the balcony. The other members of the family took the rooms. Contrary to common perception of the neighbours, she loved sleeping on the balcony. After locking the door, it turned into her own private space. The balcony had now given her another advantage of keeping an eye on Avinash. He had changed so much. He now had a full-fledged beard. Avinash regularly came home drunk. She had seen him getting down from some or the other car, completely sloshed. Most of the time, the watchman had to take him to his flat.

Sanam was now a Mass Media Post graduate diploma holder and worked in a Women's magazine as a junior features writer. The pay was not great, but she loved her profile and enjoyed the work. She had made a few inquiries about Avinash with the film beat editor. It was common knowledge that his career had gone downhill in the last two years with many of his movies proving to be a dud at the box office. She had watched a few of the movies he had written. They were not great, but they were good. Avinash wrote extensively for the likes of Charan Dohar. These were primarily opulent romantic dramas and commercial potboilers with huge and expensive sets where women in chiffon saree danced to romantic tunes in the snow-clad mountains of Switzerland.

"When you are so intelligent, why do you write ridiculous commercial movies?" She often asked out the imaginary Shastri ji in her dreams but would never get an answer. All she would get was a pat on her hand in her dreams.

She also got to know that there was a strong rumour that Avinash's girlfriend of three years Super Model Nitika had broken up with him. He had also been accused of sexually harassing a female colleague that led to him being disowned by his billionaire writer father. Sanam did not believe any of the allegations.

The complexities of his life really saddened her. The problems had taken a toll on him. She could not find the positive person she had met two years back. She found a troubled soul who was struggling to fight the battles of life. Sanam started doing Japji Sahib in his name. She believed that reciting the entire Japji daily balanced all aspects of oneself and activated one's soul.

Every morning after her household chores before leaving for office, she would go into his wing, on the pretext of meeting this elderly couple, the Bajwas. Mrs. Bajwa always had a soft spot for her. As she would pass the third floor for the fourth, she would tenderly touch the doorknob...trying to feel his touch on the door, reciting the final verses of Japji Sahib for him, hoping that God will give him strength to endure the harsh realities of life.

It was just another morning when she stepped into his wing. She was busy reciting the verses when she extended her hand for the knob with her eyes closed as always when a hand came out and pulled her into the flat. She gasped loudly and found herself pinned against the wall staring into the face that had taken away every ounce of peace she had ever known.

"Avinash!" escaped from her lips.

He was just gazing into her eyes with anger. It was unnerving her. His one hand kept her pinned to the wall while the other lifted her chin to make him look into his eyes.

"Hello, cute Punjaban!" he said in a heavy voice.

"Ooh!" Sanam exhaled as she realised that he still remembered her.

"Your 'payals' (anklets) wake me up every single morning...I often wonder why you faintly knock my door every day and then leave in a hurry. Will I get an answer today?" he asked in a menacing tone.

Contrary to the fear Sanam was supposed to feel, Avinash's contact and proximity sent delicious shivers in her body. Her eyes started drooping in anticipation. Her entire skin broke into goosebumps. It was getting difficult to breathe. Her chest was heaving, and her legs were fast turning into jelly.

Avinash touched her forehead with his index finger and traced the path from her forehead to the bridge of her nose ...finally stopping at her lips.

"Tell me sohni Punjaban...are you still as innocent as you were two years back. Have your luscious lips been kissed till now?" he asked in a sultry voice that belied his desire for her.

Sanam stood there frozen.

"Tell me...have you ever been kissed? Speak up!" he asked in anger, grabbing her cheeks and squishing them together.

"No!" Sanam blurted out. She was going through a gamut of emotions. She was overwhelmed with desire yet scared at the same time-a heady mix.

"You should get what you came for! So that you can also brag to your friends that the great Avinash Shastri has kissed you! That Avinash Shastri desired your flesh and could not control himself," he declared as he came nearer and claimed her lips with his.

The kiss started as a punishment but quickly turned into a passionate one. Initially, Sanam was taken aback by the force of the kiss but recovered fast and to her own surprise kissed him back.

His hold on her softened and her hands found his neck. Her fingers snaked into his thick wavy hair caressing his neck all the way up, igniting him more. His hands cupped her bottom and brought her closer. The heat of their bodies made a clear declaration of their mutual need.

He headed for her nape and claimed it as his own. He bit her there again and again, getting more and more excited by her moans. His fingers searched for the front hooks of her kurta and his lips claimed the ample supple bosom she had to offer. His hands cupped her perky mounds, and she moaned his name louder.

"Yeh kya ho raha hai? [What the hell is happening here?]" someone shouted, bringing them both back to reality. Sanam gasped, brought her hands up to cover herself and hid behind Avinash.

In the throes of passion, they had not bolted the door and now nosy neighbours had witnessed the entire scene.

As soon as she could, Sanam ran out of his flat. She was shocked, she did not know what had just happened there. She made her way to the Gurudwara, completely in a daze. She sat there for the entire day.

As the darkness approached, she realised that she would have to eventually head home. Her instinct was asking her to run away from all of this, there was no one of her own there in that home...but she chose to not to be a coward. Her heart was in her mouth when she entered the building. She saw everyone looking at her in a weird way. Sanam understood what had happened. In a span of a few hours, she had become a whore.

CHAPTER- 3
BOUND IN HOLY MATRIMONY

The incessant knocks at the door rudely woke up Avinash. He opened the door to find an emotionally distraught teen at his doorstep.

"You have brought disgrace to my sister! They are marrying her off to an old man..." the teen broke down.

Avinash just stood there frozen.

"You have done this to her...She tried killing herself because of what you did! I will never forgive you," he was sobbing uncontrollably.

Avinash was lost for words. Although he had a massive hangover, he understood it was about Sanam. Her brother was correct, it was his doing.

"Listen, you are her brother? Come on...get up! Take me where it is happening? Get up!" he told him.

It was an old temple on the outskirts of the city. Sanam lay there helpless. She had been drugged so that she would be co-operative. She had already made a failed attempt to kill herself by slashing her wrist. In exchange for a hefty amount, her Uncle and Aunty were getting her married to a twice married man with kids. The podgy groom sat there waiting for the Panditji to start performing the pooja. He was continuously leering at his soon-to-be bride imagining the deflowering in which he will soon indulge. Sanam, although in a state of delirium, felt nauseous at the sight of the said person.

A pall of gloom descended on her. This was the end. Nothing would get better after this. Her ever-positive soul was about to break down. For the nth time she asked Waheguru what she had done to deserve this fate. Just as she had lost all hope, she heard a commotion around her.

Avinash entered the temple and kicked the havan kund that had been lit with fire. His kick was so forceful that people looked back in shock.

"You cannot do this! To whom are you getting her married? I will call the police!" Avinash screamed at her relatives.

Avinash was furious. His hungover eyes were murderous. He was shaking with anger. He charged at the so-called groom, caught him by his shirt and punched him twice.

Seeing his anger and aggression, her Uncle and Aunty were fast losing their nerve. A huge crowd had gathered around the mandir to watch the high-octane drama that was unfolding there.

Avinash then moved towards Sanam's Uncle and slapped him across his face.

"This is our daughter; we will marry her off with whomever we want. Who are you to object?" Aunty cried trying to save her husband from Avinash.

Avinash was still holding the Uncle, but the Aunty had his attention now.

"Tum ne isko kahin ka nahi choda...ab aisi ladki se kaun shaadi karega? Tum karoge? [You have sullied her name, who will marry her now? Will you?]" Sanam's Aunty somehow gathered her wits and almost challenged Avinash.

The venomous words found their mark. Avinash felt as if someone had poured icy water on him. He looked at Sanam who was sitting listlessly still in the corner. She had been beaten black and blue. Her arms had bruises that had developed into a shade of deep rude blue, telling him that she had been subjected to this treatment for days. He saw a bandage on her wrist, half hiding a deep gash that was meant to have ended her life.

"I will marry her...Panditji, shlok padhiye! [Panditji, start the rituals!]" Avinash let go of the uncle and told the petrified pandit.

They were married according to the Hindu religion. The pandit also gave them the certificate of wedding as was the legal compulsion. It read 'Bound in holy matrimony- Sanam Kaur Bedi and Avinash Shastri'.

A few hours later, Sanam woke up on an unknown bed, completely disoriented. She looked around. It seemed familiar. She got up and peeped out of the balcony-it was Avinash's home. Memories came rushing back. She was still in the wedding finery.

Avinash had married her. It was surreal.

Sanam dozed off again. She woke up around midnight, Avinash still had not returned. She was now on the edge.

It was almost one at night. Sanam had been waiting for her newly wedded husband to come home. Her heart was beating with concern. She did not know what to do. Just then, a key clicked in the main door of their one room apartment. Avinash barged in drunk and with a girl in his arms. Their mouths were locked in a deep and passionate kiss. His hands were exploring every curve of the girl's body, much to Sanam's distress. Sanam stepped back in shock, breaking a glass tumbler in the process. The sharp sound caused everyone in the room to pause.

"Shit!" Avinash muttered under his breath.

"Who is she?" the girl asked.

"My wife...I had forgotten about her!" he said.

"Get out...come when I call you," he screamed at Sanam.

She quickly made way to the small balcony and shut the door behind her, leaving them to get on with their business. She shut her ears to shut off the loud moans that tore the air. As she sat there crying, she cursed her luck for never ever being worthy enough to be loved.

Sanam woke up on the bed. Over the course of the night, she had somehow shifted from the balcony to the bed.

She saw Avinash sitting across in the chair deep in thought. She sat up, looking around for her dupatta.

"Freshen up...We need to talk," Avinash said, throwing her dupatta at her.

She went to the washroom and could not recognise the girl who stared back at her. She looked a pale shadow of herself.

A while later, she sat there sipping hot tea that Avinash had brewed for them.

"I cannot stay married to you...I am in love with Nitika. We have had a few misunderstandings. It is just a matter of time; she will come around. You should look for another accommodation!" Avinash said in a monotone.

"Whatever you did…You did not need to, but you still did! Thank you!" Sanam said, keeping the teacup down. She got up and walked towards the main door.

"What the fuck are you doing?" Avinash screamed, scaring the life out of Sanam.

"Leaving…you just asked me to leave," Sanam said softly.

"You are such a…*Gadhi* [addle-brained person!]! Where will you go now? I meant you will have to leave in a few days. When you decide what to do next. Kya tum sach main akal se paidal ho? [Are you really that dumb?]" he gave her a good scolding.

Sanam hung her head low and went back and sat in the chair.

"Do you have any relatives in this city?" Avinash asked her.

"No…no one at all," she said, and Avinash huffed.

"Just give me a few days, I will leave," she assured Avinash.

"Ok…you go and change now," Avinash told her.

"I…I don't have clothes!" she said nervously.

Avinash stood still for a moment.

"Come along with me," he said, pulling her along.

In five minutes, they were at her Uncle-Aunty house. Sanam stood there damn scared. As her older cousin Bunty opened the door, Avinash pushed him aside and asked her to take whatever was hers.

"Sanam take your stuff," Avinash told her. Sanam looked around in fear. Her Uncle and Aunty came running at the door.

"Sanam, don't get scared…your husband is here! Take whatever is yours…no one will touch you," Avinash declared, throwing an open challenge to all her relatives.

"How dare you? You are a complete *Gunda* [hooligan]!" Bunty said, rolling his sleeves showing Avinash a punch and trying to play the superhero.

The very next instant, Bunty had been lifted off a few inches off the ground and then put back at Sanam's request.

Avinash twisted Bunty's one arm and asked, "Let me see who will stop me?" calling out the entire family.

Bunty was now openly crying in pain.

"Deepu, go help her!" Avinash ordered Deepu.

Sanam with Deepu's help packed her few clothes and possessions. While leaving, she stopped at her Aunty.

"These earrings are my mother's!" Sanam told Avinash.

Avinash twisted Bunty's arm again…Bunty yelped, and Aunty gave the earrings to her.

Sanam then went to her Uncle.

"My debit card?" she extended her hand in front of her Uncle who quickly took it out of his wallet and gave it to her.

"If any one of you even breathes the same air as Sanam I will make you repent!" Avinash threatened the entire family.

Sanam now had a bounce in her step. She felt avenged and had a huge smile on her face.

"Don't be so happy! You are not my wife…neither am I your husband…this was acting to teach them a lesson," Avinash said in a tone laced with acid as they entered his home.

The smile that had been playing on Sanam's lips died a sudden death.

CHAPTER- 4

MISTRESS OF THE HOUSE

Avinash had left after dropping her home. At least she could breathe now. Every moment with Avinash since morning had felt like a rigour. She wanted to disappear somewhere. His smouldering looks burnt her skin. She had sensed a deep resentment in him...towards herself. The thought saddened her. She did not want to be a cause for anyone's sadness.

"Enough mopping...get up and do something," she told herself.

She looked around the house. It looked as if it had not been cleaned since ages. She got to work.

In the coming hours, she cleaned, dusted, changed the bed sheet, washed his dirty clothes, and ironed the clean ones.

She finally went into the kitchen and looked around. She decided to make a simple meal for him. Sanam had never begrudged work, had it been at her Uncle's place or the sewa at gurudwara. But doing all these simple chores for Avinash were giving her a lot of pleasure.

"Will he like my cooking? I wish I knew something fancy!" She spoke aloud to herself.

Finally, she was happy with her hard work. The house looked as if it had gotten a makeover. She was smiling.

"What the fu*k is this? Why did you touch my things? Who allowed you to do this? Is this your home?" Avinash turned around and questioned Sanam when he arrived in the evening. Every word from his mouth spilled venom.

"Dinner..." she spoke softly. She had been standing there with a plate of food in front of him while he had been ranting about her indiscretions.

He looked at her with anger and resentment and threw the food plate against the wall.

"You are neither the mistress of this house nor my fu*king wife....do you understand?" he screamed.

Sanam stood there shocked.

"Or do you want to become my wife? I know all these days you have been eyeing me with lust, trying to entice me with your innocence and charm. Let me tell you Ms. Sanam Kaur Bedi, although I find you very appealing, Avinash Shastri has now stopped trusting women like you who lust after me for whatever reasons. However, now that we are here...let me pay you for the hard work you have done to get into my good books," Avinash said in a slow and menacing tone.

He pinned Sanam against the wall, took off her dupatta and covered her lips with his own. While his one hand kept her pinned, the other hand went to the back and pulled the zip of her kurta down, giving him unfettered access to her abundant cleavage. His mouth left her lips to travel to her breasts. Avinash suckled and bit her breasts, extracting loud moans from her. Her skin had broken into goosebumps.

He let her go for a minute to take off his T-shirt, exposing his well-toned rippling torso to Sanam. Sanam was left dumbstruck by the beauty of his finely built body. He was correct. She did lust after him, but who would not? He was so dishy; any warm-blooded girl would desire him.

Avinash laughed at her discomfort as he put his hand in her denim pants touching the very core of her being. As his deft finger started to touch there, molten desire scorched her body. She held onto him because her legs were fast turning to jelly. Her moans were enticing him more. The huge bulge in his pants clearly conveyed his desire.

"I knew it...you too are like those other middle-class girls...my body is what you want. This is what you will get," Avinash said with sarcasm.

The words were like a slap across her cheeks. She came back to reality. A lonely tear escaped her eye as a reaction to Avinash's insult. Suddenly, she felt herself going unresponsive. Tears were fast flowing now from her eyes.

Avinash realised it too. Although she did not stop him, his passionate kisses couldn't get her to return those.

"What the fu*king hell!" Avinash released her and went for a cold shower.

Sanam quickly adjusted her clothes, cleaned up the mess and retired to the balcony. Her heart was heavy, and tears just wouldn't stop coming.

Next morning, she got up early, got ready and left the flat. Avinash was still sleeping.

She headed towards the gurdwara. She spent an hour just sitting there...she prayed...she needed sanity and strength. Her Waheguru had never disappointed her before, it did not today.

Sanam went to her office from there. She had gone AWOL on them in the last week. She met the editor Mrs. Banerjee and convinced her to let her keep her job. Mrs. Banerjee was a gruelling task master and an astute judge of character. She had witnessed Sanam's struggles in the last two years since the time she had joined them as an intern. Although Sanam had never shared her life story, the bruises on her body were enough to tell Mrs. Banerjee the hardships she had been facing in her personal life.

As Sanam headed home, she was happy to have her job and friends back after so many days. As she reached Avinash's flat, she felt her heart beat faster. When she opened the flat with the spare key he had handed her over yesterday, she breathed relief. He was not there. She quickly went to the bathroom and changed. She had eaten a vada-pav and cup of cutting chai at a street stall to avoid entering his kitchen. This was all she could afford. She had only a few hundred rupees with her, and a few thousand in her account as she had discovered today. Her Uncle had withdrawn every single penny that he could. She had to manage the remaining few days of the month with the meagre amount she had now. On top of it, Sanam had to arrange for her accommodation.

She retired to the balcony and drifted into sleep. The next two days, she followed the same routine. It was the fourth day when she entered the flat a lot later than the previous days.

She had stopped at the Gurudwara to have food. She knew 'langar' was for the needy, but she had been hungry to her bones. Vada-Pav was not appealing to her on the fourth day after having it for three days straight.

"I must make an extra donation to the gurdwara in the coming month," she told herself.

Sanam was happy after having a full meal. She was humming a tune when she entered Avinash's flat.

"Where have you been?" asked Avinash, startling her.

Sanam had not expected him to be there. Every day he had been returning late.

"You have a boyfriend?" he asked.

"No... I went to the gurdwara," she said.

"Why do you have to go to gurudwara every day so late?" he asked her sharply.

She kept quiet. She would prefer dying rather than telling him the real reason.

"Where were you the whole day?" he asked.

"I have a job," she replied.

"I feel responsible for you...that's the only reason I asked you," Avinash said.

"Voh...I wanted to tell you something," Sanam said. "A friend of mine has arranged for a place for me at a local PG. It will be available in a week. I will shift then," she spoke and left for the balcony.

CHAPTER- 5
TURMOIL

It was Sunday again. One full week of her OMG-did-it -really-happen wedding. Sanam laughed loudly at her own witty self. Sitting, pondering, and mopping had never been her style. She loved to embrace whatever life dished out at her. In another week, she would be out of here. She had taken the change in her life positively. She had gained freedom from her Uncle and Aunty. She had married the most eligible bachelor of Bollywood...married? Sanam laughed to herself.

"Chalo...acha hai...whatever it is. Imagine if I had gotten married to that old leacher!" Sanam told herself. The thought itself sent shivers down her body.

It was almost seven in the morning when she escaped from his flat and headed for the gurdwara. It was a Sunday and there was no office. She quickly stopped at the tapri for her regular cutting tea.

There was this awkwardness between Avinash and her. She had not tried to resolve the issue at all. It did not matter. In a few days, she will be gone from his life forever. This thought was not a happy one, but life is life, she placated herself.

The entire day she spent in the gurdwara doing sewa. She slept there for an hour in the afternoon with other older women. Gurdwaras and temples were a sanctuary for people like her who had absolutely nothing much happening in their lives or to say 'everything bad happening in their lives'.

"But never mind, God helps those who help themselves," she told herself. She closed her eyes as she was damn tired. At one point of time, she imagined she had seen Avinash looking at her from afar.

"Stop being delusional Sanam!" she told herself and went off to sleep.

She reached his flat late that night. She was exhausted and thankfully Avinash was not there. She took a breath of relief and proceeded towards the balcony. She was still thinking about the bare-torso Avinash she had been lucky enough to see till the sleep claimed her.

Sanam woke up the next day in the morning in the bed, with a heavy arm weighing her down. For a minute she freaked out...then turned and saw Avinash was sleeping next to her and it was his arm around her waist. She tried to get out, but he rolled her back. Somehow, she got out and got ready. The arm had given her a moment of comfort but then she had remembered that she was nothing to him, and that saddened her for a few minutes, but not for long.

Avinash was in her thoughts the full day. She kept on relishing that comfort she felt in the morning.

She was happy, so decided to splurge on herself...she ate a masala dosa and felt very guilty later on.

She was in her own world-humming and talking to herself. Avinash was not at home again. She changed quickly and made her way to the balcony. It was a full moon night. Sanam wondered if she would ever get a chance to look at the simple wonders of this world with someone special.

A sharp ache rose in her heart....and words came out from her mouth in the form of a folk song...

Roi naa...je yaad meri aayi ve...

She let out her tears and felt lighter after that. Her eyes were almost drooping when the balcony door opened.

Sanam woke up with a start and looked around for her dupatta.

"You should not sleep on the balcony, I have no place to smoke," he said harshly.

Sanam got up and picked up her mat and her bag which functioned as a pillow and proceeded towards the kitchen.

"I keep going to the kitchen at night," Avinash told her.

"You tell me then?" Sanam asked with a lot of hesitation. Sanam had not been able to talk to him since the night they had almost made love. His opinion about her mattered to her a lot. She was hurt but also understood where he was coming from. Still, she had no intention of conversing with him and the very thought of talking to him put her into a panic mode.

"Stay in this room…do you have an issue with the AC?" he asked.

"Nope…" Sanam shrugged and put her mat down, as far from his bed as possible.

"It is a small Room…I will trample on you when I get up at night. You should sleep on the bed…it is big enough for the both of us," he said with a matter-of-fact tone.

Sanam gasped but recovered quickly.

"I am not used to sleeping on a mattress," she stuck her ground and laid down the mat.

"Sanam, you really test my patience…till the time you are here, you will listen to me!" Avinash warned her, picked her up, and dropped her on the bed.

Not one to take it lying down, Sanam got up from the bed. She knew she was playing with fire but somehow, she wanted to rebel.

"Why am I behaving like this?" She asked herself. She did not know…or did she?

"My life, my decision. It is an inconvenience for a few days. I am leaving this Saturday…I will sleep down," she asserted.

"You talk a lot!" Avinash pulled her towards him by the waist and took her lips. This kiss was gentler than what they had shared before. He sucked at her lips, tasting the sweetness of her mouth. His hands were all over her back. Just as she welcomed the warmth of his lips on hers…it was gone.

"You will sleep on the bed, and it is not negotiable!" Avinash said while looking at her well kissed face.

Sanam nodded. She was suddenly very tired. She gently lay down on the bed and gave up. Over the night both invariably snuggled into each other, having a perfect night's sleep.

She woke up to his arm across her again. This time she smiled and tried to get out of hold again.

"Running away again?" asked a sleepy Avinash, bringing a blush to her cheeks.

"Ji…I need to go to the office!" she said nervously.

"Liar! No office opens so early. It is six now…sleep now," he pulled her back to the bed.

"Ji, I need to go to the Gurdwara and perform 'seva' [community service]!" she said softly.

"Why don't you start charity from home?!" he said.

"Ji …tell me,"She asked, confused.

"A cup of tea please!" he asked her.

She got up, made one cup of tea for him, and handed it over to him.

"What about you?" he asked.

"I don't want anything," she said as she picked up her clothes and headed towards the washroom.

Her mind was in an emotional turmoil. She understood the angry Avinash, but she could not understand why he was making it so difficult for her by being nice. His every action rubbed salt in her wounds. She wrapped both her fingers around the cutting chai glass seeking comfort from the warmth of the hot tea struggling to contain her tears.

CHAPTER- 6

COCOON

The next few days, Sanam stayed clear of Avinash. She would make breakfast for him but escape quickly without having anything. The Christmas cheer all around made her aware of how alone she was in the big, bad world. Soon, it was the NewYear's Eve and Sanam was feeling incredibly low again. She just wanted to rest it out. She left the office and chose not to go to the gurdwara in the evening and came directly to the flat.

"I think I am coming down with something," she told herself and went directly to the bed. After the whole tantrum that night, she has started sleeping on the bed. She must have slept for an hour when the doorbell rang.

Sanam got up and opened the door. A tall, hefty man wearing a weird hair wig was standing with a thick envelope.

"You? Here?" Sanam asked in shock. She had seen him a few times before. He used to hang around with a few notorious boys from their neighbourhood. He had even publicly proposed to her once, which Sanam had rejected unceremoniously.

"Ahem…I am Saurabh Chhabra…Advocate Mehta has sent some papers for Mr. Avinash," he said nervously. He was clearly taken aback but was still checking out Sanam from head to toe. His gaze was mentally undressing her, the gaze repulsed her.

"He is not at home and not expected soon. Give me the papers," she almost snatched the envelope from him and tried to shut the door in his face.

"Why are you always so rude? You think I do not deserve respect?" Saurabh stuck his foot inside the door and asked menacingly.

"What the hell? Get out of here! I will call my husband!" Sanam cried aloud when Saurabh barged in and shut the door.

Saurabh kept a hand on her mouth.

"I know what kind of a wife you are and what kind of a husband he is! You had rejected me because I am poor and now you have trapped Shastri, giving him all the benefits. Do you know how much humiliation I have suffered because of you? You will pay today!" he said, sending shivers down her body. Tears were rolling down her eyes.

Saurabh had one hand on her mouth and the other one had twisted her arm capturing her. Her petite body was unable to fight him.

He threw her on the bed and climbed on top of her. His hands were all over her, tearing clothes. She was fast losing consciousness when she felt the dead weight lift from her.

Sanam got up to see that Avinash had barged in and lifted Saurabh off her. Avinash banged his head on the wall.

"Haramzade...how dare you touch her? How dare you touch my wife? I will kill you!" he was punching him continuously.

"Aviiiiinash!" Sanam called out as she fainted.

Avinash left Saurabh to catch her. Seeing an opportunity to flee, Saurabh ran from there.

A few minutes later, when Sanam gained consciousness, she was in Avinash's arms. He was gently caressing her. As she recollected the incident, she started shivering like a leaf.

"It is ok Baby! Nothing will happen to you, I am here!" he said gently.

Sanam got up and dashed to the washroom. She stood under the shower and rubbed herself till she could take no more. She could hear Avinash screaming on the phone but registered nothing. Somehow, she got out of her clothes and wrapped herself in a towel hanging on the rack. She came out dripping and shivering. All she wanted to do was to lie down.

Avinash quickly got another towel and started drying her hair. He got his T-shirt and made her wear it. The T-shirt reached till her thighs. She was oblivious to whatever was happening. As the shock of what had happened finally started sinking in, tears started flowing and she collapsed on the bed.

He held her as she cried her heart out. Finally, when he felt she was completely spent, he went and fetched a hot towel to clean her face. A hot cup of ginger tea followed next. She eventually dozed off in his arms.

Late at night, the doorbell rang, waking up and scaring Sanam. She whined as she felt Avinash leaving her, she held him closer.

"Baby let me go, I will be right back," he said softly.

She had been wrapped in a heavenly cocoon of warmth that she did not want to leave. But she recovered soon after spotting Avinash with a big box of pizza. A small smile spread over her face. However, she lay back again, she did not have any energy to stay up.

"Let's eat pizza," Avinash said gently.

"No, I don't feel like eating anything," she almost whispered.

"Either we both eat, or I throw this away," Avinash spoke harshly now.

Summoning up courage from somewhere, Sanam got up and accepted a slice from him.

Sanam bit into the pizza and it kicked her hunger. In no time, she went for another one. Those two slices of pizza were fast working their magic on her. She giggled when a kernel of corn got stuck in his full-grown beard, making him smile.

"He looks so handsome while smiling, but his 'high and mighty' attitude!" Sanam was busy conversing with herself, not realising that she had said the whole sentence aloud.

"You said something?" he spoke with a dry tone.

"Hayo rabba...Did I?" Sanam could barely hide her embarrassment. She got up to wash her hands and realised that she was only in his T-shirt-no inner wear or bottoms- and this is how she had slept in his arms. Awareness shot up in her body tightening her nipples into beads. A slight blush crept up her cheeks, but she realised surprisingly that she was not embarrassed. She tied her hair in a bun and bent down to get herself in more than a skimpy garment before Avinash alleged a seduction attempt by her.

She giggled at the thought of seducing Avinash. And then a warm feeling...like her core was melting, took over.

She turned around to find Avinash lounging in the balcony smoking a cigarette not aware of the storm raging in her heart.

She came out a few minutes later, appropriately clothed...well almost. She was feeling adventurous. She had not worn her bra; she just wanted something to happen. It was worth a try. Her twin mounds had been in captivity for many days and nights. It was time they tasted some freedom. She giggled again, stealing a glance at Avinash, who was lost in his own thoughts. She dozed off faster than she had thought. In her sleep, she felt warmth take her over again. She hugged the bundle of warmth and delicious smelling cologne. She felt heady and a sigh escaped her lips when her delicate legs entwined with a certain someone's stronger ones. The comfort and the warmth she felt that night, she had not felt before in her life.

CHAPTER- 7
SIZZLE AND DRIZZLE

"Running away again?" Avinash repeated as he had done previously, but Sanam felt the tone was a wee bit warmer than before.

Sanam had woken up at the same time as she did every morning-body clock.

"Ji office," she said softly.

"No office is open on the first January and you are not well...don't go," he said, yawning and pulling her back in the bed.

"Our office is open, and they will cut my salary if I don't go," she said.

"I will drop you, there is still time. Now for heaven's sake woman-sleep!" he took her in his arms and slept.

Sanam's skin broke into goosebumps at his touch. He had his arm around her, and she had her head on his chest listening to his heartbeat. Her soft breasts were digging into his chest, she was feeling ecstatic and a little high. He had already gone off to sleep so she had an amazing chance to observe him. His features were classic. She had seen him clean shaven and had taken her breath away then. He looked even more fascinating now with a beard. He had been the object of her dreams for the last two years.

"Dreams do come true!" she chuckled thinking to herself.

She knew he had been hurt...deeply...her heart felt for him. Remembering how he had taken care of her yesterday, she knew that underneath all the anger and resentment, he was the same 'good' guy whom she had fallen in love with ...fallen in love or infatuation? She did not have the answer-only time will tell. She dozed off snuggling closer to him.

"Sanam...wake up...you will get late," Avinash woke her up.

"Oh Shit!" Sanam woke up with a huge gasp.

"It is ok! We still have time," he said, offering her a hot cup of tea, which she accepted gratefully.

"Who brews better ginger tea? That road stall tapriwale or I?" he chuckled, moving to the balcony for his morning smoke.

Sanam burnt her tongue and choked. "He knows it...he fucking knows it!" she thought mortified. Her cheeks had gone red, and she bit her lower lip in embarrassment.

She quickly finished her tea and ran for the bath. Officially, it was supposed to be a holiday as it was the first day of the new year. However, there was a tradition of conducting a small pooja in the office that day, so things were going to be a little easy. All the women had decided to wear a saree. Sanam too was pretty excited. The fact that she owned only one saree and had worn it last year as well, did not dampen her excitement even one bit.

She came to the kitchen after the bath to wrap the saree.

"Ahh...the blouse has gotten too loose," Sanam sighed. She removed the blouse and took out a needle and thread to sew it.

"Fuck cockroach! Oh God!" Sanam screamed as she spotted her arch nemesis.

Avinash had just stepped under the shower when he heard Sanam scream. He quickly grabbed a towel and went out. The next moment he opened the kitchen door with a huge thud. Avinash stood there dripping wet with only a towel around his torso.

He saw Sanam standing clad in a black demi-cup bra showing off a massive amount of her tantalising cleavage and a petticoat exposing her entire midriff particularly the belly button.

Awareness spread in both their bodies...although Avinash's was more obvious, observed Sanam with a chuckle and bit her lower lip to calm herself down.

"Amma cockroach!" Sanam started panicking again as one crept on her petticoat.

Avinash took a newspaper lying around, lifted the cockroach on it and quickly threw it out of the kitchen window.

Sanam was still openly staring at him, she could not take her eyes off his sinewy arms and well-built chest. Desire was kicking off in her core.

Avinash looked at her and went out of the kitchen, closing the door and leaving Sanam crestfallen.

"I am not exciting enough for him," she told herself ruefully, trying not to cry. She was unable to take his paradoxical behaviour.

Just then the kitchen door opened again.

"Are you sure Sanam you want me to be your first?" Avinash was standing there with an unmistakable desire flecking in his eyes. His body betraying the calm in his voice.

Sanam nodded and closed her eyes in the anticipation of ecstasy. She was not disappointed. Avinash's lips settled like petals on hers...he was taking it slow. His hands were all across her body. Sanam too was exploring him. She had her fingers in his thick wavy hair and was now moaning in pleasure.

"Aviiiiiiinash," Sanam moaned in pleasure, extracting a groan from him.

The kisses were now passionate, putting both on fire. Avinash left her mouth for the enticing cleavage that was beautifully presented in the demi-cup bra. He was biting her creamy skin leaving a trail of his claim all across. He lifted her in his arms and took her to the bed. Even though the AC was on, they were both on fire.

Avinash's towel had long left him...his stiff manhood teased her to no end. Her bra and petticoat soon joined the towel on the floor. He was alternatively sucking and kneading her breasts, sending her into a pleasure comma.

"Please Aviiiiiiinash," she rasped, begging him to make proper love to her; that she was scared at the same time was very visible.

"It's ok baby...I will try not to hurt you," he said, kissing her.

She cried when he entered her...but the pain soon changed into pleasure and Avinash and Sanam climaxed together amidst their love cries.

"Don't go to the office today...call them and tell them you are not well!" he ordered.

"Okay," she said, glad that she could be with him the full day. They lay in each other's arms after making love. Her body felt sore in places she did not know existed. She did not want it to end. She had only one day more with him and then she would shift to the Paying Guest accommodation. The thought saddened her to no end.

She borrowed his phone and called up the office informing that she will not be able to come in.

They just lay there silently hugging each other.

She took a quick bath and washed the bed sheet that had borne the evidence of her innocence. Later, she moved towards the balcony and tried to soak in the sun. There was no view from the balcony as such- just the main road with the regular hustle bustle. However, across the hustle bustle there was this BEST bus depot which at night had all the red buses lined up. This view wasn't visible to her from her Uncle's flat but from the last few days she had been oddly enough enjoying it from this balcony.

But today, Sanam was feeling like a bird suddenly out of the cage.

Soon Avinash too joined her there. The silence they shared was not lonesome...it was beautiful.

"Are you going to feed me something?" he almost ordered in a dry tone.

"Attitude...sorry bhi nahin bolta!" Sanam thought with a smile as she headed to the kitchen, tying her hair in a knot.

In some time, she came out with a plate of poha and a cup of tea.

"Do you survive on air?" he asked.

Sanam smiled and got one for herself too.

"I do not like eating alone! Remember that!" he said.

Sanam did not feel like telling him that the day after tomorrow he will be all alone. She just smiled and let it be. She was not going to let anything upset her today.

"What would you prefer for lunch?" she asked once they were done with breakfast.

"You!" he said and pulled her onto his lap. Her heartbeat quickened in anticipation. He cupped her breasts eagerly looking at her face for reaction. She moaned in pleasure and her pleasure aroused him more. He scooped her and took her to bed. He pulled down the zip of the kurta and took it off in an instant, surprising her. Her legging went down next. As he reached for her bra, she stopped him. She sat on her hunches and cupped his face slowly kissing his face starting with his forehead, then eyes and nibbled at his earlobes extracting a sigh from him. The bulge he had in his pants was growing painful by every passing minute. He attempted to disrobe himself, but she refused to let him do so. She took off her last stitch of clothing and straddled his denim covered manhood arousing him more.

"You are such a minx!" he said, biting her cheeks. Ultimately, unable to bear more torture, he broke free, put her down and claimed her as his own...again.

Lunch was forgotten for more rewarding pleasures. It was already five pm when they woke up.

"Feel like going for a ride?" he asked.

Sanam nodded happily.

She opted for a black sleeveless suit while he was in his signature long white kurta and jeans. They went to the Bandra Bandstand. It was a beach front with a promenade i.e., a long walkway. They sat there on the edge holding hands, watching the beautiful hues that were colouring the sky and the angry waves rocking the shore.

They dined at the Beach Cafe where she tasted 'sizzler' for the first time.

Avinash spoke in monosyllables and did not speak at all for most of the time. But Sanam was comfortable with the silence. It was just soothing for the soul. She had not felt happier than she did today.

As they were riding back, Sanam felt this intense desire to touch him...up and close. It was drizzling a little and she was in the mood! She put her hand inside his kurta. His body jerked with the unexpected touch. Her index finger traced the outline of his abs, leaving a trail of fire. This time Avinash could not stop himself from responding. He took her hand out and caught it in his hand while managing the bike with the other. For Sanam the time had suddenly lapsed...to her it seemed like the ride two years back.

Avinash opened the door and moved aside to let Sanam in. As she came in, Avinash locked the door and groped her from behind.

"Aviiiiiinash...." she moaned.

"Baby...You do not know what you made me go through on the bike. You should be punished for it!" he said huskily, biting on her earlobe.

He opened the zip of her kameez and put her against the wall, with her back facing him. Avinash put her hair aside and started plundering the arc of her shoulders with feather kisses.

"Baby ...you are so fuc*ing sexy!" he groaned while kneading her supple bosom.

"Aviiiiiiinash," she moaned too.

In a few minutes, they were naked, and the room was full of moans.

"One minute...hold on…. third time is allowed?" Sanam asked Avinash while he was wearing protection.

"What the fuck are you saying woman?" Avinash was baffled by her query.

"Nahin matlab...third time in a day is allowed? Can we do 'it' so many times?" she asked innocently, sending Shastriji into a fit of laughter.

He rolled on the bed clutching his stomach rocking with laughter.

"You are real...right?" he touched her cheeks while laughing even harder.

By this time Sanam knew she had goofed up. She bit her lower lip and looked innocently at him.

"Oh God...baby!" he said as his lips captured hers to do everything that their hearts allowed.

A little while later, Avinash got up to light a smoke... Sanam got up to look out for a T-shirt to wear for the night. As she was wearing that particular piece of clothing when her eyes went to the parcel of papers that came in yesterday. It was now open...a partial word caught her attention. She took out the papers and read: DIVORCE.

CHAPTER-8

SOMETHING IS BETTER THAN NOTHING!

DIVORCE...it was a stamp paper with a proper government seal. Sanam could not understand at all...her mind went blank.

"We need to talk," Avinash said, dousing his half-smoked cigarette in the ashtray. He gestured to her to sit.

"Sanam, there are two sets...one is official divorce papers and the other is an MOU (memorandum of understanding). You should read these papers," Avinash said.

"Why don't you tell me?" Sanam said quietly, every word came out of her throat with a lot of difficulty.

"Our marriage is legally binding. My lawyer registered it the day after we got married. He is going to file a divorce petition the day after tomorrow. The court is most likely to recommend a six months 'cooling off' period. Generally, when a couple files for a divorce, immediately after getting married, the court suggests a 'cooling off' period to give them time to rethink their decision. My lawyer will act on it again after the end of six months of our marriage. The divorce will get finalised after almost one year...court procedures usually take time," Avinash said and waited for her reaction. He got none.

"Sanam, I came here to write a film script and to get rid of the writer's block that has been troubling me for the past one and a half years. I did not intend to marry you or anyone for that matter, but whatever happened with you happened because of me. You are my legally wedded wife; I am not denying that. I will never deny that! We need to stay together for at least six months. I have something planned in New York in a few months, so everything will fit in perfectly. The rent for this flat has been paid for another ten months. You can stay here till then" Avinash spoke, turning towards Sanam to gauge her reaction.

"Anything else?" she asked blankly.

"The MOU says that you will be paid rupees one Crore at the end of the year once the divorce comes through. If we have physical relations…when we have physical relations, you cannot get pregnant. If you do become pregnant, I will not be liable for paternity. I will not give the child my name and you cannot ask me for its upkeep. There is also a non-disclosure agreement. You cannot talk about your personal life to anyone or ask about mine. You cannot disclose our agreement to anyone," he spoke in a matter-of-fact tone.

Sanam was still numb, trying to soak in information. She went into the washroom, changed into her own clothes, and lay down on the bed, trying to fall asleep.

"It was a memorable day. Good night," she said in a monotonous tone.

As the right side of the bed dipped, she knew he had joined her. Involuntarily, her body turned towards him and instinctively he too turned towards her, pulling her into his embrace. She instantly felt safe and secure.

"Please say something!" Avinash said softly.

"I am at a loss for words now! All I can understand is that you have made an awfully expensive deal. All you had to do was to ask me, I would have signed the papers right away. Anyways, I am not selling myself!" Sanam said. She was trying to keep her emotions in check but was failing miserably.

"Sanam listen up…I am never going to repeat this! A lot has happened in my life in the last two years and everything bad. I have been cheated upon and betrayed by those claimed to have loved me. I was in love with Nitika…maybe I still am… we broke off six months back…since then it has been a downhill. My personal life…professional life…everything went for a toss. Then, I came here and met you again. You know this thing between us…this physical attraction…has always been there. I could never understand why two years back I came all the way to the suburbs just to spend some time with you. Or why every day I used to wait for your payals to announce that you are so near me? Why am I spellbound by every action of yours? It is physical Sanam! It is the undeniable chemistry that pulls us towards each other, but it's not love. I am incapable of loving anyone now. It is a wasted feeling. Do not fall in love with me Sanam...please I beg you! I had not planned to seduce you...it happened. I have not cheated on you in our marriage. I had sent that girl back after I remembered that you were there. I have only money to offer to you. I am very rich, but at the same time insanely poor. I am not offering you money to buy your body...quite the contrary, I am offering you myself for the coming months. Ghate ka sauda hoon main Sanam tumhara sirf nuksan hoga...par mujhe tumhari zaroorat hai [I am a loss-making proposition, but I need you]," Avinash spoke in his signature matter-of-the -fact tone.

His words were a soothing balm for her bleeding soul. Avinash was asking for her help...he needed her, just as she needed him. Her hands of their own accord went up to cup his face, pulling his lips to her own and sealing the agreement.

"Having you for a few months is better than not having you at all, Avinash. Seeing you in person every day for a few precious months is better than staring at your picture. Feeling you inside me for a few nights is definitely more than pining for you in the silent nights for my hollow self-respect. It is better to have loved and lost than never have loved at all. I do not think I can fight the love I have for you Avinash! Come to think of it, I will sell myself without batting an eyelid if I can have you for a while in my life. Something is better than nothing!" Sanam thought of all this but did not tell Avinash.

"He would freak out if he heard all this," Sanam thought and giggled.

Avinash was staring at her, seeking an answer. He was perplexed that a few moments back this incredibly beautiful face was in despair and now it cracked into a giggle. He heaved a great sigh of relief when she touched his lips with hers assuring him that she will not leave him alone with himself. She was an angel. Sleep took them over before either of them could think more. They lay there fitting into each other like a glove in a hand, their bodies and destinies entwined.

Sanam woke up again at the same time the next day, but that day she stayed in bed in his embrace. She loved the warmth his body gave her. She waited for her mind to reject the decision her heart had made last night; it did not happen. She felt happy. Now that she thought about it, she did not feel like leaving her husband behind...her husband! This was the first time she had addressed him as her husband. Well, he had addressed her as his wife-twice in two days. She relished the feeling of warmth that enveloped her heart. She kissed him on his cheeks and nuzzled up against his neck extracting a whimper from him.

"Go to sleep, woman!" he said.

Sanam giggled and tried getting out of his grip, but he did not let her go.

"Please ...I need to go!" she whispered in his ears.

He pulled her over himself in such a manner that she was lying completely horizontally on him.

"Early in the morning?" Sanam asked, shocked.

"Huh?" Avinash took a few moments to realise she was referring to 'the morning wood.' He smiled in response, showing his perfect teeth.

"You know Sun is not the only thing that rises in the morning!" he said sheepishly, earning a guffaw from her.

"Ganda baccha [Bad boy!]," she said gently, patting his cheeks and biting her lower lip as she sat up on him.

He looked into her eyes seeking confirmation of the sudden desire. Desire was written all over her face. In a moment, she was underneath him. Avinash dipped his head and claimed her luscious lips earning a moan from her. He went on to lick, suckle and bite every inch of her creamy skin. Their lovemaking was urgent and passionate...they climaxed together satisfying more than the body's hunger for each other.

Sanam quickly took a shower and went into the kitchen to make breakfast and lunch for her husband. They had their morning tea and breakfast together.

"Haye Rabba!" Sanam exclaimed loudly, almost giving Avinash a mini cardiac arrest.

"What happened?" Avinash asked her from the balcony.

She stood in front of the mirror and stared at herself in despair. Numerous love bites had appeared after their full night and morning love making sessions.

"How will I explain these?" Sanam whined.

Avinash came and laughed at her distress.

"So what? You are married!" he said, holding her tightly at the waist.

"I haven't told anyone about our wedding in the office!" she said softly.

"Why? Do you have a boyfriend in the office?" Avinash said in a dangerous tone.

"Arre…how could I explain that I am looking for a PG accommodation if I have a husband!" she justified.

"You can tell them now that you belong to me!" Avinash said tersely, pulling her closer.

Sanam stared back at the uncharacteristic display of emotion.

"But remember that my name is Avinash Kumar not Shastri!" he said abruptly.

"Ok," Sanam was taken aback by the sudden change in tone and loss of warmth.

"Now what do I do with these?" she looked at him in anger pointing towards the love bites.

"Acha now it is 'what do I do with these?' Last night it was 'Oh Aviiiiiiinash'… 'yes baby'," he mimicked her, extracting a deep gurgle from her.

He pinned her to the wall with a gaze so intense that quickened her heartbeats in an instant.

"Tell everyone that you are married now! And do not you dare go to that tapri wala…hai leches at you!" he said, warning her.

"Well…you also lech at me!" she winked at him.

"I am your husband…it's my right!" he said, sprinkling her throat with feather kisses.

"Hide this with a dupatta…Chalo, I will drop you today," he said, giving her a deep parting kiss that left her wanting more.

"Will you be able to warm up the food?" she asked him while locking the door.

"Ji maate [madam]! Shall we?" he said sarcastically, earning a big smile from her.

She took out a black bead necklace from her bag-her mangalsutra. She had bought this in the local train the other day for fifty bucks but did not have the courage to wear it till now. She was happy now. She wondered if this was not love then what was it? This had to be love! Nothing else made sense.

He dropped her in the office building, where a few of her colleagues witnessed Avinash kissing Sanam's hand before riding away. Even with his head covered in a helmet, it was easy to make out that he was the owner of a perfect physique.

The women pounced on her asking her who he was. The fact that she was wearing a mangalsutra added fuel to fire. 'Sanam ki shadi' became the hottest gossip of the office.

She had cooked a backup story citing him to be her boyfriend of a few months and a quick wedding at the mandir not giving out any particulars. She even ordered a 'samosa-jalebi' party for everyone. The day could not have gone slower. She just wanted to run back to him. Before she could ring the bell, the door opened, and Avinash pulled her in.

"How did you know?" she asked, astonished at his accurate timing.

"Your payals!" he said, kissing her full on her lips.

CHAPTER- 9
ROUTINE

The next day Avinash dropped her at the office in the morning. She bid him bye and was about to run when he caught her wrist and pulled her back. He took off the helmet to kiss her palm all the while watching her intently. A deep blush crept on her cheeks. She bit her lower lip and then almost ran to her office.

"Oh, my my! Your husband is so handsome! Tu toh chuppi rustom nikli! [You turned out to be a dark horse!]" Parul said, giggling away to glory.

"He looks like a film hero! Pata nahin tujhe kaise mil gaya! How could he marry someone like you? You are so behenji (a plain Jane), no style at all," Meena added acerbically.

Sanam felt this intense need to bang someone's empty head on the opposite wall. However, she listened and ignored them. She was too happy to spoil her morning listening to these horrendous and vile women.

Parul Singh and Meena Sharma had been her nemesis the whole last year. Parul came from an influential family and happened to be the main investor of the magazine and Editor Banerjee's family friend. Parul was a senior features writer whose only talent was to encroach upon junior writers' articles and parade them as hers. How she had managed to survive for so many years, no one knew. Meena, on the other hand, was a junior writer just as Sanam. In fact, they both shared the same cubicle. Meena loved to trade gossip and harboured a lot of animosity for Sanam. Maybe, that was the reason Parul and Meena gelled so well.

"Oye! How did you marry such a good-looking man? Did you force him to marry you?" Parul barged in again. Meena joined Parul with her fake laughter.

"*Iski toh ho gayi...aapki kab hogi?* [Sanam got married, what about you?] Did the suitor who came last week reply?" Madhu came to Sanam's rescue from the adjacent cubicle.

"Very funny," Parul scooted away from there.

"Gun or *khanjar* [dagger]?" Madhu asked Sanam seriously.

"Both...first I will stab Parul's eyes out then shoot her! Bitches are trying to make a pass on my husband!" Sanam said in anger.

Madhu burst into laughter.

"Both your language and thoughts are colourful today!" Madhu said, trying to control her laughter. Sanam smiled too. She liked Madhu. They were not best friends or so but were friendly with each other.

"Parul must have never imagined that you would get married before she got married. She is burning in jealousy!" Madhu tried to get Sanam in a better mood.

Sanam giggled at her friend's response.

"Acha, what happened at the base of your throat!" Madhu teased her in the lunch hour a little while later.

"Shit it is visible! I thought I had hidden them!" Sanam thought to herself and went red while adjusting her dupatta.

"Well, it is ...it is a skin allergy!" Sanam said and blushed further.

"Skin allergy? Ha-ha...I am joking! You are happy right?" Madhu asked Sanam.

Sanam nodded.

"Touchwood. You deserve it!" Madhu said, hugging her.

Sanam felt moisture in her eyes. No one had ever told her before in her life that she had deserved happiness. She hugged Madhu back.

"Do not get sentimental now that you are married. By the way, when was the last time you hit the parlour?" Madhu asked Sanam, observing her face closely.

"I cannot remember!" Sanam tried to jog her memory.

"You that you are getting some action…uhmm…I mean you are married, you need waxing asap," Madhu teased her.

Sanam blushed red as she understood her implication.

"We need to go shopping as well…. vaise wali [adventurous]," Madhu winked, leaving Sanam blushing away to glory.

Sanam was late that day. Avinash was getting worried and pacing their bedroom and balcony. He opened the door the moment he heard the familiar tinkle.

"Where have you been?" he roared, almost shaking her up.

Avinash found her eyes were swollen red. It seemed as if she had cried a while earlier.

Sanam was perplexed. Of all the things she had expected, she had not expected Avinash to be this angry with her. Tears threatened to flow again in her eyes.

"What happened Baby? Why have you been crying? Did someone touch you?" he asked her urgently.

Sanam nodded in a 'no.' She went ahead and kept her bag on a chair and went to the balcony to grab a towel.

"Why are you walking like this?" he asked her sternly.

"Like what?" she asked.

"What happened? You are scaring me. Your office was supposed to get over by four today: Saturday. Where did you go after that?" Avinash was now losing his patience fast.

"Parlour!" Sanam spoke softly.

"What parlour?" he asked, baffled by the line of conversation.

"Beauty parlour," she said.

"Why have you been crying then and why are you walking like this?" He wanted answers fast.

"Uffo Avinash…let me take a bath…it's hurting…really hurting," she said crying bitterly.

"What is hurting?" Avinash was about to pull his hair.

"I will just come in a few minutes," she said, rushing to the washroom.

A few minutes later, Sanam stepped out wrapped in a towel and stood in front of him. She unwrapped the towel after a few seconds.

There was not even an inch of her body that Avinash had not seen but the way she had unfurled the towel made desire kick in his groin and then the realisation hit him.

"Ahh...bikini wax!" Avinash broke into a fit of laughter.

Looking at the pained look on Sanam's face, he calmed down.

"Did it hurt baby?" he said gently, tugging her to sit on his lap.

She nodded, found himself and reached out for a hug. Avinash felt his manhood stiffen further. He made her sit aside and went to the fridge.

He returned with a pack of frozen peas to function as an ice pack and sat on the bed signalling Sanam to come to him. He made her lie down and applied to the area which had now turned an angry red.

"Who asked you to get it done? I like the way you are Gadhi!" he told her.

"Madhu suggested it. She said it will make it better. You do not think so?" Sanam asked with a pout.

"I think it will baby!" Avinash replied, feeling himself stiffen beyond control.

Sanam did not realise when Avinash's lips had replaced the ice pack and she had been taken to heaven and beyond, moaning away to glory. In between their moans and raptures, they became one yet again.

It was Sunday and she took the liberty to sleep in late. It was also two full weeks of their wedding. She was happy. Madhu's words had struck a chord somewhere.

"I deserve happiness," she reminded herself. She visited the gurudwara and quickly returned.

She went through the daily household chores and thought of preparing an elaborate brunch: Aloo puri and halwa for dessert.

She was working away at the mortar and pestle making chutney when Avinash entered.

"What are you doing?" he asked.

"Chutney," she said.

"So, use a mixer! Who does this nowadays?" he said.

"Well…you don't have one," she said.

"Hmm!" he said.

They enjoyed their brunch.

"Hum kahan jaa rahe hain?" Sanam asked him as she sat behind on his bike.

He took her to the main market and parked in front of a crockery shop.

"Buy whatever you want!" he said.

Sanam felt as if someone had brought her into a candy store.

"Bhaiya mixer dikhaiye [show me the mixer]!" Sanam went all bonkers in the store. She bought more than she could hold sitting behind the bike. They went again to the Bandstand smiling all the way enjoying their Sunday just like any other happily married couple.

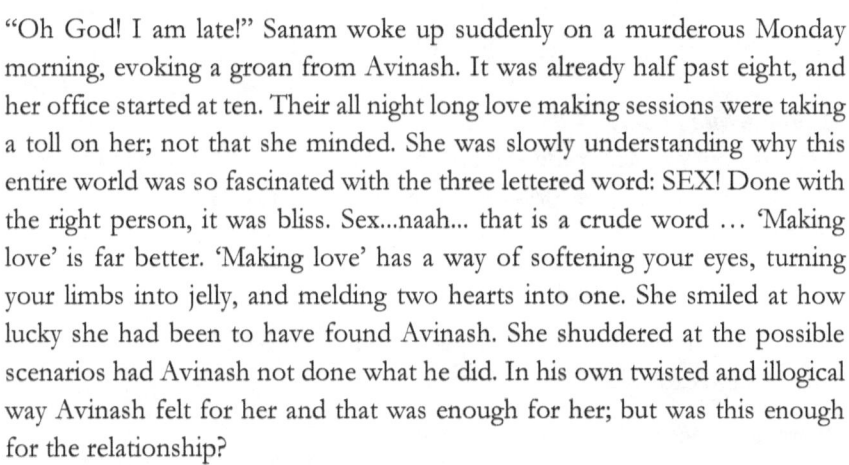

"Oh God! I am late!" Sanam woke up suddenly on a murderous Monday morning, evoking a groan from Avinash. It was already half past eight, and her office started at ten. Their all night long love making sessions were taking a toll on her; not that she minded. She was slowly understanding why this entire world was so fascinated with the three lettered word: SEX! Done with the right person, it was bliss. Sex…naah… that is a crude word … 'Making love' is far better. 'Making love' has a way of softening your eyes, turning your limbs into jelly, and melding two hearts into one. She smiled at how lucky she had been to have found Avinash. She shuddered at the possible scenarios had Avinash not done what he did. In his own twisted and illogical way Avinash felt for her and that was enough for her; but was this enough for the relationship?

"Do you have a relationship or are you guys role-playing a 'happily married couple'?" her mind questioned

"I deserve happiness," she reminded herself yet again. Sanam brushed the doubts that were troubling her under the carpet. "I will cross the bridge when I come to it," she assured herself.

She smiled as she again tried to get out of his embrace, and he wouldn't leave her. This was fast becoming the highlight of her day. Sanam had always pined for someone who would hold her and not let go...even if it were for a few months.

"Let me go!" she whispered in his ears.

"Go after a while," he answered sleepily.

"I need to cook," she replied.

"Don't cook," he said groggily.

"What will you eat then?" she said, pecking him on his lips.

"I didn't die of hunger before I got married to you!" he said, now fully awake.

"Haan...mangwana mutton biryani...mere haath ki daal roti thodi na achi lagti hai! [Order out, you do not value home food]" she answered back.

"All right...take a day off!" he suggested.

"I don't have leaves!" she whined.

"You are confused...what do you actually want?" he snapped.

"Ok...I will sleep for another half an hour!" Sanam patted his head. She knew she could not win him over with words.

A little while later…
"Is this how you will come along?" she asked Avinash, looking at him from head to toe. Avinash was dressed in grey gym shorts and a 'USS Polo' T-shirt and trainers.

"Why? Is that an issue?" he asked.

"No... but your fans will die with excitement!" she replied. He looked at her with a blank expression.

"Parul and Meena," she further explained.

"Who?" he asked.

"My colleagues...who apparently can't believe how you chose me!" she said, earning a kiss from him.

As predicted, Parul and Meena had been waiting for Sanam and her husband. The moment the bike stopped, they pounced on them.

"Hi…I am Parul, and she is Meena," an over-enthusiastic Parul introduced themselves.

"Hi," Avinash said, not taking pains to introduce himself. He took off his helmet, took Sanam's palm and kissed it.

"Bye baby!" he said, completely ignoring the other two women and riding off!

For the next few days, they settled in a nice routine…But some things are not meant to be.

CHAPTER -10
BHRAMASTRA

"This is for you," Avinash gave a gift-wrapped box to Sanam a few days later.

It was the latest I-phone.

Sanam was dumbfounded. Avinash was looking at her expectantly.

"This is an I-phone?" Sanam said looking at the phone in her hand in amazement.

Avinash just smiled.

"For me?" she asked, and Avinash nodded.

"It must be very expensive?" Sanam asked with a melange of emotions in her eyes.

"Should not matter to you baby!" Avinash said, kissing her full on her lips.

"Avinash…I cannot afford it! It is three times my monthly salary!" she said softly.

"Baby you don't have to, it's my gift for you!" he said, cupping her face.

Tears welled in her eyes.

"Avinash don't get me wrong…No one has ever given me a gift…so I can't tell how grateful I am to you…but I can't accept it…it's too expensive," she said with a lot of hesitation.

Sanam saw Avinash's face go blank.

"You do not have a phone and I need to contact you at times. Here is a phone. I cannot understand why you cannot take it?" Avinash did not understand how illogical Sanam could get at times.

"You have already done a lot for me Avinash...please understand I can't take it," she said, trying to kiss him.

"Enough...you do not want it, I get it. Now drop the topic," he said, getting back to his laptop. He had started spending a lot of time writing these days.

Sanam did not know how to explain to him. It was something that had been her spontaneous response. Yes, he was her husband, but what was their relationship? She could not accept it in the current scenario. She could neither explain it to him nor to herself. For a junior writer, she was surprisingly inarticulate when it came to expressing feelings.

She had offended him somehow, she realised that now, but it was still not acceptable to her.

Sanam tried to talk to him, but he would not budge.

They had dinner together but there was this discomfort. He was clearly put out, but Sanam did not know what to do. She tried talking to him, but he just brushed her aside.

At night she tried again. He ignored her completely citing work. She waited for him in the bed, but he kept on working till late.

It was late when he finally came to bed. She expected him to hug her as he did every day, but he disappointed her. She tried hugging him but that did not work either. She silently cried the whole night till sleep claimed her.

This went on for two days. Avinash refused to hug or kiss her. In the mornings, Avinash would come to drop her but would not give her the customary kiss.

"Did the love birds fight?" Madhu asked.

"How do you know?" Sanam asked her. Madhu's tender inquiry had brought a fresh bout of tears for Sanam.

"Do din se madam ki smile aur glow dono gayab hain! [You have not smiled in two days!]" Madhu added.

Sanam told Madhu her attempts to placate her husband and the zero-success rate she had had till now.

"Did you use *Brahmastra* [the ultimate weapon]?" Madhu asked Sanam and then whispered something in her ears making Sanam giggle.

In the evening, Sanam came home late. She did not try to pacify Avinash today. She made dinner and served him his food. She saw he was stealing glances at her.

"So, I have his attention! Good!" she told herself. She was just dying for the night to progress. Around an hour later, Sanam went for a shower and came out dressed in a wine-coloured negligee. It was a sheer net garment that had noodle straps and stopped just above her knees. She sprayed perfume on herself and tried catching his attention.

Avinash had caught a glimpse of her and understood her play. He showed no interest in her actions, in fact he completely ignored her.

Sanam could not believe that 'the Bhramastra' could fail. She could not believe her bad luck either. Disheartened, she tried the last trick in the bag. She faked sleeping facing him, giving him an unobstructed view of her ample cleavage.

When nothing happened, she finally gave up and went into the kitchen feeling wretched about herself. She needed something to dull her disappointment and senses. Sanam took out a tub of Choco-chips ice-cream and put a spoonful of it in her mouth.

A while later, Avinash came inside the kitchen and stood next to her. By now Sanam was too disappointed to expect anything from him. She was just into her ice cream tub.

"Aww… you are such a baby!" Avinash came near her ear and said softly.

"I am not a baby," Sanam responded sharply.

Avinash pulled a strap of her flimsy negligee down and captured her peak with his mouth for a fleeting moment.

"Hmmm…. correct …you are not a baby…you are a fully grown woman!" he said suggestively, making her shiver in anticipation.

"I want ice-cream," he said.

Sanam extended the tub to him after stuffing a spoonful in her own mouth.

"Not from here...he thrust his tongue into her mouth to taste the creamy desert and even sweeter mouth. Their passion soon claimed them both.

That night he took her on the kitchen counter. Their one room flat resounded the whole night with their sighs and moans.

The next day the husband was back kissing his wife bye at the doorstep of her office.

Two people happened to witness this scene, but the reactions were completely opposite. Madhu cooed and Dhruv experienced a sharp pain as if he had been branded by hot iron on his heart.

Dhruv Gulati was a freelance photographer in her magazine. He was a reasonably tall guy with a well sculpted body. He was a charmer and the heart throb of the female population that had been deprived of good-looking men in the 'Kaleidoscope' magazine's office. The only other males were sixty-year-old accountant Mr. Murthy and an editor Vikram Singh, who could not hold a candle to Dhruv in looks.

Here women swooned over Dhruv, but his heart only fluttered for Sanam. He had returned that morning and witnessed his own heart break into a million pieces.

"Sanam ...Congratulations! I did not know that I would go on leave for a few days and return to a shocker!" Dhruv congratulated Sanam.

"Thank you!" Sanam smiled and went about with her work.

"Aaj mujhe Dhruv se Devdas wali feel kyun aarahi hai! [Why does he look like the tragic hero 'Devdas']" Madhu whispered in Sanam's ear.

"Oh please! He must have broken up with some model!" Sanam responded unperturbed.

"Oh, by the way, 'Brahmastra' worked...right?" Madhu teased Sanam, causing Sanam to blush from ear to ear but put her head into the computer monitor rather than answering her friend.

That day was particularly busy for Sanam. Parul had taken a half day leaving her work on to Sanam. It was almost 8pm when she was done with her work. On a normal weekday, by this time, she would be done with dinner. She was damn scared of what Avinash would say. As it is, things had gotten better after many days with him...she did not want to mess it up.

As Sanam left the office, she realised that BEST buses (the local transport in Mumbai) were on strike since afternoon. She tried for an auto rickshaw but in vain.

Sometime later, a bike stopped on the road.

"Sanam, may I drop you?" Dhruv asked.

Seeing no other option, Sanam reluctantly agreed. Dhruv had dropped her home earlier a few times, so she did not feel awkward with him.

"Thank you, Dhruv!" Sanam said when they reached her building.

"Sanam," Dhruv grabbed her wrist as she was about to move away from him.

"Dhruv what are you doing?" Sanam was completely startled.

"Why did you lead me on? You know I love you...everyone in the office knows I love you! When did you become so heartless? You broke my heart!" Dhruv spoke overwhelmed with emotion, shocking Sanam who had no idea about his feelings for her.

"I am married!" Sanam said.

"Just tell me one thing, had you not married your husband would you have married me?" Dhruv almost begged her not leaving her wrist still.

Sanam was caught up in a quandary. She just wanted to run away before Avinash witnessed anything.

"Yes," she said empathising with him...her heart was breaking seeing his pain.

Just then another hand came and caught Dhruv's wrist.

"Leave my wife's wrist or I shall not even take a minute to break your hand," Avinash roared.

Sanam started shivering with fear. Her worst nightmare was unfolding, and she could not do anything about it.

CHAPTER- 11

PUNISHMENT

"Leave my wife's wrist or I shall not even take a minute to break your hand," Avinash roared.

"All yours, brother," Dhruv said, leaving her wrist.

"Remember Sanam, I truly loved you, but you broke my heart!" Dhruv said.

Avinash caught the collar of his shirt in an instant and was about to punch him when Sanam hugged and begged Avinash to let Dhruv go!

"Avinash let him be! Dhruv you please leave!" she told Dhruv, dragging Avinash away.

By the time they reached their flat, Avinash was in a rage. His eyes were red with anger and veins around his neck were so strained that it looked that they would almost pop out of his neck anytime.

"How dare he touch you? Who was he?" Avinash roared while pacing the room.

Sanam shivered with fear.

"I would have broken his nose, why did you stop me?" Avinash just screamed at her without giving Sanam a chance to say anything.

Avinash caught Sanam by her shoulders and gave her a good shake as he threw another volley of questions at her.

"Where have you been all this time? Why were you with him?" he spoke in a dangerous tone.

Sanam did not find words to answer.

"How could you say that you would have married him?" he broke a glass flower vase kept on the table. He was now out of control.

"Woman, why are you testing my patience? Say something Sanam!" he literally barked at her.

Sanam was now crying. In tears she told him why she accepted a lift from Dhruv.

"You do not bother calling in... Oh yes, why? Oh, madam doesn't have a phone! Does not even matter if a phone is there in the house but madam's self-respect takes a blow! Of course, if not me then someone else! Of course, it always must happen with me! You have been cuckolded Avinash...yet again!" Avinash was spitting venom that was tearing her apart.

"Avinash please you must trust me! How are we going to have a relationship if you do not trust me?" Sanam tried to reason out with him.

Rather than calming him down, Sanam's words added oil to fire.

"What relationship are you talking about? We...We do not have a relationship! Our relationship is purely physical. How many times do I have to tell you, woman...I love Nitika! You are nothing to me!" Avinash was pulling at his hair with his own hands.

Sanam stood there stunned. She was in a daze after hearing him out. But Avinash was not done yet.

"You want to know what our relationship is? He asked, coming dangerously close to her.

Avinash threw her dupatta away and ripped open the neckline of her kameez, exposing her bra and navel. Avinash pulled her into himself.

"This is our relationship...purely physical" he said while furiously biting her nape.

"This is what you desire, Sanam Kaur Bedi!" Avinash said, taking her to the full-length mirror.

"Look at yourself Sanam...this is what you are! A bag of bones and desire. *Main nahin toh koi aur sahi* [if not me then someone else]," he whispered in her ear as he tore off the rest of her clothes.

"Every single time, innocent looking women cuckold me!" he laughed bitterly.

Sanam was numb. She had absolutely no idea what had hit him.

By now Avinash was in a different zone. He was biting her across her body. He took to kneading her breasts…almost mauling them. Sanam was largely unresponsive.

He took her mouth in his own and bit her lips to evoke a reaction from her. Sanam hissed in pain.

Avinash was all over her, but this time instead of pleasure, the motive was hurt.

"He wants to punish me…I have hurt him," Sanam told herself. She understood what was coming her way. She prepared herself for the pain.

As Avinash stripped his clothing, Sanam cried aloud in fear and closed her eyes. She was completely dry and was shivering at the thought of the impending pain.

Instead of pain tearing through her, she felt Avinash's breath on her nape. The fear in Sanam's cry had acted as a whiplash for him. He let her go instantly.

"I have become a monster!" he cried aloud in disgust. He turned around and left.

The moment Avinash left, Sanam collapsed on the bed and broke down. She pulled a sheet on her almost naked self, cried till she could cry no more and eventually dozed off to sleep.

A few hours later Sanam woke up from a deep slumber. Her whole body was burning with fever and aching in places. Avinash still had not returned to the house.

She washed her face and put on some clothes. Her torn clothes were lying around the whole room. As she picked up her torn clothes, a few wayward tears escaped. By the time she was done, flood gates had opened. She sat down on the floor and howled, cursing her bad fate, and nursing her broken heart.

Sanam was in no condition to go to the office the next day. She went to the local store and dialled her office from there making appropriate excuses. It was afternoon and Avinash still had not returned.

Sanam played their conversation repeatedly in her mind. By the evening she was barely able to get up. Avinash still had not returned and now she was in knots. She had been crying since last night. Her heart was sinking, she looked at her hands again and again as if her life were sand which had just slipped out of her fingers.

It was almost midnight when she got up to use the washroom. Her body had been burning up the entire day. As she got up, she suddenly felt giddy and tried to steady herself but lost balance. Sanam hit herself at the corner of the bed and fell due to the impact. A small pool of blood formed where she had fallen.

CHAPTER- 12

ANGER

As Avinash opened the door of the flat, he saw Sanam on the floor unconscious and bleeding from the forehead.

He quickly took out his phone and dialled a number.

"Bittu…you have not gone far right, come over quickly…my wife needs a doctor. Get your medical box," Avinash literally barked into the phone.

He carried Sanam to the bed and tried to wake her up. He thanked his lucky stars that his doctor friend had just dropped him home.

A little while later, Avinash sat on the bed holding Sanam's almost lifeless hand. She still had not gained consciousness. The doctor had sedated her.

"She is anaemic and malnourished," his friend told him. "I know it is your personal life, but I did not know you were a brute Avi! She is delicate, please deal with her humanly," the doctor said with a hint of derision. He gave Avinash a list of medicines and left.

Avinash was ashamed of himself. He knew that was responsible for her pain. When he woke up from slumber the night before, he realised what he had done to Sanam. He left her because he was not able to face her or himself after being such a brute to her.

He looked at her. Her neck showed the brutality that he himself had inflicted on her. Tears of shame fell from his eyes.

"Will there be enough punishment for me?" Avinash asked himself. He caressed her cheek. Her fever had gone down for sure. He looked around and picked the pile of torn clothes that he had created that night. A look of utter distaste crossed his face.

"They were right…I have become a monster!" he told himself with self-loathing.

Sanam woke up late morning in Avinash's arms. She liked the warmth that she had been enveloped in. She liked the weight of the leg that had been there since sometime.

However, her throat was parched.

"Water," she tried to search for water. Avinash woke up and handed her a glass of water.

Sanam still felt very weak. She lay down and in no time was asleep again.

Sanam woke a few hours later feeling better. Her eyes took some time to get used to the brightness. It was afternoon. She got up but miscalculated her step and was about to fall when a strong pair of hands caught her. The next moment she found Avinash looking into her eyes. Her first reaction was relief…but then their last encounter flashed in front of her eyes. She remembered what had happened when he had almost forced himself on her. Fear crept into her eyes and her body shivered. These tremors were not of delight but of fear.

Avinash immediately looked aside and set her on her feet. For the first time in the past few weeks, things were awkward between them. Avinash was ardently trying to avoid eye contact. Sanam was not interested anyway.

Sanam felt stronger now. She went for a bath. As she returned, she caught a whiff of a burning toast. She turned towards the kitchen and saw Avinash unsuccessfully trying to toast a slice of bread. Sanam almost smiled at the cute picture he made- a six feet muscled man struggling with a slice of bread. She headed to the stove and switched it off. She changed the flat pan (tawa) and toasted the slices. She observed he had already cooked eggs. She took off the toast and served it to him on a plate.

"It's for you," finally a few words came out of Avinash's mouth leaving a shocked expression on Sanam's face.

"I don't feel like eating," she said looking away, and went and sat on her side of the bed.

He followed her with the plate. And a glass of milk.

"You need to eat something to take the medicines," he said in his trademark 'matter-of-fact' tone.

"I do not feel like eating anything. I will make tea for myself!" she said softly.

"What is wrong with milk?" he asked.

"No one ever gave me milk to drink, so I guess I am not used to it," she said politely and formally as she went to the kitchen.

She soon returned with two cups of tea and a few biscuits for herself.

Sanam sat on her side of the bed with her back to him. Physically, Sanam felt better after the tea and biscuits but emotionally she was in another zone.

"Please take medicine," he said softly, handing her a glass of water.

Sanam stared at the medicines, she looked at them as if she would squish them into powder by her stare.

Although he had said this very politely, she felt her anger simmering. She wanted to scream; she was outraged. She was angry: at him…at herself…at the life she had been living…at her own helplessness. She hated him for making her fall in love with him. She hated herself for falling in love with him. And for the first time, she was angry at God…for taking away her parents so soon…for the unloved childhood…for reducing her to this state of helplessness.

Sanam did not realise the intensity of anger she felt. She had been clutching on to the glass so tightly that the glass broke in her palm. The shards of glass cut her, and blood oozed out of her hands.

Normally she would have cried buckets at this much pain, but today she did not feel the pain at all. All she felt was emptiness and cold, where her heart used to be.

Avinash stood there frozen in shock. He had not witnessed this aspect of Sanam in these weeks they had stayed together.

Avinash was awashed with guilt.

"What have I turned her into?" he asked himself this rhetorical question.

He recovered to take the glass shards from her hand. She had cut herself badly. He picked up in his arms to avoid the glass shards pricking her feet. She wore a stone-cold expression on her face. He wrapped her hand in a towel temporarily and cleaned up the mess. She did not respond. She was angry. He knew that.

He brought out the first aid box. She was still sitting in the chair. He sat down on the floor, took her bleeding hand in his and gently cleaned the wound.

"Had I been gentle before, all this wouldn't have happened," he told himself with bitterness. Once he was done, he did not want to move. He sat there kissing her hand gently. When she did not respond, he put his head in her lap and put his arms around her waist like a small child seeking comfort from the problems of this world.

Sanam still did not respond. She was just absentmindedly stroking his hair.

"I am sorry baby!" he told her, tears slowly falling from his eyes.

Sanam just looked at him…. her eyes did not have the warmth he was so used to looking into…they had something else…hard, cold anger and loathing.

CHAPTER- 13
FORGIVENESS

Sanam had not felt so dazed and unfeeling ever in her life. She could see Avinash was repenting and crying, but she felt nothing...zilch...nada! It seemed that she had zoned out everything from her mind.

Avinash was speaking to her. She did not respond. He tried twice, but she did not respond.

Avinash then made her stand and took off her kurta and then the bra. As chilly air touched her body Sanam realised that she was topless. He was now mechanically working removing her lowers.

She looked at him sceptically. She could not believe it was happening to her again. That was not her Avinash.

In a matter of a few moments, she was completely naked in front of him. She shivered with fear. Sanam closed her eyes and crossed her arms protectively around herself in anticipation of pain...but that never happened. Instead of pain, she felt the cold balm slowly warming on her skin. Avinash wasn't ravishing her; he was applying medicine on her cuts and bruises that spanned her whole body and he was crying. She could see the tears silently flowing down his eyes. Once he was done, he got a T-shirt of his and made her wear it. She stood there...frozen...unable to move but tears were slowly welling up in her eyes.

He picked her up, laid her on the bed and tucked her in.

As he turned to leave, Sanam held him back by wrapping her fingers around his little finger, gesturing to him to join her. He came as she bid, she wrapped herself in his arms. Gone was her fear...her reluctance. He was still her haven, still her salvation. Her pent-up anguish and anger were now coming out as tears. She hid herself in his chest and cried as much as she could.

"I am sorry baby! I am really sorry!" he begged her forgiveness as he rocked her against his chest. He let her cry her out.

"Sorry, meri jaan!" he kissed her forehead as he adjusted now asleep Sanam in the nook of his arm.

"My punishment has just begun" he told himself as he patted her to sleep.

Sanam woke up in Avinash's arms, to find him already awake and looking at her tenderly. Had it been a week before, they would have been making passionate love at this time. She suddenly missed that part of their relationship. It suddenly struck her; Avinash had not been wrong there…their relationship was all physical…driven by desire. There were so many aspects that completed a relationship. All they had between them was this desire…this passion. They had never talked about their personal lives with each other…oh yes! They were not supposed to…according to the MOU. She smirked to herself. Come to think of it, she knew nothing about him…what he thought about so many things-his family…his friends. They did not even know about her existence. He had clarified it earlier on many occasions that he was not hers. Still, she had harboured the hope that maybe he will fall in love with her one day. Those hopes had been dashed two days back. She felt so sorry for herself. There was this physical pain that was there in her chest. She felt restless.

Avinash was watching the changing emotions on her face. He knew what was going on. He knew that his punishment had just begun. With a heavy heart, he got up and headed to the kitchen to make tea. Maybe one day she will be able to forgive him. He hoped that day would come soon.

Sanam now felt the resurgence of her anger and restlessness. She knew there was only one place which would get her relief. She got ready and picked up her dupatta.

"Where are you going?" Avinash asked her.

"Gurudwara," she said, trying to control her irritation.

"I will come along!" he said.

"No, I will go alone!" she said sternly.

"Please! I will stand outside" he said softly.

"Your wish!" she said, moving out of the door.

He took her to the Gurdwara and went along with her inside. What she needed, he needed too…salvation.

Once they had done the 'Darshan' she sat down in the inner sanctum, where the path was happening.

Avinash sat on the men's side of the hall.

Sanam found herself calming down. In a few minutes, a lot of people congregated there. It looked like an Anand Karaj (a Sikh wedding). She sighed. Today of all days she did not want this.

Sanam was about to get up when the groom entered.

"The Groom is tall and handsome, just like my Avinash," she thought with a smile.

He was dressed in cream colour sherwani and had a customary sword. The bride came soon after. She was dressed in pink. The couple's height difference was like theirs. Sanam stayed back…somehow, she now wanted to witness this union.

As the Anand Karaj started, a beautiful silence fell on the congregation.

It was time for the first Lavaa to be read…

{*The laava (singular laav) are the four Shabads (sacred hymns) of the Anand Karaj (Sikh wedding ceremony). They form the central part of the marriage ceremony. The "four rounds" ("char phaara") as they are sometimes called form a central part of this auspicious occasion.*

These central Shabads that are the key element of the Sikh marriage ceremony are from the Guru Granth Sahib}

Keethaa lorreeai kam so har pehi aakheeai - This Shabad is by Guru Nanak Dev Ji in Siree Raag:

pourree || keethaa lorreeai ka(n)m s har pehi aakheeai || kaaraj dhaee savaar sathigur sach saakheeai || sa(n)thaa sa(n)g nidhhaan a(n)mrith chaakheeai || bhai bha(n)jan miharavaan dhaas kee raakheeai || naanak har gun gaae alakh prabh laakheeai ||20||

(Pauree: Whatever work you wish to accomplish-tell it to the Lord. He will resolve your affairs; the True Guru gives His Guarantee of Truth. In the Society of the Saints, you shall taste the treasure of the Ambrosial Nectar. The Lord is the Merciful Destroyer of fear; He preserves and protects His slaves. O Nanak, sing the Glorious Praises of the Lord, and see the Unseen Lord God. ((20)))

Suddenly, Sanam felt this all was happening for her. These words were not words. She had vowed herself to Avinash and she had gotten scared at the first sight of trouble.

"No matter how the marriage had happened...when Waheguru was there, why did I get scared? I have been a fool to fear her own husband. Yes, he has wronged me, but I know who he is under all the anger, and I have behaved like everyone else in the world behaved with him," Sanam thought regretfully. Tears of pain fell from her eyes.

Laavan 4

This Shabad is by Guru Arjan Dev Ji in Raag Vadhans: pooree aasaa jee manasaa

pooree aasaa jee manasaa maerae raam ||

mohi niragun jeeo sabh gun thaerae raam ||

kahu naanak mai var ghar paaeiaa maerae laathhae jee sagal visoorae ||4||1||

(My hopes and desires have been fulfilled, O my Lord. I am worthless, without virtue; all virtues are Yours, O Lord. All virtues are Yours, O my Lord and Master; with what mouth should I praise You? You did not consider my merits and demerits; you forgave me in an instant. I have obtained the nine treasures, congratulations are pouring in, and the unstruck melody resounds. Says Nanak, I have found my Husband Lord within my own home, and all my anxiety is forgotten.)

By the time, the fourth Lavaa was read Sanam had gained clarity in thought.

She had promised herself to her husband. What he thought about it did not matter to her. They were bound by the invisible threads of destiny and love.

"What was I doing? What was I trying to do? I was seeking love in exchange for love! Is that even love? True love does not seek love in return. You saved me, Waheguru! Thank you," Sanam begged forgiveness from the almighty.

"It is going to take time for me to forgive you Avinash, but everyone deserves a second chance!" Sanam told herself as the Anand Karaj got over.

She looked around for Avinash. She found him sleeping in a shady corner of the corridor on the 'Dari' kept for all. He looked so peaceful while sleeping.

She did not want to disturb him. She sat beside him fanning him with her dupatta to fend off the flies. Sometime later, Avinash woke up with a start.

"Sanam," he spoke in his semi aware state, completely disoriented. Sanam cupped his face with her hands.

"You are fine?" he asked her.

In a few minutes, he gained clarity and was awake.

"Gosh...I fell asleep here!" he told her, smiling sheepishly.

"Chalen?" Sanam smiled. Her smile lit up his face.

Avinash's face looked relaxed now. He even flashed a smile at her.

"Vaise Chinese pasand hai tumko?" she asked him.

They left the Gurdwara holding hands, smiling.

CHAPTER- 14

SHOPPING

"Gosh...what happened to your forehead?" Madhu pounced on Sanam as soon as Sanam entered the office.

"Long story baby!" Sanam said.

"You tell me...how was the office in my absence?" Sanam asked in return.

"Heart breaking news...Dhruv Gulati resigned the very next day he had returned," she said.

"It was so boring! He was not here, and neither were you!" Madhu kept on speaking, not registering Sanam's expressions. A lone tear escaped Sanam's eye.

"Hey bhagwaan, why are you crying? Didn't your man kiss you today? Did the love birds fight again?" Madhu said softly.

Madhu was referring to Sanam and Avinash's morning ritual. Madhu usually came walking from the train station approximately at the same time as Avinash dropped Sanam. To stop the Parul-Meena menace, Sanam asked Madhu to wait for her so that those women stop coming near them. Not that Madhu minded...She would religiously stand there and wait for them. Then wave at Avinash or engage in a light banter with him to shade Parul and Meena. Sanam often laughed at it. Madhu did not have malice at heart...she was honest, outspoken and bindaas...qualities that Sanam greatly admired. And at the end of the whole scene Avinash would sneakily lean in and kiss her hand.... making Sanam blush every single day!

"Madam what happened?" Madhu was now intrigued.

"Should we talk during the Lunchtime?" she told Madhu.

During lunch time, Sanam updated Madhu with a partial narrative of what happened with Dhruv, how Avinash came at the last moment…how they fought…her fever and her fall…everything but not how her husband wronged her. However much she was saddened by Avinash's behaviour, she could never degrade him in front of others.

"You really didn't know Dhruv was crazy about you?" exclaimed Madhu!

"No baba!" Sanam said, getting irritated by having to answer the same question so many times.

"So why do you think he would entertain us standing at our cubicle? Why would he treat us to coffee so many times?" Madhu asked.

"For you!" Sanam said innocently.

"For me?" Madhu guffawed.

"Please spare me the stare!" Sanam pouted.

"Sanam how are you obtuse?" Madhu guffawed again.

"If anyone else is interested in me let me know now before my husband gets to know and creates a scene!" Sanam told Madhu.

"Hmm…there are two-both in our office!" Madhu declared!

"Shit…you mean Mr. Murti?" Sanam was scandalised.

"Shit…shit…I wish I could unhear this!" Madhu exclaimed, muttering an apology in her heart to the old man.

"So, who?" Sanam asked.

"Arre Vikram!" Madhu blurted.

"Oh F**K!! But he is your ex-boyfriend!" Sanam was now truly scandalised.

"Ex hua toh kya hua, ladka toh hai woh [he is still a man]. I had broken only his bums not his ding dong!" Madhu said it with exasperation referring to the incident when Madhu and Vikram were in a living in relationship. During a fight, Madhu had chased Vikram in the whole housing complex and had battered his posterior with a frying pan in front of the society residents.

Sanam burst into laughter when she heard Madhu. Madhu was unpredictable and damn funny. Sanam laughed so hard that tears came in her eyes. Madhu had told her this incident once they had become really friendly. Sanam could not forget the look of fear that had passed Vikram's face the day he joined the magazine and saw Madhu as he was being introduced to the whole staff. That day Sanam had fought to contain her laughter when Madhu told her that Vikram Singh was the same guy.

"Acha coming to the point...who is the other one?" Sanam asked.

"Apna company ka CA" Madhu said.

"Haye woh toh uncle hain..." Sanam was losing it.

"Abey buddhu...CA ka beta...woh bhi CA hai!' Madhu could not believe Sanam was so dense.

"Haye is saal dono ko rakhi bandh doongi," Sanam said with utmost sincerity.

Madhu could not stop laughing.

A few days later...

"I will return late today. I am going out shopping with Madhu," Sanam politely informed him.

"Enjoy," Avinash said smiling.

"I have cooked food," she said softly.

He looked at her for a few moments, smiled and got back to his writing. They had not gotten physical again after that fateful night. Initially, they tried sleeping apart but, in the morning, both found themselves entwined with each other...they gave up.

They had settled into a nice rhythm. In the mornings Avinash would drop Sanam to the office and head to the gym. In the evenings he would generally work furiously at his laptop, read a book or watch news on the TV.

Sanam, once done with her household chores, would settle down on the bed and scribble away or explore his book collection. Once he saw she was interested in reading, he made a few suggestions which Sanam was enjoying a lot. They hardly communicated. Words were rarely used between them...this is how it had always been. In the initial days, Sanam had observed and understood so many things about him. She would cook and plate his food every morning. By the evening, the leftovers on the plate would tell her his likes and dislikes. He loved Daal-rice and sabzi. He was not fond of oil...preferred butter or ghee. He did not like khichdi much. He loved yellow pumpkin sabzi...which he thought was potato sabzi. Sanam had not corrected him. She knew he had a sweet tooth. He loved besan ke ladoo, gajar ka halwa, and suji halwa...tolerated kheer and disliked barfi. She knew he liked salad and eggs with his drink. He was not a fan of Chinese or any other cuisine but went along to accompany her.

"Wow! You are looking so cute and hot- both at the same time," Madhu exclaimed looking at Sanam.

Sanam had chosen a cute and funky kurta for herself at 'Eastside', an upscale shoppers' paradise in the mall. It was costlier than what she normally wore but it was worth the cost and Sanam was already in love with it. It had totally transformed her personality. She liked what it did to her.

"This makes you a little livelier and classier!" Madhu told her.

Sanam also bought a decent but low-cost phone for herself with Madhu's help. She had wiped her account clean but felt happy doing so. They ate at the food court. Sanam had not had fun for a long time.

As they exited the mall, Avinash was waiting for them. Sanam squealed in delight. She had not expected him to be there. He had taken Madhu's number in the morning when he had gone to drop Sanam.

Sanam was happy. She had a fabulous time on her outing and now Avinash had come to pick her up. Her day could not have ended better.

She was just dying to try her new dress again. Sanam hugged Avinash and did not realise that she kissed his back plenty of times, making him smile all the way.

Avinash could not take his eyes off Sanam as she posed in front of their full-length mirror. She looked extremely happy with her new kurta. Avinash wondered how someone could be happy with so little. He had been observing her in the last few days-her wants were very few and lifestyle simple. Her wardrobe was extremely limited. He had often seen her sitting in the corner and sewing her dresses which had a tear or so. Avinash had seen the state of her only pair of sandals that she owned. It pricked his heart that she had been going through such penury but greatly admired her self-respect. He had all the money in the world, but she would not take it. But something needed to be done soon. Today, looking at her had given him an idea!

Next day...
In the evening Sanam received a message from Avinash.

"When will you get free? I will come to pick you!" it said.

She had shown Avinash the phone yesterday and given him the number. Contrary to her expectations, he had not said a thing. He had taken it and spent half an hour on it-feeding the Wi-Fi password, his number in the phone, making her personal mail id, installing messaging and music apps.

"Avinash, where are we going?" Sanam asked him as she met him outside her office.

"Haan, I need your help! You know I have this coupon for some Eastside store...It will expire today. Nihar, my personal assistant used to take care of this, but he is in Delhi now. So, I have two options, either I shop, or I let it go to waste. And I am never able to shop alone...will you help me?" he asked. He had bought the coupon online in the morning, but Sanam did not need to know this.

"Of course...oh it is the same mall that Madhu and I visited yesterday," she said.

"Acha?" Avinash hummed.

"What is the coupon worth?" she asked him.

"Twenty thousand rupees," he said casually. He had gone to great lengths to hatch the plan. It was time to execute it.

"What?" she was astounded.

"Arre chill...our company is a shareholder. But today is the last day! If we like something we will pick, or the money will get wasted...now what else can we do!" he said casually.

"Rupees twenty thousand waste!" Sanam exclaimed.

Avinash smiled to himself; his plan was working.

"Tum ameer log bhi na…paise ki kuch value nahin hai…that's why capitalism flourishes!" she gave him a sermon.

"Let's shop…we have only a few hours left for the store to close," Avinash told her.

They went to the men's section and bought some T-shirts which they liked.

"I am done…I don't like anything else," Avinash said half an hour later.

"Do you want to buy something for yourself or the house? We still have fifteen thousand to burn…or else the money will go back to the company," he said an hour later.

"I can buy a few things…why let the money go to waste?" Sanam said thinking aloud.

"Chalo!" Avinash said with a smile.

Sanam went crazy like a child in a candy store. She hopped from one stand to the other showing him the selection…asking for his opinion. Avinash just watched her being her happy self.

She bought an array of kurtas, dresses, cosmetics, and footwear. Bed linen and a few other things for the house were thrown in.

By the time they were done shopping, she was bone tired and incredibly happy. So was he.

CHAPTER- 15

VIXEN

"Baby, you are getting late!" Avinash called out to Sanam who was taking longer than usual to get ready. Truly so because for the first time in life Sanam had been spoiled for choices. She could not decide which kurta to wear to the office from her new wardrobe.

"Sorry!" Sanam came out and stood in front of their full-length mirror and started combing her hair.

Sanam was so occupied with the time that she was completely oblivious to the fact that she was looking like a stunner. First thing in the morning, Sanam had cut the front section of her hair into bangs, which now covered her forehead. She was wearing a pastel blue and green kurta with matching leggings and a beautiful dupatta. Her kohl rimmed eyes were looking fetching, just as the small round bindi on her forehead which brought out her cheekbones and the heart shaped cut of her face.

Sanam was combing her hair when she stole a glance at Avinash. Avinash was busy with his phone. It seemed to her that he had not noticed her hair cut. The brightness of her face dimmed a little bit.

Avinash had dropped her as usual, and as always, she turned as he caught her hand, but just entwined her fingers with his, smiled and left. Since that ill-fated day, Avinash would just hold her while sleeping and kiss her forehead off and on. He had stopped getting intimate with her. It had been almost a month now and she missed him -missed *'them'* so much! Sanam sighed thinking about the state of affairs with her husband.

"Sanam...dhyan de!" Madhu poked a pen into Sanam's stomach. It was the weekly editorial meeting, but Sanam was completely lost. Madhu had seen Editor Mrs. Banerjee eye Sanam once or twice.

"Cinderella ka dhyaan hi nahin hai! Banerjee ke haath maregi aaj," Madhu rolled her eyes and muttered to herself. Madhu had started calling her Cinderella when she spotted her in the morning with a complete makeover.

Sanam was completely oblivious to her surroundings. Madhu was right, Sanam felt like a Cinderella today and the fact that she had a Prince Charming was like a cherry on the cake.

Prince Charming huh... sirf charming ? Prince stunning... hot... delicious... tempting piece of meat. He was like this ice-cream sundae with all the marvellous toppings. Gosh! She wanted to lick the cherry on the sundae. The thought scandalised her and cracked her up at the same time. The result was a funny noise that sounded like the mating of a moan and a laugh.... suggestive and sexy!

"Sanam, we are talking about obituaries, and you are laughing! Who will write the tribute to this slain writer? Will you for the next fortnight's edition? Since you find it so funny, you will write it," Editor Banerjee screamed at the top of her lungs.

"Ok madam...Sorry Madam," Sanam was visibly embarrassed. The meeting finished soon, and the editor left.

"Kiske baare main soch rahi thee Cinderella? Tera Prince Charming milega tujhe, do ghante hain abhi," Madhu teased her purposely in front of Vikram and Parul.

Sanam blushed a deep pink much to the chagrin of a disappointed Vikram and an irritated Parul.

By the time she reached home, Sanam had made up her mind to do something about the dissatisfactory situation at home.

"Yeh kaisa hai?" Sanam asked as Avinash was working on his laptop once they were done with dinner.

"Nice," Avinash smiled looking at her enthusiasm. Too tired to try her new purchases last night, Sanam was trying them on now. Having caught his attention, she tried two more dresses with compliments from Avinash.

"What do you think about this?" Sanam asked Avinash but got a stunned silence from him.

Sanam was wearing denim hot pants and a demi-cup bunny patterned pink bra she had picked up from the lingerie section of Eastside. She was feeling bold today, she needed this and he did too!

She walked towards him, holding eye contact between them. She pulled his chair towards herself and put her legs across to sit in his lap in a straddling position. Her arms went around his neck.

"What do you think of this Shastriji?" She brought her lips near his and spoke seductively.

"Ahhmmm...Very nice," Avinash could barely manage to speak.

"So, what will you do about it?" Sanam said while running her fingers in his hair.

Avinash almost groaned.

"Sanam I am trying to control...what I did to you last time was unforgivable...I can't let it happen to you again!" he said in a despondent tone.

"I forgave you long back. It is time you forgive yourself Avinash!" she said softly. She stroked his cheeks gently, but he looked away.

Sanam pulled herself up, disappointed with the turn of events.

"Avinash, what is that stain on your T-shirt? At the back? Is it blood? Take it off!" Sanam almost yelled in alarm.

"Oh no, it is on your shorts!" Sanam spoke in horror as he pulled down his shorts.

Soon Avinash Shastri stood in his briefs looking puzzled trying to find the stains that did not exist, till he heard a huge slap on his well-rounded bottom and the penny fell. This innocent minx had conned him...if the oxymoron ever existed!

"Excuse me madam! Did you just spank me?" Avinash asked her with a look of disbelief.

"Can you see anyone else here?" Sanam was trying to control her giggle, hoping for a positive reaction from him.

A naughty glint now came into Avinash's eyes. His member had been teased a lot today and he needed to settle the score with his tormentor. He wanted her to be his again and wanted to belong to her.

Avinash ran towards Sanam, who squealed and jumped on the bed trying to run away yet dying for the punishment. He caught her soon and both wrestled and fell on the bed as she tried to get out of his grip. Ultimately, he spanked her bottom twice. Her bottom was so supple that his fingers refused to move on and lingered there for quite some time, drawing invisible patterns on the mounds while his lips ultimately captured hers. Sanam let out a moan when Avinash put his lips where they belonged-on hers. They could not keep their hands off each other. Their now offending inner garments were quickly removed. Both their bodies were parched for each other's touch. It seemed they could not get enough of each other.

Avinash moaned loudly as he entered her. His patience giving up with every stroke he was thrusting in her. His hands had clutched on to her abundant breasts. He felt the last of his sin wash away with the last thrust where they both became one.

As Avinash dropped her next morning, he caught her hand like he always did and pulled her towards himself; but today Avinash just stood there, his gaze transfixed on her. Sanam looked into his eyes, she could see a flame of desire in his eyes, which did not fail to scorch her.

"Aviiii late ho raha hai!" Sanam reminded him shyly.

Avinash pulled her to himself and instead of kissing her hand, kissed her cheeks and whispered in one ear 'Miss me!"

Sanam did exactly that.

They fell into their earlier routine and time literally flew for Sanam. The next few months passed in a wink.

"The six months period has come and gone! Anytime now Avinash will get up and throw in the towel. You do not have to feel bad then…do not be heartbroken! Remember, you knew what you had walked into...Something is better than nothing!" Sanam consoled herself time and again.

Long back she had decided to sit back and enjoy married life, even if it meant a 'role-play' kind. Sanam knew Avinash was going to be her first and the last and that she would treasure every moment spent with him. Still there were times when her heart lurched as the month changed. Sanam and Avinash had not talked about the end of the 'cooling off period.' They had married in the middle of December, and it was the first week of August now.

"I don't want to wish it on myself!" Sanam decided that she wasn't going to broach the topic.

"Uffo...what are you thinking about?" Madhu interrupted her.

"Nothing much!" Sanam tried to evade Madhu's question.

"Acha dekh, tera hero aa gaya!" Madhu exclaimed.

Sanam's dull face morphed into a glowing one as she watched her husband come from far, riding his Royal Enfield looking as dashing as ever.

"Avinash...are you free for the evening tomorrow?" Madhu asked Avinash as he stopped his bike.

"Depends...tune date par jaana hai mere saath?" Avinash flirted with Madhu as Sanam burst into laughter.

"Haan...karega double date? I need to introduce someone to you!" Madhu said with a blush.

Avinash looked at Sanam, she smiled and then said yes.

The next day, Avinash reached Sanam's office before time. He had been missing his wife too much. Sanam came out with Madhu a little while later. As always, few words were exchanged between the couple but enough got said in glances. Madhu, unaware of the non-verbal communication happening, kept on talking without waiting for a reaction. After waiting for a brief while, a tall and lanky guy came towards them.

"Rohan!" Madhu squealed and hugged him.

"Arre baba! Tu blush bhi karti hai?" Avinash mocked her.

"Guys this is Rohan...mera hone wala fiance!" Madhu said, blushing further.

"Haye...Sachi! Congratulations Madhu!" Sanam jumped and hugged Madhu in excitement, making others burst into laughter.

They went to a trendy restaurant to have dinner.

"Baby will you drink?" Avinash asked Sanam tenderly. He had his arm protectively around her waist since they had entered the restaurant declaring her taken. It was a very Alpha male thing to do. Sanam smiled to herself as she saw him throw a 'I-will-murder-you-if-you-look-at-her' look at the other men present there. The look, which Sanam so easily recognised now, would have offended some women but made her happy...incredibly happy. She always longed to belong to someone.

"Baby...baby will you drink? You are so lost today!" Avinash told Sanam.

"Haina? Teri cute biwi kab se lost-lost hai!" Madhu added.

"Is it so baby?" Avinash asked her softly, caressing her cheek. This small gesture sent shivers of want in Sanam's body bringing in feelings that he knew too well.

"Yesterday again Sanam got herself into a soup during another editorial meeting," Madhu said and went on to tell the entire escapade leaving Sanam completely red faced.

"Another means?" Avinash asked her.

"Since the time you have gotten married, Sanam keeps on daydreaming during the office hours. She escapes in her own world at the drop of the hat," Madhu explained and then went on to tell Sanam's recent escapades much to the embarrassment of Sanam.

"By the way, you never told me about Rohan!" Sanam accused Madhu.

"Sorry Sanam...it happened so quickly," Madhu looked at Rohan and blushed.

"Details!" Sanam asked them.

"Will you do the honours?" Madhu asked Rohan.

"So, we were classmates!" Rohan started.

"Oh, childhood sweethearts! Aww!" Sanam cooed and everyone laughed.

"No...we were just friends till last week!" Madhu blushed.

"Well, I always liked her but never had the guts to tell her. I shifted to the US some years back and we lost touch. Our mothers met last week and casually my mother told her that I was here for a potential match. We met last week, and I guess the rest is history!" Rohan blushed.

"So, the wedding is in three weeks and then I will shift to America with Rohan," Madhu dropped the bomb.

"Three weeks? So soon Madhu? And that means you will leave the office?" Sanam said. She felt happy for her friend, yet there was a corner of her heart that was sad at the thought of losing her only friend.

"Sorry Sanam!" Madhu said across the table.

"It's ok baby!" said Avinash, kissing a lone tear away.

"Par tu three weeks main khana banana kaise sekhegi?"Sanam asked innocently, cracking everyone at the table. Rohan laughed so hard that he spilled his bear on himself.

"Nahin vaise YouTube hai...main tujhe videos bataungi...woh banana!" Sanam said with Avinash gesturing a big no behind Sanam's head, that Sanam caught with the corner of her eye and gave him a deadly stare.

"Baby if looks could kill, I would have been dead by now!" Avinash took an imaginary dagger to his heart and mock stabbed himself.

"Bataya kyun nahin ki acha nahin laga?" Sanam was no mood to forgive her husband.

Madhu and Rohan went into a laughing fit looking at the couple bicker.

"Arre North Indian tak theek tha...Woh Punjabi Chinese too much ho gaya...Yaar hakka noodles main Paneer sirf Punjabis daal sakte hain!" Avinash said, trying to control his laughter like others.

"Bahut jyada bahadur ho gaye ho!" Sanam said in a threatening tone.

"Sorry baby...sorry!" Avinash begged his wife, peppering her hand with feather kisses.

"Oh God! This guy has been kicked out of the kingdom of eternal bachelorhood. He has been domesticated. A six feet guy scared of his petite wife! What a scene!" Rohan rolled with laughter.

"A kingdom you will soon leave! Aur Sanam ke hurt hone se darta hoon…usse nahin!" Avinash said sheepishly, earning a blush from Sanam.

As they rode home, Sanam and Avinash had a happy smile on their faces. Rohan was a great guy and Madhu and Rohan seemed to be in love. Their first evening outing as a couple with friends had been a success.

Sanam was just coming out of the bathroom after changing, when Avinash pulled her and pinned her to the wall. He was a little tipsy and completely in the mood.

"Avinash…Kya kar rahe ho?" Sanam asked him, blushing away.

"Madhu said you are lost in thoughts in the office. Whose thoughts?" Avinash asked her sternly, earning a grunt from Sanam.

"Whose do you think?" Sanam asked, teasing him.

"Tell me quickly woman before I die!" he asked, biting the nook of her throat.

"Ahh…yours baba!" Sanam spilled the beans earning a wide grin from him.

"What kind of thoughts?" he asked in a seductive voice.

"Gande wale!" Sanam spoke, licking her lips before biting his chin.

"Tell me…describe what you thought!" Avinash was dying with curiosity now.

"Let me show you!" Sanam said as she unpinned herself and brought his shorts down to take his throbbing member into her mouth.

Avinash was reduced to a moaning groaning mess in a minute.

"You are such a vixen baby!" Avinash groaned as he reached climax.

CHAPTER- 16
CRITICAL CONDITIONAM

It was finally a long weekend. Saturday was a holiday on the occasion of Rakhi. Sanam felt a little prick. Till last year she used to tie Rakhi to Deepu, but her Uncle's family had shifted lock, stock and barrel to Punjab soon after her wedding. As much she could gather from the gossip, they had run away with the money taken from the Lala who wanted to marry her. She had been surprised that Lala had not come to their house to recover his money…maybe Avinash's anger had scared him. They were back to the earlier routine. Sanam felt peaceful and happy for the first time in her life. She looked around…although it was just one room, it was her entire world. She was blissfully happy with her husband…. never mind the future…she was happy in the present. Sanam looked across to Avinash, he was furiously typing away. He had been writing since morning…around six -seven hours had passed. Watching him write was her favourite hobby on the weekends because on the weekdays she was hardly around. He had recently acquired reading spectacles that sat very cutely on his long nose completing the 'writer' look. His strong fingers typed away gently at the laptop. They had woken up late today after a stormy night of lovemaking. She blushed at the memory of the wild night they had and suddenly she wanted him again…but he was writing…she huffed with a pout.

"Baby chai pilla na!" he said absentmindedly.

Sanam got up and on a whim took off her kameez and wore his discarded T-shirt which still smelled like him. She wore her denim hot pants underneath…it was getting too hot.

As she kept a cup of tea next to the laptop, he held on to her hand and kissed it absentmindedly and went back to work.

Sanam's plan had failed.

"TV dekh loon? Will you get disturbed?" she asked him, putting her arms around his neck from behind and kissing his shoulders.

"Haan…go ahead…vaise bhi I will be done in half an hour!" he replied.

Sanam was surfing the channels when she came across 'Hasee toh Phasee'…her favourite movie. She had only watched the trailer as at her Uncle's place she wasn't allowed to watch the complete movie. And they did not appreciate such a subtle movie.

"Wow! 'Hasee toh Phasee'", Sanam screamed and did a victory dance.

In a span of a few minutes, she was completely engrossed in the movie oblivious to the surroundings. She was commenting, laughing, and blushing as the movie proceeded.

Sanam did not even know when Avinash joined her on the bed. She made an alluring picture. She was sitting on her hunches and bouncing with emotions. The bigger size T-shirt had slid across one of her shoulders exposing the full strap of her bra-the bunny pattern one which was his favourite. His hands went to explore firm breasts only to be jerked aside.

"Avinash tang mat kar…movie dekhni hai," Sanam was now in a different mood.

"Haye Avinash kitna handsome hai! Muah…muah!" Sanam exclaimed.

"Thanks baby!" Avinash said while giving her a love bite on her exposed skin on the shoulder.

"Arre Avinash Malhotra ki baat kar rahi hoon! Iss film ka hero!" Sanam said innocently but did not turn back to see the fallen face of Shastriji.

Avinash realised he was not getting what he wanted any sooner…might as well enjoy the movie and try and maximise his chances. He pulled her into his lap as she was crying and comforted her. Soon she was sprawled between his legs, and both were enjoying the movie. By the end of the movie, Avinash had dozed off leaving Sanam at loose ends again. Once the movie got over, Sanam chanced upon 'Aiyyaa.'

"It's my lucky day!" Sanam gave a yelp. She had heard the story from a friend but had not watched the movie due to the obvious reasons.

Avinash had woken up on her yelp.

"Another movie? Oh baby…thoda rest kar le…aaja," he pulled her towards his chest.

"Arre, you have to watch this one…mujhe hamesha dekhni thee…tum bhi dekho na Avinash," she pulled at his T-shirt.

"Haan baby dekh raha hoon," Avinash said…but his baby was not paying attention to him at all.

Avinash was now frustrated. He took off her T-shirt, but Sanam was so into the movie, she did not even realise that her T-shirt was gone. Avinash got to work. He started kissing her collarbone and biting her ears. Without much ado, his hands went straight away to unfasten her bra. Sanam was now sitting on her hunches with just a pair of hot pants on!

"Oh Avinash…you are such a darling! How did you know my boobs were feeling constricted with the bra?" Sanam massaged her naked breasts with her hands and then took the discarded T-shirt and wore it.

"Thanks baby! Tumhe sab pata hai!" Sanam said sweetly, planting a kiss on his cheek and went back to the movie.

Avinash was now completely lost. He had no other option but to watch the movie, which he did dutifully.

Soon Sanam started dancing on the raunchy number… "Dreamum Wakeupum.." pulling Avinash along…who had no idea what to do but went along with the flow. Sanam could not believe herself when she saw Avinash dancing, she squealed with laughter. As the song ended, they both collapsed on each other…laughing. Avinash tried his luck again, but Sanam went back to the movie after a little petting.

"Hai kya muscles hain!" exclaimed Sanam looking at the hero Prithviraj.

Shastriji had completely given up. He was HUNGRY now. 'Hungry' being the operative word.

"Baby khana kya hai?" he asked gently.

"Hay rabba..khana toh banaya he nahin!" she says suddenly with guilt.

"Pizza chalega?" he asked.

"You are such a darling!" She kissed him full on his lips and before he could take it further, she went back to the movie.

Once the pizza and the movie were over, Sanam hugged Avinash. She had discarded her shorts and was now only in his T-shirt. Avinash's hopes that had risen, were dashed the next minute when he realised that Sanam was already asleep. Shastriji tried his best to wake her up... but nothing worked. Peace and sleep eluded him leaving him high and dry.

CHAPTER- 17

MISSED SUNSET

Next day was Sunday. Sanam woke up and went to Gurudwara. Generally, Avinash always went along with her, but he was deep asleep. Sanam was feeling guilty for not making dinner last night and thought of going out of her way to make an elaborate feast for him.

Avinash woke up to an empty house. All he wanted to see was his girl, but this peace had been eluding him since yesterday. He found his breakfast made and tea in the flask. He quietly had his breakfast.

He went to the balcony for a smoke when he saw two people lifting his bike.

"Oye…what are you doing?" he screamed and went down to the building compound.

The Bajwas stayed on the fourth floor in their building wing. Their recently Dubai returned son had bought a new car, which he was trying to park in the spot where Avinash's Royal Enfield had been parked.

"What the fu*k! Why are you guys touching my bike?" Avinash yelled at the men.

"I told them to make space," a young man stepped out. He was in his late twenties and a flashy looking guy. Avinash had seen him smiling at Sanam a few times. He was Bajwas' son.

"Myself Balraj Bajwa," the young guy put a hand forward towards Avinash, who just stood there grunting.

"Why did you move my bike?" Avinash asked in his 'Don't-mess-with -me' tone.

Senior Bajwa, who was the secretary of the building, sensing trouble, called a few people over. Soon there were a sizable number of people waiting for the show to start.

Avinash signalled the other two guys aside. He went and took his bike and parked it where it had been parked earlier.

"We own a flat and we can park our car anywhere we want. You are a tenant ...you will have to listen!" Balraj spoke in a condescending tone. Avinash saw red.

"Tenants do not stay for free. Why cannot you park where the others have parked their car. I have been parking my bike here since the last few months...it will stay here. Now let me see who will touch my bike!" Avinash threw an open challenge.

"Such an unreasonable man he is!" Mrs. Bajwa jumped in the discussion in defence of her son.

"Haan bewada hai...koi baat kahoge toh usse toh apni izzat ka kuch nahin hai...par hum toh izzatdaar hain na!" Mr Bajwa poured oil on the fire.

"Haan, I used to get drunk.... but of my own money. I did not ask any of you! Did I?" Avinash said, fuming at them.

"Such a goonda...bechari Sanam phas gayi!" Balraj said, dramatically provoking Avinash.

Avinash had had enough. He pulled Balraj by his T-Shirt collar.

"Yeh teri car...yeh meri bike...issme meri biwi ka naam kyun aaya?" Avinash shook in anger. The others watched in horror.

"How dare you take my wife's name in this argument? How dare you bring my wife into this? I will kill you if you take my wife's name from your mouth!" Avinash lifted Balraj off the ground.

All hell broke loose.

Sanam was returning from the Gurudwara when she saw commotion in her own building compound.

"Kya hua?", Sanam asked one elderly uncle.

"Bajwa aur aapke husband ki ladai ho rahi hai," he said.

Sanam ran towards the crowd. She saw Avinash holding Balraj and people trying their best but Avinash not letting go.

"Avinash please chodo!" Sanam ran towards him.

"Baby tujhe lag jayegi...side ho ja," Avinash told her.

"Aviiiinash jaane do usse! Tujhe meri sar ki kasam!" Sanam yelled at him and that was it.

Avinash let go of the idiot.

"Avinash please chalo yahan se...please," she pulled him towards herself.

"Ab kissi ne meri bike ko touch kiya ya meri biwi ke baare mein kuch bola to tang tod kar haath main de dunga!" he put out an open challenge.

Sanam tried to move him but could not.

"Baby chod...kuch nahin karunga!" he told Sanam.

They reached home, she made him sit and gave him water. His eyes were red, nostrils were still flaring.

"Avi kya hua? Itna gussa? Sir phat jayega!" Sanam said kissing his forehead and hugging him.

"Saale samajhte kya hain? Kuch bhi bol denge! They called me a bloody drunkard...do you believe it?" Avinash was still enraged.

Sanam gave him a pained look.

"Aur tum agar woh Bajwas ke yahaan gayi toh dekh lena!" he warned her.

"Sanam tu kitni achi hai.... tu kitna acha khana banati hai...sab meetha meetha bol kar tujhse kitna kaam karwati hai...kitna khoon jalta hai mera!" he said.

"Acha acha nahin jaungi," Sanam tried to pacify him.

A little while later she gently coaxed him to have lunch and fed him with her own hands when he threw a tantrum like a five-year-old child.

Avinash was in no mood to write; he picked up a book when Sanam put it on the TV.

This time she chanced upon "Hum Mil Gaye!" and put it on. She had caught this movie in bits and pieces and was now happy to watch it in one go.

Avinash too gave up reading, hugged her, and started watching the movie. It was fun. They laughed together and enjoyed the songs.

"Haye mast movie thee!" Sanam exclaimed.

"I like the lead pair!" Avinash said.

"I think Pareena Kapoor ki jagah koi aur hoti toh acha hota!" she said. "She was a little over!" Sanam added.

"Arre tum acting ke baare main kya jaanti ho? She was the best choice for the role," he said in an irritated tone.

"Matlab...mujhe lagaa maine bol diya!" Sanam added casually.

Little did Sanam know that he had been the Assistant Casting Director for this movie, and it was the first job he held in Bollywood.

"Bas saari duniya tumhare hisaab se chalti hai! Madam ko superhit pair nahi pasand!" Avinash was now in a foul mood.

"As an audience I have full right to say what I observe!" Sanam said in anger.

"Woh kamina Balraj tumhe taadta hai...tumhe pata nahi chalta... woh observe nahin karti...tumhe lagta hai sab ache hain...toh sab ache ho jate hain?" he was now really pissed off.

"Avinash...tum itna gussa kyun ho gaye?" Sanam was now in tears.

"Kabhi yeh aunty...kabhi woh aunty...apne ghar ke liye tumhare paas time hi nahi bachta!" he growled.

Sanam fell silent. Her heart was heavy with emotions. She took a book and started making an effort to read it.

A little while later...

"Yaar yeh ghar hai ya ajayeb khana? Where in the hell are my reading glasses? Bas kaam karna hai...productivity ho ya na ho! Kahin bhi kuch bhi rakhna hai!" Avinash yelled to himself moving around the room like a mad bull.

Sanam now had had enough. She made him sit on the chair and took his specs off from his head.

"Oh!" was the only word Avinash could manage to utter.

Sometime later she served him his evening tea and snacks. He held her hand, but she jerked it away.

"Shit!" he let out a muttered oath as a little tea fell on fingers.

"I will return in a few minutes," Sanam turned around and left.

Sanam returned in fifteen-twenty minutes and saw Avinash had not touched the samosas she had so lovingly made for him. A tear escaped her eyes.

"Baby, I was waiting for you! I do not like eating without you!" Avinash said, noticing her gaze.

"Hmm," Sanam hummed with a small smile, signalling that her anger was almost over now.

"Let's warm up the tea!" he said, walking towards the kitchen and bringing the tea for her.

"Movie dekhen?" he asked her gently as he fed a bite of samosa in her mouth.

Sanam shook her head in a no.

"Bandstand chalen?" Avinash said, earning a sweet yes from her. They shared the samosas and had tea from the same cup.

"Baby chalo...sunset miss ho jayega!" Avinash called Sanam out a few minutes later.

"Haan Chalo...ready" Sanam said, coming out of the washroom.

"Yeh kya pehna hai?" Avinash was shocked.

Sanam was wearing a Burqa.

"Abey yeh utaaro.... aise feel aarahi hai ki kisi aur ki biwi ke saath ja raha hoon!" Avinash said.

"Kyun...tum hi toh bolte ho…yeh tadta hai...woh tadtaa hai...mujhe pata nahi chalta! Koi mujhe tadta rahe...mujhe bas tu dikhta hai! Samajhe?" Sanam gave it back to him.

Avinash started laughing as her purpose sank in. He rolled on the bed as tears of laughter escaped his eyes.

For minutes he sat down and laughed his heart out.

Sanam was still standing where she had been but had taken off the burkha.

Avinash came to her and put his mouth on hers.

They never witnessed the Sunrise from the Bandstand that day.

CHAPTER- 18

OBLIVION

"Acha suno...I need to go out of town for a few days," Avinash told Sanam later that night.

"Kab?" Sanam asked politely.

"Tomorrow morning, I will leave! You will be fine na?" he asked her.

Sanam lowered her gaze and nodded a yes.

"Kab aayoge wapis?" Sanam asked cautiously so as not to offend him.

"5-6 days...maybe a little later," Avinash said casually.

"Ok!" Sanam said softly, heading towards the kitchen to avoid reducing to an emotional mess in front of him. Staying with him for almost nine months, these five-six days away seemed like an eternity. Sanam went to the washroom to have a good cry. She composed herself and came out a while later. Avinash was busy on the phone co-ordinating a few things at his end and did not notice her.

They retired early as Avinash had to leave in the morning.

Sanam unknowingly clung to him, her heart beating a sullen rhythm, wondering how these five-six days would go...And what if he does not come back? Her heart started beating faster resulting in a tighter hug. She was literally glued to him that night, trying to find solace in his heartbeats...wishing sleep would take her over so that her mind would stop conjecturing scary scenarios.

Avinash woke up early and packed his backpack. Sanam too got up and made tea for him.

"Please don't travel by train...for two stations...go by bus or auto...actually take a cab...promise?" Avinash took her in his arms.

"Haan...ok" Sanam said, trying to smile.

"Aur khana khogi time par?" Avinash asked sternly.

"Door theek se lock karna," Avinash was now looking worried.

Sanam smiled and cupped his face to claim his lips. Their lip lock went gentle to passionate in a matter of a few seconds with them ending up in a quick and intense coupling as if scared to let go of each other even for a few seconds let alone for a few days.

"Aaj aapke mister nahin aaye?" Madhu teased Sanam.

Tears escaped Sanam's eyes in reply.

"Hey, what happened?" Madhu asked in concern and laughed loudly when Sanam told her the reason.

"Uff yeh mohabbat!" she further teased Sanam, making Sanam laugh along.

"Aaj kya karegi ghar jaakar?" Madhu asked her.

"Safai? Maybe I will read a book!" Sanam said thinking hard.

"Why don't you stay at my place tomorrow night?" Madhu offered.

"Won't it be bothersome for your family?" Sanam asked.

"Arre na yaar....my friends keep on coming! In fact, you will be awesome for my reputation! My most sane friend. Otherwise, my Aji(grandmother) keeps on cursing my choice in friends!" Madhu said laughing.

"Avi se pooch kar bataun?" Sanam said in excitement and immediately pinged her husband.

"Go ahead...Enjoy!" he replied a few hours later.

True to her word, Sanam started 'Safai Abhiyaan' the moment she reached home. She changed the bedsheet, ironed Avinash's clothes to perfection, cleaned the kitchen and made besan ladoos for Avinash and a few for Madhu's house. Still Sanam had some time left, so she turned on the TV and listlessly surfed channels. Avinash still had not checked his messaging app. Sanam had not hoped for much...he rarely checked his cell phone.

This one room flat looked so huge and cold without her husband. Sanam had been holding her tears for the entire day...the dam broke, and she spilled her anxiety out. This love was all consuming. She was deeply, irrevocably in love with her husband, and it was a bad one. It had been almost ten months since their wedding. As the days were passing by, a dread was filling up Sanam's heart. What if this week is the last one? She had no idea what she would do once Avinash left her. She prayed to her Waheguru to give her strength and wisdom.

"I love you Avinash...even though I know you will never love me back!" she cried again, hugging a pillow with his T-shirt on it.

The next day was turning out to be a little more bearable than the day before. The excitement of going out and meeting new people was finally catching on. She had never done this before...but was looking forward to it. Madhu lived not very far from the office...just two stations away. Sanam and Madhu reached her home early in the evening.

"Toh, tu hai Sanam? [So, you are Sanam?]," Aji said, laughing in her tutti-futti Hindi and pulling Sanam's cheeks.

"Chaan mulgi haighh! [She (Sanam) is a good girl]," Aji told her daughter-in-law.

Madhu's family was a typical Maharashtrian family...simple, warm, and welcoming. Madhu's father was a government servant, and her mother was a homemaker. Her younger brother Mayank was taking his tenth boards. Madhu's grandmother, fondly called 'Aji' (father's mother), stayed with them.

"It is a small and loving family," thought Sanam with a touch of envy.

"Hmmm...amazing...Aji yeh kya hai?" Sanam asked while biting into a dark savoury pancake.

"Tujhe acha laga?" Aji grinned.

"Bahut zyada! Yummy hai!" Sanam was licking her fingers.

"Thalipeeth kehte hain isko! Chal main batati hoon kaise banate hain!" Aji was beaming.

Madhu's Aji was short, fair and an adorably stout woman. She wore kastha saree *[A Kashta saree is a back tuck at waistline of the fabric that's draped on the bottom..it is 9 yards long]*. With a toothless smile and a walking stick, she looked nothing short of a sweet old teddy bear.

"Sanam tell me are you ok in your head? You are friends with Madhu! Who in her right mind will be friends with this goondi?" Aji grinned, pulling Sanam's cheeks again.

Aji had asked Sanam to sit down and was massaging oil into Sanam's hair.

"Haww Aji!" Sanam could not stop laughing. She felt this affinity to the cute old furball. She was getting something that she had never experienced (after her own mother) in her life-maternal love.

"See I told you na Sanam...My Aji does not value me at all! She does not realise that I am she incarnated. You have no idea what all kands Aji has done in her youth!" Madhu said dramatically only to be hit with a stick by the old lady.

"Dambis! Laaj naahi vaate tula? [*Aren't you ashamed of yourself?*]" Aji said, spreading her toothless grin.

"Donno drama!" Sanam laughed.

"You know Aji and Ajoba (grandfather in marathi) had a love marriage and Aji had proposed to him! Can you imagine? At her age in that era?" Madhu said excitedly.

"Wow Aji! Tell me your love story na!" Sanam begged Aji.

"Arre he was ten years older to me…. tall, dark, and handsome. His family had just shifted to the neighbourhood. He had studied Law in London and I was in the first year of my college. We saw each other for the first time on the terrace. Vaise I too was exceptionally beautiful then as well," said Aji dramatically earning a guffaw from the girls.

"Dinner is ready!" Mayank announced, interrupting their story.

Dinner was a simple yet delicious fare. Varan-bhaat [Daal-rice] and the signature shrikhand with aloo puri.

Sanam requested Aji to continue her story after dinner was done. Sanam, Madhu and Aji were in Madhu's room. Her mother and father had retired in their own room and Mayank was studying outside.

"Madhu…chal dawa gheyun aa [*Madhu…get the medicine*]," Aji winked at Madhu.

Madhu returned with three glasses. And brought out the bottle of Vodka she hid in her cupboard.

"Ek drink ke bina love story ka maaja nahin aata," Aji winked at the girls. Sanam was shocked for a moment but joined in as they laughed.

"Acha toh…I fell in love with her Ajoba…hero maafik dikhta tha…kitna cute..kitna handsome thaa! Koi bhi ladki marti uspar. But my bad luck…he turned out to be 'Shareef.' I would ogle at him, but he would refuse to look towards me. One day I got tired. I jumped the terrace wall and went to him. He was reading the newspaper and grew so nervous around me that all the papers flew in the morning breeze. I went and kissed him on his cheeks," Aji said blushing.

"Aww…so cute. Phir kya hua?" Sanam was already in love with Aji.

"Bas bol diya…you must marry me! Teri kissi aur se shaadi nahin hone doongi! I then went to my parents and told them that I liked this boy and if they did not say yes then I would elope. We got married next month!" Aji grinned and blushed.

"Chal you too have some Vodka and tell your love story," Aji told Sanam.

"Arre, I don't drink!" Sanam was flabbergasted.

However, Madhu and Aji made her drink some…. enough to loosen up her tongue.

"Pata hai Aji…mera Avinash bahut tall aur handsome hai…sabse achi baat hai he is an amazing person! Main jitni tareef karun utni kam hai…Vo itna acha hai! Par jab gussa ata hai toh ekdum khadoos ban jata hai! Uske bina zara dil nahin lagta…rona aata hai uske bina…Mera bas chale toh khud ko aur usko kamre main band karke chabi phenk doon," Sanam was for the first time sharing about what she felt about Avinash with someone. It felt so good!

"The way he smiles…the way he talks..is so…perfect. Aur uski aankhen! Haye they are so deep..so intense!" Sanam was blabbering and Aji was just grinning from cheek to cheek.

Madhu had already gotten drunk and hit the bed. Sanam was pressing Aji's feet and talking about what she liked no... loved about Avinash. A few minutes later it hit her that Aji too had dozed off. Sanam smiled to herself and picked up her phone. Avinash had not seen his messaging app till now...but there was an SMS sitting there for her!

"Kaisi ho?" it read.

These two words made her heart race.

"Main theek hoon...tum?" Sanam wrote before dozing off.

In the morning, Aji made Amboli (marathi equivalent to uthappa) and fed her with a lot of love. She packed some for the girls' lunch boxes. Aji gave her the pre-mix of Thalipeeth too! Sanam profusely thanked the family for their hospitality.

Sanam had asked Madhu to come to her house for the next day, but Madhu had to run various errands for her own wedding.

The rest of the day was a mix of happiness and warmth of meeting such good people and a longing for her husband.

The next two days seemed like a month to Sanam as Madhu too had taken casual leaves.

Finally, on Friday Madhu returned and things started looking better.

"Aji aur sab kaise hain?" Sanam asked Madhu!

"All fine...Aji toh is missing you so much!" Madhu said with a smile.

"Haye sachi?" Sanam said in excitement at which Madhu giggled.

In the evening, they decided to eat panipuris at the chaat wala stall just outside their office.

Sanam had gotten in the habit of checking her phone every second minute in the hope of getting a text from her husband. Just as Sanam was about to eat her first Golgappa (panipuri), her cell buzzed. She gave her piece to Madhu and checked her phone.

"I will stay out for three more days" - Avinash had messaged.

Tears rolled down her cheeks in an instant. She refused the Golgappa, suddenly losing all appetite.

Her cell pinged again.

"Panipuri kyun nahin khaa rahi?"- Avinash had messaged.

Sanam wiped her tears and started typing when it struck her.

"How does Avinash know?" Sanam said aloud and looked around to see him standing next to his bike...a little far away.

Sanam dropped her tiffin bag and everything else in her hand and ran towards him.

Avinash broke into a big smile watching her drop everything and run towards him, tears streaming down her eyes. He lifted her in his arms as she reached him oblivious to everything around them.

CHAPTER- 19

HUNGER!

Avinash could not stop himself from hugging her. He kissed her forehead and cheeks many times.

"Bas Jaan!" he said, gently pacifying her as she hugged, not letting him go!

"Ghar chalen?" He asked her gently to be rewarded by a nod and a sweet smile on her tear-stained face.

"Arre, don't forget your bags!" Madhu came running after them.

Sanam hugged him tightly on the bike with both her hands in his one, while he managed the bike with the other. They held onto each other till they reached home.

"I need to bathe," Avinash said the moment they entered home. He stripped off his kurta and headed towards the washroom. Sanam was taken aback, she had expected at least a kiss the moment they entered.

She sullenly picked up his discarded clothes. It seemed like he had returned home first and then headed to pick her up.

"Sanam towel de na!" Avinash yelled ten minutes later. As Sanam handed the towel, he grabbed her wrist and pulled her in.

Sanam gasped as Avinash pulled her to himself and claimed her lips. His wet dripping body soaked her clothes too...but she was not complaining. The kiss spoke of hunger and desperation. They were under the shower, but their bodies were on fire.

"I was full of grime Jaan! I needed a shower but now I need you!" he said, taking off her clothes swiftly.

"Did you miss me, Jaan?" he asked, pinning her against the wall with one hand and cupping her breast with another.

"Aviiiinash," Sanam moaned. She was slick with desire in an instant.

"Bol na Jaan? Did you miss me?" Avinash now roaming his tongue on her nape.

"Bahut miss kiya," she said, cupping his face to claim his lips.

Her hands roamed around his sinewy arms. She tore off her lips from his to kiss his chest and biceps.

Avinash's breathing became laboured as she cupped his behind. His manhood that had stiffened long ago was eager to find release. Sensing his need Sanam bent down and took it in her mouth....

Avinash could not stop himself from grunting in pleasure. He placed one hand on the wall to support himself and the other on her head. After a few minutes, Avinash lifted her, put his lips on her and consumed her in a passionate kiss.

"I can't wait to take you!" he lifted her, and she instinctively wrapped her legs around him.

"You want to do it standing? It will be painful later!" he asked her.

"I have fantasised about it ...a lot ...with you!" Sanam told him in a sultry tone.

Her words tripped him over the edge of desire. His strokes became deeper as Sanam moaned his name again and again driving him mad.

Sanam was delirious with pleasure. She thought she would die if he stopped.

"Avinash!" Sanam screamed in pleasure.

His strong strokes quickly led to earth shattering orgasm for her. She collapsed on him, spilling him with her hot, molten flow.

"I missed you, Jaan!" he grunted as he climaxed. Avinash had to hold the wall with both hands for support. Sanam unwrapped herself from him and would have fallen had Avinash not supported her. Her legs had turned to jelly, but a delicious sense of fulfilment had taken over her body.

"Baby wait here!" Avinash wrapped a towel around himself and walked out. He returned in a jiffy bringing in two soft and fluffy towels. He tied one towel around her torso and the second around her hair.

He lifted her and took her to the bed covering her with the duvet, joining her right away. The warmth of their cuddle after the cold shower sent her to heaven.

Sanam could not take her eyes off him. She wanted to soak every inch of him…his jaw cut…his deep beautiful brown eyes, his abs, his stocky hands…everything.

"Like what you see?" Avinash said in a naughty tone.

"Immensely!" Sanam kissed his chest and grinned like a Cheshire cat.

"Taad rahi ho tum mujhe!" he teased her.

"Bilkul! Tum tadne ki cheez ho…Totta ho!" Sanam said lifting herself from his chest and resting her head on her arm to get a better look at him.

"Totta..what's that?" he asked with a grin.

"Hmmm… 'Totta' is the cheesy Punjabi equivalent to the sophisticated 'Handsome hunk' in English" she teased him. "What do you prefer? English or Punjabi version?" she chuckled.

"You are too much!" he grinned ear to ear and tried hiding the blush that had crept in.

"And you are too strong!" she said with a short breath recollecting their recent tryst.

Her comment sent delicious shivers down his body. He pulled her to himself and kissed her thoroughly. Their towels had been long undone, she could feel his stiffness poking her in the right place. They would have gone ahead for another steamy session of love making had Avinash's stomach not growled …loudly.

Sanam guffawed.

"Bhook lagi hai Jaan! I will eat you later, give me food first, woman!" he said.

Sanam got up quickly, wore one of his T-shirts and bolted to the kitchen.

He soon joined her in the kitchen, hugging her from behind.

"Thalipeeth! Wow..it's my favourite! Tumhe kaise pata?" he was as excited as a kid who had just been handed over a huge bar of chocolate.

"I learnt it from Madhu's Aji!" Sanam said, putting the water on the stove for ginger tea to go along with thalipeeth.

"This is delicious!" Avinash said as he gorged on Thalipeeth laced with a huge dollop of homemade white butter. Sanam had followed Aji's instructions to serve it with a mound of homemade butter. Making butter at home was the first thing Sanam had done after returning from Madhu's place.

Sanam watched Avinash eating with a lot of happiness. She had cooked all her life but watching the way Avinash enjoyed food cooked by her filled a void in her heart.

"Handsome ...one more thalipeeth?" she asked him.

"Irada kya hai tumhara Biwi...kya baat hai?" he teased her. Sanam was almost going to drop the besan ladoos she was plating on hearing 'Biwi' from his mouth.

"Huh?" Sanam asked.

"Yeh 'handsome' kabse bulana shuru kar diya tumne?" he asked her with a ridiculously cute smile.

"Jabse 'Avinash Malhotra' ko handsome bolne par problem hui tumhe!" she giggled as he blushed.

Sanam kept the ladoos in front of him and kissed his cheeks. He held her hand and made her sit in his lap. She hugged him and sat contentedly for some time as he relished the besan ladoos.

"Shit I am so tired…" Avinash thought aloud sometime later.

Sanam made him sit down on the floor and brought out a bottle of oil to massage his hair. Sanam was never going to know that Avinash's luxury car had broken down in the middle of nowhere in the rural area of the state. He had travelled in state transport buses (changing three buses) to reach in time to pick her up. His back had borne the brunt though.

"Oye handsome chal...so jate hain!" Sanam shook Avinash who was dozing off.

They snuggled in and both slept properly after quite a few nights.

CHAPTER- 20

MARRIED BUT NOT BLIND

Next weekend...

"Haye…. you can't really trust gadgets these days," Sanam came out of the kitchen with a look of irritation as she gave Avinash his morning cup of tea.

"What happened?" Avinash asked her.

"The mixer has stopped working. It was working fine till last night," Sanam told him.

"Hmmm…" Avinash hummed.

"Let me see!" Avinash entered the kitchen armed with a screwdriver and took over the mixer.

"Arre jaane do…I will take it to the market today," she told him.

"You do not need to …. I will mend it!" Avinash said with confidence.

"Tumhe aata hai?" Sanam could not believe her ears…Never in her dreams had she ever thought that Avinash would be so hands on!

"Bas husband par trust nahi karna…. Woh gair aadmi ki baat par bharosa hai tumhe!" Avinash said while taking the mixer outside to his writing table. He had just finished a gruelling writing session, and this promised to be fun.

"Suno, Kuch Khaa lo na," Sanam said to a busy Avinash sometime later.

Avinash had gotten so busy that his tea and breakfast were getting cold.

Giving up on him…Sanam started feeding him herself. Once done she shifted her focus on getting the lunch done.

An hour later lunch was ready, but the mixer was not. Avinash had opened every damn part of the mixer ….barring the base. If one did not look at the base, from where one could guess that this mess of nuts and bolts would have once been a mixer!

"Chalo lunchtime handsome!" Sanam gently kissed him on the cheek.

"Bass almost done..." Avinash said while concentrating on the job in hand.

"Avinash bore kar diya tumne aaj," Sanam whined.

"We could have done so much today.... socho na kitna kuch!" she tried to tempt him.

"Bas baby.... Tera toh one track mind hai! "Avinash teased her.

"Theek hai...track nahi pasand toh track badal deti hoon!" Sanam said, taking it seriously.

"Nahin Jaan...I was kidding. Let us have lunch!" Avinash tried to pacify her.

"Abey yeh kya hai?" Avinash wondered aloud.

"Gatte ki sabzi!" Sanam replied.

"Main nahin khaunga.... kaisi hai yeh!" Avinash made a face.

"Zara taste toh karo!" Sanam tried to coax him into eating it.

"No!" Avinash threw a tantrum like a kid.

"Tumhe meri kasam!" Sanam used the last resort.

"Kya Yaar...tum fayda uthati ho Mera!" Avinash said while dipping his chapati into the rich gravy.

"Holy hell!! This is.... ummmm...yummy! "Avinash said while relishing the food to be rewarded by cute kisses on his cheeks by his wife.

"Mixer is ready...chalo try karte hain!"Avinash said enthusiastically.

The moment he fixed it in the jar, the whole structure collapsed, spilling the contents of the jar and the parts of the mixer everywhere.

"Bhaiya iska kuch ho sakta hai?" Sanam opened the rummages of once-upon-a-time-mixer that had been wrapped in a piece of clothing.

The shopkeeper looked baffled.

"Behenji yeh kya hai? Yeh kaise ho Gaya?" Sanam wanted to laugh but looking at Avinash's grim face chose not to.

"Woh... hamari building main ek hain…. ghar par repair karte hai …. unhone Kiya!" Sanam was struggling to keep a poker face.

"Problem kya thi? Achanak chalna band ho gaya?" the shopkeeper asked, leaving Sanam and Shastriji surprised.

"Child lock lag gaya hoga! Yeh dekhiye!" the shopkeeper showed them a small button at the base of the mixer.

"Nausikhiya hai repair wala aap ka...aage se kuch bhi ho... bande ko yaad rakhiye!" he said sweetly, raising Shastriji's temper.

"Lekin ab iska kya?" Sanam asked the shopkeeper.

"The repairs are going to cost you Rs. 2500...if you add Rs. 500, you can buy a new mixer," he said.

A little while later Sanam and Shastriji left the store with a new juicer- mixer in tow. Sanam with a grin and Shastriji with a deep blush.

"Chalo baby! Let us go!" Avinash called out to Sanam who was dressing up for the evening. Rohan and Madhu were going to meet them over dinner. Sanam came out with skinny jeans and a light pink peach chikankari short kurta looking resplendent.

Avinash had discarded his Kurta for a trendy T-Shirt and jeans that emphasised his sinewy arms.

As they were riding the bike, on the opposite side of the road, Sanam spotted a busty girl in a skintight top walking with a bounce. As they crossed her, she saw Avinash turn his gaze to check the girl out. Sanam felt furious at this and instinctively gave a sharp slap on his helmet making him aware that she had registered his checking out the girl.

Sanam was in a bad mood by the time they reached the restaurant and joined Madhu and Rohan.

Madhu and Rohan got up to greet them. Sanam tried to sit with Madhu, but her plan was slyly foiled by Shastriji who held her by her shoulder and made her sit next to him on the sofa. Shastriji tried holding her hand or extracted a smile from Sanam but failed.

"Aur bata Lady Killer!" Rohan teased Avinash.

"Abey kya bol raha hai?" Avinash tried to douse the fire that promised to burn him later.

"Tere andar aate hi...Woh girls ki nazar tujh par atak gayi hai!" Rohan said while pointing out a table full of girls openly drooling over Avinash.

Sanam gave those girls a bad look.

"Abey bas kar ...vaise bhi bahut bhadki hua hai aaj!" Avinash spoke in Rohan's ears.

"Isn't it too quiet today?" Rohan said after a few minutes observing the cold vibes between the otherwise romantic couple.

Avinash looked nervously at his wife.

"Is it the quiet before the storm?" Rohan teased Avinash.

"Acha yeh batao...galti kiski thee?" Madhu teased Sanam and Avinash.

Sanam gave a look to Avinash. "His. He has hurt me!" she said.

"Maine? Main kyu hurt karunga? Yaar these Indian women na... seriously.... they are so narrow minded," Avinash spoke in his defence.

"What are you trying to say?" Sanam budged in.

"Interesting!" Rohan chuckled.

"Abey....it wasn't my fault. I was...we were... on the bike and there is this ...this ...well ...well-endowed sexy girl walking rather briskly.... you understand na Rohan?" Avinash was trying to tell Rohan not willing to articulate it!

"Ooh...wah yaar...wow...lucky yaar!" Rohan said, gushing.

"Ouch!" Rohan screamed when Madhu smacked his arm.

"And Sanam has picked up the fork to murder her husband...and rightly so!" Madhu commented.

Avinash took the fork from her hands and kissed her. However, Sanam still had that murderous expression.

"Arre Indian girls need to understand that we are MARRIED but not BLIND!" Avinash and Rohan burst into laughter.

"Nature has distributed so much beauty...let's appreciate it! I was just doing that... appreciating it!" Avinash rested his case with Rohan siding with Avinash and Madhu siding with Sanam.

"Zayada na intelligence mat jhado Avinash!" Sanam told Avinash.

"Baby main intelligent hi paida hua hoon!" he said bragging. He knew Sanam was getting pissed off, but he liked his Sanam feisty now and then.

"Dekhi maine aaj intelligence- Mixer bhool gaye?" Sanam said sarcastically.

Avinash blushed and groaned. Sanam then launched into the whole Mixer fiasco leaving everyone in splits.

"Aur itne intelligent hai ki janab ko aaj tak aloo aur kaddu (yellow pumpkin) ki subzi main difference nahin pata chala!" Sanam got back, giving Madhu a high five.

"What? Woman, you have been feeding me kaddu?" Avinash said, genuinely surprised.

"Feeding nahin...you have been practically begging for kadoo!" Sanam laughed with Madhu joining in.

"Saare husbands ek jaise hote hain...Apne aap ko supersmart samajhte Hain!" Madhu looked towards Rohan.

"Madhu tune jo us din pilaaya tha na mujhe ...woh mangwa," Sanam said sweetly now in the mood for fun.

Madhu ordered a vodka with thumbs up for Sanam and herself.

"Jaan you will drink?" Avinash asked. He was not aware that his girl had started drinking.

"Wives bhi na bahut controlling hoti hain," Rohan chuckled.

"Husbands itne budhu hoon toh wives kya karen!" Madhu replied sarcastically.

"Arre wives ke pass toh hathiyaar hota hai na...bhrasmastra!" Avinash added.

Sanam and Madhu looked at each other shocked.

"I didn't tell him! I swear!" Sanam told Madhu who just would not stop laughing.

"Kya?" Rohan asked, baffled by the women's reaction.

"Kasam! Jab koi logic nahi chalta toh KASAM!" Avinash said.

This reply brought wholehearted laughter from the girls.

"Inke lagne pe duniya chalti hai," Avinash added.

"Bachelor life zyaada achi hai na?" Rohan said

"Haan bey!" Avinash added.

"Chal toh bachelor life main vapis chal!" Rohan told Avinash.

"Kaise?" Avinash asked him.

"Do you play football? " Rohan asked him.

"Of course...college team captain!" Avinash said.

"Sab ladkiyaan marti thee Football captain par! Hai na Avinash," Sanam added sweetly.

"Tumhe kaise pata?" Avinash asked Sanam.

"Bas jahaan par the handsome hunk Avinash ho vahan toh ladkiyaan pagal hongi na!" Sanam said dramatically. Her every word reeked of sarcasm. The alcohol was kicking in now. She was not tipsy but just a little high!

Avinash was now getting worried with the way this evening was turning out.

"I need to do some damage control otherwise I will be just twiddling my thumbs at night!" he told himself.

'Toh kal football match final?" Rohan confirmed.

"Confirmed," Avinash replied and sealed the deal.

Avinash gestured him to wrap up the party as the women left for the washroom.

"Madhu dekh woh ladkiyaan kaise humare boys ki taraf dekh rahi hain!" Sanam told Madhu.

"Arre humare wale bhi toh 'Married but not blind' ka jhaap kar rahe hain,"Madhu scowled.

They had been observing the guys from the washroom. The men would off and on look at that side and smile.

"Sabak sikhana padega! Are you in?" Sanam asked Madhu.

They sealed the deal with a high five and a hug.

CHAPTER -21
SWEET REVENGE

Sanam was a little miffed with Avinash and had been ignoring him since the last one hour. She had quickly changed into one of his T-Shirts and feigned sleeping.

Avinash understood that he had majorly goofed up his chances for the nightly bliss. He mentally kicked himself for not foreseeing the ramifications of his being 'a smart Alec'. He thought of a plan to coax her into his evil designs for the night.

"Baby your skin is so dry...let me apply some moisturiser!" Avinash told Sanam.

He got a bottle of moisturiser and started applying it on Sanam's arms. He had taken off his T-Shirt to make a stronger case.

Sanam knew where this was going but remained impassive.

Avinash started on her legs.

"It is actually feeling so bloody good," Sanam told herself. She did not realise that she had moaned in pleasure already, raising hopes for Avinash.

"Should I play with fire?" Sanam asked herself and then decided to go for it.

"Handsome, do my back too please!" Sanam said taking off her T-shirt.

Avinash gasped. He had not thought it would be so easy to convince her, but he was in for a surprise.

He turned her around and started massaging her stomach ... sneakily going up...way up in circular motion.

Sanam moaned!

"Hmmm.... this feels so good....so relaxing! Gosh..I am so sleepy!" She yawned as well.

Avinash felt like he was standing outside the best chocolate boutique of the world but had no money to buy anything. This window shopping was killing him. "Whose fault is that?" his heart asked quietly.

"Let's try harder," his mind told him. 'Harder' being the operative word.

Since massaging her mounds did not work, he chose to go for the deep valley.

His one hand went underneath her and wrapped her breasts. Slowly his other hand stroked her lower tummy and then sneakily dipped lower stroking her core with his magical fingers. It was not before earth shattering orgasm rocked her...almost undoing her resolve!

"Thanks baby...Goodnight!" she turned and kissed him and went back into the duvet stifling her laughter as she saw expressions on his face.

He had lost all hope when suddenly Sanam turned around and straddled him..... playing with him.

"Masseur...Masseur khel ho gaya ho toh kuch dhang ka karen?" she said, unable to control her laughter.

Avinash immediately shifted his weight to bring her down and towered over her.

"I thought you would never ask sweetheart!" Avinash now completely stoked with desire laid claim to her lips.

Rohan had been a member of a local football team during his engineering days. Since the time he had returned from the US on his two month long 'Wedding holiday' he had been playing with them. This team had reached the finals of a local championship. Unfortunately, one player had fractured his leg and had withdrawn at the last minute. Rohan as a last resort had asked Avinash and was happy that this worked.

Avinash left early in the morning for the football game practice so that the team could get to know him and vice versa.

Avinash came home incredibly happy. He was crazy about football and had a wonderful time in the morning practice session. He returned home, freshened up, ate, made love to his girl, and went off to sleep to leave again in a few hours. All this while he was so preoccupied with strategizing the match that he completely missed the naughty glint in his wife's eyes who was planning to serve him a new dish: Revenge…. best served cold.

Avinash reached on time, half an hour before the match and met Rohan and others. He was a talented player and the team had seen that in the morning. His leadership qualities quickly made the team respect him.

It was a big muddy ground. There were no stands. Each team's patrons stood around the boundary. On one side a few bikes had been parked. Some people were sitting on the bikes to watch. The atmosphere was electrifying. The public broke into a big applause and cheers when the teams arrived on the ground.

The opposing team was a team of brutes. Rohan had not been wrong when he had told him that the opposing team played very rough and tough. Avinash had realised this in the first five minutes of the play when he got into a confrontation with the captain of the opposing team 'Shekhar'.

Shekhar was a tall, well-built guy and extremely aggressive.

Avinash was playing offence and scored the first goal in the sixth minute of the game. The team was rocking it till the fifteenth minute, when Avinash noticed the members started getting distracted. A weird energy came into the group. Not only his team, but the opposing team also started slipping up. Avinash was baffled with this sudden change when he spotted the source of trouble. From his peripheral vision he saw two very good-looking girls, now seated on his bike, watching the match. All he could see was two pairs of sexy legs.

"Huh! No wonder all the men are off their game!" turning to carefully observe the beautiful ladies when he got the shock of his life…the girls were none other than Sanam and Madhu. And the worst thing was that all the men on the ground were lusting after them.

"What the fu*k! Concentrate guys…concentrate!" Avinash yelled with frustration.

"Rohan woh dekh," Avinash told Rohan.

"Half time main dekhte hain!" Rohan told Avinash, but Avinash was now a devil incarnate.

He went towards their side and asked why in gestures. However, the girls refused to look at him. They were busy admiring Shekhar and his gang who were passing smiles to them.

"Mujhe substitute kar," Avinash told the captain.

"Abe koi hai nahin...kaise karun?" the captain told him.

Avinash was now completely frustrated. He was finding it difficult to concentrate on his game.

"I have no one but myself to blame," he told himself wanting to murder all men on the ground.

Finally, the half time was declared. His team was able to score another and give away two. The score was two all.

"Guys concentrate!" the captain said in frustration.

"Ek minute de! Rohan chal!" Avinash told the captain.

"Madhu," Sanam said softly and smiled when she saw the men running towards them.

Madhu was wearing khaki shorts with a sleeveless top that accentuated her svelte figure. Sanam was wearing a floral-patterned maroon half jumpsuit that showcased her long legs and a ponytail with lip gloss.

Avinash had a million emotions playing havoc with his heart and brain.

"Madhu, what in hell are you guys doing here?" Rohan asked Madhu in anger who moved away dramatically. Rohan went after her trying to placate her.

Avinash just stared at Sanam with a weird expression on his face. He was aware that a lot of men were staring at them. He came near and picked her in his arms and turned towards the ground and placed his lips on hers claiming her in front of the whole ground.

The kiss was a passionate one. It was a claim Avinash laid on Sanam warning everybody to steer clear of her.

He could hear a collective gasp and many hearts breaking.

Rohan too had returned after placating Madhu.

Avinash and Rohan returned after claiming their women to a few disappointed guys.

"Oye...bhabhiyaan hain tumhari...game par dhyan do," Avinash said sternly, pulling everyone up.

The second half started. Both the teams were at each other's throats.

The play was getting rougher by the minute. At that very moment, it started raining.

Shekhar had realised the opposing team's best player's weakness…. his girl.

He came near the women and took off his jersey in front of Sanam making a play for her.

The next moment he was knocked down by Avinash who was aiming at him rather than the goal post. A fight broke out with Avinash punching Shekhar in the face. They were thankfully stopped by their respective teams, who intervened to broker peace.

"Whoever looks at my wife will not leave this ground on his legs," declared Avinash. His face was bloodied in the fight, but Shekhar's was worse. Avinash left him and went towards Sanam. He kissed her on the lips again, took off his jersey and threw it at her. He was now shirtless with a bloodied face in the middle of a muddy football field on a rainy day.

Sanam could not take her eyes off Avinash. He looked so attractive...so dashing….so devilish. She realised she had fallen for an ultimate bad boy…the devil himself and this realisation put her body on fire.

Somehow Avinash intuitively guessed her thoughts and blew a flying kiss to her before going back to the game.

The men were now fighting for their life on the field. Both the teams were kicking each other's asses. Madhu was almost in tears when Rohan fell and got hurt.

Sanam was faring a little better. If Avinash was getting beaten up, he was beating the others too. He looked like an anti-hero full of angst. Sanam loved this side of her man. He was macho and virile: her dream man. It felt as if her fantasy was playing out.

Ultimately, after a gruelling second half, Avinash's team won with two goals in the last minute. One done by Rohan and another by Avinash.

As the buzzer sounded, the teams celebrated. Avinash left everything and ran to his wife. It was still raining and there she was looking like a siren soaking in rain. He claimed her lips again. She was like this drug in his system...he was unable to get enough of her.

"So?" Avinash asked her.

"So.... Married but not blind?" Sanam asked, trying to stifle a laugh.

"Married and BLIND," Avinash said as they both burst into laughter.

CHAPTER- 22

TRUTH

"Arre yaar biwi...it hurts!" Avinash could not stop hissing in pain.

Although it was exhilarating to play a hero on the ground, the consequences were not that exciting. Sanam had spent the entire night putting hot water-compress on various parts of Avinash's anatomy.

"Abey yaar pyaar se… husband hoon tumhara…roti nahi jise garam-garam sek rahi ho!" Avinash whined after another hot compress.

"Heropanti karte hue yaad rakhna chahiye tha!" Sanam giggled.

Avinash had a swollen eye, a badly scraped knee, and a bloodied elbow. Bruises were scattered across his body.

Sanam had taken a holiday the next day to tend to her husband. He was worse than a child when injured. She had to coax him into eating food and painkillers.

"You are not going anywhere," Avinash declared, putting his head in her lap.

He was clinging to her like a kid, which secretly gladdened Sanam. She felt so protective towards him. She knew he was stronger than she is, superior to her in strength, but she wanted to protect his tender heart.

He was a giver in life. He gave his heart and soul in whatever he invested his time. Sanam would often observe him writing, thinking, and dwelling on things which were best left alone.

She often noticed his eyes...they were full of sadness sometimes. She wanted to heal him from the hurt he had suffered...wanted to fill his mind with happy memories.

His drinking and smoking worried her to no end. He had almost given up drinking but was still smoking a lot. Sanam thought of doing something about it. She kissed his sleeping face and tried getting out of his embrace to answer the call of nature. Getting out was futile because he had gripped her so closely. She gave up and rather enjoyed his warmth.

A few days later...

Avinash parked his bike inside a palatial mansion located in an upscale Sea facing residential area of Mumbai. He had lived his three decades of his life here...in his 'home'. It had been almost a year that he had shifted out. Now that modest one room apartment felt more homely rather than this huge, imposing, and opulent dwelling. He felt indifferent towards it. This bothered him. He had not left this house in happiness...but nothing could be done about it. Today was Ganesh Chaturthi. He never missed it. He owed this to his parents, no matter how bad the relations were.

"I do not need to think now! Let us get this done with!" he told himself as he threw his bag on his shoulders and walked into the mansion.

"Montu (Avinash) has come!" his mother almost cried in delight as she watched him enter the main door. Handing over the stuff she had in her hand to a house help standing nearby, she stood there with moisture in her eyes.

"Aai!" Avinash bent to touch her feet. His mother tried her level best to hide the moisture in her eyes but some treacherous bit of it spilled out.

Avinash hugged her out and kissed her forehead.

Mrs. Karuna Shastri was a petite woman. She had warm and kind eyes. Life had been kind to her because she looked younger than her fifty- five years. However, a lot of wrinkles and sorrow had crept on her face recently.

"Last year wasn't kind to you too Aai!" Avinash thought to himself with dismay.

"You came earlier than I expected. Chalo, you can have breakfast with us! Bhattji (Panditji in marathi) came in the morning and did the sthapana of the murti," Karuna was blabbering on quite uncharacteristically. Her son had returned home after almost a year.

"Papa and Baba?" Avinash asked her.

"Kab aaya beta?" his father came from behind. There was a little awkwardness between the son and the father, but Avinash took the initiative and bent down to take his blessings. His father in turn hugged him. Alok Shastri was a medium built sixty-year-old man with keen eyes. He had mousy brown hair and a moustache. A pair of black spectacles sat perched on his high bridged nose giving him a dreamy look which so many women were still crazy about, much to the dismay of Mrs. Shastri.

"Papa has lost a lot of weight!" Avinash made another observation with a prick of guilt.

"Oye Montu! Mera bacha!" an elderly voice called Avinash from behind.

"Baba!" Avinash already had a huge smile on his face.

"Bansi kaka...get baba some coffee," Karuna said, trying to fill the silence on the breakfast table between the father and son. The table was full of delicacies, but Avinash felt his hunger ebb somewhere. Yet, he wanted to make an effort today. He attacked the food with gusto.

Avinash wanted to reach his home early so had not eaten anything since morning, barring the morning tea Sanam and he had together. Sanam. Although his mind had argued that he could not have brought her here, his heart had whispered otherwise. He was already missing her. Avinash had not been very keen on leaving her alone at a festival, as it is she had no family except him, but he had ultimately given up in favour of his mind.

"Montu take this sabudana khichdi...I made it especially for you!" Karuna served him, breaking his train of thought.

"Yummy! Khoob chaan Aai *[very delicious]*," Avinash said.

"Papa, take some khichdi...it's nice!" Avinash asked his father.

"I ...I..will try!" his father fumbled while speaking. It had been over a year since his son had spoken to him. Mr. Shastri almost broke down with emotion but held himself back.

"Kaisa hai tu Montu?" Baba asked him, patting his shoulder, his voice heavy with emotion.

Baba was Satyendra Kumar Shastri, called Satti by his friends. He was a business icon of his times and the founder of the Shastri Empire. He was a medium built but extremely handsome guy for eighty years. Baba was Avinash's paternal grandfather, his mentor, and his best friend.

"Theek hoon Baba...dekho weight put on kar liya hai!" Avinash joked showing his flat tummy.

It was a lame joke, but his parents could not stop smiling.

It seemed their only son was slowly returning to them. The bitterness and the anger were not visible today.

"He is smiling...after years...he is smiling!" Karuna stole a look at her husband, who was as overwhelmed with emotion as she was. She thanked Ganpati Bappa for the positive change she was seeing in her son.

It was after a long time that family members were talking at the dining table.

"Acha how did the Sholapur Farmhouse deal go?" Baba asked Avinash to divert his attention as everyone ran out of things to talk at the table. The men started talking and went to Baba's room to complete the discussion. They were still talking when a house help came and called Alok out.

"Let me show you the projection Baba," Avinash said, reaching for his backpack for the laptop.

As he was taking his laptop out, a small lunch box fell out.

"Ladoo," Avinash said aloud. Since he had refused breakfast, Sanam had put some ladoos for him in his backpack. A huge smile came to his face as he thought about her sweet gesture.

"Besan ka ladoo!" Baba exclaimed as he snatched the ladoo from Avinash leaving Avinash in splits. His old man had a sweet tooth, how could he forget.

"Wah...maza aa gaya! Kisne banaya?" Baba asked Avinash.

"Woh.. woh...Halwai ke yahan se laaya!" Avinash fumbled.

"Barkhurdaar Halwai ke ladoo main itna swaad kahan! Chal sach sach bata kya naam hai uska?" Baba coaxed him gently.

"Kaun? Kis ladki ka naam bataun?" Avinash now on full alert.

"Ghar ka ghee...ghar ka ladoo.... ladoo dekh kar yeh smile. Hum gadhe dikhte hain?" Baba teased him.

Avinash blushed.

"Aur waise maine nahi bola ladki...tumne bola ladki!" Baba was smiling now.

Avinash knew he was trapped now. Anyways he had never been able to hide anything from Baba.

Baba was the only one who had never doubted him...no matter what or how bad the circumstances had been. His love had been unconditional for Avinash. And that was the reason Avinash loved Baba more than he loved his parents, and they knew it. Sometimes he felt his own father felt jealous of the bond he shared with his grandfather.

"Acha ...let me close the door," Avinash went and bolted the door and returned to Baba sitting at his feet.

Avinash told Baba everything that had happened including the marriage and divorce papers in brief.

"Toh bola ki nahin usko?" Baba asked him.

"Kya?" Avinash seemed puzzled.

"Wahi...I love you!" Baba smiled as he spoke.

"LOVE? Love nahin hai Baba...Love thodi na hai...Love hai hi nahin! Emotional attachment hai!" Avinash was trying hard to convince himself more than he was trying to convince his grandfather.

"Chalo...koi na! Ek peg marega?" Baba asked.

"Abhi? Subah subah hai...aur Ganpati Ji aaye hain! Kya baat karte ho Baba?" Avinash appeared to be shocked.

"Chod use...tere face par kya hua? Ladai hui?" Baba gave him a worried look. The aftermath of the football match was still visible on Avinash's face.

"Football match main hua!" Avinash averted his gaze but caught his grandfather grinning at him.

"Kya...Kya hua? Why are you smiling like you just cracked a deal?" Avinash was now flustered.

"Chal ready for analysis?" Baba asked him. This had always been the most happening part of their conversation. Avinash had always brought his problems to Baba and then they did SWOT (Strength, Weakness, Opportunities and Threat) together. Together they had found a solution to his dilemma on career, problems with peers, his proposal to the first girlfriend and breakups! They were a team.

"Pichle teen saal se tune har roz subah uthkar daaru maari hai...aur aaj alcohol does not interest you! You hardly drank during your Sholapur trip. Your skin tone has become better...smoking has reduced. Nails have been cut...did you cut? No because you cannot...till last year your mother used to do that for you! Your face is glowing...means you are eating a balanced diet with lots of fibre...only a girl can do that. You have already finished your script after years of a writing block but postponed the New York plan...means you want to stay here. You have started talking to your parents. And the most important evidence...you are smiling! If this is not love, then pray tell me...what is?" Baba rested his case leaving Avinash completely SHOCKED!

"That's the truth Avinash...accept it!" Baba said gently.

CHAPTER- 23
HAPPINESS

Avinash was left speechless and was thankful when Bansi Kaka interrupted.

"Memsaab ne coffee bhijwai hai!" Bansi Kaka came in with a tray with tastefully arranged Pistachio and cashew cookies, Avinash's favourites.

"Chalo...at least because of you I got to eat these," Baba said, attacking the plate.

"Baba...diabetes!" Avinash warned Baba.

"Oho...Kuch nahin hota!" Baba ignored enjoying the goodies, willing to let the matter slide.

"Chal yaar...photo toh dikha!" Baba told Avinash.

Avinash took out his phone and showed him a few photographs. These were the pictures he had taken secretly before leaving for Sholapur. A few were of her sleeping.

"Yeh iski naak thodi tedhi hi na...Aur bunny teeth bhi hain?" Baba observed.

"Arre that's the cutest thing about her," Avinash responded and blushed when he realised Baba was stifling his laughter.

"Baba meri class le rahe ho?" Avinash said with a sigh.

"Arre nahin Montu," Baba was laughing harder now.

Avinash was flustered.

"Bahut pyari bachi hai...Naam kya hai?" Baba said in a serious tone.

"Sanam Kaur Bedi," Avinash said.

"Punjabi hai? Oye balle balle!" Baba was grinning from ear to ear.

"Mani hoti toh khush hoti!" Baba said softly.

'Mani' or 'Rukmani' was Avinash's paternal grandmother, Baba's wife. She had passed away fifteen years back due to health complications. She belonged to Delhi. During her lifetime, Rukmani Shastri had been incredibly happy that her only son married a genuinely nice and beautiful girl, Karuna; but the fact that Karuna was not a Punjabi pricked her at times. The mother-in-law and the daughter-in-law had a good-natured Punjabi-Marathi tug-of-war always on.

"Does she scold you?" Baba asked him.

"Kabhi kabhi," Avinash smiled fondly at the memory of the few times she had taken his class.

"Do you enjoy it?" Baba asked

"Immensely!" Avinash said sheepishly.

"When will I meet her?" Baba asked excitedly.

"Not soon...you are a flirt!" Avinash said defensively.

"Yaar bada kharaab hai tu! You are scared that she will leave you for a hunk like me?" Baba teased Avinash bursting into laughter.

"Flirting to tune mujhse seekhi...Vaise teri flirting ki aadat gayi ki nahin?" Baba asked him.

"Gayi...gayi...fas gaya iski wajah se!" Avinash said and then went on to tell Baba about the Football match and how Sanam brought him to his knees. Baba was in splits hearing his grandson's marital woes.

"Milwa de na Montu...Badi pyari bachi hai...Mani ki yaad aa gayi," Baba said with longing, feeling a weird connect with Sanam.

"Montu...see who has come!" Karuna called out while opening the door.

His maternal uncles and aunts had come especially from Pune, bringing along their families. Avinash was happy to see his mother's side after a long time. His mother's family was a famous family of Nagpur, settled in Pune from the last two generations.

"Arre Avinash...Kasha ahes tu? (How are you?) Meet my wife Sayli, she too works with us at the firm," Sagar dada proudly introduced his wife.

His cousin, Sagar Kulkarni, son of his older uncle (Mama), had recently gotten married. Avinash could see the newly married couple glancing at each other, passing a secret smile when they thought that no one was watching. This made his heart ache for his Sanam.

"Was it really what Baba was saying?" he asked his own aching heart.

Karuna sat there watching Avinash mingle with her side of relatives. Avinash had taken after his maternal family in looks. Although she herself was petite, her brothers were tall and well built. Though his physique had taken after the Kulkarni clan, his face bore a deep resemblance to his paternal side. He had the signature Shastri traits: bright with a creative bent of mind. He was fiercely competitive, another Shastri trait. There had not been even one competition where he had participated and not won. "He is one of the brightest minds I have met!" Baba always said.

"Avinash has taken the best of both sides," Karuna remembered her own mother's observation about Avinash.

"Vahini [Sister-in-Law] ...look at this," her younger brother's wife called for her attention pulling Karuna out of her thoughts.

Lunch was a gala affair. Not because it was a lavish feast but because one could see the Shastri family happy and light-hearted after a long time.

Avinash smiled as he bid farewell to his relatives. It felt nice to meet his various relatives and cousins today. Baba had retired to his room for siesta.

Avinash decided to look around the house where he was born. His hands reaching out to the walls that he had probably coloured with crayons so many times as a kid. It felt like yesterday.

He remembered the day his mother had caught him defacing the walls and given him a gentle scolding. His grandmother had immediately come to his rescue and ordered him to colour all the walls of her bedroom. His grandparents had not gotten the walls whitewashed for a long time to retain his handiwork till his own father got someone to photograph the walls and hang the prints as a souvenir.

Avinash did not realise when he found himself standing outside his father's study. The door had been ajar…he peeped and saw his father seated in his recliner smoking and lost in thought.

Avinash went inside and sat on the comfortable couch next to his chair. His father's study had often been 'off-limits' for him, as he had his storytelling sessions here. It was a huge room with sun windows overlooking the sea. A gentle breeze came in, throwing the curtains into a tangle every now and then. One whole wall had a huge book collection. In the corner of the room, there was a sophisticated bar offering every variety of alcohol under the sun.

"Kab aaya Montu?" his father asked as his gaze fell on Avinash sitting next to him.

"A while back Papa," he answered.

"How have you been bacha?" his father asked, his voice heavy with emotion.

"Fina Papa...but you haven't been keeping well!" Avinash asked his father.

"I met Sudeep that day...he just couldn't stop praising your script...he is very excited about the project going on floor next month!" Alok Shastri told his son with pride. Sudeep Misra was an internationally acclaimed off beat movie director. His movies were known for cinematic depth and strong characterizations.

"You wrote the screenplay too? Script and screenplay both in the last year?" He asked Avinash, drawing another cigarette and offering one to his son.

"Yes papa!" Avinash said, lighting it for him.

They sat together smoking in silence. Once they were done, his father offered him another which Avinash refused, startling his father.

"I am trying to quit smoking Papa!" Avinash said.

"Arre wah! That is nice...I could never...but great that you are!" his father added.

Avinash and his father sat in silence for some time. Finally, Avinash got up to leave and headed towards the door.

"I always knew you had it in you, Montu...I just couldn't find a way to tell you!" Alok said at the retreating figure. Avinash heard him and turned to find his father in tears.

"I was too harsh on you, Montu! I thought my sarcasm might make you leave that commercial rut you had gotten yourself stuck into for the sake of your friendship. I never thought that in the process I would lose you. I was so scared of you getting used to mediocrity when you are such a bright mind. I did not know how to reach out to you. Instead, I pushed you further away! I am so sorry beta!" Alok said overwhelmed with emotion.

"I am sorry I wasn't there for you when you needed me the most...I am sorry I couldn't be a good father!" Alok Shastri was now shaking with remorseful tears.

Avinash was shocked to see "Hitler Shastri", a moniker he had given to his father, broken down.

He went and hugged his father.

"I was an idiot papa! You did right...I would not have listened otherwise!" Avinash said, consoling him. Avinash's all misgivings about his father were gone in an instant.

Unknown to both, Karuna had been standing outside the study and had witnessed the whole scene. She was reduced to tears. She knew Alok loved their son to bits. The last few years had been the hardest on him. To see your only bright son as a failed alcoholic was painful for any parent especially when one felt that one had contributed to that failure.

Avinash made his father get up and took him into his parents' bedroom and made him lie down.

"Papa, you sleep! You are too tired!" he told his father gently.

"Will you be gone when I wake up? Don't go!" his father asked him.

"No papa...I will be here...In my room! Sleep now," Avinash urged and sat there till his father slept. It struck him how the roles had reversed. There was a time when his father used to put him to sleep and now his father felt like a kid to him.

Avinash turned to see his mother crying.

"Aai!" Avinash hugged her.

"Let's go to my room, Papa is sleeping here!" he took his mother to his own room which was just down the corridor. Like his parent's room, it had a huge balcony overlooking the sea.

His room remained exactly like he had left. It had been aesthetically designed with masculine tones. It had a huge sand bar for his boxing practice. The balcony had a swing on which he and his grandmother used to sit on after he returned from school.

They sat on the bed once his mother stopped crying.

"You didn't miss me, Montu!" his mother complained to him.

"I did Aai!" he said, which was hundred percent true. He had missed his mother a lot.

"I missed your thalipeeth and varan-bhaat a lot!" he said, making her laugh.

"Chal hat...Petu..bas khane ke baare main sochta hai! Kabhi socha...teri Aai kaise rehti hogi tujhe dekhe bina?" Karuna started crying again.

"Sorry Aai...main bahut bura hoon!" Avinash said. He was at loss of words realising he was not the only one who had suffered in the past year.

"Memsahib garam tell!" a domestic help came in and handed over a small vessel of warm oil. Karuna made him sit down for a head massage.

Avinash was doozy after the massage and did not realise when he rolled into a blissful sleep.

He woke up a few hours later, just in time to catch the beautiful sunset. Avinash had not imagined that he would laugh or even smile today, but he was surprised at himself. He felt happy...it felt like a tonne of baggage was off from his heart.

"Sanam ko hona chahiye tha...such a beautiful sunset!" realising that the only missing piece to his happiness was his wife.

"Baba...sab chai ke liye wait kar rahe hain!" Bansi kaka called Avinash out.

He changed into a T-shirt and shorts and proceeded to the dining room. The Shastris had an enjoyable 'high tea' with all members happy and warm with love for each other.

Avinash proceeded to take a bath and got ready for the evening pooja in a new kurta that his mother had bought for him. His mother always chose the kurta for him for the aarti. The rich peach coloured silk kurta made him look dashing.

It was a yearly ritual for the Bollywood industry to turn up at The Shastri Mansion for the first day aarti. Although this year the invites had not gone out as they did every year, still a lot of his father's contemporaries turned up.

The Shastris were gracious hosts. A professional music group had been called for the aarti. The evening was a hit.

It was almost one o'clock at night when the last of the guests left.

"Aai, I should leave now!" Avinash said, bringing tears to his mother's eyes.

"Will you come for Visarjan tomorrow?" Karuna asked him.

"Yes Aai," Avinash told her.

"Come back home, Montu! This is nothing here without you!" his father said, surprisingly.

"I will Papa...soon..I will come back home!" Avinash said. "With someone," his heart added.

Sanam had drifted off to sleep when she heard the doorbell ringing. She saw the time it was almost two at night.

A moment later, her phone rang.

"Avinash pata hai koi doorbell baja raha hai! Mujhe bahut darr lag raha hai! Amma...kya karun?" Sanam whined.

"Abey main hoon...darwaza khol" Avinash laughed.

"Sachi...kha kasam!" Sanam still not out of the sleepy daze.

"Kasam...gadhi!" Avinash laughed.

Sanam opened the bolt and the chain she had put on the door to see Avinash grinning ear to ear...and suddenly she felt a blush creep into her cheeks.

Avinash put aside his backpack and a bag full of goodies his mother had insisted on giving.

He locked the door and stared at her, making her conscious. Avinash had not looked at her for almost twelve hours and now his heart was racing. He just could not keep his emotions in check anymore. He pulled her to himself to smash his lips on hers to kiss her senseless.

CHAPTER- 24

RED AND WHITE

Two days later…

"What the Fuc*! Baby meri white shirt!" Avinash exclaimed.

Avinash had just come out of the washroom, when he noticed his white shirt lying on the stand with pink blotches. The colour from some other cloth had run over his shirt, spoiling it.

"Yaar it was my favourite shirt!" Avinash said, trying to calm his aching heart.

"I know Avi…sorry for your shirt, shorts, jeans and t-shirt," Sanam said seriously, anticipating his outrage anytime.

"T-shirt and jeans …kaunsi t-shirt?" Avinash said in a shock. He clearly had not expected this turn of events.

"Woh Super-Dry green colour wali!" she said softly.

"Abey yaar What the fuc*!" Avinash felt his anger pop up.

"You need to look at what you are putting in the washer! Please woman…meri sab favourite thee! Why do you do so much work? How many times have I told you let us keep a maid…but you no… want to do all the chores yourself and then mess up the whole thing! I so wanted to wear that one today…I have a meeting at ten o'clock! Shit yaar!" Avinash was now very frustrated.

"Phir toh acha hi hua!" Sanam did not realise that she had spoken aloud.

"What did you say biwi?" Avinash said in a dangerous tone.

"Nothing at all!" Sanam kicked herself for speaking aloud and continued with her kitchen chores to make herself invisible.

"You were saying?" Avinash asked her again, standing at the kitchen door draped only in a towel.

"Why do you even wear your shirt...when you must keep the full front open? The first three four buttons are always undone...even your mole is visible. Isse acha hai mat pehno," Sanam blurted out whatever came to her mind.

A small smile was now playing on his lips thinking how she was possessive of him. Avinash was much calmer now.

"Baby now onwards keep your coloured dresses out when light coloured clothes are going in... Ok?" he told her politely.

"Wahi...Wahi toh problem ho gayi...it was not a dress that bled colour...it was... you know woh jo meri new red panty hai na...woh jis pe ek dil bana hua hai ...woh jo teri favourite hai," Sanam blushed while speaking.

Avinash just smiled, enjoying her blushing.

"Woh panty pata nahin kaise teri shorts main aa gayi thee. I knew its colour runs...Pata nahi kaise chali gayi!" Sanam said in a puzzled tone.

Avinash now just stared at her.

"Anyways I am really sorry handsome! Maaf karde!" she said, pecking him on his lips and leaving for a bath.

"Red panty! Red panty!" he repeated and then the panty ...uhh...penny fell for Avinash.

Two days before, Sanam had bought a new red coloured printed negligee which had driven him mad. She looked like a goddess in that. They had made wild love the whole night. The next day, she had left for office, but he could not get that image out of his head. So, he had grabbed the thong type red panty and had given himself to her fragrance and his own lust for her. Once done he had put the panty in his short's pocket, forgotten about it and thrown the shorts in the washer at the end of the day.

"Shit...it was my fault! Isse bataya toh band baja degi...full on drama karegi aur raat ko kuch karne bhi nahi degi!" Avinash told himself.

He was in his thoughts when Sanam walked out of the washroom wearing his white shirt looking as tempting as a cupcake with a topping of chocolate ganache and marshmallow. The front three buttons were open, and her beads were jutting out...teasing his manhood to no end. He now understood the 'Dilemma of the front three buttons!'. He wondered if Sanam did this deliberately...to teach him a lesson?

Meanwhile, Sanam had forgotten that she was still holding the white shirt while she was talking to Avinash about the clothes. She had taken the shirt to the washroom instead of her clothes. When she was done, she realised her mistake...she adorned the shirt as it was spoiled now...better make good use of it.

She hung her towel on the balcony and went to the kitchen unaware how seductive she looked in her current avatar. She was chopping vegetables when a pair of hands groped her from behind. She knew it had to be her husband.

"Kaam ke time par yeh sab soojhta hai usko!" she chuckled.

"Avinash leave me...I need to make food!" she took the rolling pin and gently tapped at him.

Not discouraged by her actions, Avinash kept on working his way around the shirt. He focussed on kneading her supple bosom.

Sanam could not control the moan that escaped her lips. Encouraged by her moans, Avinash slipped his hands into her lace panty. The move hit Sanam like a bolt of electric current. She started squirming as his fingers worked their magic around her core. She held onto the kitchen counter to balance herself. She was now squirming and shivering with pleasure. Working his fingers on her, his mouth was at the nape of her neck drinking on her honeysuckle skin. His manhood was getting painfully heard by every passing minute. Sanam soon orgasmed loudly, much to Avinash's delight. He loved giving her pleasure...and loved being the reason for her pleasure too. He opened the buttons of the shirt and took her arms above her head. He then pulled the shirt up, tying it around her wrists.

Avinash then picked her up on his shoulder and took her to their bed smacking her round bottom all the way! He already felt like a caveman who had picked up his woman for pleasure. Sanam was squirming in anticipation. Her lips were yearning to claim his.

Avinash removed his towel and stood there looking at her, drinking in the sight till he could not hold any longer. He aligned himself to her...she was more than ready for him and moaned loudly when he entered. Her warmth was enveloping him with every thrust. He pumped his desires into her.... realising that he had not felt like this for anyone till now...realising that she had spoiled him for anyone else. His body and soul craved only for her. She was the only thing that had kept him sane in his darkest time...she was his light at the end of the tunnel. She was his...only his. Avinash grunted loudly as he came in, filling her with ecstasy.

They lay down in exhaustion. Suddenly Avinash heard her giggle uncontrollably.

"Kya hua?" he asked her.

She nodded her head in nothing but kept on laughing.

"Ab bologi kya hua?" Avinash lifted himself on his elbow, eager to find out what was tickling her.

"You know, I moan very loudly!" she said giggling.

"Umm...Yeah and that drives me crazy!" he said, licking her cheek.

"Tujhe lagta hai awaz bahar jati hogi?" Sanam asked him.

And for the first time Avinash thought about the thin wall separating their only room from the corridor of the building floor.

"Oh no! I never thought about it!" he confessed.

"You know our friendly neighbourhood aunties have been giving me bad looks for months...I realised why after you moaned today!" she said, abandoning herself to her laughter.

"Fuc*..they aren't getting any from their husbands …. right baby?"

Avinash said before claiming the peak of her breast.

"And here I am getting all fantasies fulfilled!" Sanam said lazily, enjoying what his lips were doing to her. She took his lips off her breasts and brought to hers for a deep kiss.

"Tell me about your fantasies!", Avinash asked her, gently pulling her into his embrace.

"Almost saari fulfil ho gayi hai," she said with a blush.

"Adhoori kaunsi reh gayi?" Avinash asked her.

"Bathtub wali!" she said, hiding herself in his chest, making him laugh.

"Teri bata!" she asked him in return.

Avinash thought hard for a while and then said, "I will tell you in good time!"

CHAPTER- 25
GANPATI BAPPA MORIYA

They had dozed off after their laborious lovemaking. Avinash had to cancel his meeting to reschedule it to another day. The shrill ringing of the phone woke them up.

"Avi tumhara phone!" Sanam spoke gently, nudging him to wake him up.

Avinash on the other hand turned and hugged her, refusing to take the call.

However, the caller was persistent. Avinash had to take the call on the third ring.

"Hello...Rohan!" Avinash spoke as a yawn escaped him.

"Saale...dopahar ke do baje kaun sota hai?" Rohan chuckled.

"Arre nahin...woh raat ko I was working till late ...aankh lag gayi thee! Tu kaisa hai? " Avinash tried to change the topic.

"Sanam kahan hai?" Rohan asked.

"She is ...she is…in the kitchen yaar!" Avinash fumbled as he realised in an instant that he was on speaker as his answer was received with a couple of chuckles which he guessed was Madhu.

"Sanam was supposed to come over for lunch at our home Avinash…we have our Ganpathi visarjan today!" Madhu jumped in.

"Bhai tum log aajayo, yahaan ek item hai jo tumhare bina khana nahin khaa rahi!" Rohan told Avinash. Avinash too had put the phone on speaker.

"Haaye I had promised Aji!" Sanam said, waking up with a yawn.

Avinash slapped his hand on his forehead as Madhu guffawed and Rohan broke into laughter.

"Haraami mat has itna...teri shadi ke baad main poochhunga!" Avinash told him sarcastically.

"Par main sab sach sach bata dunga!" Rohan teased good naturedly.

"Tum log jaldi aa jao! We are waiting for lunch!" Rohan said.

"Tumne sar par haath kyon maara?" Sanam innocently asked Avinash, snuggling into him.

"Abey jab maine bol tha tu kitchen main hai...to boli kyun? They kind of got a hint!" Avinash said.

"Hint about what? Sanam asked again.

Avinash looked at her. They were both without a stitch of clothing covered only by the soft duvet. She looked like a sight for sore eyes. Her hair was ruffled, eyes were droopy, and lips were swollen, but she looked beautiful.

"Jaan tum itni intelligent ho... phir kabhi kabhi itni gadhon wali baatein kyun karti ho?" he asked her while pecking her lips.

"Mujhe aur kiss chahiye!" Sanam whined.

"Chal baby...chalte hain varna they will tease us to no end!" Avinash urged her to get up after kissing her thoroughly.

"Madhu, they are here!" Rohan yelled as he gave a big hug to Avinash and smiled at Sanam.

Avinash felt the warmth in the hug. Rohan had become a very dear friend to him in very less time. Of course, the Sanam- Madhu bond was an instrumental factor in them coming closer, but Avinash had found a genuine and clear-hearted friend in Rohan. He was intellectually stimulating as well. They had bonded well on the football field. Now Rohan seemed more like a brother to him.

"Sanam aali ka? (Has Sanam come?)" Avinash heard an excited voice from behind.

"Aji!" Sanam went and hugged the excited, chubby old lady who had come out. The scene brought a huge smile to Avinash's face.

He could not take his eyes off the duo. It was genuine warmth that he was witnessing.

"Sanam is so warm and sweet! Who would not fall in love with her?" Avinash pondered on the rhetorical question and still not understanding how it highlighted the entire irony of the situation.

"Tera Avinash kahaan hai?" Aji asked in excitement, making Sanam blush.

"Avinash...Yeh Madhu ki Aji!" Sanam introduced her husband to Aji.

"Aah...Hero sarkha disto! [He looks like a hero]", Aji chuckled, making Avinash laugh. He quickly bent to touch her feet to take blessings.

"Tu mala nahi kadhi bolalis hero! [You never called me a hero!] ...I hate you Aji!" Rohan said dramatically, pulling Aji's cheeks.

"Hat..tu Nilu Phule disto…. Dambis! [you look like Nilu Phule (a famous Marathi villain)..Rascal!]" Aji said, delivering a playful slap on Rohan's cheeks making everyone present laugh.

Rohan introduced Avinash to Madhu's parents.

"Chalo, let us have lunch! Aji has been waiting for you!" Madhu said once the couple had taken the blessings of Ganpati.

It was a traditional Marathi fare. Varan Bhaat, batata bhaaji [aloo pakora], Paale bhaji [Leafy vegetable] and Vaal chi bhaji[a kind of soybean preparation], puri , puranpoli, modak and shrikhand.

"Puranpoli mast aahe…Modak pan! [Puranpoli and modaks are amazing!]," Avinash spoke in fluent marathi.

"Tulla marathi yete? [You know marathi?]," Aji said, startled.

"Majhi Aai marathi aahe! Kulkarni...Nagpur chyabajucha Sonegaon [My mother is a Maharashtrian. Surname 'Kulkarni' and hails from Sonegaon near Nagpur]

"Khankaneet Marathi boltoy ha! [He speaks Marathi perfectly!]" Aji said with glee.

"Aika..me khara sangatey… Sanam itka bolli Avinash…Avinash..mera Avinash yeh..mera Avinash woh….mujhko laga…yeh koi hero hi hoga….jo itni sundar ladki mili usko[I will speak the truth….Sanam has spoken so much about 'My Avinash' that I wondered it must be a hero who would have married a beautiful girl like Sanam !" Aji said, making Sanam blush like crazy and everyone else laughed.

"Kya Aji you are embarrassing my friend!" Madhu said.

"Meri bhi beti hai par main jhooth thodi na bol sakti hoon?" Aji said, making everyone laugh again.

After lunch, Aji and Avinash sat together. Aji on the bed and Avinash on the floor near her feet and they talked heart to heart.

Soon it was visarjan time. Madhu's family had kept a five-day Ganpati and took it to the nearest beach for visarjan. Soon Mayank's, Rohan's and Madhu's friends joined in. Rohan's football friends had joined in too, but they were at their best behaviour that day calling Sanam 'Vahini [bhabhi]'…no one wanted to cross Shastriji. They had learnt their lesson on the field that day.

There was a big musical band to take Ganpati Bappa back to his abode. The aarti was phenomenal. Although Sanam did not understand the words, she was surprised that Avinash knew most of the verses. He was singing along with the others. It was so comforting for Sanam to see him completely absorbed in something like this.

"Haye…ghar jaa kar nazar utarungi Avinash ki…nazar na lag jaye!" Sanam told herself.

Avinash was clearly the most handsome and impressive personality in the room. He was receiving a lot of admiring glances from almost everyone. This made Sanam's heart swell with pride.

"Aise mat dekho mujhe Biwi! Aarti chal rahi hai!" Avinash whispered quietly in her ear, smiling and making her blush.

Once the aarti was over, Madhu's father picked up the idol and took it to the back seat of an SUV and everyone hailed "Ganpati Bappa Moriya…Pudche varshi lawkar yaa [Hail Ganpati Bappa…return to us early next year!]"

In the SUV, Aji took her seat next to the idol to distribute the prasad. It was customary to keep the idol company on the way to visarjan.

Sanam had never participated in a visarjan before. She had seen processions from the balcony but never had experienced one. That it was electrifying was an understatement. They had brought in holi colours.

"Oye meri cute Punjaban!" Avinash said, pulling her to himself and before Sanam knew, she was full of red 'Gulal". Sanam took the gulal and coloured his face too. They had changed into their rough clothes as they knew it was going to get messy. Avinash had changed into a ganji...he looked at a sight in his vest. His rippling biceps looked like a work of art. And his smile...it was his smile that made Sanam's heart do somersaults.

"Bappa please, I cannot live without him! Please do something!" Sanam prayed to Bappa with her tears mixing into her smile.

Everyone was full of colour. The procession started with the band leading and the dancing party following with the SUV.

The men had begun dancing like crazy. They were dancing in a circle keeping the women in the circle to keep the untoward attention away. Sanam, Madhu and the other women made their own group and having a fun time. However, the one who stole the show was Avinash.

Today was a revelation for Sanam.... her quiet and taciturn husband was a cracker of a Visarjan dancer. It soon began raining. Visarjan without the rain was no fun at all.

Avinash was having a ball. He had not felt so liberated since years. With Bappa's blessings, it felt like his tough times were over. He was carefree. He was happy. He felt drunk. He felt drunk on happiness. Off and on he would pull Sanam in the circle of madness and would always sneak in a kiss or two. Rohan had again pulled him in for a 'Naagin' dance. Their naagin dance brought in applause from everyone with Madhu and Sanam laughing the loudest. A few moments later, Avinash's eyes searched for his wife, troubled for a moment when he could not find her. He got his breath back when he spotted her with Madhu's mother taking care of her.

Soon, they reached the beach. The barricades did not let the car go nearer to the shore. Aji till last year used to manage, but this year she did not think she would be up to it. Aji and one other elderly woman thought to call it quits as they could not walk that much.

"Aye...kai zhala darling? [what happened?]" Avinash inquired.

"Damli mee! [I am tired!]" Aji replied.

Avinash called Rohan and told him something. Together they went away for a while.

"Where are Avinash and Rohan?" Madhu's father asked.

"Hey Aji!" Avinash and Rohan screamed from afar, pushing a handcart [Haathgadi]. They had rented the handcart from a guy who was taking it back once done with his customer.

They made both the elderly women sit on the cart and the two kids that were in their party and pushed the handcart. Aji could not stop her toothless grin.

"Bagh...[watch] Sanam...bagh Madhu!" Aji screamed in excitement, waving at them.

"Aww...aren't our men darlings? Aren't we lucky?" Madhu said dreamily to Sanam.

"Very...very very lucky!" Sanam replied in an equally dreamy voice.

"Mooshik vaahan modak hast, Chaamar karn vilambit sootra, Vaaman roop maheshwar putra, Vighna vinaayak paad Namaste"

Meaning: *O Vinayaka! The remover of all obstacles, the son of Lord Shiva, with a form which is very short, with mouse as Thy vehicle, with sweet pudding in hand, with wide ears and long hanging trunk, I prostrate at Thy lotus-like Feet!*

Once the last aarti on the shore was over, they followed the professional swimmers, who took Bappa into the sea. The immersion in sea symbolises a ritual see-off of the Lord in his journey towards his abode in Kailash while taking away with him the misfortunes of his devotees.

Sanam felt a sadness encompassing her heart. All this while it was exciting, fun and frolic, but the farewell pained a little. It felt like a family member was going away for a long time.

"Bappa bless me…make me that capable that I am able to bring you home… to my family!" Sanam pleaded to Bappa.

Avinash saw the play of emotions on Sanam's face.

"I know it's tough Jaan," Avinash came from behind and caught her hand. His fingers entwined in hers, warming her heart again.

"Maybe Bappa would hear my plea!" thought Sanam, hoping against hope.

CHAPTER- 26
VINES AND CREEPERS

After Visarjan, Sanam and Avinash had left for home. A while later Avinash stopped at a roadside Pav Bhaji stall. Hunger was gnawing at their insides. The rainy weather and roadside Pav bhaji were a hit pair. The buttery amalgamation of vegetables spiced with a unique blend of spices teased their senses. The sizzle of buttery pav getting fried on the hot tava brought them down to their knees.

"Are you sure Avinash?" Sanam asked him in amazement.

"Haan jaan!" Avinash gave her a sexy grin and parked his bike. Against his better judgement Avinash had stopped at the stall, royally ignoring the shocked expressions from Sanam.

Since the day Avinash had gotten to know that Sanam was malnourished and anaemic, he had become a martinet with her on food. That meant milk and fruits regularly and street food very rarely. Sanam was happy to comply, whatever made her husband happy.

Avinash made her sit on the bike and took the extremely hot plate from the vendor. He took a morsel of the buttery pav and dipped it in the bhaji, blew on it slowly to bring down the temperature and fed it to Sanam, taking her by surprise.

"Ohhhh God...Sooooo..Gooooooooooood!" Sanam couldn't stop herself from moaning, embarrassing the daylights out of Avinash.

"Baby kya kar rahi hai? Bhare bazaar mein lafda ho jayega!" Avinash said with a mixed expression of lust and embarrassment.

"Hmmm... Yeh kitni yummy hai na?" Sanam licked his fingers, finishing off the morsel of buttered pav smattered with Bhaaji.

Avinash bought a bottle of soft drink from the next stall and handed it over to her and soon broke into a smile watching Sanam struggling with the cap of the plastic bottle.

"You are such a baby!" he said tenderly, bringing warmth to her cheeks. Both were so involved in themselves that they didn't realise that a group of young college-going girls standing at the stall were observing them keenly, cooing and giggling at their antics.

As they got ready to leave, Avinash and Sanam realised those girls were looking at them and whispering to each other. The girls called Sanam over. Sanam went there and started talking to them, returning a while later with a huge smile on her face. Avinash looked at Sanam quizzingly.

"Kya hua?" he asked her.

"Ghar chal batati hoon" she said waving at the girls.

"Bye….bye!" the girls screamed dramatically, almost teasing them. Avinash was most surprised at the turn of events but thought it better to ask his wife once they reached home.

"Biwi, what about those girls? What did they want to tell you?" Avinash asked once they settled for the night.

"Ek minute," Sanam picked her phone from the side table.

"Wow!" Avinash exclaimed.

The girls had clicked a few candid pictures of them and sent those to Sanam.

"Achi aayi hai na?" Sanam asked him and he nodded silently in return.

She smiled and snuggled into him and dozed off to sleep instantly.

Avinash picked up her phone and sent the pictures to his own phone. To say that he was shocked out of his wits was an understatement. He just could not stop looking at the images. Avinash stared at the photographs for a long time. Sleep had vanished from his eyes and the secret that his mind had embedded in its depths was making its presence felt. A lot of questions came along with that forbidden feeling. Avinash was tired of answering those questions. All this while he just lay down with a naked Sanam in his arm clinging to him like a creeper plant clings to a wall.

This reminded him of the 'The curtain creeper' plant he had back at home.

'The curtain creeper' plant had been put in their mansion by his father. His father was a keen gardener. If he wasn't writing, then he would be easily found in a garden.

"Papa, why do you like the creeper variety of plants? They are weak!" a thirteen-year-old Avinash asked him. They had a string of Bougainvillea and a variety of climbing vines all across their house.

"But they are so beautiful! A creeper finds it difficult to climb without support. The slender stems climb up and then fall beautifully over a wall or railing. The tender stems hang down to form a curtain. They look magnificent! Imagine climbing all the way up just to hang down!" his father told him.

"But aren't they parasitic? They cannot stand on their own and take support of a wall or a railing! Wouldn't it be suffocating for the walls?" Avinash asked his father.

"You have a point there Avinash! But I do not know why I have always felt otherwise. Why do we always assume that the wall would hate it if the vines cling to it? It could be a fulfilling feeling too. Some walls like to be clung on to! To be loved by someone so dearly that their life depends on you...that's sheer love. True love never suffocates you...it grows on you...Lucky are those who get to see such a pure form of love!" his father explained.

The thirteen-year-old Avinash had not understood much but this thirty-five-year-old Avinash today understood what his father meant that day. Somewhere in the dark wilderness, Sanam had creeped in like a climbing vine and entwined herself around his heart taking his loneliness, angst, and heartache away.

He looked at the pictures yet again.

"I will be a fool to deny it any longer", Avinash realised.

He was ...he certainly was...absolutely was ... in love with Sanam.

CHAPTER- 27
PYAAR AND SANSKAAR

Sanam woke to a loud crash.

"Aviii," her mind registered in shock. She quickly wore a discarded T-shirt and reached the kitchen.

"What happened?" she asked him rhetorically.

Avinash was standing there dumbfounded with an upturned tea pot which had slipped from his hands while he was trying to fill the beautiful glass carafe(a fancy kettle)with tea. The carafe had broken with the impact shattering into tiny glass shards.

"Avinash tumhe lagi toh nahin?" Sanam asked him.

Avinash froze in his place but there was a huge grin plastered on his face. He did not know how to react. He wanted to surprise her, but his actions had probably done the opposite.

"Handsome, please come out...I will clean!" Sanam came into the kitchen.

Avinash just stood there.

"What were you doing Avinash? Mujhe utha dete...mera favourite carafe tha! Ab chalo...out," Sanam slapped on his ass to shoo him out.

Avinash felt a blush creeping into his cheeks. It was not for the first time that she had called him 'Handsome' or spanked his behind...but today he was acting like a teenager.

In some time, Sanam made breakfast and brought it out to the table for Avinash.

"Yeh kya only one plate poha? You are not eating, baby?" Avinash said disappointed.

"Maine dabbe main dala! It's getting late!" Sanam said swiftly.

"Aise thodi na hota hai? Share with me jaan!" Avinash took the plate of poha intending to walk towards her to feed her. However, destiny had conspired something else. He hit his knee on the table while getting up which led to the poha spilling over him. He tried to balance himself and, in the process, knocked out the cup of tea with his other hand.

Sanam stood there looking at the royal mess that he had again created.

"Baby don't worry...I will clean it!" Avinash said grinning sheepishly.

"Yaar, aaj hua kya hai tujhe Avinash? Chup chap bed par baith ja...mujhe kitna late ho gaya hai! Daayan aaj mujhe mar dalegi!" Sanam said in exasperation.

"Kaunsi wali Daayan...tere office main toh bahut saari hain?" Avinash said innocently.

"Aviiiinaaaash irritate kar rahe ho aaj mujhe tum!" Sanam banged her hand on her head.

Avinash just stood there smiling goofily.

"Uhhhhhhhhh....... main maar dalungi aaj tumhe!" Sanam picked the broom and aimed at his well-rounded bottoms.

"Acha sorry...sorry jaan!" Avinash said and went to hug her.

"Hilana nahin..chup chap baitha reh!" Sanam screamed at him like a lioness.

"Ok..Ok" Avinash sat down on the bed and kept a finger on his lips, all the while smiling.

Sanam cleaned up the entire mess and went to the washroom.

"Hilna nahin bola tha na!" Sanam growled at him when she saw him moving around.

Avinash rushed to his previous position on the bed.

Sanam came out a few minutes later with a cup of tea, a tiffin box and a spoon.

She sat in front of him and started feeding him with her own hands.

"Tera tiffin hai...tu kya khayegi lunch break main?" Avinash refused the spoonful of poha.

"Main mangawa loongi! Tu khaa...raat ko bhi dhang se nahi khaya...hear your stomach growling!" she told him in a stern tone.

"Tu kha pehle..." he said, making her smile.

Together they shared a cup of tea and a plate of poha.

Soon Sanam came out with a couple of red chillies, mumbling something continuously. She revolved the chillies around his head a couple of times and went and burnt it on the flame.

"Yeh kya tha?" Avinash asked, grinning at her behaviour.

"Tune apne ko dekha hai subah se? Ajeeb ajeeb harkaten kar raha hai! Aur hasee ja raha hai! Koi chudail to nahin chipak gayi?" Sanam said innocently, cracking him up.

"Ab bataunga kaun si chadail chipki hai toh gussa ho jayegi!" Avinash thought as he laughed harder.

"Sachi gadhi hai meri jaan!" he observed.

"Oye meri sohni punjaban!" he called her out, holding her hand to claim his customary kiss, making her blush yet again.

Sanam could not stop blushing! She ran towards her office as she was already late. She looked back and found him still waiting there for her to enter the building. Sanam found warmth enveloping her entire being. She knew she loved him to the moon and back but was there hope that he might feel for her some day? She scolded herself for going down that road where there was nothing but pain for her.

"Aagayi maharani!" Parul taunted as Sanam entered the office.

"Uff! Dayan!" Sanam let out a muttered oath. Parul and Meena had started taunting her more since Madhu had left the office. Sanam was now seriously thinking of switching jobs.

"Kaise kaise log hote hain!" Sanam exclaimed and got on with her work. The next few hours went in a wink.

"Sanam madam aapka parcel aaya hai!" her office boy came and put a big pizza box on her table around lunch time.

"Mera? Maine kuch order nahin kiya!" Sanam was shocked.

The name was hers…surely but..Before she could think more, her phone rang and brought a smile on her face. It was her husband.

"Hello Jaan!" he whispered.

"Hi…tumne bheja?" she asked, trying to mask her smile.

"Kuch khaya toh hoga nahi tumne subah se! Haina?" Avinash told her. It sounded more like a statement rather than a question!

"How well he knows me!" Sanam thought to herself.

"Mangwane wali thee! Tumne kuch mangwaya?" She counter questioned trying to divert his attention.

"Haan biriyani!" he said smiling, thinking about his gadhi.

"Aviiiinash arre bola tha na…. non vegetarian nahin Ganpati main!" she said.

"Arre VEG biryani hai…it's an oxymoron but yet called for it!" Avinash said, hearing her giggle as an answer.

"Oh god, the giggles! How I love her giggles!" Avinash told himself.

"Baby chal garam garam khale…isse pehle ki woh Parul aajaye tera lunch khane ke liye!" Avinash told her.

"Haye tujhe kaise pata?" she giggled again looking back at the pizza box and indeed Parul was standing and examining the box.

"Madhu ne bataya tha!" Avinash said laughing.

"Aagayi woh pizza dekh kar!" Sanam said, ending the call quickly. Today Sanam was determined to eat what her husband had sent for her.

Sanam shut down her desktop and opened the box. It was her favourite…onion, corn, and bell peppers! The pizza came with a portion of chocolate mousse.

"Thanks for the amazing lunch…As I promised, I didn't even offer a morsel to Parul today..Ate the whole thing myself!" she wrote the message to him.

Avinash read the message with a huge smile and then went on to eat his veg biryani.

"I will tell her today!" he told himself, smiling with confidence.

But by the time evening came, Avinash grew nervous again. His newfound knowledge about his own state of heart was perplexing. Avinash was completely wound up. He had been fumbling and goofing up since morning. Last time he had been this nervous proposing to a girl was ...sixteen years old maybe? All his bravado left him at the last minute. He had been waiting outside her office since the last half an hour

"I will get free in half an hour!" Sanam texted him as was their routine. For many months now, Avinash had been picking her up.

"I am there already!" he wanted to say but did not.

He parked his bike at a nearby cafe and ordered a cappuccino-Sanam's favourite. He was not a cappuccino person at all...he liked filter coffee or homemade instant coffee...but not the frothy cappuccino. But his wife had a strong liking for it.

"Come to the cafe!" he pinged her.

He was brought back from his thoughts with a round of applause. A young boy had bent on his knees and proposed to the girl amidst the cheering of the crowd. The girl said 'yes' and the couple was now ecstatic.

"I have to do something special for her!" he told himself.

"I have been obnoxious to her...putting her through so much!" he reminded himself with sadness. He thought it was best to wait for that special day when his film will be announced, which would be any day in the coming month. He was going to work with Sudeep Misra, the National award-winning director. The groundwork had already begun. The shoot would begin in a few days. It was a momentous occasion for him. His work will be put on celluloid after three years. Avinash felt his fears dissolve in a grin.

Mindlessly grinning is how Sanam found him at the cafe.

"Oye Handsome...theek ho na?" She asked him, checking his forehead for fever.

"Aagayi Baby!" Avinash gave her a sterling smile and ordered another cappuccino for her.

A few days later...
The building had organised a 'Maata ki chowki' and Avinash and Sanam went down to take the blessings. They were about to leave the pandal when Avinash got a call. Sanam stood outside to wait for him to get done. Sanam noticed there was this group of Society women who were looking towards her and talking. Most of these women were friends of her Auntyji.

"Biwi...Sorry, I have to postpone our dinner...I need to leave asap...work!" Avinash pulled her close, kissed her forehead, and left. He already had his bike keys with him, so he left right away.

Sanam walked towards the building, walking past the gossip mongering women who were chatting at the entrance of her building.

She had climbed two storeys when she realised that she had left the plate in which she had taken prasad down in the pandal. She quickly turned back and went down but stopped as she heard her name.

"Sanam badi arrogant ho gayi hai aajkal!" said one lady.

"Haan itna handsome ladka jo mil gaya hai! Palalng tod romance chalta hai aajkal E-302 main!" said another lady, making everyone laugh.

"Lekin Anita behenji maine suna ladke ke maa-baap koi nahin!" said another lady.

"Haan, vaise sach hai! Kahan ka hai...kis family ka hai...kisi ko pata nahi...Sansakaari toh bilkul nahi...dekha nahin kitna chumma-chati chalti hai khullam khulla!" the lady who had spoken before said.

"Che-che aise log sharifon ki building main kaise aa gaye!" She continued.

"Dekhna aise ladke bas ladki ka pair bhari karke gayab ho jate hain...kisi ko kya pata kahan ke hain! Bas aish ki...aur furrrr!" the woman said, laughing scornfully.

The women were so engrossed in their acerbic exchange that they did not realise that Sanam stood behind them.

Sanam just wanted to run away, but she knew she could not.

"When these women had no fear of God, then I would not run away. I will look into their eyes and face them!" she thought.

"Excuse me!" she said loudly, clipping the group's laughter.

"Anita behenji …Haye usne sun liya!" one lady said regretfully.

"Sun liya toh sune…mujhe kya dar mara hua hai!" The lady who was leading the mudslinging said.

Sanam took her steel plate and returned to the entrance where the women were still there. As she was passing by, Mrs. Anita took another dig at her.

"Jinohene taras khaa kar itna bada kiya unko toh apne gunde pati se pitwa kar bhaga diya…kya hi umeed ki ja sakti hai aise logon se!" Mrs Anita said.

Sanam was almost on the verge of tears and this barb was like a nail in the coffin. She turned towards them with determination.

"Anita aunty, jin logon ki aap baat kar rahi hai na…woh mere parents ki crores ki property bech kar khaa gaye aur das (10) saal mujhe naukarani bana kar rakha. Phir ek din, mujhe ek budhe ke haath bech diya. Unko yahaan se mere husband ne nahin, us budhe ne bhagaya hai jiska paise khaa gaye!" Sanam said. She was not done yet!

"Haan hum palang todte hain…par woh mera pati hai! Marriage registered hai humari! Legal hai… Anita aunty aapki tarah boss ke sath nahi hoti promotion ke liye! Aur yeh bhi aapki best friend 'Mami ji' jinke jaane ka dukh hai na aap ko…unhone bataya…sabko pata hai building main!" Sanam stopped for a breath.

"Aap log jo sanskaaron aur purity ka roona ro rahe ho…..aap logon ke bacche kahan se aye…asaman se? Aap me se ek ka pati ka affair chal raha hai…building main hi. Aur Anita aunty aap apne bete ko sambhaliye…. uski aankhen laal studies ki wajah se nahi hoti…par aap zaroorat se zyada samajhdaar hai…aapko kya batana!" Sanam said sarcastically.

"A real woman never puts another one down…no matter what! What is the purpose of having a 'Mata ki chowki' when you are going to worship one woman and degrade another at the same time! I feel sad for women like you! Kuch zyaada bol diya ho toh maafi!" Sanam folded her hands and left the dumbfounded women behind.

Sanam entered her flat and went into the washroom to turn on the shower and cool herself. Sanam's heart was drumming in her ears with rage. When the anger subsided, Sanam broke down in a loud wail, crying till she had no more tears left.

CHAPTER- 28

I LOVE YOU!

For hours Sanam sat like this till her survival instinct kicked in. She got out of her wet clothes and got into the T-shirt Avinash had worn in the morning. She could still smell him on the comfortable piece of hosiery. It felt that he were here, hugging her. She never felt weird getting into his used unwashed T-shirt. A year before she would have scrunched her nose at the unhygienic scenario. She had of course heard about couples sharing the same things, sticking to each other for twenty-four hours and had never been able to understand why people would do that. Today she understood every bit of it.

Another wave of emotion hit her, leaving behind tears in her eyes. As she sat on the bed, Sanam hugged herself and rubbed her upper arms.

"Control yourself ...you don't want Avinash to know about this!" she told herself. "Get a grip on yourself ...this is not the first-time people have been mean to you ...it's ok! You are strong!" she kept on telling herself.

As if by telepathy, her phone buzzed with a message from Avinash.

Jaan, I am stuck at a creative session here…. escape doesn't seem easy..might return by tomorrow morning. Need to return to the meeting now. Bye! - 10: 45 p.m.

Kuch khaya tumne? - 10: 46 p.m.

Nahin khaya hoga! Chalo Chai banao! Music lagao! And please have those cookies. I know you like them! - 10: 47 p.m.

A smile came to her lips...He knew her so well! She got up to follow her husband's order.

Nothing that cannot be fixed with a cup of tea and music. A few months back, Avinash had bought a sound bar to which he rarely listened, but she was completely into it.

She put on her playlist, went to the kitchen, made elaichi tea and dug into the jar of Pistachio and cashew cookies that Avinash's mother had sent for him. Sanam had avoided eating those because they were meant for him, but Avinash had realised it and since then made her eat the same every time he had them. The hot tea warmed her throat...his thoughts warmed her heart. It was surreal how Avinash was so present even while being absent, Sanam wondered. Her hands moved to the other playlist that she used to listen to named 'Avinash's favourites!'

Sanam put on 'Katra Katra milti hai...', a track from the movie 'Ijaazat', sung by the legendary Asha Bhonsle and written by Gulzaar Sahib.

She listened to it on the loop for the longest time. A few days earlier, Avinash had forcefully made her watch the movie.

"Avi bahut boring hoti hain purani movies!" Sanam had tried to make him change his mind.

"Nahin baby..this movie is awesome..Gulzaar Saheb ki hai! See, I watched woh Kartik Aryan ki movie for you ..now you have to watch it for me!" Avinash countered her argument.

Sanam had watched the movie and enjoyed it. But today she realised that it was a love triangle too! A guy torn between his girlfriend before marriage and his wife whom he had married under pressure. The parallel tore her.

The dam of patience she had retained till now broke somewhere, engulfing her in raw emotions. Sanam drowned in her tears, whimpering at the pain that threatened to consume her.

"I will always be alone! Woh bhi chala jayega ek din! This is all temporary! Waheguru...take away this pain please!" Sanam cried and cried till she drifted to sleep.

Sanam woke up with a throbbing head, a pair of swollen eyes, an aching back and a broken heart. She realised that she had slept on the floor wound up in the foetal position and recoiled as the previous day's events came to her.

Unwillingly, Sanam dressed up and set out for her office with a heavy heart. Avinash had not called in the morning or messaged neither did she. The day dragged on becoming increasingly unbearable by every passing minute. Finally, he called her around evening.

"Baby kahan hai?" he said sweetly.

"Office main! Aur kaha jaungi!" Sanam said in a sullen tone.

"Kya hua jaan?" he instantly realised she wasn't her chirpy self.

"Nothing...kuch nahin..." Sanam tried to dismiss his concern.

"Acha kab free hogi? Main try karunga time par pahuchne ki! We are still at the meeting," he said, stretching himself and yawning.

"Aaj editorial meeting Avinash...der lagegi, don't know kab free hogi...I will come myself!" Sanam told him.

"Nahin tum kaise aayogi akeli? Give me a tentative time, I will wait for you!" Avinash insisted.

"Avinash tumse shaadi se pehle main akele travel karti thi...ab hamesha toh tum nahi honge na...akeli thi hamesha...I can manage myself!" Sanam almost screamed into the phone earning puzzled looks from everyone around.

"I have to go!" she said and cut the call in a haste and headed to the washroom to get some privacy.

"Sanam mere articles edit kyun nahi kiye abhi tak? Release karne hain!" Parul came in gobbling a banana and uttering half eaten words.

"I am not your servant Parul!" said an irritated Sanam.

"You are my junior and you should have done it by now. Editor Banerjee has been asking for it since morning!" Parul almost screamed.

"So, for once do your own work! Or better still...ask your best friend to do it for you!" Sanam said without glancing at her even once.

"O madam don't cross your limit!" Meena turned around and answered.

"I am well within my limit, but you girls have crossed it many times!" Sanam replied acerbically.

Parul gave her a bad look and left huffing and puffing away.

"Oh Madhu! Why did you have to leave?" Sanam sighed for the nth time.

The Parul-Meena drama was getting on her nerves.

"They left without any drama...this isn't over!" Sanam told herself.

Sanam's intuition was correct. It was their weekly editorial meeting.

"Parul, have you fixed the appointments I asked you to?" Editor Banerjee asked Parul.

"Sanam was supposed to do it...she didn't!" a defiant Parul passed the buck to Sanam for the weekly appointments that had to be fixed by Parul.

"Parul, why haven't your articles been filed? How much more time will you take? I cannot understand some of your articles that are so nicely written and well researched and some so badly written, as if written by a high school student who doesn't understand English. You are a senior reporter; you should set a good example for the juniors!" Editor Banerjee said furiously.

"Ma'am Sanam did not edit my articles...it's all her fault! All my articles are excellent, sometimes Sanam deliberately tampers with them, lowering their quality!" Parul told Editor Banerjee.

This was the last straw for an already simmering Sanam.

"Haanji sab kaam Sanam ka hai...Parul yahan sirf khana khane aur muft ki salary lene aati hai! Oh nahin...nahin...jab tak madam kisi ko mentally harass na kar len...inka khana hi hazam nahi hota!" Sanam said in a voice dripping with sarcasm.

"Sanam chill!" Vikram Singh tried to calm her, but Editor Banerjee gestured to him to be quiet.

"Aur haan high quality articles? Woh kis chidiya ka naam hota hai Ms. Parul Singh? There have been so many articles that I have rewritten for you, and you f*cking know it! You know what Ms. Senior reporter there are a few things you need to know as a writer...There is nothing like 'ALRIGHT!': Those are two words...ALL RIGHT! There is nothing as 'prepone' and for f*ck's sake the spelling of VIDEO is not V-E-D-I-O! I cannot take this anymore...I QUIT!" Sanam picked her bag and walked out of the meeting room.

Sanam did not hear others calling her…she almost ran out of the building.

She was about to cross the road when a bus came in front of her, freezing her in the middle of the road. Sanam closed her eyes and braced for the impact when a strong pair of hands pulled her out of the harm's way.

The bus stopped with the terrifying screeching of brakes. The driver and conductor stood there throwing a volley of expletives.

She opened her eyes to find herself in a tight familiar embrace. Sanam lifted her eyes to look at a furious Avinash.

"Chalo ghar!" Avinash said sternly.

Had Sanam been in her senses she would have seen an eager Avinash waiting outside her office.

"Baby…!" he had called out to her when he had seen her trying to cross the road without looking around.

Avinash parked the bike in the building compound. He literally dragged her along to their flat.

Sanam was still in shock.

"Tum dekh kar kyun nahin chal sakti? Kuch ho jata tumhe toh?" Avinash told her furiously when they reached home. He was in a murderous rage as he paced their small room; still trying to come to terms with what he had witnessed. Cold fear had gripped his heart when he had realised that she was walking blind. He had run as fast as he could, thankfully he had reached in time. What if…he didn't want to go there..he didn't. He now felt faint with anxiety.

"I can manage myself…Yahi kaha tha na? Kya kiya? Kuch bologi Sanam?" Avinash was on the edge. He turned around when she sat like a statue.

A soft whimper caught his attention. Sanam was shaking now with sobs. Avinash went and hugged her as she broke down.

"I quit my job!" Sanam said as she broke down again.

"Acha kiya…but why did you not see where you were going baby? Tumhe kuch ho jaata toh meri jaan?" he hugged her.

He took her to the washroom, cleaning her face and urging her to change into a T-shirt.

He left her on the bed and went to the kitchen to make tea.

A little while later, Sanam told him what happened at the meeting.

"Mujhe koi like kyun nahin karta Avinash?" Sanam looked away dejected.

"We cannot expect everyone to like us, baby! Even if one person really likes us it should be enough" Avinash told her.

"Kaun mujhe like karta hai?" she asked him, looking at him with her innocent cocker spaniel eyes.

"Tum khud!" Avinash said light heartedly.

"Hmm!" she gave a shy smile.

"Kitne log tumhe like karte hain...Madhu, Rohan, Aji...!" Avinash told her, pulling her closer into his embrace.

"Haan!" Sanam said softly, trying not to get disappointed.

"Aur main!" Avinash said softly.

"Main tumhe pasand hoon?" Sanam chirped up. "Kya like karte ho?" She asked him.

"Hmmmm...bahut sochna padega!" Avinash said dramatically, but she just smiled weakly, her eyes drooping.

"You are amazing...you are sensitive, kind-hearted, and beautiful not only from outside but also inside. I almost died today Sanam seeing you.... I do not know what I would have...I wanted to burn the world then. I lied to you ...I do not just like you baby...I love you with all my heart!" Avinash said looking at the ceiling because he would not have been able to say looking at her.

His declaration of love was met with pin drop silence. Avinash turned around to see Sanam had already fallen asleep.

"It's a sign Avinash...make it special for her!" Avinash told himself as he drifted into sleep, his heart oddly at ease.

CHAPTER- 29
AFTERSHOCKS

"Avinash...Avinash...!" Sanam cried in her sleep.

Avinash woke up to her whimpers. He realised that she must be suffering the aftershocks of the previous evening incident. He hugged her tightly.

"Baby I am here…! Baby…look at me!" Avinash shook her lightly.

Sanam opened her eyes and looked at him.

"Woh…mujhe nahi samajh aa raha kuch! Oh Avinash!" Sanam broke down and hugged him tightly.

"Bas mera bacha…you are with me…I won't let anything happen to you!" he assured her.

"Tum chale jaoge...mujhe chor kar!" Sanam cried into his chest.

For a few moments, Avinash was lost for words.

"Is this how much I have hurt her that she fears that I will leave her one day…I am an a*shole!" he cursed himself.

"Baby sun main nahin jaunga tujhe chor kar…I will be there for you Jaan," he tried to soothe her, but she was beyond herself crying. Her cries were piercing his heart.

Avinash took her in his lap and patted her back to pacify her. He took her in his arms, wiped her tears and started dropping feather light kisses on her cheeks tasting her salty skin. When nothing worked, Avinash cupped her breasts and started working on them. In a few moments, Sanam was pulled out of her misery. She gave in to the delicious sensations that were sending her in a whirlwind of emotions.

"Baby you are so exquisite! I could keep on kissing your luscious lips forever! Your doe-eyes pull me towards them!" Avinash said, trying to be seductive.

Sanam chuckled. Encouraged by her response, Avinash thought of taking it further.

"Baby, your breasts are so big and beautiful...I can suckle on these honey mounds forever!" Avinash said, continuing his tone and his work on her breasts.

This time Sanam could not control herself. She let out a throaty laughter. She rolled on her stomach right out of his lap on the bed, leaving a completely puzzled Avinash staring at her.

Sanam's body was shaking with laughter. She was trying to control herself looking at Avinash's hurt face.

"Ab batogi kyun itna has rahi ho?" Avinash said innocently, completely at loss why a passionate scene had taken this turn.

"Batati hoon...ruk!" Sanam said, trying to compose herself.

"Tere dialogues...aur teri tone...ekdum Prem Chopra sunai de raha thaa tu! Itni cheesy lines kaun bolta hai?" she said, going into a fit of laughter again.

A smile played on Avinash's lips and transformed into a grin.

"Toh bade nahi hai? Yeh bolun?" Avinash asked her in a light tone.

"Hai maine aisa kab kaha? Matlab words theek the tone funny thee!" Sanam said blushing.

"Acha? So those words meant nothing to you?" Avinash asked her sincerely, coming closer to her cupping her well rounded bottom which was now left exposed to his gaze by the T-shirt.

"It's just that ...that you never talk while...!" Sanam now becoming weirdly conscious of him.

"While what baby?" Avinash pulled her closer.

"Tu screenplay main bhi itne cheesy dialogues likhta hai?" Sanam asked while trying to divert his attention but gasped a moment later remembering that a few months ago, he had not liked her commenting on his movies.

"Isse bhi cheesy!" Avinash said, winking at her, surprising her.

"Woh yaad hai 'Don't underestimate the power of the uncommon man' from Ludhiana Express?" Director ko kitna samjhaya tha maine ki ...yeh kya hai? But he said, "Give me cheesy line Avinash, jis par theatre ki audience paise phenke!" Avinash told her, grinning away to glory.

"Matlab itna cheesy dialogue thaa..kya bolun...par wah re janta...hit ho gaya!" Avinash said, reminiscing the good old days.

"Aur woh movie 'Mera suit hai Armani'...It was Farheena Khan's movie. Those dialogues were just not happening!" Avinash said.

"Woh movie tune likhi thi?" Sanam said, making a face.

"Nahin..... sirf dialogues likhe the!" Avinash said. "Pata hai Sanam, Papa did not talk to me for days after watching the movie. He felt embarrassed that I was associated with such a project. The movie tanked at the box office, and so did my career" he said sadly.

"Ek baat puchu, tu gussa toh nahin karega?" Sanam asked him cautiously.

"Bol na Jaan!" Avinash replied.

Gathering all her courage, Sanam said, "Tune kabhi koi different movie try kyun nahin ki? Hamesha Charan Dohar ki romantic movies kiye...! You are so intelligent...so sensitive and so intellectual!" Sanam asked.

"Arre wah! Meri biwi itna acha sochti hai mere baare main?" Avinash said with a smile making Sanam blush. Listening to such adjectives from her warmed him. He took her lips and gave her a passionate kiss. He did not want the kiss to end but he wanted to tell her what he had never told a living soul.

"FEAR!" said Avinash.

"Huh?" Sanam asked bemused.

"Fear of failure...fear of failing where my father excelled. Art movies or parallel cinema was...is... his forte...even the commercial movies he did were blockbusters and intellectually appreciated. I trained as an engineer because I could not gather courage to write, when I did, I took the easy way out! Charan, Farheena and I were childhood friends. Same circle you know. Our fathers worked together, and we grew up together...same schools, same parties etc. Charan was making his movie 'Abhi Khush, Abhi gone' when his regular writer bailed out on him. We were partying together when he came in - upset. He pleaded with me to bail him out...I did that without thinking much about it. The movie became a hit...but my father was extremely critical of my work. At that time, I was craving for his appreciation and approval. I hated him once he frowned upon my work. Now I look back, he was correct. He tried to tell me what I was doing...where I was going wrong; but I took it as an umbrage and retreated in a shell. There is nothing wrong with the Charan Dohar type of movies...it takes a lot of effort to create something like that...and to convince people with a good romance; but those movies never brought creative satisfaction to me. My father knew this...he knew me more than I knew myself, and he tried to save me from my own mediocrity, I just did not let him. Once I settled in that comfort zone, I was too scared to experiment. To try and fail in front of my father and give him that satisfaction that he was correct all along…was an ego issue for me!" Avinash did not realise when his eyes got clouded with unshed tears.

Sanam pulled him closer and hugged him.

"I think you must have misunderstood him...No father will be happy to see his son fail Avinash," Sanam told him.

"I know now...I was a fool...I ruined my career. I gave my parents so much pain! I hope I make them proud someday Sanam," Avinash broke down hugging her. She was a source of so much comfort for him. He was feeling lighter getting this off his chest. Since the day of Ganpati, he had been feeling guilty.

"Tum bahut ache ho Avinash...mujhe pata hai! Tumhara dil bahut acha hai!" Sanam said smothering his face with kisses.

"Biwi...aur kya acha hai mere main?" Avinash asked his wife, smiling amidst tears.

"Well, your eyes are very kind!" Sanam said, looking into the beautiful brownish black irises and wiping his tears away.

"Aur?" he asked her in a child-like voice.

"Aur tumhare baal…. I love to weave my fingers through them," she said, doing exactly what she had said.

"Aur?" he asked again.

"Aur tere lips...they are like waterbeds…succulent and juicy!" Sanam said, biting her lower lip.

"Aur?" Avinash did not want her to stop tonight.

"Teri chest...is so hard!" Sanam said while running her fingers on his chest, exciting him completely and knowing that she was in control today.

"Aur?" he asked, catching his breath watching her cheeks blush. He was completely under her spell.

"Aur tere well rounded bums!" she said, lowering his shorts and spanking one of them. The spanking broke all the dams of control both had.

Both their lips met in urgency, knowing the mutual desire that needed to be satisfied. They took pleasure in pleasuring each other; taking each other to the peaks of ecstasy and collapsing once the embers of passion had burnt out for the night.

Avinash woke up to a pickle-y aroma in the late morning. Instantaneously, he realised that she was still upset and stressed. He knew after spending all these months with her that Sanam cooked when she was stressed. Their kitchen was full of a variety of pickles, jams and Sherbats concoctions. Sanam's pickles and especially the Sherbats were his favourite.

"Sending Sanam to a cooking class was the only thing her Aunty had done right!" Avinash thought.

"Chalo lets see what's cooking in the kitchen and in my biwi's mind!" Avinash told himself.

"Baby kya bana rahi ho?" Avinash asked Sanam, hugging her from behind.

"Nimbu ka achaar!" Sanam said.

"Par woh toh hai na ghar par?" Avinash asked, although he knew she would come up with some other reason to make it. It was her stress buster.

"Haan that's red…this is black wala!" Sanam said with a cute pout which Avinash could not resist and quickly bit her lips.

"Aaah…kitne kamina ho tum Aviii!" Sanam tried to fend him away, but Avinash stuck to his place.

"Main na yeh garam garam laga doongi tumko!" Sanam warned him, showing the hot spatula.

"Hai main darr gaya!" Avinash said dramatically, trying to control his laughter.

Sanam scowled at him.

"Biwi...tum apne pati parmeshwar ko marogi?" Avinash continued the drama.

"Mera pati parmeshwar nahin.... Prem Chopra hai! Hawas ka pujari!" Sanam said, pushing him away. But Avinash kept on his 'Never-say-die-attitude' and kissed her neck again.

"Haye rabba! Mera achaar khraab hua na toh I will kill you!" Sanam finally took a rolling pin and spanked him.

"Ouch Jaan!" Avinash knew she meant business.

"Haan jaa raha hoon, bahaar aa jao breakfast lekar!" Avinash said while finally leaving her alone.

"Baby what is bothering you?" Avinash asked her once the breakfast was done.

"I quit Avinash!" Sanam said gloomily.

"Koi baat nahin bacha...you will get another job!" Avinash tried to console her.

"Should I talk to some people?" Avinash asked her.

"Bilkul nahin...I will find one for myself!" she told him.

"Actually, Editor Banerjee pinged me a while back! She wants to talk to me! I cannot go back and face those people after what happened!" Sanam told him the reason for her worry.

"Oh! But why can't you face them? You did no wrong! You must talk to Editor Banerjee! You have worked with her for so long... she deserves a parting word at least!" Avinash made Sanam understand.

"I will take you today! And I will come inside too!" Avinash told her.

"Tu chalega mere saath?" Sanam asked with relief.

"Haan baby...Hum saath main chalenge!" he said, pacifying her.

A few hours later, Sanam walked into the magazine office.

"Ma'am may I come in?" Sanam asked Editor Banerjee.

"Aao Sanam...How are you doing now?" Editor Banerjee asked her.

"I am good ma'am!" Sanam said confidently.

"Gussa utra? Tumne kal bahut kuch bol diya Parul Singh ko!" Banerjee told Sanam.

"I am sorry ma'am but not for speaking my mind but just quitting the way I did. It was not respectful to you …you stood by me in my time of need!" Sanam said in a matter-of-fact tone.

"Main Parul Singh ko nahin nikal sakti…Financer ki niece hai woh! Isliye this letter is for you! You have been removed from the post of Junior reporter!" Editor Banerjee said with nonchalance.

Sanam had been expecting this.

She took the letter from her and kept it in her purse and said, "Thankyou Ma'am for everything!" and got up to leave.

"Sanam you will not read it?" Editor Banerjee asked her.

"No…not now…maybe later!" Sanam said, trying to sound unaffected.

"Sanam, sit down and read now!" Editor Banerjee said sternly.

Sanam quickly sat down and opened and read…

Dear Ms., Sanam Kaur Bedi,

We are glad to inform you that you have been promoted to the post of senior reporter….

Sanam took a few minutes to soak in the news.

"Oh ma'am…I didn't expect this…I thought you were going to fire me!" Sanam was so excited she went and hugged Editor Banerjee.

"Sanam…control yourself!" Editor Banerjee told her sternly.

"Yes, I know what you were expecting that; but I have been waiting for you to step up for a long time! I have always known that you were writing Parul's articles…in fact doing most of her work. But I could not help a person who did not stand up for herself. How can you expect someone else to do justice to you when you yourself do not have the guts to do right by your own self. Once you learnt the lesson, I stepped up too! But please understand I still cannot lay-off Parul Singh. It is not an ideal world. Let us hope she does not find another Sanam Kaur Bedi to do her dirty work. So now off you go…enjoy today and come tomorrow!" Editor Banerjee said.

"Thanks a lot ma'am! You are such a bad ass!" Sanam told her, jumping gleefully as she left her cabin.

"Haha...Bad-ass and a bitch who was exactly like you twenty years back!" Editor Banerjee said reflectively as she saw Sanam leaving her cabin.

Avinash stood outside her office while Sanam went to meet Editor Banerjee. Sanam had asked him to wait because she did not want to appear weak in front of her colleagues. His eyes were on the main gate...he was pacing the pavement anxiously. Avinash got anxiety every time he would spot a BEST bus coming. He did not want anything repeated...they had been lucky yesterday.

"Aviiiinash! Aviiiinash!" he heard his wife screaming. He turned to see Sanam running excitedly towards him and finally she hugged him.

"All well baby?" Avinash asked her.

"Haan.... thanks for being there for me!" Sanam gave him her million-dollar smile.

"Toh phir chalen?" Avinash asked.

"Kahan?" she asked.

"Somewhere special!" he said.

CHAPTER- 30
SERENDIPITY

"Avinash...Pehle sun...mujhe Senior reporter bana diya! Now I will have my own by-line...Written by Sanam Kaur Bedi," Sanam exclaimed.

Avinash took her into an embrace.

"Sanam Avinash Shastri baby!"Avinash thought to himself...soon! It will happen soon.

Baba had left for America just after the visarjan to attend some business.

"Once Baba will be back, I will ask him to talk to Aai and Papa," Avinash told himself.

Avinash envisaged no issues once he agreed to further his grandson's case. Baba already loved Sanam and in fact he had especially called to talk sense into him. He had been ecstatic when Avinash had told him that he loved Sanam insanely.

"Brilliant choice!" Baba had said after eating the ladoos Sanam had prepared for him. Avinash had told her that his friend's grandfather loved the ladoos and the next day she had made a big jar of besan ladoos. This was his Sanam...loving...sweet...kind.

"Sanam Avinash Shastri! Sounds fantastic!" Avinash smiled to himself.

"Avinash...kuch bolta kyun nahin? Kab se smile kari jaa raha hai!" Sanam asked him.

Avinash smiled at the more casual way his wife had started addressing him. At times she called him 'tu' instead of 'tum' and that gave him happiness, brought him closer to his wife.

"Aviiii," Sanam patted his shoulder.

"Arre this is awesome baby! Meri Senior Reporter madam! Aaj toh celebration hogi!" Avinash said, hugging her. He was happy for and proud of her.

"Kahaan chalen?" Sanam asked him.

"It will take us half an hour to reach there!" Avinash said.

Sometime later, Avinash stopped his bike right outside a one storey building teeming with intellectual hustle and bustle.

"This is Prithvi theatre!" he told her as she gasped.

'The Prithvi Theatre' is a small, cosy place tucked away in a by-lane adjacent to Juhu Beach, a place home to some wonderful drama, built by veteran actor Shashi Kapoor and his wife Jennifer Kapoor in memory of Prithviraj Kapoor, Shashi's father and a stalwart in Bollywood.

Sanam had always heard about Prithvi theatre but never visited it. Whatever plays she had watched were in her college because of the old manager.

"Baby the play is at 7pm… that means we still have one and half hours to spend. Let us have coffee," Avinash took her to 'The Prithvi cafe'.

Sanam could not keep her excitement down. It was a cafe operating out of hut shaped counters. There was green everywhere you looked. The cafe was built around the trees, not the other way round. The vibe of the place was simply different: intellectual, creative, and funky.

Sanam was smiling looking at the eclectic and passionate discussions happening at different tables. Avinash fitted right in with his white kurta and jeans.

"Irish coffee try karegi Jaan?" Avinash asked her.

"Woh kya hoti hai?" Sanam asked.

"Ruk …abhi aaya!" Avinash returned a few minutes later with a sleek and beautiful Hurricane glass (shape of the glass) with dark brown liquid with a thick layer of whipped cream lacing it.

"Wow…kitni sexy lag rahi hai!" Sanam could not control herself from exclaiming.

She took a sip excitedly expecting something sweet but the very next instant her expressions changed as if she had taken a bitter pill.

"Yuckkks kadvi hai!" Sanam scrunched her nose at the sexy looking drink that had cheated her.

"Biwi jis ko tum yucks kar rahi ho...log special aate hain peene ke liye!" Avinash could not stop smiling at her.

"Irish coffee is a hot cocktail. It has hot coffee, Irish whiskey, sugar and topped with cream. Vaise iska ek specific glass hota hai...but aaj yeh hurricane glass main hai!" he told her.

"Vaise, I knew whisky would be too bitter for you," Avinash told her sweetly.

And as if on cue...someone came and served them a huge slice of vanilla chocolate pebble cake and a hot piping cup cappuccino.

"Haye tujhe kaise pata mujhe cake khana tha aur cappuccino peena tha?" Sanam said, giving him a sweet smile and attacked the slice of cake with relish.

"Teri smile ke liye toh jeete hain baby!" Avinash told himself as he sipped on his Irish coffee.

"Omg! Yeh toh Naseerudaullah ka play hai...Manto par!" Sanam clapped her hands and jumped in her seat when Avinash showed her the tickets.

"Chalo... We need to stand in a queue to get the best seating space...that is the style here!" Avinash told her.

Sanam looked around and found a serpentine queue forming at the entrance.

Half an hour later, they sat in the best seats in the theatre.

"There is no separate seating here, just long extended sofas. Maybe the makers wanted the audience to have a feeling of the drawing room when they watched the plays...like a cosy gharwali feeling!" Sanam thought to herself as she awaited the play to start. It had been almost three years since she had watched any theatre.

The play was a modern interpretation of Saadat Hassan Manto's stories. Sanam sat there almost in the arms of Avinash who had kept an arm behind her. He gently nudged her to take his handkerchief at one point when he heard her sniffles.

Avinash felt as if their life had come full circle. Their meeting three years ago was at a play like this...at Naseerudaullah Sir's play and he had been watching her more than the play ...like he was doing now. It was nothing but sheer serendipity that he had met her again the next day. Since then, this girl had not left his imagination.

"Avinash!" Sanam whined tugging on his kurta bringing him back to the present. It was the interval and she wanted to go to the washroom.

"Chal, I will tell you where it is!" Avinash told her.

As Avinash was waiting for her to return, a sultry voice came from behind revealing its owner to be an equally sexy lady.

"Avinash! Kurte main toh bahut dashing lag rahe ho!" the lady said and hugged him tightly.

"Oh…hi Aparna! Kaise ho?" Avinash said with courtesy.

Aparna moved in the same circles as he did a few years back. She had been a successful model till a few years back. Now she was hunting for a sugar daddy.

"Kissi din date par chalen?" said the sultry voice.

Avinash was saved by the ringing of the bell indicating the play was about to resume.

"I need to go," Avinash told her quickly and left to look for Sanam. He found her just getting out of the washroom.

Sanam was just getting out of the washroom when she spotted a sexy lady hugging her husband. Her Husband did not resist it. Had it been the Sanam of two or three weeks back, she would have cried and felt horrible. She did feel horrible today, but since the day the ladies of her society had taunted her, she had realised the ephemeral existence of her love. Sanam knew it had already been over ten months that they had been together…it would be over soon. She had promised herself that she will be strong from now onwards and start detaching herself from him. Sanam took a deep breath and went inside the washroom again as she saw Avinash look for her.

"Wow…amazing play!" Sanam told Avinash.

"Ruk zara!" Avinash told her, making her sit back while the others were leaving.

Avinash wanted the Aparna lady to move out and wanted to introduce Sanam to the cast of the play.

"Jaan come!" Avinash led Sanam to the centre of the stage towards the cast.

"Salaam sir!" Avinash bent down to touch the great actor Naseerudaullah's feet.

"Arre barkhurdar tum? Kaise ho? Huh...all well?" Naseer Saab grinned and hugged Avinash.

"All well sir! Ma'am!" Avinash turned towards Mrs. Ramona Shah and touched her feet too.

"Oh God…Avinash what a pleasant surprise! Karuna kaisi hai? Aur Alok bhai sahab?" Mrs. Shah asked Avinash with genuine concern.

"Inse introduce nahin karwaoge?" Naseer Saab looked towards a nervous Sanam.

"Yeh Sanam hai," Avinash told him, before he could say much, Naseer Saab got called by someone.

"Beta kya karte ho aap?" Mrs. Shah asked Sanam, trying to make her comfortable.

"Avinash...idhar aana!" Naseer Saab called Avinash.

"Yeh jo mohtarma hain...yeh sirf friend hai ya special friend hain?" Naseer Saab said with his signature intonation.

"Ji special hai…bahut special hai!" Avinash blushed. He wanted to inform his parents about his marriage himself…he owed them this much at least.

"Kitni pyaari aur bholi hai. Alok aur bhabhi ko pata hai?" Naseer Saab asked him. Naseer Saab and Alok Shastri had been close friends for decades. They and their gang met once in a month at least.

"Nahin, I am going to tell them soon! Was thinking of introducing her on the film release!" Avinash told him.

"Haan haan...good idea. Screenplay zabardast likha hai tumne! I fell in love with the character. Let us see how it pans out. Sudeep is damn excited! Excellent job Avinash!" Naseer Saab hugged him.

Just then a musical sound of giggling pulled them out of their conversation. Avinash knew the sound so well.

"Chalo dekhen what these women are cooking!" Naseer Saab chuckled.

"Bharabhai vs Bharabhai was so much fun!" Mrs. Ramona Shah was sharing anecdotes from that serial and Sanam was struggling to stifle her giggles.

"We will take your leave now Ma'am...Sir!" Avinash said, joining his hands.

"Come over someday Avinash and bring Sanam too!" Mrs. Shah told him.

"Don't they make a lovely couple, Naseer? Such chemistry! Karuna is going to love her!"

Mrs. Shah exclaimed at the retreating couple while Naseer saab smiled knowingly.

"Sanam...What a coincidence!" a tall and handsome young man exclaimed.

Sanam had been sitting at the table in the restaurant they had planned to have their dinner.

Avinash had gone outside to attend a call.

"I am sorry...I didn't recognise you!" Sanam was trying to recognise him. He did seem familiar, but she could not put a name to his face.

"I am Praveen...I used to be Shruti's...umm...friend!" the guy said embarrassed.

"Arre haan...Shruti's boyfriend! How have you been? Shruti kaise hai?" Sanam said without abandon.

"Arre woh toh break up ho gaya...two years back!" he said, embarrassed to the core.

"Can I have your phone number?" the man pulled his wits together to ask.

"Huh...kya karoge number?" Sanam asked with her trademark innocence.

"Umm...woh," the guy was looking for words.

Avinash had been on a call when he saw Sanam talking to a very good-looking young man. He immediately finished his call and walked towards them.

"Sorry baby! The call took longer than expected!" Avinash kept his hand on her shoulder.

There was an awkward silence when Sanam caught on the drift that she was supposed to introduce.

"He is Avinash…and he is Praveen …meri ek classmate thi…uska ex-boyfriend!" Sanam said.

By this time, the lad was too embarrassed. He immediately bid a goodbye and left the restaurant. The rest of the dinner went without a hiccup.

"Why didn't Sanam introduce me as her husband? Does it mean she does not want to tell others about me? Does she love me or not?" Avinash was pondering upon these questions at night as Sanam lay cradled in his arm, hugging his bare chest. It had been a hectic day and Sanam had slept the moment they had hit the bed.

It was the first time Shastriji had thought about something he had taken for granted till now. "It was serendipity for me to have met her when I did…was it for her too? Or did she just bow down to the circumstances? Does Sanam really love me?" This question gave Shastriji a long, sleepless night.

CHAPTER- 31

THE GIFT

A few days later....
"I will be late today...I need to buy a few things!" Sanam messaged Avinash.

"Me too...stuck at the shoot!" Avinash replied.

"Avinash has been stuck at shooting a lot nowadays...Chalo, hope things are working for him!" Sanam smiled and sent a silent prayer to her Waheguru.

"Take care baby...ghar jaa kar message karna!" Avinash pinged her and smiled.

Avinash's screenplay had already started taking shape on reel. The shoot had started one month back. Two schedules were already over. That was the unique style of Sudeep Misra. He always shot before the film announcement to keep the subject out of the hands of the 'ultra-creative people' who often got inspired by the storyline. Sudeep often worked on very tight schedules, taking bulk dates of all the actors and crew. In the time of smartphones, he still managed to shoot most of his movies without the media getting a whiff of it. It required a lot of planning and every crew member had to sign a non-disclosure agreement. Twenty years of being in the industry, he had worked with only a handful of writers...Avinash was extremely lucky that Sudeep Misra had taken out time and listened to his script. The rest was as they said history!

Avinash had never felt better, more creative, and more peaceful than what he had been feeling in the last one year...precisely since he got married to the most adorable munchkin in the world: his wife.

"Sir aapko director sahib bula rahe hain!" the assistant director came and told him, bringing Avinash out of his thoughts.

Sanam reached home around 10 pm, Avinash had not returned yet. She immediately kept her shopping aside and started preparing for a quick meal. Once done with the meal preparation, she set around to make a list of the last-minute purchases for the dinner they were hosting tomorrow for Madhu and Rohan.

Madhu and Rohan were coming over to hand them their wedding invite. Sanam was excited for the first ever dinner she was going to host. She had an elaborate menu planned and had taken a half day off from work.

Once the dinner was done, Sanam talked Avinash into cleaning the utensils.

"Biwi, ab tum apne pati-parmeshwar ka fayda utha rahi ho!" Avinash teased her.

"Haan toh? Pati bhi mera fayda uthata hai …roz raat aur subah ko!" Sanam said dramatically, kissing his cheeks teasing him to no end.

"You owe me one baby…tonight!" Avinash winked at her.

"Nahi…thak gayi hoon baby!" Sanam tried to make him understand.

"Haan toh tum kuch mat karna…main smabhaal loonga!" Avinash told her with a poker face.

"Haww…Kitna kamina hai tu!" Sanam said, truly shocked at Avinash, sending him into a fit of laughter.

"Aaj bahut dino ke baad chances are bright!" Avinash exclaimed. With her promotion, Sanam's workload had increased leaving her exhausted and somewhere down the line, it had impacted their coupling. Sanam generally was not left with the energy to do it in the morning leaving Shastriji craving for more.

"Baby yeh kya hai?" Avinash exclaimed once he came out of the kitchen. His hopes were dashed when he saw that Sanam had emptied all the contents of her closet on the bed.

"Tsunami aayi ya toofan?" Avinash asked her.

"Yaar, I am unable to find my blouse, I need it for measure to give the new blouse for stitching. Aur teri side ki cupboard locked kyun hai? Khol na…vahan na challa gaya ho!" Sanam exclaimed. She was bone tired and wanted to hit the bed soon.

"Arre, toh main thodi naa pehenta hoon tumhare blouse!" Avinash replied, startling her.

"Khol de na baby...I need to sleep...I need to give my blouse for stitching tomorrow," Sanam tried to cajole him.

"Arre tum toh ek dum lady Sherlock Holmes ban gayi ho!" he exclaimed with a guilty expression on his face.

"Avinash …. kya chakar hai? Tujhe pata hai mera blouse kahan hai?" Sanam asked him sternly.

"Nahin yaar ...tum toh police ban gayi ho! Mujhe nahin pata!" Avinash said in a terrified voice. His expressions betraying his words.

"Tujhe meri kasam!" Sanam used the ultimate resort.

"Abe yaar…....yeh galat hai! Exploitation hain...mardon ka!" he huffed and paced the room as if trying to come to a decision.

He then came to his cupboard and opened the lock to take out a few cardboard boxes. Tumhare blouse ka raaz!" Avinash showed Sanam.

"Kya hain yeh?" Sanam asked him, puzzled, opening the first box.

It contained an exceptionally beautiful maroon coloured banarasi silk saree. It had a thick gold border with small polka dots all over the body of the saree. The pallu was an intricate design of delicate gold threads. Sanam had never seen anything so exquisite and was tongue tied for a moment.

"But where is my blouse? Aur yeh saree kiski hai?" Sanam was unable to understand anything.

"These sarees are for you! Aur woh blouse gaya hai measurement ke liye taki the rest of the blouses can get stitched," Avinash said exasperatedly showing her the other two sarees. He had planned on surprising her, but her investigation had ruined everything.

"Tumhe pasand nahin aayi?" Avinash asked, watching her go quiet.

Sanam sat on the edge of the bed quietly with her eyes full of unshed tears, scaring Avinash out of his wits.

"Baby why are you crying? Blouses kal ban kar aa jayenge! Please do not cry!" Avinash was completely baffled by her reaction.

"Abey saree ko dekh kar kaun rota hai?" he continued.

"Avinash, are you embarrassed by my dressing sense and clothes?" Sanam asked him clearly when the penny fell for Avinash.

"No... are you mad?" he asked, completely bewildered by her accusation.

"Toh yeh sab kya hai? These sarees must be awfully expensive!" Sanam asked him in a flat tone trying to hide her pain.

"Baby...I was just passing by the shop when I saw this saree..and thought of you!" he said trying to make her understand but it was looking quite difficult.

"Maine kaha tha tumse.... I do not need your money!" Sanam's tears were just not stopping. Avinash cursed himself. He had gone overboard. In his attempt to make her feel nice, he had done the opposite. He should have known how self-reliant she is.

"Baby I did not think much...if you do not like these sarees, I will throw them out! Mujhe bas tumhe in sarees main dekhna tha...Please jaan...do not cry!" Avinash said with utmost sincerity, chewing his nails away.

Listening to his sincere tone Sanam stopped crying. She got up and started clearing away her clothes. By the time she got over, she was in a better mood. Avinash had gone off to sleep on the chair where he sat waiting for her to clear the bed. Sanam looked at him and her heart warmed up.

"Zyada react kiya maine shayad!" Sanam thought with guilt.

She turned to pick up the boxes but stopped midway. The maroon saree was so beautiful. She kept the box aside to open the rest of the boxes. which had sarees too.

One was a black silk Kanjivaram saree with bronze brocade and pallu. It was a beauty. Sanam had never seen something sexy yet subtle. The third saree was a mint green base floral printed chiffon saree. It had a delicate print of pastel-coloured flowers and tapering of gold beaded lace. If Sanam was floored by the elegance of silk earlier, she was now won over by the breezy chiffon. Avinash had gone to a lot of pain to get her something exquisite.

"Bura laga usko...dil dukhaya maine uska!" Sanam mused to herself.

"Jitna door jaane ki koshish karti hoon, tum utna hi kareeb kheech lete ho Avinash! Jab jab dekhti hoon tumhe, pyaar aata hai tumpar!" thought Sanam and sighed to herself.

She kept the boxes properly and went to Avinash to make him sleep properly on the bed.

"I will have to make it up to him but how?" She thought while kissing him to sleep. She thought for a long while, then an idea came to her, and a huge smile shone on her face.

"Do nothing and everything will happen!" She told herself with the grin of a cat that got all the cream Sanam had observed during their earlier fights that the moment she would apologise to Avinash, he would show attitude. So, let him be under the impression that she was still upset and hopefully he would make love...patch up sex was amazing, she had realised over time. Sanam felt guilty again. She had been so rattled by the society incident that she had been putting him off love making in the last two-three weeks. It had been difficult. It had been futile. It had been draining.

Sanam had never been the one to hold back...if she had, she gave. Denying him the simplest of pleasures, had cost her peace of mind.

"I am so done with resisting him...he is so sexy...so handsome...so precious," Sanam told herself and felt desire kicking in her core.

She jumped back into the bed and lightly kissed Avinash's cheeks. As expected, Avinash moved in his sleep and pulled her over into his arms. Sanam snuggled more into him, earning a delicious sigh from a sleeping Avinash.

The alarm on his phone woke Avinash up. He reluctantly opened his eyes and felt her weight on his arms. He switched off the phone alarm and turned himself towards her thinking of stealing a kiss before she woke up. She was always a sight that Avinash could never get enough of. But today's sight left him shell shocked. She was wearing an inviting skimpy white top.

"You are a vixen, woman!" Avinash chuckled and kissed her full.

"Sarees achi lagi?" Avinash asked her tentatively once they had relished each other.

"Bahut...they are so pretty! Thank You Avi!" Sanam said with enthusiasm and spattered his face with wet kisses.

Avinash grinned from ear to ear at her reaction.

"You don't know what you are for me...," Avinash had just formed those words when the phone rang. It was Sudeep Misra on the other end.

"F*ck...wrong timing!" Avinash cursed in his mind as Sanam looked back at him, puzzled by the weird expressions on his face.

"Acha...don't forget raat ko dinner hai...Madhu and Rohan are coming!" Sanam reminded Avinash while serving him breakfast.

"Hmm," Avinash answered as he stuffed Aloo paratha in his mouth.

"Acha suno...see what I bought for Madhu!" said an excited Sanam, showing him a bag full of shopping while he was eating.

She took out a beautiful teal embellished saree with a zari border.

"You know this blue saree is for Madhu. This was the best in the store!" Sanam told her husband.

"Best thee toh tune kyun nahin le?" Avinash asked, unable to understand the logic.

"Arre, If I am gifting someone, I will give the best to them...right?" Sanam explained, earning a smile from him.

"Aur woh kya hai? White in colour?" Avinash asked her inquisitively.

"Nahin yeh kuch nahin...aise hi," Sanam tried to hide the bag.

Avinash was now completely intrigued.

"Arre, dikha na baby!" Avinash got up and took the bag.

He found men's lucknowi kurtas. Two white and one navy blue coloured. By size he could gauge one white was for Rohan and the rest two were his size...for him.

"Wow...kitne ache hain...mere liye layi...toh de kyun nahin rahi thee!" Avinash asked Sanam who was trying to evade his eyes.

"Kya hua baby?" Avinash was baffled by his wife's reactions.

"Nahin...woh...woh tumhare standard ke nahin hain!" Sanam said her eyes stuck on the floor.

Sanam had bought the kurtas for Avinash and was going to show him the shopping last night. After seeing the quality and price of the sarees, she realised that her gift was inexpensive. Sanam had tears in her eyes. He was meant for finer things in life, and she had bought something so banal for him.

"Tum mujhe aisa samjhti ho Sanam?" hurt was evident in Avinash's voice.

Avinash had been so happy to see the kurtas. Her gift meant so much to him. He could not believe she had decided to hide these for some materialistic notion she had about him.

"Do you think I am so cheap Sanam that I will compare your emotions with money? Tere mere beech main paisa kyun aata hai hamesha?" Avinash uttered these words with difficulty.

"I am sorry Avi!" Sanam said while she hid herself in his chest; tears flowing freely from her eyes. Eyes that were trying to hide the shame of judging her husband by the societal stereotypes.

CHAPTER- 32

ICE-CREAM

Later in the evening…
Avinash had come home just in time to welcome Madhu and Rohan to their humble abode…However one look at the usually happy couple was enough to tell Sanam and Avinash that there was a storm brewing in the happy lands.

"Haye aa gaye tum log! I was missing you so much Madhu!" Sanam said, hugging Madhu, who seemed to have been fighting off tears for a long time. Madhu broke down and Sanam looked helplessly at Avinash and Rohan.

Rohan massaged his brows with his fingers in an exasperated expression.

"Arre Rohan chal na yaar…beer le kar aate hain!" Avinash said, taking control of the tricky situation. Rohan agreed in relief.

"Kya hua Madhu? Tu theek hai na?" Sanam asked once Madhu had emptied her pent-up feelings in the shape of tears.

"Haan woh…jo…aayi hai na Australia wali kamini…usne laga di hai life ki!" Madhu said shakily, trying to breathe through the tears.

"Kaun aayi hai? Woh Rohan ki bua (Aunt…relation being…Father's Sister)!" asked Sanam.

"Haan yaar jabse Aatya (Aunt in Marathi) aai hai na tab se jeena haram kar diya hai…Yeh saree halki hai…yeh elegant nahin…woh cheap hai…bloody bitch!" Madhu cursed.

"Yaar she is so interfering…meri wedding saree par drama kiya…yellow-green hi honi chahiye…chalo if Rohan's mother speaks then I can still take it…but she has no business speaking!" Madhu's sobs had now turned into war cries.

She was breathing now…but she was breathing fire.

"Forget that...I can understand yellow, and green is a tradition. She had absolutely no business speaking on my reception lehenga! Beh@n@@@d she tells me 'Marathis wear sarees, not lehenga! She has the audacity to tell me which colour will suit my complexion! Behe@ ki L#@% teri shaadi nahi hai...meri hai!" Madhu spit out the choicest of expletives and now looked far better than what she did when she had arrived.

"Yaar Vodka hai?" Madhu asked Sanam.

"Haan na! Avinash sab le kar aaya tha..." Sanam almost told her the latter part.

"Tujhe pata hai...aatya itni buri nahi hai jitni uski bahurani hai.... Savitri! Saara din Rohan ko chipakti rehti hai...Her husband is such a nice man, but she is such a sl@t!" Madhu said dramatically.

"Tu un sabko ignore kar na! Ek hafte ki liye shaadi par aaye hain...Phir tu doosre continent main...wo doosre!" Sanam tried to calm her down.

"Yaar main toh kar doon...Rohan bhi kare na! He bloody cut my call yesterday because he was having a bloody chai with his Vahini (Sister-in-law)!" Madhu took in the 60 ml shot of Vodka in one go.

"Yeh 'Vahini' kya hota hai?" Sanam asked, cutely drinking her soft drink.

"Bhabhi.... uski 'Savitri Bhabhi'!" Madhu said dramatically.

"Hawww...woh 'Savitri Bhabhi'?" Sanam exclaimed. Avinash had once shown her a popular adult comic series to expand her 'general knowledge'.

"Haan wahi hai!" Madhu said seriously. Madhu had meant it as a joke, but Sanam at times was not able to understand the thin line between pretence and truth. She was scandalised to the core.

"Lekin chai hi toh pee na bechare Rohan ne! Toh itna kya gussa?" Sanam tried to reason it out with Madhu.

"Tujhe pata hai woh handsome ladkon ko chai, coffee aur ice cream kaise offer karti hai? Pehle yun jhukti hai...phir saree ka pallu girta hai...itte se blouse main do bombs," Madhu said dramatically.

"Haye rabba! Kinni besharam hai! Durr phite mooh!" Sanam said. "Madhu tu mujhe ekdam sahi lag rahi hai...kar gussa Rohan ko...bada aaya bhabhi ka devar!" Sanam told her.

"Chal tu garam-garam tikki kha...aur dande laga Rohan ko!" Sanam tried to lighten up the mood. Madhu was already feeling better.

"Oh my God! Chai ko lekar barasi tujhpar?" Avinash asked Rohan.

"Abey tune vahini ko dekha nahin hai! Kya bolun...full aadamkhor bandi hai yaar...You know woh kehte hain na... 'hot...maal'...you know," Rohan tried explaining with gestures.

"Oh...L-O-V-E-L-Y!" Avinash said dramatically, taking another swig at his beer. They had gone to a nearby Wine shop to buy a few beers and were drinking in his car parked on the roadside.

"Bhai...tu sambhal kar rehna...tere 'type' weakness hai uske! Kahin Sanam woh football match ke din wala roop dharan na karle!" Rohan reminded him.

"Oh! I do not want that!" Avinash came out of the appreciation mode in the memory of 'Married but blind' promise.

"Chal abhi tak Sanam ne theek kar diya hoga Madhu ko.... waise bhi aloo tikki aur chole banaye hai usne...yaar meri dadi jaisa khana banti hai! I cannot eat outside now...she cooks so well," Avinash said with pride.

However, as they returned, the women gave them no bhav. Madhu and Sanam were laughing together, absolutely ignoring their better halves.

"Yaar tera samajh mein aata hai, par mere wali?" Avinash said in a surprised tone.

"Baby kya hua?" Avinash asked Sanam, hugging her from behind as she was heating food in the kitchen.

"Kuch bhi toh nahin!" Sanam replied. Avinash by this time knew that 'Kuch bhi nahin' meant a lot. He put his questions on the back burner and went off to the room to Rohan who was faring way better than before. Over the course of dinner, things had normalised to quite an extent till Rohan received a phone call...actually a series of missed calls from his 'Vahini'.

Madhu took one look at the phone and lost it yet again.

"Yeh aurat tumhe phone kyun kar rahi hai? Sirf tum hi reh gayo ho is duniya main?" Madhu asked him in anger.

"Baby all she wanted was a few things from the market...please don't get angry...she is my brother's wife...what am I supposed to do?" Rohan asked Madhu, pleading his case.

"Sach main Rohan...you should not hurt Madhu like this! She loves you too much!" Sanam jumped in the support of Madhu.

"Abey yeh gadhi kyun ghus rahi hai unke beech mein?" Avinash thought to himself.

"Sanam chal ice cream le kar aate hain!" Avinash told Sanam.

"Arre par kheer banai hai....," Sanam said.

"Rohan hum ice-cream le kar aaye," Avinash told Rohan.

"Sun... take my car...Aur Bandra se le kar aana...Candies se!" Rohan said winking, while throwing the keys of his brand-new SUV to Avinash.

"Hai...par Bandra se aate aate toh melt ho jayegi!" Sanam exclaimed.

"Chal Gadhi..." Avinash said.

Before Sanam could say anything controversial, Avinash whisked her away.

Sometime later...
"Mujhe aloo tikki khaani hai!" Avinash whined for the nth time as they parked in a secluded corner at the Bandstand.

"Arre par do already khai tumne! Ab ghar jayenge toh garam-garam khilaungi," Sanam said lovingly as if she were talking to a child. At times, her husband behaved worse than a child, but she could not blame him. His whining was in a way a compliment to her! Her husband was crazy about her cooking, and this was a tag Sanam wore with pride.

It was the couples' dinner night that she had waited for days. They were supposed to have been at home enjoying the goodies she had spent the entire day making.

Instead, here they were sitting in the car...Rohan's car...which was parked at the bandstand...holding hands...listening to music.

"Kya soch rahi hai baby?', Avinash asked her, absentmindedly stroking her arm with his thumb.

"Bas kuch nahin.... ghar jaa kar kitna kaam hai pata hai? Bartan dhone hain .... kitchen sambhalni hai...Bedsheet dhoni hai!" Sanam said.

"Bedsheet is new baby...you just put it up an hour earlier," Avinash said absentmindedly.

"Avinash ...sachi?" Sanam gently slapped him on the shoulder.

"Ouch baby...oooooooooo!" Avinash said, realising what Sanam was trying to say.

"Chee...How can you talk like this baby? Ewww...I wish I could unhear this! I almost imagined it!" Avinash said, shocked.

"Tujhe kya lagta hai wahan bhajan kar rahe honge? Patch-up sex best hota hai!" Sanam almost moaned at the memory of their morning tryst.

"Baby do not do this.... main control nahi kar pa raha hoon," Avinash took her hand and kept it on his stiff member.

"Haww.... Avinash tu toh ek minute main ready ho jata hai!" Sanam said blushing.

"Baby usse bhi kam...Tu apne aap ko underestimate karti hai humesha!" Avinash said, taking her mouth and sneakily putting his hand up her kurti and stroking her bare waist.

"Avinash koi dekh lega," Sanam said, breaking the kiss.

"Baby kuch nahi hoga! Dekh main kya karta hoon!" Avinash switched on the car and did something with the temperature control and in a few minutes the car's windshield and windows turned foggy.

"Mere paas aaja baby!" Avinash pulled Sanam towards himself and took to her lips.

"Avi...mujhe darr lag raha hai!" Sanam said, trying to get her breath back but Avinash paid no heed.

"Avinash...tu kitna desperate ho raha hai! Car main karna hai kya?" Sanam asked him innocently.

"Gosh baby tu kaise kaise thoughts daal deti hai mann main! Uff...you are driving me crazy!" Avinash went back to her lips and breasts making her moan in his mouth.

Their lovemaking was interrupted by a sharp tap on the car window.

"Oye Romeo.... khidki khol na .... kuch de de..." a eunuch banged incessantly on the car window.

"Shit...shit!" Avinash exclaimed nervously.

They took a while to make themselves a little presentable and then he rolled down the window.

"Kya hai didi?" Avinash addressed the eunuch.

"Haye...kitna chikna hai! Aye Sarla, Bimla, Laxmi...dekh film ka hero hai koi.... saath main heroine bhi hai!" the eunuch used her signature clap to summon others.

In a few moments there were around six-seven eunuch clapping and demanding money from them.

Avinash tried to put the car in reverse, but they would not let him. They summoned more eunuchs and made him roll down the window.

"Baby don't get out or roll down your window," Avinash told Sanam.

"Arre main koi hero nahin hoon didi!" Avinash told them.

"Toh apna hero mafik face toh dikha ache se," a eunuch said, making him roll down his window more.

"Biwi hai meri woh," he tried, sweetly talking to them.

"Haan...haaan...hum kab kah rahe hain nahin hai!" the eunuchs tried teasing him in a good way, making him blush.

The lady who had discovered them, Babita said, "Chal humare liye kuch dede...aaj sab kangal aashiq mile! Chal de varna pappi kar dongi!" the eunuch said sweetly, making Sanam roll in laughter...Avinash could not help turning red.

He dug into his wallet and took out a note of five hundred. "Bas itne hi hain!"He tried to patao her.

"Bas 500? Haye itna hot hai...itne dole-shole hai aur dil itna sa hai! Tu rakh yeh apne paas...bus hum sab ko ek ek kar ke pappi de de," Babita said, trying to pull him in for a kiss.

"Arre nahin...nahin...yeh lo...giving them the two thousand rupees note he had tried to hide.

"Thank you, mister...Babita naam hai mera...kabhi koi kaam padhe toh idhar kisi se bhi poochna! Madam ka khayal rakh...item hai!" Babita whistled her team to let the car go.

"Bye hero!" They all cried as the car left and laughed loudly.

"Fu*k... saare paise le liye!" Avinash chuckled trying not to look at his wife who he was sure was simmering with anger.

"Abhi bhi pant tight hai toh kuch kar doon?" Sanam asked him sarcastically.

"Sorry baby!" Avinash said meekly. He knew he had taken an unnecessary risk today.

"Poori raat tum yeh sab karte ho... main mana karti hoon? Subah bhi chahiye...did I say no? But walking, talking, eating all you want is a F-U-*-K! Kabhi tum nahin milte toh I look for you between my legs!" Sanam said in a fit of anger.

Avinash was dying to laugh but thought otherwise.

"Baby...that's not true...aaj subah tumhe chahiye tha!" Avinash said, never failing to make a point.

"Seriously Aviiiinash?" Sanam wound up her fingers in a fist.

Avinash thought it was better to shut up.

A little while later, they entered their own house to find Madhu and Rohan sitting in each other's embrace.

"Hey guys...tum ice-cream nahin laye?" Rohan asked them.

"Long story!" Avinash said grumpily.

CHAPTER- 33

PHOENIX

"Could you pack this dress?" Sanam asked the lady attendant and handed her the dress.

Madhu had informed Sanam that the cocktail party was a western formal thing. Sanam was fired up completely. Till now she had not worn anything western or for that matter attended any party. It seemed this was going to be another first for her...her first party ever and her first party with Avinash. There had been so many firsts that she had experienced with Avinash. Her first bike ride...her first Ganpati...her first shopping trip...her first story getting published... her first by-line...her first date...her first kiss and her first time. This thought brought a deep shade of pink on her cheeks and a pool of delicious wetness between her legs.

The ringing of the cell phone brought her back.

"Baby I am outside...aaja!" Avinash told Sanam over the phone.

Avinash had not been able to come to the mall for shopping but had given his approval over whats app. The approval session had tested his control and pushed it to the brink. Sanam had sent him sultry selfies of herself. She had purposely tried dresses that he knew she would never wear anywhere. He was furious with her.

"Avinash," Sanam came with a couple of bags and hugged him. Avinash's anger disappeared in a moment.

"Who could remain angry with such a munchkin?" he asked himself.

"Happy baby?" Avinash asked her, seeing her excitement. Her smile was contagious. He could not stop himself from grinning.

"Aaj toh maar dala Biwi!" Avinash said dramatically, earning a huge grin from her.

"Ready for the punishment baby?" Avinash asked her.

"Waiting!" Sanam whispered in his ear while biting his earlobe.

They were grinning when they parked in the society compound and making their way towards the staircase when they heard someone calling them.

"Didi" a hoarse voice called out to her.

Sanam turned towards the voice and froze.

"Deepu!" Sanam answered in a teary voice as she rushed to hug her cousin. Deepu was her only cousin who had ever shown affection for her.

"Arre, tu kitna lamba ho gaya!" Sanam exclaimed as they hugged.

"Kaisa hai Deepu?" Avinash asked him as Deepu bent to touch his feet to take his blessings.

"Chal upar chal!" Sanam held his hand happily.

Anyone who saw them could have vouched that they were a real brother-sister duo and not cousins.

"Didi maine disturb toh nahin kiya?" Deepu looked around awkwardly. He was but a young boy of sixteen who had come for the first time to his married sister's place. Avinash understood that.

"Arre bilkul disturb nahin kiya…Acha laga tujhe dekh kar!" Avinash said, handing him a glass of an aerated drink.

"Sab ke saath aaya Deepu?" Sanam asked him.

"Nahin…apne Mama ke saath Nanded ke Hazur Sahib aaya tha. Unko Mumbai dekhni thi aur mujhe apne friends se milna tha. Dupar ko aaya tha main…Watchman ne bola aap log late aaoge," Deepu spoke in one go. He spoke like Sanam- from the heart.

"Aaj raat rukega na?" Avinash asked him nicely.

"Arre nahin…train pakdni hai…teen ghate(hours) main Dadar se," he replied.

"Kitna acha hai na tu aaya...maine kal tere favourite chole bhature banaye the...khayega na?" Sanam asked, jumping in joy. She was really attached to her cousin.

"Baby tera bhai aaya hai itne dino baad, tu use vegetarian khana khila rahi hai? Butter chicken order karte hain!" Avinash said.

"Nahin jiju ...didi ke haath ka khana khaye zamana ho gaya," Deepu replied.

However, Avinash insisted and ordered butter chicken.

"Didi sun," Deepu extended one small pack towards her. It was a half kg rasgullas from her favourite sweetmeat shop. And a small rakhi.

"Rakhi baandh de!" Deepu whispered.

Sanam could not control her emotions and broke down. She went in and made an arti thali and tied rakhi to him.

"Itna bada kab ho gaya tu Deepu?" Sanam gently patted her brother's head.

"Deepu sab kaise hain?" Sanam asked him while serving food.

"Haan theek hain...Apko pata hai...Amrita didi ne ghar se bhaag kar shadi kar li," Deepu said.

"Kya? Aisa nahin karna chahiye tha! Maa Baap ko dukhta hai!" Sanam said.

"Didi, why are you so nice? Aap unlog ka kyun soch rahi ho jinhone aapko sirf dukh diya? Woh toh aise maa-baap hain jo khush ho rahe hain ki shadi ka paisa bach gaya! Sharam aati hai unhe maa-baap kehne main!" Deepu said regretfully.

"Beta parents ko aise nhin bolte...Chalo woh sab chod...khana kha!" Sanam said.

"Acha woh Tanya mili thee teen-chaar baar...tera number pooch rahi thee!" Sanam said dramatically.

Deepu almost choked on the butter chicken making Avinash chuckle good naturedly.

"Number de kar jaana...ki already de diya?" Sanam asked with a smile and Deepu turned the shade of the butter chicken gravy.

"Didi woh sirf friend hai!" he said, trying to evade eye contact.

"Haan, mujhe bhi wahi laagi...Good friend!" Sanam said grinning ear to ear.

"Deepu, how are studies going?" Avinash decided to change the topic.

"Phir kab aayega Deepu?" an emotional Sanam asked him when it was time for him to leave.

"Nahin pata didi. Next year rakhi par try karunga...promise. Aap apna khayal rakhna," an equally emotional Deepu replied.

"Deepu tu yeh rakh...pehle pata hota toh kuch lati!" Sanam gave him some money, but Deepu refused.

"Bacha...rakh le teri didi ki promotion hui hai!" Avinash said as they all burst into laughter.

"Deepu take care and ping me when you board the train," Avinash told him as he dropped Deepu at the station.

"Jiju maine aapke drawer main ek white envelope rakha hai...didi ko ghar jaa kar dena," Deepu told Avinash.

"Kya hai usme?" Avinash gave a puzzled expression.

"Didi ki family ki photos hain. Sometime back, we had gone to a relative's house, and they showed us their wedding album which had Sanam's didi's parent's pictures. I stole those pictures. I did not give her earlier because I knew she would cry. I could not see her crying anymore. Itne saal har roz rote hue dekha hai usko. Aaj pehli baar khush dekha hai jiju. Thank you!" Deepu said and hugged a stunned Avinash.

"I never asked about her parents. I never gave her the comfort to share her grief with me. How did she hide so much sadness in her heart? I claim to love her, but I know nothing about the fears that ail her!" Avinash reprimanded himself.

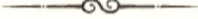

It was early morning and Avinash still had not been able to sleep. As expected, Sanam had broken down looking at the pictures of her parents. They had been clicked just a few days before the cruel accident that had taken her family from her. Tears just would not stop coming. She lay down drained in his arms till sleep claimed her.

"Main kyun zinda rahi...zinda rehna mushkil hai...marna aasan tha Papa!" she had wailed in grief while Avinash just held her looking on helplessly.

It broke his heart to see in so much pain. He was unable to put in words the deep ache that he felt in his heart. Tears found their way out his eyes as Avinash cradled her head in his arms and drifted off to sleep.

"Chai pe le bacha!" Avinash said softly, offering a cup of hot ginger tea in the morning. She had woken up some time back but was sitting like a zombie.

"Avinash mujhe Gurdware le chalega?" Sanam whispered as she sipped the tea.

Avinash looked at Sanam as they walked out of the Gurdwara. She still looked broken. The glow was missing from her cheeks, the smile was missing from her eyes.

The visit to the Gurdwara had managed to calm her down, but the Avinash could not get away from the guilt that had been gnawing at his soul.

"I never asked. Why did I never ask? Why did I not share my feelings with her? How could I be so indifferent to her pain? Am I crazy only for her body or do I really love her? People who love others do not behave callously like me!" Avinash was deep in introspection.

"Baby we need to fuel up the bike," Avinash told her as they left the Gurdwara and stopped at the petrol station.

While they waited in the queue, Sanam got down to check the small pup that was playing with a few pebbles in the corner. Avinash's mind was still pondering upon the uncomfortable questions that life had thrown at him. On top of it, the bike behind was honking incessantly. He fuelled the bike and made a beeline for the exit.

Avinash had reached a little ahead of the petrol pump when a passing biker asked him to stop.

"Aap apni wife ko petrol pump par bhool aaye!" he said grinning, shocking Avinash to his wits.

It was then that Avinash realised that Sanam had gotten down at the petrol pump and had been so caught up in introspection that he royally forgotten her behind.

"Oh God! I am so screwed!" He immediately turned the bike around.

Avinash had not been this scared of his wife, but he had firm belief in his own good looks and cuteness that she would forgive him.

"Baby sorry! Raat se tere liye upset tha...subah se kuch khaya bhi nahin...Galti ho gayi...maaf karde!" He at once joined his hands begging in front of a furious Sanam who watched his antics burst into laughter and her beautiful laughter reminded Avinash of a few lines he had read somewhere...

"And just as the Phoenix rose from the ashes, she too will rise. Returning from the flames, clothed in nothing but her strength, more beautiful than ever before." -Shannen Heartz

CHAPTER- 34
LAILA MAIN LAILA

"Baby late ho jayenge hum!" Avinash called out to his wife. It was already seven and he did not want to be late for the cocktail party.

Sanam just smiled at the nervous Avinash but kept on putting make-up on her face.

She had been furious when she realised that he had forgotten her behind. Despite her resolve that she will give him a tough time, she could not control her laughter watching him grovel. He had her heart, and his one smile was enough to melt the Ice Maiden's resolve.

"See, is the look complete?" Sanam asked, stepping into black wedges a little later.

Sanam was prancing around wearing a cap sleeve knee length black party dress. It was elegant, sophisticated yet extremely sexy. It settled around her curvy body in the most fascinating way.

"Nope...kuch missing hai!" Avinash said, dulling her smile.

Avinash turned around, opened his wardrobe, and took out a jewellery box.

Sanam was shocked when he brought out a delicate gold necklace, with an infinity sign diamond pendant. He bought out a ring and earrings in the matching theme. He slipped the ring in her finger as Sanam watched in shock. The small diamonds set in muted gold were glittering like stars. A wayward tear escaped her eyes.

"Baby please mana mat karna!" Avinash said, licking her tears and kissing her lips softly.

"You look so beautiful!" Avinash said, kissing her forehead as she tried to hide herself into his arms.

"The cab has come!" Sanam said, pulling him towards the door.

"Oh yes! We are ready to party!" Avinash exclaimed happily.

"Zyaada flirt nahi karna...jyada peena nahin...smoke bilkul nahin karna," Sanam ranted off directions to Avinash.

"Jee Maate! Aur kuch?" Avinash joined his hands together.

"Aur sun ...woh chudail Savitri Bhabhi se door rehna!" Sanam issued a final warning to Avinash as they left their home for the party venue.

The cocktail party was yet to start. They had reached early as ordered by the couple of the hour.

"Wow...looking so pretty baby girl!" Madhu exclaimed the moment they entered, hugging Sanam.

"Tu bhi," Sanam said, admiring her red body con wonder.

"We were so waiting for you! Maza ayega!" Madhu exclaimed, clapping her hands. The entire vibe was exciting and bubbly.

"Meet my cousin Akriti and her husband Naveen," Madhu introduced the couples. Akriti and Naveen were newlyweds and about the same age as Madhu and Rohan.

"Hi Sanam! I have heard so much about you!" Akirti said excitedly. Akriti she was short, slim, and blessed with sharp features- a typical Marathi Mulgi(girl).

Madhu pulled the women away towards the girl gang. In no time the girls were giggling and bubbling away.

Avinash saw Sanam jump and laugh with the girls.

"Just what my baby needed," Avinash observed with a smile.

"Apni-apni biwiyon ko baad main tadna! Pehle, we need to discuss our performance!" Rohan told Naveen and Avinash.

"Kissi kamine ki wajah se Madhu ko mera plan pata chal gaya hai!" Rohan said glaring at Naveen.

"I am so sorry yaar...Akriti se kuch bhi chupana impossible hai! If you message someone, she gets angry that I am secretly messaging some girl. Tere surprise ke chakkar mein meri bayko (wife in marathi) mujhe talak de deti! Avinash, you tell him how wives are!" a frustrated Naveen asked him. Naveen was fair complexioned, lean as a reed, had a mousy crop of brown hair and wore thick spectacles. He was one person who was always fidgety and fiddle-footed.

"Sanam bhi aisa karti hai kya?" Rohan asked Avinash.

"Nahin aisa nahin karti...par uska alag drama hai! Meri abhi abhi class lagi hai...Teri (Rohan) shadi abhi nahi hui na...you do not know!" Avinash taunted Rohan.

"Kuch bhi!" Rohan responded, punching Avinash gently in his solar plexus.

"Jabse Savitri bhabhi ka naam suna hai, Sanam ka tandav chalo hai!" Avinash said. "Vaise hai kahan teri vahini! Hum bhi toh dekhe hai kya cheez!" Avinash told the men.

"Yaar tabahi aa jayegi...kyun apna ghonsla jalana chata hai?" Rohan tried to warn him.

"Sanam, tujhe pata hai boys kya plan kar rahe hain?" Madhu asked her.

"Nahin toh...kya plans?" Sanam asked innocently.

"Tera husband bhi shamil hai planning main!" Madhu said, giggling away at Sanam's shocked expressions.

"Ab bata na Madhu!" Sanam urged her.

"Rohan is going to give a surprise performance for me!" Madhu said excited

"Wow, that is great! Par isme Avinash kya kar raha hai?" Sanam asked her, confused.

"Arre woh bhi dance kar raha hai!" Madhu told her, making Sanam burst into laughter.

"Avinash dance karega? Haww...tab toh stage gaya!" Sanam laughed away.

"Arre hume bhi karna hai unko…Surprise!" Madhu told her the plan she had hatched. Akriti and Madhu also showed them the dress they had bought from the market in a hurry.

"Yeh thoda chota hai Madhu!" Sanam exclaimed.

"Arre nahin yaar…hoga tujhe…hum dono discuss karke laye!" Madhu reassured her.

"Are you sure yeh ho jayega Madhu? Haye Avinash gussa na ho jaye!" Sanam expressed her reservations.

"Akriti ka husband bhi toh hai…kuch nahin hoga! Chal pehle decide karte hain phir washroom main chalte hain!" Madhu said.

"Ruk…pehele woh terrorist kahan hai?" Sanam asked, looking around.

"Kaunsi terrorist?" Akriti asked, shocked.

"Woh bombs wali!" Sanam elaborated.

"OOOH woh! She is talking about Savitri Vahini!" Madhu said laughing.

"Haan wahi teri Savitri Bhabhi! Akriti nazar rakhiyo apne wale par… suna hai badi harami hai!" Sanam said dramatically.

Initially, Madhu and Rohan had decided to keep things simple at their wedding. They had hardly got a month to plan everything. The cocktail party was intended to be a small one but last-minute additions and inputs by the extended family had made it a big occasion. The venue was a huge lawn of a sports complex beautifully decorated with infinite fairy lights. A dance floor had been built in the corner of the lawn. The rest of the lawn had tables and chairs set up. The pleasant September evening was the perfect weather for a celebration. The cousins on both sides had planned surprise performances which were not much of a surprise now…thanks to the overexcited uncles and aunties.

People started arriving and soon the party was in full swing. A young cousin of Madhu started hosting the performances. It was a cute, family fun occasion. Madhu roamed around everywhere with Sanam in tow…making her feel a part of her family.

Madhu's younger brother- Mayank and cousins gave a performance on a popular bollywood number. The bride and groom's parents gave a performance on a Marathi chartbuster. The cutest act was put up by Madhu's Aji with her two sisters in tow dancing on "Navrai majhi….".

Everyone was enjoying the performances when suddenly the lights went out and the spotlight shone on a scantily clad buxom woman, wearing a scintillating red one piece and a faux fur boa. She came out shaking a leg on the song 'Laila main laila' from the movie 'Qurbani.'

"Yeh Savitri bhabhi!" Madhu whispered to her girl gang as the women across the hall gasped.

Sanam gulped down her thumbs-up and looked startled as the woman swayed like a Nagin (snake) around the male population present. Rohan, Naveen, and Avinash were standing a little away from the stage enjoying their drinks. The woman scanned the men around and zeroed in on their men. Madhu, Akriti and Sanam collectively gasped when the woman reached their husbands. She danced away seductively around them, especially around Avinash.

A look of horror crossed Avinash's face. He tried to escape her claws, but the lady would not leave him. She roamed her hands around his broad chest, going as far as his stocky thighs. Avinash looked helplessly at Sanam who stood frozen in her place looking furious.

By the end of the performance, every wife at the venue wanted to rip off a certain someone's throat except one…the lady's mother-in-law.

"Bagh bagh(watch) Madhu…this is performance…this is dance!" Rohan's Australian Atya (aunt) taunted Madhu.

"Yeh Rohan ki Atya (bua) hai…Madhu pointed towards a purple-coloured gown clad lady in the 60s.

"Haye…full dayan hai! Chal ab toh in naagino ko dikhana hi padega!" Sanam told the girls.

"Chalo…let's show the Kangaroos what we can do!" Madhu told the women, indicating that it was time for their performance. Rohan's Australian Aatya had rubbed the Madhu-Sanam-Akriti trio the wrong way.

"Stop…the boys are coming this way!" Sanam said observing that Avinash and the other two boys were walking towards them.

"Sweetheart…I did not do anything…woh khud chad rahi thee! I swear Married and BLIND!" Avinash pinched his Adam's apple.

The terror on his face instantly pacified Sanam.

"Sacchi?" Sanam asked in a baby voice.

"Haan baby!" Avinash said with relief. For him no one, absolutely no one mattered but his wife.

She gave him a killer smile and bit her lower lip and whispered in his ears seductively, "Shastriji…dhyaan stage par rakhna!" and walked towards the girls, giggling away.

"Thank God…kaand nahin hua!" Avinash let out his breath, snatching away a piece of chicken tikka that Rohan was about to eat. He had not realised that he had forgotten to breathe in the anticipation of Sanam's reaction.

"Naveen, tell me one thing…Why were you pacifying Akriti for? No one even came near you?" Rohan asked all the while trying to control his laughter.

"Precaution is better than cure. Main gaya usko bola -Babe, she tried to come near me, but I stepped back. Avinash and Rohan stood frozen there but not your husband!" Naveen said sheepishly.

"Abey saale…harami," Avinash swore, hitting Naveen playfully in the stomach. The trio laughed and enjoyed the snacks for a while.

"Yeh humari wives DJ ke paas kyun khadi hai?" Avinash asked the men while observing the scene carefully.

The women went towards the DJ to explain the line-up of the songs. The DJ was a buffed up, extremely fair guy in his mid-20s. Unfortunately for Avinash, some would call him good looking too.

"Yeh DJ hai yaa model? Kahan mila tereko yeh piece?" Avinash asked Rohan.

"Kaun Kasim Ijaaz? Haan woh model hai, DJing bhi karta hai…my friend suggested," Rohan answered.

"Dekh humari biwiyon ko kaise taad raha hai BC!" Avinash was almost about to lose it watching him smiling and fawning over his Sanam. The moment DJ kept his hand on her shoulder, Avinash lost it.

"Fu*k! How dare he touch my Sanam?" Avinash said, throwing away the fish fry he had picked up from the waiter and proceeded towards the stage.

"Arre, now the girls are moving Avinash Bhai…jaane do! Scene mat create kar! Girls' ka mood kharab ho jayega. Usne wapis dekha na Sanam Vahini ki taraf toh main uska muh tod kar aaunga! Aai Shapath (Maa Kasam)!" Naveen spoke with full passion.

For a moment Avinash and Rohan both were shocked. They had never expected such a statement from Naveen. A very lean and nerdy Naveen bashing up a beefed-up stud like Kasim was a little hilarious.

Rohan and Avinash burst into laughter. The situation was under control for the moment.

"Thanks man!" Avinash told him, pulling Naveen into a hug.

Waiting for their cue, the women stood nervously in the annex next to the stage and DJ setup.

On the other hand, the audience especially, the husbands were waiting with a bated breath for the girl's performance.

The lights went out and the girls came to the stage under spotlight and the husbands collectively held their breath. The girls had dressed in school uniforms…red pleated plaid mini cheerleader tartan skirts, white shirts, and matching ties. They were oozing oomph.

The ladies one by one danced on popular numbers and culminated the performance with the remix version of 'Tu tu hai wahi dil ne jise apna kaha' from 'Yeh wada raha.' They exited the stage to a thunderous applause. The girls went behind the screen that had been constructed for the event and hugged each other. Sanam gasped as a strong arm pulled her. She knew the touch…it was Avinash.

"Kitni sexy lag rahi ho!" Avinash said and claimed her lips.

They broke up due to the teasing cat calls made by the other two pairs.

"Seekho romance…tum!" Madhu complained to Rohan.

"Noted babe!" Rohan smashed his lips on Madhu's, making the others cheer loudly.

"Guys seriously…thank God the backlight is off now…otherwise the whole silhouette would have been visible to the audience!" Naveen said in relief.

"Kya yaar Akriti…tere husband ko thora chill karna sikha!" Rohan said.

"Girls you were awesome…I could not take my eyes off you! Guys, are you Ready?" DJ Kasim came and went without waiting for an answer.

"I could not take my eyes off you ...tabhi T-shirt nikal di! Saala B****nC@@d," Avinash swore.

DJ Kasim had whistled and taken off his T-shirt during the girl's performance and it had taken the combined strength of Rohan and Naveen to stop Avinash from banging Kasim's head to the wall and a reminder that the girls were enjoying themselves a lot.

"Avinash Bhai C-O-N-T-R-O-L!" Naveen and Rohan begged him, while the girls were oblivious to the undercurrents.

The men shooed the women towards the guests and started their performance. They looked dapper. They had lost their blazers and ties. Had retained the waistcoats and had rolled up their shirt sleeves.

They opened their sequence with "Pyar humein kis mod pe le aaya" from the movie 'Satte pe Satta'. Rohan was at the forefront and the other two were in the background. The entire audience broke into a thunderous applause. The women went crazy too...but laughing.

The reason was that the men were not great dancers...honestly, they were not even good…and that was the reason none of them had the guts to give a solo performance. But the effort and passion all three had put forth was worthy of praise.

Naveen, who was a huge Sunny Deol fan, danced to "Main Nikla Gaddi Leke " making Akiriti squeal and hide her face. The whole gathering could not control its laughter as Naveen did end up looking like the emaciated version of Sunny Deol...the dude danced just like his idol.

Finally, Avinash took the lead with "Chand mera Dil...Chandni ho tum" making Sanam blush all the way.

The guys wound up the performance with the foot tapping number "Make Some Noise for the Desi Boyz' from the movie 'Desi Boyz'. Once or twice Sanam ducked under the table watching Avinash doing thumkas on a certain line of the song. The last number was 'Subha Hone Na De' from the same movie. The plan was that all three men would start the number and as the song would progress Avinash and Naveen would get Madhu to dance with Rohan.

Before Avinash and Naveen could get Madhu, Savitri Bhabhi entered from backstage to perform in the female voice….

Tu mera hero (O o o...)

The men were shocked! Not only had their plan been foiled, but their married lives were also in jeopardy. Avinash took the decision in a split second and jumped from the stage towards his girl, signalling the others to follow suit. The men were now on their knees in front of their girls lip-syncing the song and saving their marriages. Savitri Bhabhi was dancing alone on the stage when DJ Kasim took to the stage to dance along with her.

Although Avinash had moved in good time, a certain lady's appearance was enough for Sanam to understand the situation. Sanam instinctively knew that the Ichchadhari Nagin (a mythical shape-shifting serpent creature in Indian folklore) had taken a liking to her husband. Sanam was mentally suiting up with imaginary ammunition to guard what was hers.

The two women- Savitri and Sanam shared a momentary eye-lock. The war was ON.

Once the performances were over, people took over the stage. The men took their women to dance. The three couples stuck together for the next hour or so. Savitri Bhabhi did try to budge into their circle but was cleverly dodged by Sanam, Avinash and others.

After a few drinks, the guys came into their desi avatar and grooved on "Appadi podu remix" and 'Zingat' putting the stage on fire.

Finally, they sat down to dine. Sanam was feeding Avinash when the Nagin slithered in,

"Oh my God...you guys danced a smashing number!" Savitri Bhabhi came to their table complimenting all the men but eyeing only one.

"Fake accent hai tera Dayan!" Sanam observed while gritting her teeth.

"Tum kya kaam karte ho?" Savitri Bhabhi asked, unduly stressing the word 'Kaam"!

Avinash almost choked on his food.

"Woh Vahini...he is a translator," Rohan said looking at Sanam's reaction. He was trying to douse the fire that was soon threatening to engulf the whole evening.

"Really Honey-Bunny? Lagta toh gym instructor hai...yeh Dole-shole...yeh thighs!" Savitri Bhabhi said followed by a sinister laughter that shook her assets making the other women cringe and swear.

"No one has offered me a chair till now, toh chalo Hunny-Bunny ke thighs main kitna dum hai yahi dekh lete hain!" Savitri Bhabhi said, eyeing Avinash.

In a split second, Sanam bounced off her chair and jumped into Avinash's lap taking Savitri Bhabhi off-guard and leaving her visibly fuming.

"My husband, my throne...and please take the chair. This is the least we can do for our elders!" Sanam told Savitri with a challenging smile.

"Arre haan haan...I was just joking Hunny-bunny! Main bhi apne husband ka bahut khayal rakhti hoon! Parag toh mujhe kehte hain ki mera naam Savitri ki jagah 'Sati-Savitri' hoona chahiye tha! Aaj kal ki ladkiyon ki tarah nahin hoon main!" Savitri Bhabhi threw her venomous words at Sanam.

Sanam had just taken a big sip of water but as she heard 'Sati - Savitri,' she could not control and spit the drink out. Since Savitri Bhabhi had just taken the chair next to Avinash, she invariably became the target for the liquid projectile.

"Holy Fu*k! Kitne gawar ho tum log!" Savitri Bhabhi screamed at Sanam who was trying to control her laughter like everybody else at the table.

"This dress was fucking expensive!" Savitri Bhabhi stomped her foot and walked away from the table leaving behind a group that erupted into a huge bout of laughter.

"Sanam, you were Savage!" Akriti said between the bouts of laughter and the others agreed.

An hour later, only the extended family and a few close friends were left in the party. Soft music was playing in the background and the couples were relaxing. Savitri Bhabhi had not shown her face since the water-gate incident.

All the relatives were rounded up as Madhu's Aji came to the stage to say a few parting words to the about-to-be married couple.

The DJ was missing, so someone fiddled with the knobs on the console and gave Aji a mic.

"AAAAHHHH..." came a loud moan in the audio system. Aji stepped back in shock. She again tried speaking...and another moan came ...louder and clearer this time.

"Me nahin (not me!)," a shell shocked Aji explained herself.

Soon a lot more noises started coming. Noises of bodies slapping each other...rubbing against each other. 'Noises' people generally associate with SEX. It seemed like that while switching on the mic for Aji, someone had switched on the other mic which was now somewhere completely inappropriate.

Someone was grunting and someone was moaning. The audience in the lawn froze. All were shell shocked. It was not that everyday normal people heard a LIVE sex scene going.

Sanam stared at Avinash as if asking him if it was what she thought it was.... who nodded in affirmation.

"Come on Honey-Bunny...harder!" Sanam heard these words and lost her control. In the pin drop silence, a small giggle by Sanam undid everyone.

All those who had recovered from the shock were now stifling their giggles but Sanam being Sanam could not hold on...before Avinash could gag her, more giggles had escaped. Next was Sanam's full throated laughter ringing in the lawn.

"Harder ...fuck harder!" the lady screamed somewhere.

"Errr..RRR..Ghhh," some guy grunted.

Avinash had now given up on Sanam and had joined her. The whole audience laughed like they had never laughed before. People were avoiding eye contact with others and laughing. Some were trying to switch off the sound controls, but nothing was happening.

"Ooohhhoooo!" A wolf whistle from the lady announced that the act had reached its culmination.

A few minutes later, the voices were heard again.

"Come give mommy a last kiss!" the female voice said. This time however, the audience could see the silhouette of a buxom female kissing a strapping young man with a mic resting in his trousers pocket. The backlight behind the screen was ON. The kiss went so hot, that the couple lost balance and fell through the screen on the stage.

CHAPTER- 35

COMMITMENT

After the unfortunate event, the party had wrapped up while the night was still young! The three couples had not wanted the night to end so all six of them had got into Rohan's seven-seater SUV and headed to create the after party at a private party place near Mazagaon docks.

It was almost one in the afternoon and Sanam and Avinash were still in bed. They had returned at six in the morning. The three couples had spent one of the most romantic dates of their lives, cradled in each other's arms... under the beautiful blanket of glittering stars and soothing sounds of the crashing waves.

It had been a beautiful end to an eventful day.

Sanam had woken up some time back, but her body was in a delicious limbo. She was snuggled into Avinash who had held her in a tight embrace, as if she would run away if the hold slackened. He was still deep asleep.

Sanam tilted her body and looked up at his serene, adorable face. She felt a surge of protectiveness and love for him. Every moment spent with him was so special.

"Avinash is such a nice person," Sanam told herself as she remembered the last evening. She noticed his small gestures yesterday for the elderly especially Aji. This is how he was...he will not even let the other person realise but would do so many things for them. He noticed everything; he took care of everything. He deserved everything in this world. Every time she looked into Avinash's warm eyes; she would feel herself fall more in love with him.

"Haye kinna sona hai tu!" Sanam pinched his chin.

She tried tickling him, but he did not budge at all. She tried getting out of his embrace, he did not let her go.

"Avi uth na...bore ho gayi main!" Sanam whined after not getting a reaction from him.

"Haye Kumbhkaran hai mera husband. Duniya mai aag lag jayegi tabh bhi inki neend nahin khulegi! Hayo rabba!" Sanam thought to herself.

Sanam extended her free arm for her phone and happened to touch a couple of remotes. She picked up the remote when a devil's idea struck her. She giggled quietly imagining the result of the prank she was about to execute.

She picked up the sound bar's remote, connected her phone, cued in a song and closed her ears. In a few seconds, the whole society heard the loudest 'Who let the dogs out? Who? Who?" in the middle of the afternoon.

"Fuuuuuuuuuuu**kkkkkkkk..........," Avinash yelled and woke up like a bolt of lightning had struck him.

Avinash was dazed and just wanted the noise to stop. He got up and manually switched off the music system.

"Kaisa mazak tha ye baby?" a shocked Avinash asked, turning towards her only to find his wife rolled like a ball shaking with laughter. Tears of laughter trickled down Sanam's face.

Avinash's anger melted away in an instant. He stood hovering over the bed with his hands on his waist watching her lovingly. Sanam was wearing a cute pink and white polka dots on a mint green base T-shirt.

"Fuck she looks like a marshmallow! Soft, sexy, and so edible!" Avinash observed.

Instantly, his body rose to his vivid imagination. He took off his T-shirt and pulled her by the legs to the edge of the bed where he was standing.

Sanam's laughter died on her lips when she saw the intensity of desire in his eyes. His smouldering gaze scorched her, making her bite her lower lip in anticipation of ecstasy.

Avinash disposed of her t-shirt in a jiffy, and both lost the sanity they were barely clinging on.

His lips were so tempting, she was dying to taste them. Slowly and seductively her hand went into the waistband of his shorts to push down the offending garment to feel his towering modesty. He grunted loudly in pleasure and in return squeezed her supple mounds. They were in seventh heaven and Avinash was about to enter the cave of pleasure when Sanam's phone rang.

She got distracted by it and extended her arm towards it.

"Ignore baby!" Avinash said, entering her who moaned in return.

Her phone rang again…they ignored. When it rang incessantly for the third time, Sanam's concentration broke.

"Baby lagta hai important hai!" Sanam got worried.

"Yaar KLPD mat kar!" he said grunting. But Sanam's curiosity had been awakened. She lifted the phone and saw that Madhu was calling.

"Madhu hai!" Sanam said.

Avinash froze midway.

"What is more important?" he grunted.

"You baby!" Sanam understood as she was on a STICKY wicket.

"Aviiiinash" Sanam moaned in joy as he entered her.

"You are fucking HOT PUNJABAN baby!" Avinash was increasing his pace when the phone rang again. They ignored. Then Avinash's phone started ringing. They both knew who it was.

"Kya chahiye usko…. banda apni biwi ko pyaar bhi nahin kar sakta! Wtf!" Avinash was furious now.

"Pick it up now! Tera dhyan toh udhar hi hai!" Avinash got up and went to the washroom abandoning their enjoyable exercise!

Sanam picked up both their phones and kept them on silent and followed her husband.

Avinash was now pissed off! Reaching the cliff and walking back was hell frustrating. The next moment he heard a loud knock on the washroom door! He switched off the shower and opened and Sanam walked in.

"Shastriji aapne bola tha ek din…. Shuru main karta hoon aur end tak jata hoon!" Sanam said seductively. Avinash captured her mouth with fierceness and did not let go until the job was done.

"Madhu tu theek hai? Kya hua?" Sanam called her the moment she got free from tending to her husband. There had been 26 missed calls from Madhu in the last fifteen minutes.

"I am video calling you Sanam!" Madhu said.

"Nahin...sun video call mat...I just stepped out of the shower! Tell me aise hi" Sanam said.

"Arre usme kya hai..jo tere pass hai...wahi mere paas hai...bas size different hai!" Madhu said in a matter-of-fact tone.

"Acha kya hua yeh bata?" Sanam asked a very upset Madhu.

"Yaar woh BC tailor ne shadi ki saree ka blouse kharab kar diya!" Madhu wailed loudly, breaking into tears.

Madhu and Sanam had gone to the tailor for stitching of her blouses for her wedding trousseau. Madhu had ordered one stylish yet sexy back-sleeveless blouse for a saree meant for her honeymoon and a traditional blouse for her wedding saree. Unfortunately, the tailor had swapped the designs. Madhu now had a traditional designed blouse for her honeymoon saree and a sexy blouse for her traditional Marathi wedding. It was a big problem.

"Main ek ghante main aa rahi hoon!" Sanam consoled Madhu.

"What happened baby?" Avinash asked.

"Siyapaa baby! Siyapaa!" Sanam replied.

An hour later, Sanam and Avinash were standing dutifully at Madhu's place. Madhu was in a bad state. Akriti had been having a tough time managing the Bridezilla.

"Sanam.... yeh mere saath hi hona tha? Bhagwan se meri khushiyan dekhi nahin jaati? "Hamari shaadi sabko yeh sab kaand ki wajah se yaad rahegi...sab hamare bachon ko bhi bolenge...tumhari mummy -papa ki shaadi par yeh kaand hue the!" Madhu cried.

"Aww...feel bad for you Madhu...Main jisko bhi bolunga...unko bolunga aage nahin bolna!" Avinash chuckled, making Madhu bawl harder.

"Avi seriously?" Sanam gave a sharp nudge to her husband.

"Arre pagal hai kya Madhu? Chal dikha blouse!" Sanam tried to calm her friend.

The blouse had been ruined but it could still be salvaged.

"Madhu showed me the saree. She took the saari and asked Akriti to accompany her to Aji. They chatted for a while and called Madhu.

"Yay! I think we can do something! I just need two hours! I will quickly go and return!" Sanam told Madhu.

"Arre no...no Haldi karke jaana," Madhu's mother told them. Sanam and Akriti did the haldi for Madhu quickly and left for the tailor accompanied by their spouses.

In a few hours, Sanam had gotten the blouse done by adding sleeves with a matching net and border from the upper part of the saree which anyways went into the petticoat. The result was a sophisticated contemporary blouse- by no way traditional but not unbecoming like before.

"Thanks, Sanam...I know you will always be there for me!" Madhu started crying again. The bride was definitely having a meltdown.

Avinash and Naveen had dropped the women at Madhu's place and headed to Rohan's place. Since the bride and groom were not allowed to leave their houses once haldi was done, the guys wanted to meet him as he hadn't sounded himself. His haldi they had missed in the whole Blouse-gate kaand but still wanted to meet him.

"Yaar tu theek hai?" a concerned Avinash asked Rohan.

"I don't know yaar!" a lost Rohan mumbled.

"What happened?" Naveen asked.

"Kuch bhi nahin aur bahut kuch!" Rohan sighed after taking a swig of beer. The men sat perched on the water tank platform on the terrace. Rohan's mother had sent some hot bhajiyas(fritters/pakoras) for them.

"Abey drama queen...itna serious kabhi nahin dekha tujhe...What happened?" Avinash chided him.

Rohan was now fiercely pacing the terrace. Twice he opened his mouth, but nothing came out. Finally, Rohan started speaking.

"Yaar what to tell...mood is a little off because of Savitri Vahini and Parag Dada! Parag Dada touched down today and got to know the whole scandal. His mother has already refused to attend the wedding...she is too embarrassed. Dada too might not attend the wedding as well," Rohan paced furiously.

When the great revelation happened, the lady in question (read: questionable...) made a beeline for the exit leaving her mother-in-law bawling and her partner in crime at the mercy of the audience. DJ Kasim had been beaten up by a few of Rohan's relatives. Avinash too punched him twice or thrice to settle his score, before saving him from the angry crowd. DJ Kasim's shirt had been torn and his fair face promised contrasting blue-black bruises by the next day.

Rohan's Australian Aatya had refused to go to the Groom's home (where maximum relatives were staying) and chose to go to a cousin's place.

Avinash and Naveen just empathised silently.

"On top of it, Madhu is having a meltdown. Yaar blouse ko lekar dimag ki dahi kar di. Hum launde toh shirt ko lekar kabhi nahin rote! I do not know...it is so overwhelming. This commitment thing. You know, tying yourself to one person forever. Giving your heart, your peace to someone outside your blood relations with the hope that they will not screw you up! Matlab apni g@@nd plate par sajja ke kisi hyper aurat ko de do...aur kaho...Here madam screw it! But what if I screw it up myself. What if I spoil Madhu's life? What if I cannot take care of my kids tomorrow? Madhu will get so many men better than me...Am I fu*king her life? Itna paisa kharch karke main apni hi lagwa raha hoon! Beh#$c&*d lagi padi hai meri...phat ke haath main aagayi hai!" Rohan ended his monologue.

"Isne toh 'Pyaar ka Punchnama-2.0' likh di!" a baffled Naveen whispered to Avinash.

"Abey bas bas!" Avinash hugged a shivering Rohan.

"Hota hai yaar...wedding nerves!" Avinash tried to calm him down,

"Haan yaar Dil par mat le...haath main le!" Naveen tried his hand at humour.

Avinash and Rohan, both gave him a bad look before bursting into laughter.

"You guys don't feel frustrated? Matlab's affair is fine, but Shaadi is like...jhamela!" Rohan asked the men.

"Nahin yaar...sukha khatam hota hai! Shaadi achi hai...hunt nahin karna padta...varna bhagwan ko kitna makhan lagana padta tha...kitni drinks pilani padti the pub main," an over excited Naveen babbled, shocking the other two.

"Yeh sab Akriti ko pata hai?" a shocked Rohan asked him, and Naveen nodded in 'NO'.

"Saale tu phas gaya bata ke!" Avinash teased him further and everyone laughed. Naveen's goof up had lightened the situation for Rohan.

"See bro... thousands of things can go wrong...but one thing that is right is that you two can't let go of each other. Maybe living with each other might drive you insane, living without each other will surely kill you!" Avinash told Rohan.

"Freedom is not the absence of commitments, but the ability to choose, and I think you have already chosen Madhu! Take a moment and think of a life without her!" Avinash drove his point home.

"To fall in love and to commit yourself to love, means you choose to make your loved one the one thing you cherish the most."

Avinash remembered reading this quote somewhere. He looked up towards the sky littered with numerous stars and said loudly, "I choose you Sanam!"

CHAPTER- 36
MAJNU

Next night...

Avinash was lying on the bed, with one arm around his wife who was deep asleep on his shoulder and the other supporting his head. They had just finished a hectic round of love making and Sanam had gone off to sleep instantly. The whole wedding day had been very hectic. Madhu had been the quintessential Bridezilla and had kept Sanam and Akriti on their toes. Although the girls had handled her well, it had been exhausting. Madhu and Rohan's wedding had gone in a haze and all Avinash could remember was Sanam, Sanam, and Sanam.

"Miyaan aap fullto Majnu ban chuke hain!" Avinash scolded himself.

"Abey yaar itni haseen biwi mili hai koi pagal nahin hoga toh kya hoga?" he replied to his heart.

"Majhi bayko! (My wife)," Avinash said loudly as he remembered her marathi avtaar that Aji had cajoled her into. Avinash extended his hand and picked up his wallet. He took out a polaroid and stared at it. It was their picture.

"How pretty she looked in a pink and purple Paithani Kashta saree that Aji had forced her to wear in the morning," Avinash mused to himself.

Aji had made her wear a traditional Maharashtrian Nath (nose ring) and Thussi jewellery. Avinash had been pleasantly surprised when Aji had brought Sanam out to show him. Madhu's Aji had been so happy with her ministrations that had called out the wedding photographer and made them pose together. Rohan's cousin at the wedding had a polaroid with him and Avinash had requested him to take a picture of them as well.

In the evening for the reception, Sanam was wearing the maroon Banarasi silk saree that he had bought for her. She had taken pains to get ready. A little make up had accentuated her features... brought out the darkness of her dark brown eyes and the plumpness of her soft lips. She jumped around like a teen, looking and admiring herself in the mirror many times. Her mehndi pattern looked exquisite on her and took a deeper hue than normal. This had excited her, and she had kept on staring at her hands every time she got the opportunity. He had clicked a lot of pictures of her on his phone. Some she had posed for and a lot candidly, when she did not realise that Avinash was watching her. Avinash had realised that this was perhaps the first time she had gotten ready like a married Indian lady. For some unknown reason, the thought had pricked his heart.

As Avinash stared back at the polaroid, he realised that Sanam was looking so shy while posing with him that anyone would have thought that they were a just married couple and not for almost a year.

"Wait...a year?" Avinash realised that it was last December that they had got married, and this was the last weekend of August.

"What an ass I have been to her! We have been together for almost a year, and I have already given her enough pain to last for a lifetime!" Avinash thought.

His eyes clouded with unshed tears as he remembered his venomous words and actions towards her.

"Thank you, Bappa, for giving me my love!" Avinash thanked the almighty realising that he had almost driven his happiness out of his own life with his stupid actions.

Avinash thought about his past relationships. They all now looked so superficial and hollow. Although he had had a steady stream of girlfriends since his teens, his physical chemistry had been the best with Sanam. He had never gone out of his way to spend some time with those women. He tried remembering but could not find any instance where he had been so physically attracted to someone. He had enjoyed sex off and on but mostly had been put off by the shallowness of the person. It had never gone beyond a one-night stand. Even with Nitika, it had always felt like an exercise...to keep the relationship going.

"Sanam has become my obsession!" he mused to himself with worry. The mere thought of her was enough to put his body on fire. He was obsessed with her body and her soul. Every time they made love, he would feel immensely satisfied, peaceful and loved. Every time she chatted nonsense, it felt as if a small part of his heart which felt empty earlier, would fill up with warmth. Sometimes he could not decide whether to make love to her or listen to her talking because both filled the emptiness of his soul.

As if on cue, Sanam snuggled more into him in her sleep. Avinash just could not control his smile. He looked down at her sleeping figure and smiled lovingly. Her face was glowing…. the vermilion had gotten smudged during their coupling, and the round maroon bindi still adorned her forehead. This made her look even more alluring. Avinash bent down and kissed her pout. Sanam scrunched up her nose in her sleep that made him laugh softly. Her anklets made a sweet sound with her body movements. He looked at her ankles peeping out of the soft duvet. Along with the jewellery he had bought a new pair of anklets too. A little more ornate than the ones she owned previously. He rose a little just to get a glimpse of her beautiful feet.

"Gosh! I am so gone! Every movement of hers drives me crazy. Everything reminds me of her. I feel dizzy with desire around her," Avinash groaned internally.

He chuckled at how Naveen and Rohan had teased him to no end when he just would not stop ogling at his own wife during the cocktail party performance. If she looked hot then, she looked hotter now.

"Sleep now Majnu miyan!" Avinash told himself and snuggled more into his wife.

Next morning, Sanam woke up with a start…it was 11 am and already late for Monday.

"Avinash…oh Maa! Main late ho gayi!" Sanam screamed.

"Baby…it is ok! You have a holiday today! Maine Editor Banerjee se baat kar li thee!" Avinash calmed her down and pulled her back.

"Baby bag pack kar le…We are going out for a few days!" Avinash told her, leaving her completely startled.

"Kahan?" Sanam asked him, still trying to come to terms with the surprise.

"Surprise sweetheart!" Avinash pulled her down in a hug.

By three p.m. they were ready with their luggage!

"Baby chal! Let us go! Avinash pulled her while picking up the luggage. They went down and took an auto. Avinash asked him to drop them a little ahead of their home leaving Sanam puzzled.

"Hi Bhai...hello Ma'am!" a nice voice greeted her as she got down from the auto taking her by surprise.

"Sanam ...meet Nihar Kumar, my assistant. Assistant kam, bhai zyada hai!" Avinash introduced a short, fair, pudgy guy in his late twenties. He had a cute goatee and dressed exactly like Avinash...Jeans and kurta.

"Aaiye bhabhi!" Nihar said respectfully to a black BMW SUV. Nihar kept their luggage in the boot. Avinash made Sanam sit in the passenger seat and secured the safety belt around her, pecking her on the lips sneakily once the job was done, leaving her blushing.

"Nihar sab arrange ho gaya?" Avinash asked Nihar while making sure Sanam was out of earshot.

"Haan bhai...jab tak aap jaoge tab tak sab ho jayega! Aur apne jo order kiya tha na..thats on the backseat!" Nihar smiled.

"Nice meeting you bhabhi!" Nihar took her leave.

"Bhai best of luck!" Nihar teased Avinash while dodging a punch from him.

Avinash was smiling when he sat in the driver's seat. He had asked Nihar to park the car far away from their society to keep the gossip mongers away. As they headed towards the highway, Sanam sank into the luxury of the car.

Avinash handed her a bag of goodies: pistachio cookies, wafers, chips, salted peanuts...basically everything that she loved snacking on. There was a big stash of foreign brands of caramel chocolates she often craved after making love. She blushed at the hint he was trying to give and bit her lower lip trying to stifle a smile.

"Kahan jaa rahe hain hum?" she asked.

"Honeymoon!" he replied, chuckling at her shocked expression.

"Meri movie ka promo shoot hai...kal subah shoot hoga...then we will take a small vacation till Wednesday...Thursday ko Madhu-Rohan ko see off and phir saturday ko meri movie ki announcement party hai!" Avinash told her excitedly.

"Wow! Congratulations!" Sanam jumped in her seat and hugged him.

"Thanks, biwi!" Avinash.

"Kaun hai director?" Sanam asked.

"Surprise hai baby!" Avinash said cheekily. He was a man of few words. He believed in showing in actions rather than claiming in words. Avinash was a firm believer in "When all is said and done, more is always said than done."

Sanam was incredibly happy for him, but Avinash still had not clearly invited her. The thought pricked her. Nevertheless, Sanam was damn excited for her husband.

"Acha hum jahan jaa rahe hain.... woh ek lamba sa bridge hai...woh cross karke aayega?" Sanam asked him in an eager voice. Avinash understood she was talking about the Vashi bridge.

"Yes, we will...why?" Avinash asked intrigued.

"I had seen that bridge when I had gone to Vashi with my friends on an assignment. I was fascinated by the view. You know the sea all around. I felt dizzy standing at the edge of the train compartment door. I felt a paradox of emotions then. I feared the sea, felt like a miniscule being in front of such a magnificent beast. On the other hand, I was fascinated by such a beautiful creation. It gave me goosebumps," Sanam said.

"So, have you ever been outside Mumbai?" Avinash asked her.

"Haan na...Mummy Papa Canada leke gaye the. I must have been nine years old. I had been pampered by the flight attendant in the plane. It was fun. I saw snow for the first time. My father was a well-placed bureaucrat in the Punjab Government, life was good then!" Sanam spoke with a smile. She was surprised at herself that she did not cry. Usually, she would cry at any mention of her dead family.

"Maybe, what they say is correct...Time heals. Or is it, Avinash?" her heart gently questioned.

"Why does this fantasy feel real? Why does it feel that he cares for me? Can I dare to hope Waheguru? Can I hope for the unthinkable? Will I ever be lucky to get a small place in his heart?" Sanam asked herself. Her heart felt fuzzy with warmth. Her mind went back to Madhu's wedding, when he was eyeing her openly, making her blush. Akriti had teased her to no end about Avinash being the quintessential obsessed husband. Sanam smiled and sighed. She was a little tired with their hectic lovemaking schedule. She stretched out lazily like a cat.

Avinash saw her smile to herself. He would have loved to know what was making her smile.

Sanam stretched on the seat and purred in satisfaction. She was wearing a white chikan anarkali suit, her kohl rimmed eyes were heavy with sleep. Avinash stopped the car by the road and adjusted the seat for her. Much to his agony, she chose to keep her feet on the dashboard. Now Avinash was privy to the most beautiful pair of feet, adorning the new payals(anklets) that he had got her yesterday.

Of course, he had not let her sleep properly last night. He knew she was tired. A weird sense of pride surged through him. He felt deliriously happy every time he claimed her body. He felt as if he won a trophy.

"This is such a caveman way of thinking!" Avinash admonished himself.

Yet the thought made him smile. Avinash gave up resisting her feet. He put the car on the automatic mode and handled the wheel with one hand. He took her feet and kept it in his lap, massaging them gently with his free hand. Sanam sighed in delight in her sleep, making Avinash smile in return.

"Baby we are about to cross the bridge!" Avinash woke her up a little while later.

Sanam woke up with a start. She looked out of the window in excitement at the vast expanse of sea under the bridge. Avinash turned on her favourite playlist to be rewarded with Sanam's smile.

Sometime later, they stopped at a food mall to freshen up.

"Avinash, I am hungry!" Sanam whined.

"Baby not here," Avinash tried to pacify her. She had started making small-small demands and it made him glad that she expected him to fulfil those. That felt she had a right on him.

He took her a little ahead on the highway to a very regular looking but packed restaurant.

"You get the best vada-pav and bhajiya(fritters) here," Avinash said, taking an empty bench and ordering a plate of vada pav, potato - onion bhajiyas and ginger tea.

The fare was enjoyable. Once they were done, Avinash called for something called 'Kharvas'.

"Yuuummm...what is this?" Sanam asked.

"It is called Kharvas. This sweet meat looks like paneer in texture but is essentially a milk pudding made from cow or buffalo colostrum, the first form of milk produced within one or two days of giving birth," Avinash explained.

Sanam suddenly stopped chewing on it and kept it down.

"What happened biwi?" Avinash looked at her puzzled. One minute she was enjoying the food and the very next minute she had a sombre expression on her face.

"This does not feel right Avinash. The colostrum is the right of the new-born calf. We humans are so inhuman!" Sanam said with a note of sadness.

"Not everything in this world is played by ethics, sweetheart. Almost all calves are separated from cows within hours or days of birth on dairy farms. This allows farmers to sell the milk that the calves would otherwise drink. It is all a part of the food cycle. Hunger is an ethical issue first — it is not just a philanthropic or moral issue. Some people eat meat, some eat vegetables. No one is entirely ethical. In every sphere of life, you have the big fish eating the smaller fish. Sometimes you are the big fish...sometimes you are the small!" Avinash made his argument as they drove along, pushing Sanam deep in thought.

CHAPTER- 37

LOVE AND PAIN

The hills were visible, and they were near Khandala now.

The route was pretty treacherous and went through a couple of small villages. The road was not a concrete one and was majorly unlit. Sanam was thankful that Avinash was such a skilled driver. She was just wondering where they were going in the wilderness when their destination revealed itself leaving Sanam astounded.

It looked like a huge property with cottages strewn around. The reception was grand. Everywhere one could look, there were artifacts. It spelt luxury. Sanam felt out of place in such opulence. Avinash looked at her and understood. He put his arm around her shoulders and steered her towards their cottage. Although it was pitch dark, one could see it was all lush and green. The steward guided them in the direction opposite to most of the cottages and amenities.

Their cottage was hidden by the bushes. Had the steward not been there, they would not have known there was a cottage here. These were exclusive cottages made entirely out of glass. A cottage would be an incorrect word...it was a glass house with wood supporting its structure in places.

"Enjoy your stay Sir and Ma'am! We have a separate chef dedicated to your service 24x7," the steward informed them as he left.

"It is beautiful!" Sanam gasped. Avinash was happy she liked it. This was a very exclusive resort. He had pulled a few strings to get the booking. He observed his jaan who was smiling as she explored the cottage.

It was a duplex cottage. The ground level had the seating and the dining area. One half had luxurious sofas and seating space; the other half had a huge wall mounted home theatre with luxurious recliners. The ground level further opened into a small patio overlooking the beautiful valley.

"Ohhh woooow!" Sanam exclaimed as explored the small kitchenette with a well-stocked fridge.

The first level had a huge comfortable master bed. The room had an ensuite washroom, which was as big as the bedroom.

"Oh my God...Avinash!" Sanam screamed when she spotted a huge jacuzzi in the washroom with a well-stocked bar.

"Haan sweetheart," Avinash laughed at her gleeful expressions.

Avinash slowly walked towards his wife. Sanam stood rooted in anticipation, which proved to be worth all the wait when her husband kissed her. The kiss was all desire, passion and longing. They disposed of the offending garments and moved into the jacuzzi without breaking the kiss. Once out of breath, Avinash traced the path from her ear to the breast with his lips, exacting delicious moans from her. He handed her a circular pink colour ball with small stars on it...

"Avi, what is this?" Sanam asked. She was sitting between his legs with his hands around her protectively.

"These are bath bombs! Put them in the water and see the magic," he said.

Sanam did the same and saw the bath bomb dissolving very quickly in water, leaving a rosy fizz and a light floral fragrance behind.

"One more ...one more!" Sanam took another one and dropped into the tub with a giggle. For a moment, Avinash was awestruck with the innocence on her face. He felt he was looking at a fifteen-year-old girl. But slowly as his gaze travelled south, he saw the magnificent anatomy that changed his mind and fired his desire for her more. They indulged in heavy petting.

They remained in the tub sipping on their drinks till the water lost its warmth.

"Chal sweetheart!" Avinash signalled her to leave.

"Arre but aren't we supposed to ...like do it here?" Sanam sounded disappointed.

"Baby, movies main bahut kuch dikhate hain, but it is damn uncomfortable doing the deed here. Vaise bhi you have a backache today na?" Avinash said, lifting her out of the tub.

"Oh, he noticed!" Sanam smiled at the caring facet of her husband's personality.

He lifted her quickly and took her to the bed before he lost sanity. Avinash again took them to the heights of ecstasy thrusting in her with desperation. Their long make out session had sucked all patience out of him. He had become almost an animal in heat. The room was filled with their moans and grunts.

"I love you, Jaan!" Avinash grunted as he rode her towards fulfilment, before collapsing next to her. The hectic day had taken a toll on him as within no time sleep claimed him. In his sleep he rolled towards Sanam and took her in a hug.

Sanam had not moved an inch since his declaration. She was confused if it had happened in flow or did he really love her.

His declaration had left her wide awake. She tried to get out of his arms, but he refused to let her go.

"Thand lag jayegi bacha!" he murmured in his sleep, pulling her more into him.

"Avi...loo jana hai!" Sanam told him.

"Nahin jana...so jaa!" Avinash was not willing to leave her.

"Sachi...loo jana hai!" Sanam whined again.

"Acha jaa.... love you!" Avinash kissed her forehead and turned around hugging a pillow instead.

Sanam was now completely stunned.

"Two times co-incidence?" Sanam wondered as she returned from the washroom.

"No...it can't be!" Sanam felt a warm feeling enveloping her heart.

"I-L-O-V-E-Y-O-U…...he fu*king said 'I-L-O-V-E-Y-O-U'! He loves me!" Sanam clapped her hands in glee as if she had found a treasure. Now sleep refused to come. She wore one of his T-shirts and went downstairs to raid the refrigerator. She picked up the whole tray of miniature creamy cakes topped it with half a tub of ice-cream and scooped them down. Once done, she could not believe that she had eaten so much after a heavy dinner. She tried surfing the TV, nothing could hold her interest. She tried to play games on her phone.

Finally, tired of her own ministrations, Sanam got into the blanket. A yawn escaped, reminding her that it was four in the morning. She hugged Avinash, kept her head on his chest and slept off in an instant.

Avinash got up at five in the morning. It was painful to get up early after a very few hours of sleep, but theirs was the morning shift. He had to be there by six for the shoot. Sometime later, Avinash got ready and kissed his wife goodbye.

"Baby dhyan rakhna …. Whatever you need, just order. I LOVE YOU BIWI!" Avinash whispered in her ears and left.

"I LOVE YOU BIWI!" Sanam said loudly once Avinash had left. She hid her face in the pillow in delight.

"He loves me!" Sanam realised. She suddenly felt free and happy after a long time. It felt as if a huge weight had been lifted off her head.

She felt happy and rolled off to sleep with a smile on her face. Sanam woke up later in the day with a huge smile on her face. She ordered a nice cappuccino and a plate of cookies and had it on the patio with a beautiful view of a lake.

"He loves me!" Sanam said aloud and smiled. Sanam knew it was a certainty now. She was feeling as good as if she had won a lottery. "Should I call him?" Sanam contemplated.

"No yaar…he will be in a shoot and will get disturbed," Sanam told herself.

"I am not alone in this world…you will be there for me Avinash!" Sanam said aloud and smiled like she had never smiled before. To kill time, she sat in front of the home theatre system and picked up a hindi movie "Sanam teri kasam."

"Aww…. such a lovely movie!" Sanam bawled her eyes out while watching the romance.

Sanam tried pink pasta on the insistence of the chef. She enjoyed the movie along with pasta and garlic bread. At the end, she again opted for sizzling brownie sundae.

Completely full now, Sanam decided to go for a walk to make space for more ice-cream later. She decided to explore the resort and the near-by areas. She started walking down the path that led her towards a small hamlet of kutcha houses. Someone showed her a small trek that would lead directly to the lake. Sanam looked around the wilderness. It was beautiful. The weather was fantastic. This was such a new experience for her. Sanam finally spotted the lake and sat on the bank.

"I wish Avi you were here!" Sanam said aloud.

"Acha Ji chalti hoon, mere husband ghar aane wale honge… it is already 3 pm!" Sanam told the lake an hour later, acting as if it were a friend.

On her way back, she had forgotten the route she had taken earlier. It was difficult to trace the path to her cottage or the resort property. She walked for a good half an hour and saw a lot of vehicles parked at the foot of the hill. Most of them looked like vanity vans and this looked like a shoot. Sanam took out her phone, there was no network. She started walking towards the location. Sanam was just a few minutes away from the location when she saw her husband come out of a vanity van.

"Avi!" Sanam had just mouthed those words when she saw a lady follow him. The lady went close to Avinash and hugged him. Sanam was shocked to see that Avinash hugged her back. In the next few minutes, the lady held on to Avinash and brought her lips to his. Sanam's eyes stung with unshed tears… "Nitika!" she said aloud. This one word was enough to bring her entire dream crashing down.

CHAPTER- 38

DESTINY

Avinash had a bounce in his gait today. He was happy. Last night he had not been able to control himself and had uttered the final truth. He had been too tired to keep awake, let alone explain his feelings to her. He hoped that today he would be able to explain his haal-e-dil to his wife. He wanted to finalise things with Nihar.

"Nihar all set for the evening?" Avinash pinged his assistant.

Avinash got busy with the creative meeting. The female guest star of the promo had been changed at the last minute. Someone new was coming and to top it the director Sudeep Misra had to rush back for a family emergency. Meticulously planned schedule had now gone for a toss. Avinash now had to help the Assistant Director, who was a mess of nerves, to shoot the promo.

"Fu*k... The shoot might get wrapped up late! Yaar I will miss taking Sanam there!" Avinash mused to himself.

"Sir the actress has come!" someone came and informed Avinash.

"Nitika!" Avinash spoke aloud as the female actor came and stood in the middle of the tent. Avinash was shocked. It had been more than a year since Nitika, and he had parted. It had not been an amicable separation. Nitika Trehan was a leading supermodel and his ex-girlfriend. Tall, fair, and willowy, she was every red-blooded man's dream.

"Hi Avinash!" Nitika said to Avinash.

"Hi Nitika! How have you been?" Avinash asked. Avinash waited for the rush of emotions to hit him. Surprisingly, nothing happened.

They sat under the tent that had been constructed outdoors. They got on with the scene. Avinash explained to her the requirements. Although she was not exactly the right person for the promo, they will have to work around as nothing could be done at the last moment. He sat down with the AD (Assistant Director). It was all professional. Avinash reworked the entire scene to fit into Nitika's personality, while she went into the vanity to get ready.

"Sir, madam aapko vanity mein bula rahi hain!" one of the staff members came and informed Avinash.

Avinash was deep in thought as he walked towards Nitika's vanity van.

"Nitika…May I come in?" Avinash knocked at the door.

"Please come!" Nitika said.

"You go outside and come when I call you!" Nitika told the female staff member.

"How have you been Avinash?" Nitika turned towards Avinash and asked him.

"Nice…Nitika. How have you been?" Avinash asked her. He genuinely wanted to talk to her. To him she now looked like a stranger.

"It has been a long time, Avinash. You seem to have become different. Congratulations on this movie. From what I hear, it is phenomenal! Lagta hai meri judai ne tumhe writer bana diya!"

Nitika gave a superficial laugh.

"I was always a writer Nitika…. I just did not trust myself enough," Avinash said and walked out of the vanity van.

"Avinash …I am so sorry. I did not know how to react," Nitika ran after him, hugging him.

Avinash identified a genuine emotion in her and hugged her back. But Nitika was too emotional, she brought her lips to him and kissed him.

"Nitika what the hell!" Avinash held her by the shoulders and shook her.

"Please get a grip over yourself!" Avinash admonished her.

"I am sorry Avinash. I need to talk to you. I have been missing you. I did not know why I reacted like this. Please do not leave Avinash...I need a friend," Nitika was reduced to tears.

"Ok...let's talk once we are done shooting," Avinash said genuinely.

Theirs had been a three year long relationship off and on, however those three years looked like a distant memory now. Avinash started observing Nitika, trying to understand what brought them together. He observed how Nitika talked, behaved with others: the core team and the staff. She was not exactly a cold person but was not exactly warm. She had a professional demeanour, nothing new as most of the people working in this industry had that facade going on. She looked eager to impress the right people. There was a strange mix of genuineness and artifice in her. Nitika was good looking, but her eyes did not shine when she smiled. Her skin was great, but it was fresh because of a rigorous beauty routine not naturally. Everything about her screamed artifice.

"Why am I comparing her to my Sanam? No comparison at all!" Avinash told himself and checked his phone for the network to make a call to his wife. He sent his spot boy to give a message at the reception desk of the resort which was half an hour walking from their shooting location.

By the time the shoot got over, it was already ten p.m. Avinash was eager to get back to his wife, but he remembered that he had promised Nitika too. He had managed to mail Nihar to cancel the mountain top cafe booking that he had done to profess his love to his wife.

"Let me sort out Nitika first, then I will return home and apologise to my wife," Avinash tried to sort out his next hour.

"Nitika, join me in the car!" he messaged Nitika.

"Were you ever in love with me?" Nitika asked him when they sat next to each other. The blunt question took Avinash by surprise. He clearly had not expected this heads-on approach taken by Nitika. As much as he remembered, Nitika never liked confrontations.

"Were you?" Avinash asked in return met with silence at the other end. Finding no answer coming from her, Avinash finally spoke.

"I do not think I ever loved you, Nitika. I cared for you, but it was never love. I thought I loved you, but I am so sorry Nitika it was not love," Avinash spoke in one go. He breathed a long sigh after his statement. He was not aware that he had been holding it back.

"I was in love with you Avinash...in my own selfish way, I cared for you. But I owe you a big apology, I never trusted you. I let Rashi manipulate me. I wish you could forgive me," Nitika broke down.

Avinash could see that Nitika meant her every word she had spoken. She had spoken with her heart, and he empathised with her. He hugged her out of compassion.

"You know Avinash, I used you for your money and fame. I was never there for you or for anyone else in my life. That is the reason I am alone today. My parents have stopped talking to me too! Like a lot of other people in my life, they too got tired of my selfish ways!" Nitika had a complete breakdown.

"When did this happen?" Avinash asked her.

"A few months back. I started seeing Alex Sharma and he used me exactly the way I had used you. It hurt Avinash. Karma got back to me. It took me time to understand what a bitch I had been to people," Nitika hiccupped but managed to speak her heart out.

"You have somebody in your life," Nitika spoke categorically. It was a statement rather than a question.

"Yes. I do. I love her," Avinash told her clearly.

"You know what, it shows. You look happy. You look content. I envy you Avinash...but wish you all the best!" Nitika said with a smile.

"You know what Nitika...are you still in touch with Aly Abdul Khan?" Avinash asked Nitika.

"Haan...he is still my friend. Why?" Nitika asked, confused by the question.

"I think, he genuinely cared for you. He might still...worth a try!" Avinash smiled, giving her hope while he dropped her to her own car.

"Thank you, Avinash. See you on the launch...and give my regards to your special one!" Nitika gave him a big hug.

Avinash smiled as he drove down towards the resort with this crazy urge to see his wife.

Sanam turned around alone in the huge bed. The kiss had been going on in her mind since the afternoon. She had thrown up the moment she had seen her husband in a lip lock with Nitika. It had been an extremely painful moment. She had run away from there and had somehow found her way to the resort. Once she had reached the cottage, she had received a message from her husband that he would be late on account of the shoot. For the longest time she sat on the sofa stunned with the turn her life had taken. The day had turned out to be a memorable one, not in the way she had expected though.

In the morning, her urge for watermelon and chocolate had made her realise that she might be something more than hungry. She might be pregnant. Sanam had quickly calculated and realised that she had missed periods for two months straight. Before it could sink in, her husband had given her another unforgettable memory. Although Avinash had never cheated on her, she had started hoping for a better future with him. Life had betrayed her today.

She had no intention to eat but her own condition pushed her to accept a little dal khichdi with curd. She gorged on watermelon again after a while

"Mera baby toh bahut laal-laal nikalne wala hai! Mummy is there for you baby! I will love you always…will you love your mummy baby?" Sanam gently patted her stomach and started crying and cried till sleep claimed her.

It was like this that Avinash found her. Sleeping with tear stains on her cheeks. He saw a plate with half eaten watermelon and was relieved that she had not gone off to sleep on an empty stomach.

Avinash ordered and ate food taking care not to wake up his wife. His mind was still full of his conversation with Nitika, he was thankful of the little thinking time he had gotten while Sanam was asleep. But destiny did not want it that way. Half an hour later, he got a call from Nihar which left him shell shocked. Baba had been hospitalised just before he was to leave for India.

CHAPTER- 39

FAREWELL

"Baby, we need to leave. It is an emergency," Avinash gently woke Sanam an hour after the call. She woke up with a start. Avinash had already packed their stuff and ordered a cappuccino for both.

"Kya hua Avinash?" Sanam asked him.

"My grandfather has had a medical emergency. He has been admitted into a hospital in New York," Avinash told her.

Sanam paled at the mention of New York. "Is it happening Waheguru? First Nitika, then New York!" Sanam asked herself. Nevertheless, her heart melted looking at his state.

"Kuch nahi hoga! Tu darr mat!" Sanam hugged him, rubbing his back. Avinash hugged her back as if his life depended on it.

They checked out of the resort as fast as possible and loaded the luggage in the car.

As Sanam settled herself in the front seat of the car, she felt something behind her. She looked behind and saw a scarf stuck into the seatbelt.

"This scarf?" Sanam asked aloud but she knew where she had seen the scarf yesterday.

"Pata nahi…forget it!" Avinash took the scarf and threw it out of the window. Sanam felt her emotions rise like a bile which she somehow controlled with much difficulty.

"Nitika was in the car!" Sanam realised with a sinking heart.

"Can I sleep in the back seat? I am feeling very sleepy!" Sanam asked Avinash.

"Haan baby! You are ok na?" Avinash asked with concern.

"Just very sleepy...tumhe chalega na?" Sanam asked meekly.

"Haan na! Take this blanket," Avinash settled her in the back and kissed her forehead lovingly.

Sanam lay down on the back seat, thankful for the blanket with which she could hide her tears that were refusing to stop.

Avinash dropped Sanam home in the wee hours of the morning.

"Bacha, I need to go. You will be fine right?" he asked her gently, taking her into an embrace. Sanam just nodded without saying all that she wanted to say. Avinash took her lips into his seeking warmth and strength from her, which she lovingly gave.

"You will go to the office tomorrow? Dhyan se jaogi?" he felt a lump forming in his throat.

Sanam nodded again, not having the guts to reply in words, fearing a breakdown.

"I am sorry baby! I wanted to make this trip memorable for you, but left you alone all the time," Avinash cupped her face in his palms and said with regret.

"Koi baat nahin! You take care!" Sanam said softly. Her voice betrayed the overwhelming sadness she felt.

"You take care baby! I need to go!" Avinash hugged her tightly again and left.

"Tu itna acha kyun hai Avinash?" Sanam asked the empty room and broke down crying.

Same day evening...
Avinash finally sat down with a cup of coffee after almost eighteen hours of coordinating with his friend in New York. Baba was supposed to board the flight the previous day when all of a sudden, he had experienced a sharp pain in his abdomen and fainted. Fortunately, their family friend's son had gone along to drop Baba to the airport. He had taken Baba to the hospital. It was a scare for Avinash and his family. Avinash had immediately contacted their family doctor in Mumbai and co-ordinated the flow of information and medical reports. Baba had stones in his gallbladder and had to be immediately taken into surgery.

"Chal beta...let's leave!" Avinash's father told him. Avinash bent down and picked the luggage loading it in the car. He dropped his parents at the International Airport. Their flight was due in four hours.

"Papa let me know the moment you reach! Nihar, stay connected with me at all times, even if it is early morning in India," Avinash instructed Nihar.

Nihar was accompanying Mrs and Mr Alok Shastri to New York for assistance. With a heavy heart and a prayer on his lips Avinash bid them goodbye at the airport. Avinash was supposed to join them after his film launch. He wanted to miss it, but his father had insisted that he owed it to the people who trusted him professionally and Baba would never want him to miss the turning stone of his career. Avinash had to tie all loose ends at their business and leave for New York at the earliest.

It was early morning that Avinash reached home to find his wife sleeping hugging a pillow with his T-shirt. He changed his clothes and slowly crept into the bed. Sanam turned towards him and hugged him tightly.

"Tu agaya Avi? Sab theek hai?" Sanam asked with concern. She had messaged him a lot of times in the day, but Avinash had not been able to type more than a syllable in response.

"I don't know!" Avinash said as he broke down.

Sanam held him close to her chest and let him cry. At times crying is all you need to get better. After a while when his tears subsided, she kissed his eyes and took him into a tight embrace, patting his back continuously. Avinash did not even realise when he slipped into a deep slumber.

They woke up to Avinash's phone buzzing loudly in the morning.

"Haan...I am coming!" he said to the caller.

"Baby, I need to go!" Avinash said while quickly getting up to change.

"Woh aaj Madhu aur Rohan USA jaa rahe hain!" Sanam reminded her husband as she served him breakfast.

"Oh hell! I do not know if I will be able to meet them or not! Tum chali jaana please. I might meet them directly at the airport," he told her.

"Okay," Sanam said, disappointed.

"Baby khayal rakh apna! Ok?" Avinash kissed her full on the mouth.

"I will miss you!" Avinash said, cupping her face and wiping away the wayward tears that had found their way to her cheeks.

Sanam stood frozen there once he had left. She had been feeling exhausted lately, but she had made a few decisions that she had to carry out. It was after all the question of her and her baby's future.

"Life is not a bed of roses especially when you are the small fish!" Sanam said aloud with a sigh.

"Sanam kaisi hai tu?" Madhu screamed as she spotted Sanam at her home.

"I missed you yaar," Sanam hugged Madhu and broke into tears leaving Madhu perplexed.

"Kaisi hai tu Sanam? Chal sit down first. Have some water," Madhu coaxed Sanam.

Aji hugged her and made her sit down on the bed with her.

"Kaisi hai Sanam?" Aji asked in her broken Hindi.

"Theek hoon Aji!" Sanam said, wiping her tears.

"Theek toh nahin hai" Aji said keenly observing her.

"Sanam look maa has made your favourite pineapple sheera! Take!" Madhu offered Sanam a plate full of the same.

"Madhu nakko….eh gheun zaa…tencha saathi badaam sharbat gheun aa! [Madhu don't give her sheera, bring almond sharbat for her!]" Aji instructed Madhu sharply. Madhu froze for a minute and exclaimed "Oh my God Sanam! Which month?" hugging her.

Sanam was surprised that her secret was out and broke down in Madhu's arms again.

"Arre its ok…cry…hormones I understand!" Madhu tried calming her.

"Kya hua? Your skin is glowing, but your eyes are sad. What happened sweetheart? Avinash ke saath jhagda hua?" Madhu gently patted her back.

"Nahin!" Sanam barely managed to reply.

"Phir? He knows right?" Madhu enquired gently.

"No..he does not know! He would not want the baby!" Sanam was in tears again.

"Arre mad or what?" Madhu was aghast. "He cares so much for you!" Madhu said.

"But he doesn't want a child...he told me before!" Sanam explained.

"Kuch nahin hota beta…darte sab aadmi log hain, jab hota hai bacha toh sab sambhaal lete hain. Mere paas lekar ana...kaan pakad kar theek kar dongi!" Aji said with a toothless smile.

They pacified Sanam and fed her food with love, which she really needed.

"Hope I meet you soon! Take care!" Sanam teared up again as she bid goodbye to Madhu and Rohan.

"All good things have to end...here ends an amazing period of my life!" Sanam told herself as she sat in the autorickshaw and headed home. Avinash was supposed to meet them at the airport.

"What are you saying Uncle?" Avinash screamed into his phone.

Avinash had just bid adieu to Madhu and Rohan at the airport when his phone rang, and he found Advocate Mehta on the other end imploring him to reach his office as soon as possible.

"Avinash, this tabloid 'Spotless' is planning an expose on you. I think that they have somehow got to know about your marriage! We are screwed if this happens!" a visibly shaken Advocate Mehta spoke.

"What the fu*k! How did this happen? This was not supposed to happen! How did they get to know?" Avinash was ballistic with anger. His eyes had turned red, and his flared nostrils betrayed the murderous rage he felt.

Advocate Umesh Mehta was a second-generation lawyer with their family. He had taken over the firm from his father who was a close friend of Baba. Advocate Umesh Mehta and Alok Shastri continued the tradition and remained best of friends. This was the reason Avinash had sought his help for his unexpected marriage for he knew he could implicitly trust Mehta Uncle.

The proprietor of 'Spotless' Mukund Keshwani had a bone to pick with The Shastris. Their feud went back a few years when The Shastris refused to get blackmailed by Keshwani over the slanderous articles that he had written on Avinash.

"Uncle, get me all the dirt on Keshwani and the tabloid! Hire whomever you want, I want to buy that magazine! I do not care about the price!" Avinash said in a menacing voice. The expose had been timed perfectly with the release of his movie. Baba was fighting for his life, and this was the time when the Shastri empire was at a precipice. It was a personal attack, and it was high time that scavengers like Keshwani be shown their real place.

The Mehta office kept abuzz the whole night until they hit the jackpot. A scandalous affair of Keshwani with his secretary gave Avinash the hope that his personal life will not be consumed like a cheap snack with tea by the whole country in the morning.

The first good news they got was at ten a.m. next morning. Baba was critical but out of danger now. By eleven, they had successfully stalled Keshwani from releasing the article. By two p.m. the Shastris had acquired the tabloid from the investors. And by three in the evening, Keshwani was in the lawyer's office pleading for forgiveness.

"What proof do you have for the expose?" Advocate Mehta asked Keshwani.

"I have some photographs of the couple and the contract marriage's papers," Keshwani said leaving everyone in the room shell shocked.

"How did you acquire the papers?" an angry Avinash held Keshwani by the throat.

Keshwani easily got intimidated by Avinash and begged for his life.

"Kal ek ladki ka phone aaya tha...usne raat ko papers pahunche office main!" he said.

"Who is that girl?" Avinash shook him.

I just have her number; I was supposed to keep the money ready after the expose.

"Dial the number and ask her to come here!" Avinash yelled at Keshwani.

Keshwani put the phone on speaker and dialled a number.

"Hello...yes how may I help you?" a female voice came on the other side, shocking Avinash to the core.

"May I know whom I am talking to?" Keshwani asked.

"Sanam Kaur Bedi," the voice replied.

CHAPTER- 40
BETRAYAL

Sanam returned late from the office. It was pretty dark as she opened the door to step into her flat.

As she switched on the lights, she was startled. Avinash was sitting at his writing table, sipping on a glass of whisky.

"Avinash sab theek hai?" Sanam asked. Her heartbeat just was not abating.

"Tum kab batane wali thi mujhe?" Avinash spoke in a menacing tone.

"Oh God...he knows!" Sanam's heart missed a beat. A nerve started to throb loudly in her ears.

"You hid it from me! You betrayed me Sanam," Avinash spoke with a voice heavy with emotions. His eyes were red, and nostrils were flaring with suppressed rage.

"I know meri galti hai!" Sanam broke down.

"Tumhe contract ka pata tha...how could you Sanam? Kya kami reh gayi thee? Why did you do this? You wanted to trap me for money? That cannot be true! You do not give a sh*t about money!" Avinash broke down.

"Tum kab batane wali thee mujhe? Jab bahut der ho jati? Jab zamane ko pata chal jata?" Avinash turned around to look at her with accusing eyes.

Sanam's heartbeat stopped listening to him. She just could not believe her worst nightmare was unfolding.

"I am sorry Avinash...Please understand I did not know what to do! It was an overwhelming situation!" Sanam barely managed to speak.

"I am leaving for New York tomorrow. Nihar is not there...my lawyer will be in touch!" Avinash couldn't breathe anymore. He picked up his bag and walked towards the exit door.

"Avinash please do not leave me...I am sorry! Kuch samajh nahin aa raha thaa tumhe Nitika ke saath dekh kar.... Galti meri hai...maaf kardo!" Sanam was slowly losing it. She hugged him from behind.

"Nitika ko mere saath dekha? Mujhse baat kyun nahi ki?" Avinash turned around in anger.

"The scarf was hers...you lied to me! Kya karti main, tumne kabhi assurance diya mujhe? What in the fu*k was I supposed to do?" Sanam turned around in anger.

"You betrayed me, this is the truth. I cannot stay under this roof with you! I need some space. I need a few days away from you," Avinash said in a broken voice.

"Aur tum kasam manti ho na...toh tumhe meri kasam hai...do not try to contact me. I will contact you!" Avinash spoke looking at her with red eyes and muted rage.

Sanam gasped. It felt like someone was sealing her fate and she was helpless. She stared at him to let her eyes take their fill of him. He didn't look back, just stood still for a moment before opening the door and walked out.

Avinash somehow got on to the bike and reached his parents' home. In a perverse way, he was thankful that no one was there. He locked himself in his room after talking to his father.

"Baba is out of danger but still in the ICU. Bacha sab theek hoga tu bas aaja idhar!" his father told him, sensing Avinash's emotional state.

Avinash poured a glass of scotch for himself and sat on his favourite swing on the terrace where his grandmother and he used to sit in his childhood.

"Why does this happen to me? Why me always?" Avinash spoke aloud.

Betrayal had become a recurring theme in his life. His mind went back to the time when the betrayals in his life started....

Four years back....
It was the time when Avinash had been riding high on success. He had written back-to-back seven hundred crore movies. Some claimed that Avinash had cracked the box office success secret. Success and good looks turned out to be a heady combination for Avinash. A combination that often threatens to burn down careers and lives.

It was around that time that he had met Nitika Trehan. Nitika had been a successful supermodel for years who was now trying to make a mark in acting. Avinash had had a non-committed colourful life till now. The affair with Nitika started due to peer and parental pressure. All Avinash's friends were engaged or married. His parents too had been pushing him for a more stable relationship. Initially, Nitika did tick a few boxes of being an ideal partner. His parents too loved her, they had to...she was his mother's best friend's daughter. It seemed convenient. Mutual physical attraction was there, Avinash did not give it much thought and jumped into the relationship. Had Avinash not been so drunk on success, he would have understood that it was a relationship of convenience: they kind of cared about each other but there was definitely a lack of understanding. It had been a year of their staid relationship when Avinash had met Sanam. He had been instantly attracted to her beauty and simplicity. He had often guiltily fantasised about her. Relationship with Nitika was far from satisfactory. They often fought and broke up for the first time after a year.

He had many one-night stands during this time to get over Nitika. One of them became his nemesis: Rashi Patel, a leading film actress.

Rashi Patel had fooled him into believing that she was a sweet, caring, and loving person. She slowly made her way into the Shastri household. In a few weeks, both sets of parents made Avinash and Nitika patch up, much to Rashi's dismay. Rashi then started to manipulate Nitika. Soon Rashi revealed that she was carrying Avinash's child. Avinash still remembered that fateful night when Rashi had begged him to give his name to her child. After a lot of conflict, Avinash had finally broken the news to Nitika and his family. It was followed by his parents' refusal to talk to him. Their sense of disappointment was palpable. Baba was the only one who unconditionally stood by Avinash. The Shastris reluctantly agreed to marry Avinash and Rashi.

Avinash, who had been a regular but moderate drinker, became an alcoholic in the guilt of cheating Nitika. A few weeks later, Avinash walked onto Rashi making love to his co-star. A drunk and angry Avinash beat up the co-star and slapped Rashi which ended up exposing Rashi's evil plan of trapping Avinash for his money.

A manipulative Rashi created a PR nightmare for the Shastris which heralded the downfall of the Avinash Shastri.

A month later, the real nightmare started for Avinash. Small and big tabloids started printing slanderous blind items implying that Avinash was a woman beater, substance abuser and plagiarist. Slowly these tabloids started printing the articles boldly. Rashi put a word across, and work stopped coming to Avinash. Those producers who begged him to write for them, started avoiding him. Finally, by the end of the year, Avinash became completely jobless. Dejected Avinash would often find solace in writing and alcohol. He would shut himself in his room and write. Every time his mother would force him to come down, he would suffer with the disappointment in his father's eyes, the sadness on his mother's face and the concern in Baba's demeanour. After a point of time, Avinash stopped meeting his parents. The nadir came one day when one upcoming actress blamed Avinash for sexually exploiting her. This led to a lot of media circus. Media held trials in the drawing rooms of the whole country. His mother and father took a vow of silence. They knew Avinash was innocent, but they were unable to connect and communicate with him. Only Baba could cut through Avinash's pain. Fortunately, after a few months the entire conspiracy came to light during a sting operation on the actress, done by an over enthusiastic News Channel. Although, no one spoke aloud...everyone knew who was behind the whole episode: Rashi Patel.

The day Avinash got a clean chit, he left home. He wanted to be anonymous. A nobody. He wanted to complete his film and novels for which he had lost the drive.

"I could have gone anywhere in Mumbai, why did I choose this neighbourhood?" Avinash no longer wondered. His heart knew the answer.

He let out a deep sigh and took a sip of his long-forgotten scotch. The moment the burning liquid touched his lips, he spit it out with vengeance. It tasted of betrayal.

CHAPTER- 41
A MESS

Avinash sat in the waiting area for the family members of in-house patients. Baba was still in the ICU but for observation. Thankfully, he was out of danger. It was day eight of Baba being in the hospital and day six of living without Sanam.

Time just was not passing. His mother had been feeling a little under the weather, so Avinash had asked his parents to return to their apartment.

The Shastris had some business interests here in New York too. In addition to it, Avinash himself owned a huge apartment overlooking the Hudson. His own investment was under the company name of course. The same apartment where he had wanted to take San...her.... She would have loved the glassy reflection of the sun on the Hudson.

Avinash reached the cafeteria and ordered a cappuccino for himself. He had just collected the coffee when a sweet giggle increased his heartbeat. He turned around with a smile wanting to see a familiar face but froze on spotting the source. It was not his Sanam...It was some random couple...random young couple…young couple in love. The guy had a protective arm around his girl. They shared a small kiss and moved out of the cafeteria. Avinash was so lost in the scene that he did not see around and barged into a passer-by spilling the hot cappuccino on himself.

A sharp pain rose in Avinash's heart instead. Avinash's mind had refused to remember Sanam, his heart however had refused to forget her.

After days of blocking Sanam from his mind, today his heart had finally won. He turned around and ordered another coffee.

"Sanam," Avinash spoke aloud with a deep sigh. "You broke my heart into millions of pieces and yet I still love you when every bloody piece pierces my soul," Avinash finally after days took out the polaroid of Madhu and Rohan's reception. This was the one where Sanam was wearing the maroon Banarasi silk saree that he had bought for her.

"How beautiful she looks!" Avinash spoke aloud again and the next moment his vision clouded with a film of silent tears.

He did not remember for how much time Avinash sat there reminiscing the beautiful moments he had spent with his wife. His heart ached to see her in person, to sleep taking her in his arms. The next moment, his heart pained at the betrayal he had faced. Avinash massaged his forehead with his fingers: his head was throbbing, and eyes were aching.

"Coffee!" said someone.

Avinash looked up to see two tall Pumpkin Lattes in front of him. "I didn't order!" Avinash said aloud.

"I did!" his father said, taking the chair next to him.

"Papa, you came so early! Is Aai feeling better?" Avinash was shocked to see his father return. Nihar was supposed to come and relieve him for a few hours.

"Tumhari Aai theek hai…She is resting at home. May I?" his father asked him, signalling towards the polaroid.

"Toh yeh hai Sanam? Bahut pyari bachi hai!" his father said, smiling at the picture.

"Aap Sanam ke baare mein jante ho?" Avinash exclaimed.

"Baba ne New York jaane se pehle hume bataya tha. Dekho, since Ganpati we knew there was a girl in your life. Insaan ban gaye the tum…yeh kamaal sirf aur sirf ek aurat kar sakti hai. Aur tumhare Sanam ne toh amanush(barbarian) toh manushya(human) bana diya!" his father said trying to lighten the situation.

"Aur Naseer aur Ramona bhabhi ne bhi bataya…ek special someone ke baare mein. Tumari maa toh bahut royi us din…khushi ke aansu! She was happy that you had finally met someone worthy of you!" Alok said.

"Aapne logon ne kuch kaha nahin!" Avinash said dumbfounded.

"We wanted to give you time. Nitika ke time par hum logon ne kafi interfere kiya. We realised in the last few months that we unnecessarily pressured you!

Now you tell me, why you have been so upset from the last one week. I understand about Baba, but something else is eating you up. Tell me beta...maybe I can help. Your mother is really very concerned about you!" Alok coaxed him gently.

Avinash ended up telling his father everything...almost everything that a father should listen to from his son.

"So, what did Keshwasni and Sanam discuss? Did she ask him why the expose could not get printed?" Alok asked Avinash.

"No... I could not listen beyond her name...I cut the call," Avinash said dejectedly.

"Ek minute, so the only proof you have linking Sanam with this is a landline number?" Alok questioned him.

"Haan...She accepted as well!" Avinash said aloud as if trying to tell himself that he had thought this through.

"Did she say anything specifically about papers? About the expose?" his father grilled him.

"No. She only talked about Nitika!" the conversation that had been playing like a reel in Avinash's mind.

"Did you clarify with Sanam about your meeting with Nitika?" his father questioned him further.

"No Papa. I walked out because I was furious. How could she even think that I will go to Nitika now. Didn't the past year mean anything for her? Didn't I show my love again and again in my actions? She thought so low of me," Avinash cried out.

"Montu, if I tell you as an outsider the conversation you had with Sanam seems full of assumptions. Something is just not making any sense. Why will she call Keshwani from a very traceable phone number?" Alok said thinking aloud and Avinash just looked back dumbfounded.

"Ek kaam kar...Mehta ko phone laga!" Alok instructed Avinash, giving his phone to his son.

"Umesh...I am disappointed with you yaar...But we will sort that out later. I know everything now. There is something very fishy about this incident. Hire someone to investigate this...there must be a clue...check with the courier company- their CCTV cameras. Get the person who is behind it," Alok went out talking to Advocate Mehta leaving Avinash behind with a dreadful feeling.

"Did I do wrong by her?" Avinash shivered with fear. He picked up his phone and dialled her number.

'The number you have dialled is out of coverage area.' This prompt played after every call he made to her.

His heart was sinking.

"Papa, her phone is off. I am scared," Avinash told his father just as he returned to their table.

"Koi baat nahin beta, sab theek hoga! Usne bhi gusse main phone tod diya hoga...teri tarah!" Alok tried to cover his own anxiety with jest.

"Do one thing, you return to India tomorrow! Take Nihar along with you! We will manage. Anyways, Baba is out of danger now. He is under observation. The doctor was saying if all goes well, he can be discharged within a few days. Call Nihar and ask him to book your ticket. Take him along as well, we have a lot of people here. His mother too is alone at home," Alok tried to reason it aloud with his son.

"Rohan...kaisa hai bhai? Baba is fine. I am going to leave in the next few hours. Just wanted to say that we will not be able to meet this time...next time for sure!" Avinash called Rohan and made his excuse.

"Listen if it is fine, we can come down, it is only a one-hour train ride. There is this wonderful cafe outside Penn Station. We will take the train back from there," Rohan said after discussing it with Madhu.

"For a drink you will travel two hours?" Avinash asked them, surprised by the efforts they were willing to make to meet him.

"Yaar hai tu apna! Aur phir pata nahi kab milna ho!" Rohan said good naturedly.

They arranged to meet at a cafe outside the Penn station. It would be comfortable for Rohan and Madhu to return to New Jersey where they had taken the accommodation.

"Kaisa hai bhai?" Avinash asked Rohan while giving him a tight brotherly hug.

"Madhu, looking pretty after marriage!" Avinash complimented Madhu.

"To kya marriage se pehle nahi lagti the?" Madhu whined.

"Nahin sweetheart...tu hamesha pretty lagti thee...Aur lagti rahegi!" Rohan pecked her.

"Tell me all settle here then?" Avinash asked them. He was already feeling better. Their camaraderie was easing him out a little.

"How is Sanam? And by the way, congratulations!" Rohan got up and hugged Avinash again leaving Avinash confused.

"Kis baat ke liye congratulations?" Avinash quipped.

"Oh no!" Madhu gasped.

Rohan looked around embarrassed.

"I told you not to mention it!" Madhu looked daggers at Rohan.

"Guys hold on...what are you talking about? Please tell me," Avinash asked in a sharp manner.

"See Avinash I thought maybe Sanam must have told you by now! I mean I knew she was scared that you would get angry...but I told her that you are such a caring person, you would never ask her to abort the child," Madhu said.

"Abortion.... that means Sanam is pregnant?" Avinash reasoned aloud. His eyes clouded with a melange of emotions which dropped out as tears.

"Yes...she is! She will tell you once you reach home!" Madhu tried to pacify him, but he was already lost. Somehow, he sat with them for a little more time, bid goodbye and left for the JFK airport.

"Papa, I messed up big time. I am going to become a father and I walked out on her! Will my child forgive me?" Avinash cried as he talked to his father. Life had messed up with him.

CHAPTER- 42

CRUSHED

"Why has life been so unfair to me?" Avinash questioned himself for the nth time. He took a swig of his scotch and felt this deep urge to smoke.

"No...no cigarettes...Sanam maar dalegi!" Avinash imagined her pouting in displeasure and laughed.

Once the shock of the events had worn off, Avinash suddenly started hoping for a better future.

He closed his eyes and saw Sanam with a swollen belly, smiling and looking radiant. He could see his own palm stretched over her beautiful belly. His paternal hormones were kicking in. He just wanted to hug his child. His vision suddenly changed to a small plump girl child in a pink polka dot frock, running around his parents' home. The tinkling sound of her anklets giving away her excitement. The child looked like a replica of Sanam- fair and rosy with fringe adorning her forehead. He could see Sanam happily chasing the child all across the house when the child stops, squeals in mirth and jumps into the extended arms...his arms.

"My baby!" Avinash woke up with a start.

"Kya hua bhai?" Nihar asked, shaking him up.

"Nahin...kuch nahin," Avinash assured him.

"My baby will look just like his mummy! What will my baby call me? Papa or Daddy? I like Papa more," Avinash thought with a smile. In retrospect, he realised that there had been signs all along. There had been changes in Sanam that he had noticed but not registered.

"She had started eating a little more than what she ate regularly. She was going crazy over watermelon! In the last few days, she had eaten watermelon for breakfast every day. He had found watermelon toffees in her bag and fridge too.

"Oh God! My baby is gonna be red, red gollu-gollu!" he thought like Sanam would have spoken.

Avinash's heart ached for his wife. Six days without her had been a punishment that felt like a lifetime.

"I will bear all her anger. I will grovel before her to forgive me and take me in!" Avinash promised himself.

It was three in the early morning, when Avinash and Nihar came out of the Mumbai International airport and sat in the car. As Avinash switched on his phone, he was inundated with messages and calls. He quickly called his father to check on Baba. Thankfully, he was well. Baba had been shifted to a private room, but what his father told him next shook Avinash to the core. He sat shocked for a few moments.

"Bhai...sab theek hai?" Nihar asked in concern.

"Nahin Nihar...kuch theek nahin!" Avinash was barely able to speak.

"Driver, Advocate Mehta ke ghar par lo!" Avinash instructed the driver.

Advocate Mehta was waiting for them to arrive.

"I owe you a huge apology, Avinash. Samajh nahi aa raha how could I go so wrong in recognising a person," Advocate Mehta told Avinash.

"Please tell me everything in detail. Papa just said that you had found the culprit and it was not Sanam! Please tell me everything. I will kill the person who burnt my happy home to ashes!" Avinash's veins were popping out in outrage.

"My nephew Saurabh!" Advocate Mehta spoke, his voice full of guilt.

"Kaise kiya?" Avinash asked in a muted rage.

"He befriended a girl in Sanam's office - Meena. They reached out to Keshwani the moment your movie got announced. The girl dressed up in clothes like Sanam's and went to the courier company with her head veiled. She even signed the courier slip by the name of Sanam.

Very carefully they chose a courier office where there was no CCTV camera. We were able to catch them from the CCTV camera of the opposite shop. Tomorrow morning, a complaint of forgery against the will be done in the local Police Station. I have ample evidence against Saurabh to lock him up for life. He had embezzled a lot of funds from me. I let it go as he is the son of my only sister. But clearly, he does not deserve any sympathy. All I can ask from you is forgiveness, Avinash beta!" Advocate Mehta joined his hands in front of Avinash.

"It is ok uncle! We should leave now!" Avinash told them.

"Ghar le kar chal Nihar…Sanam ke pass," Avinash spoke. His tone was barely audible. To say he was in shock was an understatement.

They reached Avinash's building an hour later. Avinash asked him to wait downstairs in the car. He was not sure Sanam would accept him or not.

Avinash entered the flat with his set of keys. He switched on the lights to find an empty flat. Things were strewn around. It seemed as if no one had been in the flat from the last few days. Avinash's heart sank.

"Nihar, Sanam nahi hai ghar par, kahan gayi hogi? Pata karo!" Avinash barked into the phone. He sat down. He had no idea what to do. His heart was sinking by every passing minute. Nihar came to the flat to see a worried Avinash pacing the room.

"What should I do? Should we wait till morning? She has no friends!" Avinash said. Panic was setting in now.

They started checking the contents of the room.

Avinash saw a yellow writing pad on the side table. Sanam used to use this a lot. She would often scribble something on this and keep it in her cupboard.

Avinash opened her side of the cupboard, and a pair of anklets fell. It was the new payal he had brought for her.

"She has removed it," his heart cried.

He looked around and found a rectangular tin cookie box with small heart icons doodled on it. The floral pattern on it had almost worn off. It was an old box, that had clearly seen better days. The lid of the box had 'TRUE LOVE' printed on it.

Avinash opened the box to find several yellow writing pad pages wrapped like letters. On the top of the pile was a very roughly folded paper. Avinash kept the box aside and opened the letter. It was addressed to him.

Dear Avinash,

Just when I had started believing in love, you left me Avinash. Like everyone else you left me. You left me alone. I made one mistake of hiding the pregnancy from you and you left me? I swear on my dead parents I did not trap you. The pregnancy was probably my mistake...I might have forgotten the pill, but the baby was NOT a mistake. WAS because it is no longer there. Yesterday, I had a miscarriage. I will not blame you; it was destiny. It was destiny that brought you to me and destiny that took you away from me. It is destiny indeed that took my baby away from me. I need to leave this house...it is eating me up. I need to go away. I can now understand your urge to run away, I feel the same.

This is probably the last letter I will ever write to you. Anyways, how does it even matter? You will never see this letter. I will burn the other letters. I know I will burn this letter later, but I had to get it out of my system.

Thank you for all that you have done for me,

Sanam.

Avinash collapsed on the floor crying. All his dreams about having a family were shattered. He clutched the tin cookie box to his heart and walked out of his flat. Somehow, he sat in the car, he was still in shock. How is a person supposed to react when he gets to know that has lost everything in life? His mind had frozen.

"Stop...stop the car!" Avinash asked the driver to stop the car as he spotted a young lady across the road.

Avinash ran like a man possessed.

"Bhai woh bhabhi nahi hai!" Nihar cried and tried to match his speed.

"Sanam..." Avinash ran across the road without realising that a garbage truck was coming from behind.

A few seconds later, Avinash lay in the middle of the road crushed by the garbage truck.

CHAPTER- 43
DECISIONS

Present day

"You betrayed me, this is the truth. I cannot stay under this roof with you! I need some space. I need a few days away from you," Avinash said in a broken voice.

"Aur tum kasam manti ho na...toh tumhe meri kasam hai...do not try to contact me. I will contact you!" Avinash spoke, looking at her with bloody red eyes and muted rage.

Sanam woke up with the same nightmare she had been having since the last nine days.

"Woh gaya meri zindagi se, why am I still disillusioned?" Sanam scolded herself. The events of the past few days played like a reel in her mind.

A few days back....

Avinash had left her alone. He was gone. He had chosen Nitika over her. Sanam sat down by the bed wailing loudly. Her heart cried tears of blood. A few hours later, the mother in her surfaced. She realised that she had a greater responsibility towards her child. Sanam got up, cleaned her face and made a cup of ginger tea. She nibbled on glucose biscuits trying to control the tears. There was this sinking feeling in the pit of her stomach.

"Nahin kuch nahin hoga...be strong my baby!" Sanam consoled herself as she started reciting the verses of Japji Sahib for mental strength.

The night was tough for her and her baby.

The next morning, Sanam dutifully ate a whole plate of watermelon: it tasted sweet and a little salty that day.

Thankfully, it was a weekend, she did not have to go to the office. It was Saturday, Avinash's film announcement. Despite whatever happened yesterday, she felt a lot of happiness for her husband...ha-ha...husband or ex-husband? Her heart asked sarcastically.

She made a light lunch for herself reminiscing the way their weekends used to go. She felt a longing for that bear hug which used to make her forget all the wrongs that ailed her life. Sleep had eluded her last night...her favourite pillow was missing. She wanted those movie marathons with him again. She mindlessly switched on the TV and tried watching before eventually drifting off to sleep. She woke up to find a lot of hot stickiness between her legs. She went to the washroom and saw a lot of bloody mucus dripping down her legs. Her legs shook while she switched on the hot shower and cried in anguish... Somehow, she gathered herself together, changed her clothes and left for the ER (Emergency Room) of the nearest hospital.

Sanam returned home after a few hours without her baby. Her doctor had warned her because she was severely anaemic, she had to be extremely careful about herself in the first trimester.

"How would this happen naturally? Why would God do this to me? Why would nature take away the life of an innocent unborn child?" The guilt of not being able to protect her baby started gnawing at her. She lay down in a foetal position till sleep claimed her.

By the time she got up next, it was already afternoon. She looked around to find loneliness staring back at her. She got up with a cold heart when her hands reached out for the newspaper which had been pushed under her door. Every day it was Avinash who would pick up the newspaper and eagerly read back-to-back. She picked up the newspaper and caressed it when a wayward tear escaped her eye opening the floodgates of emotion! The newspaper slipped out of her hands. It was when Sanam bent down to pick it up, she caught a news item in the bollywood section. It read...

'FLAME re-ignited? Ex- lovers caught getting cosy with each other at the film announcement party' along with a picture of Nitika sitting in the lap of her husband.... ex-husband.

A smouldering rage took over her. She crushed the newspaper and threw it towards the balcony. She had to vent it out. She took out her yellow writing pad and started scribbling.

Dear Avinash,

Just when I had started believing in love, you left me Avinash. Like everyone else you left me. You left me alone...You will never see this letter. I will burn the other letters tomorrow. I know I will burn this letter later, but I had to get it out of my system.

Thank you for all that you have done for me.

Sanam.

Sanam could barely hold her tears. She broke down as she signed her name. She howled and cried till she could no more.

After staring into nothingness for hours, a ping on her phone brought her out of limbo. It was from a colleague enquiring about an article she was supposed to write. Suddenly, Sanam felt that she just could not go back to her life what it used to be. Instantly, she made a decision. She took out her phone and typed a resignation letter to Editor Banerjee. She called her too and told her about the miscarriage. Sanam thanked Editor Banerjee for her guidance and love she had received from her and said her goodbyes.

"I am finished! There is nothing left in my life!" Sanam cried as reality of what had happened started sinking in. A wave of anxiety hit her.

Sanam quickly changed her clothes, stuffed her parent's pictures in her bag and left the house. Without much thinking, she took the first bus that she saw. The bus dropped her off at the Dadar station. Sanam absentmindedly started walking towards the train station when an announcement caught her attention.

"Mumbai to Nanded Special Express arriving on platform No 8 in two minutes"

Sanam ran as fast as she could and stood outside the train...frozen.

"What am I doing? I do not have any clothes.... I have nothing...What am I doing here?" Sanam started panicking and the train started moving slowly.

"Puttar Ji soch ki rahe ho... Chad jao[What are you thinking? Climb aboard]," Sanam heard an old lady call out, extending a hand to her from the train compartment door. Sanam suddenly broke out of her limbo and ran to climbed aboard the train.

"Haye...thank you betaji...aaj aapne mujhse DDLJ (Dilwale Dulhania Le jayenge) ka sequence karwa liya! Main kitty main bolungi toh jal jayengi saari ke saari! [thanks, dear..you made me enact the DDLJ sequence. If I tell my kitty friends, they will get jealous]," said the old lady.

Sanam finally registered what the old lady was saying and smiled.

"Chalo betaji...andar chalte hain...main toh pakore lene ke liye neeche utarne kagi the...gari chal gayi," the lady babbled.

The train had now caught speed. The lady took her hand and made her sit on the side seat.

"So, what's your name?" the old lady asked.

"Ji, Sanam," Sanam answered.

"Allow me to introduce myself...I am Prabhjyot Kaur Dhindsa in short Pammi!" the old lady introduced herself. Prabhjyot Kaur Dhindsa was a short, slightly dusky complexioned lady in her late 60s. She was of a medium frame with long grey hair and kind eyes. Going by the Punjabi suit she had worn, it looked like she hailed from an affluent family. Her command over English was exceptional, suggesting a good tutelage.

"What is your seat number?" Pammi asked her.

"Ummm...auntyji I think I should get down at the next stop. I do not have a ticket," Sanam said panicking.

"Oho usme kya hai...mere paas bhi nahi hai...Ticket collector se ticket katwa lenge! You do not worry; they will not throw us out of the moving train!" Pammi said in a light tone.

"You just sit here with me!" Pammi caught her hand and started talking to the family in the opposite cabin. Within no time Pammi had mixed up with the opposite family and the ones next to them.

Sanam felt the warmth of the old lady's touch seep through in her. After a long time, someone other than her husband had held her hand to calm her.

She felt her eyes wet. She looked out of the window of the sleeper class. The warm air made her sleepy and she rested her head on the window and slept off. Sometime later, Sanam felt a gentle touch trying to wake her up.

"Bacha eat something...here!" Pammi shook her, handing her over a disposable plate with two parathas and karela-potato subzi.

"Nahin auntyji you please eat!" Sanam told her shyly.

"Arre, I am eating, see my plate! Chalo you also eat shabaash!" Pammi coaxed her.

A little while later, Sanam went and stood on the train door. The family atmosphere inside was killing her. The feeling of being alone was stinging her acutely. She looked out of the door to realise that the train was crossing a river.

"This pain should end!" Sanam made yet another decision. She had just taken a step towards the door, when she felt a hand on her shoulder pulling her back.

"Puttar aise nahin sochna! Bahut choti hai tu! Waheguru sab theek karenge!" Pammi aunty hugged her.

Sanam broke down in her arms.

"Puttarji...I can't stand anymore...let's go inside and cry?" Pammi said sometime later, making Sanam break into laughter.

Suddenly Pammi's phone started ringing, making the old lady nervous. She cut the subsequent phone calls mumbling something.

"Auntyji what happened? Who is calling?" Sanam asked her.

"Ladoo, my grandson!" Pammi answered, gobbling a large piece of coconut barfi the fellow passengers had offered her.

"So, pick up na, poor child will feel upset," Sanam tried to reason it out with Pammi.

Finally, Pammi picked up the phone.

"Hi Ladoo!" She said with unusual sweetness.

Sanam was intrigued by the conversation, even though she could hear only one side of it.

"Haan toh I am a big girl. Yaar teri nurse kitni khadoos thee...koi fashion sense nahin thee. Neeru aunty ki baat na kar...jealous soul. Cards main cheating karti hai...fake bags use karti hai! Mere se full jalti hai!" Pammi spoke into the phone.

"Kahan hoon? Train main hoon. Nanded ke Hazur Sahib jaa rahi hoon. You never keep your promises. What do you mean by who will take care of me? I can take care of myself. Now I have a friend too. She will take care of me...hain beta?" Pammi threw the ball into her court.

"She is saying yes. Now stop being a mean bean handsome. See you soon!" Pammi giggled and kept the phone down with the expressions of a teen who had just taken her parents for a ride.

"Aapke grandson ko pata nahin ki aap Hazur Sahib jaa rahe ho?" Sanam asked.

"Nahin...main na, ghar se bhag kar aayi hoon!" Pammi giggled.

"Hain?" Sanam said shocked. Sanam took a moment to imagine and then laughed loudly.

"Yaar Rupanzel ki tarah qaid kar ke rakha tha," Pammi huffed. They started talking about random things till evening.

"Aunty chai peete hain...waise yeh ticket collector toh aaya hi nahi," Sanam observed.

"Aaya tha, tu so rahi thee... teri yeh upar wali seat, meri neeche wali!" Pammi said.

"Hwww auntyji sorry!" Sanam took out her wallet apologetically when Pammi got angry.

"Arre itne kaunse lakhon rupay de diye! Bas kar. Aur kya aunty-aunty laga ke rakha hai.... Nani bol...zyada sexy lagta hai!" Pammi said in a tone that one uses to scold a loved one.

Sanam got teary again.

"Ok Nani!" She said as she hugged Pammi.

"Ab Nani bola hai toh Waheguru de saun lage, gate de nede na jaien! [Now that you have called me 'Nani' swear on Waheguru that you will not go near the gates!] Nani told Sanam to which Sanam nodded.

They had two cups of ginger tea and two plates of pakoras that were especially made for Pammi by one of the attendants in the train' pantry.

"Pammiji...uhh...Nani (as she liked to be called) has a knack of genuinely befriending people and winning over them," Sanam thought to herself.

At dinner time, Nani ordered food for the family sitting opposite and in the next cabin. It was Aloo puri, off the menu, which the attendant had made especially for Nani.

At night Sanam went off to sleep using her dupatta as a cover but felt a thick blanket on her a little later courtesy Nani. She had arranged a few blankets from the AC car. Sanam smiled and slept peacefully.

They reached Nanded by eleven in the next morning. Before they got down, five six attendants came to Nani and touched her feet. They got down on the platform and were given a befitting see off by Nani's squad.

They reached Takhat Sachkhand Shri Hazur Abchalnagar Sahib around one in the afternoon. The strain of the journey was now evident on Nani's face. Sanam enquired around for a cheap place to stay. There were rooms sponsored by the Gurudwara itself. Sanam thanked the altruism displayed by the community that helped people in need like her.

She put in her and Nani's name for the Women's dormitory. She laid Nani down. She was very worried for Nani's health. Sanam observed Nani and saw her getting uncomfortable. She saw Nani sweating, shaking, and what seemed like in the middle of a fit.

Sanam ran to the reception and raised an alarm, when a strong pair of hands held her and asked, "Where is she?" he asked.

"Aap?" was all Sanam could answer.

CHAPTER- 44

REASONS

Flashback continues….

Sanam ran to the reception and raised an alarm, when a strong pair of hands held her and asked, "Where is she?" he asked.

"Aap?" was all Sanam could answer.

"Sanam?" the person stood stunned.

"Dr. Rajeev! Aap yahan?" Sanam was shocked.

"Please take me to my Nani!" Dr Rajeev urged Sanam.

Sanam ran towards their room, followed by Dr. Rajeev.

"Nani," Dr Rajeev immediately bent down and checked her pulse and pupils.

"Kal se kya khaya hai?" Dr. Rajeev spoke in a curt tone and looked at Sanam expecting a quick answer.

"Aloo puri, barfi, pakore aur subah aloo paratha!" Sanam said.

"Shit …she is in a diabetic shock!" Dr Rajeev said in an urgent tone.

He opened his medicine bag and took out a syringe to draw out a liquid from vial, injecting her. He then took out his phone, barked a few directions into it.

"Get my medicine bag," he instructed Sanam, and he picked up Nani in his arms.

"We don't have much time…let's move," Dr. Rajeev said.

"It's a small world!" Sanam thought a few hours later as she sat in the waiting area outside the ICU of a very elite hospital. Dr.Rajeev had been inside with Nani for hours with other doctors. Nurses were rushing in and out, but no one told her anything.

She had known Dr. Rajeev from the last three years. He came off and on to the Gurudwara for organising blood collection and cardio check-up camps. Many a times he had filled in for the doctors the dispensary who volunteered for sewa.

He was a tall, lean, and very good-looking man in his mid-thirties. She still remembered how her neighbour Sheetal Didi crushed on him and giggled when he smiled towards them. He always maintained decency and was courteous with everyone. The nurses who worked in the Gurudwara dispensary swooned over him...but all hearts broke the day everyone came to know he was married. Sanam remembered the day he had brought his wife along. She too was a doctor, and an incredibly beautiful one at that. All the women had been impressed with her eloquence and poise. She had always got positive vibes from Dr. Rajeev the few times she had interacted with him. No wonder he was nice; he had taken after his Nani.

Nani...tears came running at the thought of the motherly figure. Such warmth this stranger had shown to her and now here she was fighting for her life. Sanam started reciting the Japji Sahib. Waheguru had not failed her till now, hopefully he would not fail her now too.

An hour later, Sanam saw Dr Rajeev come out and take a deep sigh as he sat down beside her.

"She is still in danger!" Dr. Rajeev spoke before she could ask.

"I am really sorry, mujhe nahin pata tha," Sanam broke down with guilt.

She got up to look at Nani through the glass window of the ICU. Several tubes had been attached to Nani's anatomy. She looked an emaciated version of her former self. A whimper escaped Sanam's mouth. Her face paled and her lips became dry. She felt her vision blur as she collapsed on the floor with a big thud.

Sanam woke up to a nurse giving her an injection and Dr. Rajeev checking her pulse.

"Nurse check her Blood Pressure," he instructed.

"How are you feeling Sanam? Dizziness?" Dr. Rajeev asked her.

"Follow my finger! Good girl!" Dr. Rajeev performed the basic medical checks.

"What happened?" Sanam asked him. She still could not understand what had happened.

"You had fallen unconscious! You were out (unconscious) for almost six hours," he explained to her.

"Nurse, change the drip!" he called out to the nurse.

"Sanam please I need to talk to you! Will you please be honest with me?" Dr. Rajeev sat in the chair next to her bed.

Sanam looked back at him and nodded.

"How many days back did you have the miscarriage?" Sanam stared back shocked.

"The HCG levels in your blood were very high...We did your MRI scan and sonography to be on the safe side," Dr. Rajeev said.

"Will you please tell me what happened? Do not miss any details," Dr. Rajeev asked her.

Sanam slowly told him about the whole incident in between her emotional breakdowns.

After listening to the whole incident, Dr. Rajeev took a deep breath.

"Had your gynaecologist warned you about your anaemia? Were you put on some medication before you got pregnant?" Dr. Rajeev asked.

"The pregnancy was an unexpected one. I was using a birth control pill; I must have missed it!" Sanam said.

"That explains a lot. Sanam, what I am going to tell you is purely from the view of a doctor. You have been subjected to years of malnutrition...and as expected you are severely anaemic," Dr said looking at her.

"How do you know?" Sanam asked, completely dazed.

"Although you never vocalised, everyone at the Gurudwara knew about your circumstances!" Dr Rajeev said in a soft tone bringing silent tears to her eyes.

"So, I was saying, in cases like yours, natural miscarriages in the first trimester are quite common. Women carry the guilt of miscarriage for a long time because no one tells them that body is a machine and sometimes this machine falters. I have fixed an appointment with a gynaecologist for tomorrow, I do not think you will have any difficulty conceiving again but an expert opinion will be better. And Sanam I need to ask you something very personal...if you allow?" Dr. Rajeev asked her gently.

"Yes Doctor kahiye," Sanam said.

"With whom did you come so far Sanam? Where is your husband? Didn't your gynaecologist put you on bed rest for a week?" Dr Rajeev asked cautiously.

Sanam did not know what to answer. Finally, she decided to speak the truth.

"Doctor, my husband and I have separated recently. We are going to get a divorce. I came alone because I could not stay in the house where I lost my baby!" Sanam said in an eerily cold voice.

"Is your husband aware of the miscarriage?" Dr. Rajeev asked upfront.

"No, he left me...he didn't want the baby," Sanam said in a stone-cold voice.

"I could talk to him...make him understand!" Dr. Rajeev said gently.

"No Doctor. He did not marry me willingly; he was saddled with me. He loved someone else. He told me on day one. He did not cheat me at all; but he did reject my baby and chose someone else over us. So, he needs to know nothing," Sanam spoke with a tone of finality implying the end to discussion.

"Ok...you will be in the hospital for two days under observation," Dr. Rajeev spoke tersely and turned to leave.

"Nani" Sanam asked in a voice heavy with emotion.

"Way better...We will shift her in the ward tomorrow, then you can meet her. She has been asking for you a lot,"Dr. Rajeev said and left the room.

Sanam gave a weak smile and yawned. Soon enough she fell asleep.

"Keep her sedated, she has been through mental trauma and needs rest!" Dr. Rajeev told the Doctor on duty as he went to the ICU.

The next day Sanam woke up to the nurse giving her a sponge bath and changing her gown. Sanam felt fresh and relieved after the nurse removed her drip.

"Doctor ne soft food ke liye bola hai!"the nurse said as the ward boy put a plate of upma and a flask of tea for her.

"Ho gaya special patient ka checking?"another nurse came and teased Sanam.

"Special?" Sanam smiled, questioning them. It did not take an instant to understand what was happening. These nurses were reacting exactly like the dispensary nurses.

"Hmmm...main special ki doctor special?"she asked the nurses, turning their question on them.

The two young Malayali nurses giggled and blushed.

"Yaar he is so handsome! Kal se sab nurses apne rounds baar baar laga rahi hain. Oh man!" Nurse Rosy said.

"Seriously...he hasn't even looked at anyone till now!"Nurse Kinjal exclaimed.

"That is because he has a wife at home!"Sanam burst their bubble with a pop.

"Why are all handsome men taken?"Nurse Rosy cried in mock anguish, making Nurse Kinjal and Sanam laugh.

It was at that time when Dr. Rajeev entered, and the theatrics stopped.

"Nurses, you do not have your rounds? Update me with the vitals,"Dr Rajeev said in a profoundly serious tone.

By evening, Nani was better and had been shifted to the ward. Sanam too felt better and spent some time with Nani.

Nani smiled ear to ear looking at her.

"It's time for me to move on!" Sanam told herself as Nani went off to sleep.

"I need money to pay the medical bills!" Sanam thought. She was worried if she had enough money to pay the medical bills.

"It is such an expensive hospital," She mumbled to herself.

As if on cue, Dr. Rajeev made an appearance.

"A penny for your thoughts," he said and smiled.

"How much would the medical bill be, Doctor?" Sanam asked him softly.

"You don't have to worry about that Sanam!" Dr. Rajeev told her.

"Absolutely not. I am capable enough to pay for my own medical care!" Sanam told him indignantly.

"No one said you are not! It is just that I was saying you can pay back when you can!" Dr said, pacifying her.

Sanam was still putting together words to protest when Doctor spoke.

"In fact, I have a proposal for you! Please do not react instantly, think about it!" he said and Sanam nodded.

"I want to offer you a post of Nani's nanny!" Dr. Rajeev said, leaving Sanam shocked.

"Matlab?" Sanam asked, confused.

"Nani has become a menace. She had brow beaten and bullied five nurses. The last one left the job threatening to sue us. Nani forced me to take her to Mumbai for my seminar. I was presenting my paper the day she ran away to Nanded. She needs someone to keep an eye on her while I go out. In the recent months she has shown liking only for you. Please think about this Sanam. I have gone crazy worrying about Nani. I need your help," Dr. Rajeev said, almost pleading with Sanam.

"Maybe God led her to me for a reason," Sanam thought. Whatever the reason was Sanam wanted to be there for the lady who had given her a shoulder to cry on when she needed the most.

CHAPTER- 45

LAUKI

Flashback continues...

"Maybe God led her to me for a reason," Sanam thought. Whatever the reason was Sanam wanted to be there for the lady who had given her a shoulder to cry on when she needed the most

"There are a few things you should know, Sanam. The last year was exceedingly difficult for us as a family. My divorce came through and I lost my younger and only sister to cancer. Nani was very attached to my sister Sarah. I think she might see...I think...she already sees Sarah in you...same age similar colouring...same temperament. I shifted to Pune last year to be with Sarah and Nani. So, we come with baggage! Nani might not be the easiest person to manage, but she is the kindest soul I have seen. I hope you will give it a thought," Dr. Rajeev got up to leave the room.

"I accept," Sanam said quickly.

"Are you sure?" he asked.

"Absolutely," Sanam said with a smile.

"Itna zyada?" Sanam exclaimed when Dr. Rajeev named the amount as a salary.

"This was what I was paying the earlier nurse! Either you take this salary, or the job is not yours!" Dr Rajeev said sternly.

"I have one condition. My hospital bills get deducted first, then I will start taking the salary! And I want transparency in it," Sanam said.

"Ok," Dr.Rajeev said with a smile.

"And Doctor I do not have clothes, I will need to go out and shop" Sanam said embarrassed.

"Oh yes of course," he removed quite a few two thousand bills and handed it over to her.

"All coming out of your salary!" he said with a smile hearing her gasp.

"Sanam.... I almost forgot!" Dr. Rajeev called her as she was about to leave.

He handed over her a small ziplock packet containing her mangalsutra, infinity gold chain and ring given by Avinash and her mother's earrings.

"No jewellery is allowed in the MRI scanning room!" he explained.

"Oh mangalsutra...this is how Dr. Rajeev came to know I was married!" Sanam told herself, addressing the inquisitive thought that was troubling her.

Sanam stepped out of the hospital and asked around for shopping places. Sometime later, she found herself outside an 'Eastside' outlet. The store reminded her of a lot of things she wanted to forget, but she had no option. This store was best suited to her needs. She took a deep breath and entered the store.

Sanam bought essentials and a big duffle bag to store her clothes into. Before she entered the hospital, she bought two three novels from the bookstore next to the hospital.

Finally happy with her shopping, Sanam for the first time after so many days felt hopeful for the future.

Dr. Rajeev had booked two rooms in a small lodge next to the hospital and had pushed her to sleep at night, taking the graveyard shift himself. The next few days went in a haze. Nani was on a path of recovery and their bond had grown by leaps and bounds.

Present day....
It was Sanam's ninth night without her husband. Days were still easy to go by, but the nights were painful. Sleeping was beyond question as Sanam felt restless. The recurring nightmare was anyways stressful, but she needed to sleep. Sanam was supposed to reach the hospital by seven in the morning.

They were shifting Nani back to Pune today. Sanam could not pacify her heart so sat down to do the only thing she could think of...reciting the pauris of Japji Sahib. The morning went in a flurry, packing and shifting Nani into the ambulance. Sanam sat in the ambulance with Nani and Dr. Rajeev kept on driving right behind. They reached Pune in the night.

Sanam, along with everyone, had been too tired to register whatever was going around in the world. If she were not that tired, then she surely would not have missed the headline splashed across all the morning newspapers that day...

Famous script writer Avinash Shastri critical!

By the nightfall, almost sixteen hours after Avinash had been taken into the operation theatre and subsequently to the ICU, the doctors finally announced that he was out of danger. Although Avinash had not gained consciousness, he was out of danger.

Karuna had left New York as soon as they had gotten to know about Avinash's accident.

She reached Mumbai on the second day of the surgery.

"Nihar yeh sab kaise hua?" an emotionally overwhelmed Karuna asked Nihar.

"Sorry Kaku (Aunty)! I tried to stop him," Nihar had broken down quite a few times as he told a shocked mother about the events of the past few hours. He had witnessed the dreadful accident that had shaken him to the core. Nihar somehow, with the help of the driver, picked up a bleeding Avinash, put him into the car and rushed to the hospital.

Karuna was thankful that her brothers had taken over once Avinash had been taken to the hospital. Advocate Umesh Mehta too had rallied around informing her of how the events unfolded. Every time Karuna looked at her son's unconscious state, she felt a little bit of herself die away.

"Why did he have to fall in love with this girl? Why did this have to happen to my bacha! If something happens...No! No! He will be fine," Karuna scolded herself.

Finally, two days after the accident, Avinash gained consciousness. He had suffered multiple fractures and a few stitches to the head but had miraculously escaped any long-lasting injury to critical organs. But Avinash had failed to respond to anyone other than his mother. Since the time he had gained consciousness, he had barely spoken a few words.

Avinash woke up in incredible pain. All he could remember was Sanam.

"Sanam," he cried out in pain, he felt disoriented and lost.

Then he remembered all that had happened. His loss of a child and wife. And he broke down in his mother's arms.

A few days later, Karuna sat in the leading doctor's chamber.

"We will discharge Avinash in a day or two, Mrs. Shastri. The chances of a full physical recovery are very high! With physiotherapy, he will be walking in no time...let us say in about two months! However, it seems like he is in the middle of an emotional breakdown. We will strongly recommend a good psychiatrist!" the doctor leading the medical team told Karuna.

"He has been through physical and mental trauma, he will need your care and patience," the doctor told her.

Karuna came out of the cabin and sat down with a thud. Her worst nightmare was coming true and there was nothing she could do about it. It was the writing on the wall. Avinash had completely withdrawn in a shell. He answered in monosyllables and just stared in the empty space. That night weighed a lot on Karuna's mind. She wanted to return home today: her safe place. She was physically tired of sleeping in the hospital. Her heart was broken.

"I need my home!" Karuna told herself, trying to contain her unshed tears.

She reached home and freshened up. Unknown to herself, her feet took her to her son's room. She wanted to spend some time in Avinash's room, as she had done many times in the past one year.

Karuna switched on the light and sat in his favourite chair. Her eyes were invariably drawn to a rectangular tin cookie box with small, doodled hearts.

She opened it and saw a half-folded paper and many beautiful, folded papers which looked like letters. She picked up the half folded one...

Dear Avinash,

Just when I had started believing in love, you left me Avinash. Like everyone else you left me. You left me alone....................

You will never see this letter. I will burn the other letters tomorrow. I know I will burn this letter later, but I had to get it out of my system.

Thank you for all that you have done for me,

Sanam.

Karuna understood these were the letters that her son's wife had written to him. Even after a week of knowing, the fact that her son was married still came as a shock to her.

She looked at the cookie box again and fished out another letter.

"No... it's their personal matter...I should not read this!" Karuna's head called her out.

"Just this once," her heart whispered strongly. She picked up a letter that was pinned with another one. She opened the first letter.

Dear Sanam,

You are a bully. Kasam de kar lauki khilayi aaj! I am angry.

Yours,

Avinash.

Karuna laughed loudly. Avinash hated lauki with a passion.

"But this was the same handwriting that was on the previous letter. That means she would write a letter to herself and answer it," Karuna felt her heart melting somewhere for this unknown girl.

The second letter read...

Dear Avi,

I know you are angry at me ...It was written all over your face. Why do you have to hate healthy greens so much? Lauki is not such a bad vegetable, and I had made it well...you are just prejudiced against it. So prejudiced that my suji halwa for dessert also could not melt you.

Pata hai...I feel guilty if I do not feed you healthy, home-made food. You have been pampered and cared for so much by your family. Aisa lagta hai ki kabhi (I know it is not possible par agar kabhi...) tumhari mummy se mili toh woh bolengi mujhe ki "Thode mahine ke liye apne jigar ka tukda diya tha, uski theek se care bhi nahin kar paye?"

Toh Baby, I will feed you healthy greens till the time I can. I owe it to your mother. I do not have a mother, but I know how a mother's heart beats.

Loads of love,

Sanam

Karuna realised she had been shedding silent tears all along.

"Such a deep love!" her heart felt so much for this unknown girl, who in just a few minutes became as precious to her as her own son. Now, she was not surprised at Avinash's state. She understood what Ramona Shah had tried to tell her.

Karuna got up with a smile on her face. She picked up her phone and called out her brother.

"Dada, I might reach the hospital late tomorrow," she told her brother and was assured by him that all will be fine.

She called Nihar next.

"Everything is fine beta...can you come home tomorrow morning at eight? I need help," Karuna put the phone down with a smile.

Two days later, she brought her son home. He was still quiet. His food intake was still minimal.

Nihar and her brothers took leave after settling Avinash in.

"Chal bacha, lunch time!" Karuna brought a plate of food and sat next to him.

Avinash opened his mouth as she fed him. Lauki ki sabzi brought no response from him but glass of badam sharbat did.

"Sanam?" he looked at his mother quizzingly.

"I took the liberty of visiting your other home. Brought back the pickles, sharbat and ladoos Sanam made with so much of love for you," Karuna told him.

"Aai...she left me!" Avinash wailed, expressing his feelings for the first time since the accident.

"Bas pilu(kid)! She didn't leave you..she just got angry with you. She lost her baby beta...she is just angry! Pyaar karta hai usse toh mana kar lekar aa," Karuna said.

"But Aai she hates me!" Avinash cried.

"She doesn't hate you; she loves you!" Karuna got up and circular tin cookie box with small hearts to him.

"Aah…that cookie-box!" Avinash sighed. He had completely forgotten about the cookie box.

"Sorry, I read one...only one letter! But she is damn cute," Karuna told him to see him blush.

"But to get her to give up her anger on you, you will have to become fit and fine. So lauki now!" Karuna laughed when she saw a scowl on Avinash's face.

"Get well soon and get my daughter back," she told a smiling Avinash.

CHAPTER- 46

FIGHTER

Five months later...

"Get well soon and get my daughter back," Karuna had told a smiling Avinash.

Life however was not that easy. Avinash had hired the best detective agency to know the whereabouts of Sanam. A week later the agency had turned up with absolutely nothing. The CCTV camera footage they had been able to piece out had been woefully inadequate. Also, Avinash's accident had delayed the hiring of the agency and consequently caused a loss of CCTV footage. Government agencies delete their footage on a weekly basis. All the previous footage had been deleted. The agency had assured him that the moment Sanam used her Adhar card or Debit Card, they would intimidate him.

Week after week the Shastris got the same answer.

Avinash's only source of comfort was her letters. He had read the letters cover to cover...word to word. One of the days he had called for a copying machine to photocopy the letters himself, with little help from Bansi kaka. He did not want anyone else to read it. It was while photocopying when he came across a page on which a few figures had been scribbled. Avinash wondered what it meant. He kept it aside to think about it later.

A little later, when he was done with photocopying everything, he picked up the page. It read...

Feb- 4500

March -5500

April- 3000

May - 6000-Yay

June-7,950—WOW!!!!

Total= 25,750

making=??????

The entries on paper looked like they had been done over a period. Avinash tried hard to remember what had changed in the month of May-June.

"Aai...the mangalsutra that you are wearing, how much will it cost?" he asked his mother.

"Around two-three lakhs!" replied his mother. Avinash just stared back.

"Do you like it? Should I order something similar for Sanam?"she asked.

"Nahin Aai...I was asking for a very different doubt!" Avinash told her.

"Acha ...how much money would two threads like this and one circular disk cost? Let us say a year earlier?" Avinash drew a pattern on a plain paper.

"Arre this will not cost much beta! Hardly 25-30k!" Karuna answered while doing her work expecting to hear Avinash's response. When she did not get a response, she looked at Avinash who was smiling while tears ran down his cheeks.

"Bacha what happened?" Karuna asked him. She was baffled by the sudden change in his mood.

"Aai...she saved for months to buy those two golden threads that went around her neck. She never took a penny from me. We fought when I tried giving her an I-Phone. To gift three sarees to her, I had to struggle. When we ate out, she always offered her share. She brought in all the groceries because she lived with me. What must she have done to save money? What would she be doing now? She is self-reliant Aai...It is I, who needs her. I am so lost without her! What will I do?" Avinash broke down yet again realising how wrong things had gone.

Nani had taken a turn for the worse after reaching Pune. The next few weeks had been exceedingly difficult for Sanam and Dr. Rajeev as well. Dr. Rajeev and Sanam were stretched to their limits: physically and mentally. Their sleep cycles had gone for a toss. Both put up in the hospital and lived in constant worry. However, at the end of the sixth week of reaching Pune, Nani slowly started recovering and returned home.

"Five months!" Sanam thought aloud as she changed the calendar lying on her desk to February. It had been five months since Sanam had been abandoned by her husband, lost her child and left her home. It had also been five months since Sanam had met Pammi urf Nani. So much had happened since then. In a short span of time Nani had become more of a mother to her.

"I think this is the closest of a family I will ever get after Avinash!" Sanam thought to herself.

"Avinash…Why is my heart unable to forget you? Why do I have to remember you every time I breathe?" Sanam's heart cried while gently touching the circular disc of her mangalsutra.

"It's time to move on Sanam!" her mind told her. Sanam got up. It was six in the morning when she walked out of her bedroom to the spacious balcony of her room. The flat was actually the penthouse of a twenty-six-storey tower in one the exclusive townships of Pune. The penthouse currently had five bedrooms. Of the two guest rooms available for choice, Sanam had chosen the bedroom with a huge balcony fitted with a pod swing chair. It had a clear view of the building park, highway, and the hills beyond. There were buildings on either side of hers, but the view of the hills and the highway was clear and beautiful. It was an exclusive township, ten minutes away from the main city, complete with a mall which housed a general store and some popular brands.

There were a couple of modern building complexes with a park and a swimming pool for each building.

Sarah, Dr. Rajeev's late sister, had been a dance instructor who ran an academy that was located in the complex. One huge hall had been turned into her dance studio. Yesterday, she had seen Dr. Rajeev standing silently in the dance studio. When he had turned, Sanam could have sworn she had seen moisture in his eyes and emotion on his face before the specially crafted 'nonchalant' mask slipped back on his face. Sanam felt sad for the family that had to go through so much pain and loss in the past year.

A sad whine and a gentle tug at her kurta brought Sanam back to the present.

"Oho Daaku...you want to go down? Wait!" Sanam gently patted the dog.

Two weeks after Nani had returned home from the hospital, Dr. Rajeev had returned home with 'Daaku', a three-month-old Labrador retriever puppy. It had a rich brown fur coat and chocolate brown eyes. The puppy had suffered abuse at the hands of the owner and had lost an eye as a result. It had been rescued by Dr. Rajeev during one of his house visits to the owner. Dr. Rajeev had walked out with the puppy after calling an animal helpline and writing down a reference for another doctor and the phone number.

Nani had always been wary of pets. Sarah loved them but could not have them due to her various allergies. So, for various reasons, dogs had been a big no-no in their house.

"Eh kithon la aya...kana jeha ..Daaku lagda hai! *[from where have you got this creature? He looks like a bandit with only one eye!]*" Nani had taken one look at the emaciated puppy and told Dr. Rajeev in disdain, who had completely ignored her and gave the puppy's full responsibility to Sanam.

It had taken 'Daaku' exactly one day to wrap Nani around his little paw. He had stood at her room door and whined till she had allowed him to come to her bed. That moment onwards, Daaku had forged a firm relationship with Nani. He had his moods, and he had his Nani and Sanam to pamper him.

"This feels like family!" Sanam thought with warmth, patting Daaku's thick fur coat. Under Sanam and Nani's care, Daaku had now grown into a healthy dog.

A little later, Sanam and Nani were having a chat session after breakfast. They had already fallen into a routine. The morning tea Nani had with her grandson and at times Sanam joined in too. Breakfast they all had together. After breakfast, when the Doctor would leave for hospital, Sanam and Nani had their chat sessions. Later, Sanam would oversee the house help for domestic chores. Initially, the domestic help had objected to Sanam's ministrations but slowly she had realised that Sanam meant them no harm and had gradually opened more to her.

"Tujhe pata hai...Jaggiji (her late husband Jagwinder Singh Dhindsa) was so besotted with me, he waited six years for me to grow up so that he could marry me. I was fifteen when I first met him and gave him a good scolding for trespassing in my baag(garden). When my father asked me to apologise, I refused because I knew I was right. He was thirty-year-old then...exactly fifteen years older to me. He told me later that he had lost his heart to me right there. If he wanted, he would have gotten married to me right there. He was filthy rich. My father was a big zamindar of the Patiala district. Jaggiji was probably the richest in the state...direct descendant of the Maharaja Patiala's dynasty. Kingship was long gone but the nobility was not. Discretely, he funded my education. He made my father send me to the London School of Economics where I always wanted to go. I was twenty-one when I returned to India and met Jaggiji again. He was a tall and very handsome looking man; I had never been able to put him out of my mind since that day in the baag. I had hoped I would meet him again. One look at him, and I was full of desire. He knew, I knew we needed each other. We were married one week later. I had the best time of my life with him. That one year was full of love and romance...I had been on cloud nine. One year later, his cousins murdered my Jaggiji in front of my own eyes, in the middle of our own drawing hall, over a property dispute," Nani's voice grew stone cold.

Sanam looked back at her in shock.

"I was eight months pregnant. I had never imagined they would kill the brother who had taken care of them as his sons. I went to the police, took the case to the high court with my infant daughter in my arms. I wanted justice for the one life they took and two lives that were almost lifeless because of their actions. I was all alone. My family had decided not to support me for the fear of their lives. My daughter, Sarabjeet was one year old when the cousins aimed a revolver at me. I ran for my life...dodged three bullets. My daughter was stuck to my chest as I ran for our life. However, one bullet hit me in the back, thankfully giving just a flesh wound. At that point of time, all I could think was of my daughter, not justice. Overnight, I gathered whatever I could; met my lawyer, ceded all my rights to the property to the cousins and took whatever train that was leaving the station. I still remember the day I was ran away- I stood there with a bleeding back, a weeping infant, a bag full of jewellery and one trusted old servant. I did not know what I was doing. I stood frozen there for two minutes to wonder if I was doing right or wrong. Then I took the train. It led me to this city. Ladoo keeps on telling me not to see Sarah in you...that you are not Sarah. But he could not be more off the mark. I did not see Sarah in you, I saw myself in you that day. Sad, heartbroken, alone, confused but determined," Nani spoke the last sentence with a sense of pride.

"I do not know what your full story is...but I can say one thing for you: You are a fighter. Fight for life bache...neymat(blessing) hai Waheguru ki! Your parents up in the sky would not want you to snuff life out of the beautiful being they created. See how pained you were when you lost your baby...imagine their suffering! Promise me, you will fight," Nani said with a voice heavy with emotion and took Sanam, who had now broken down, in her lap.

CHAPTER- 47
STORY

"It has been five months Jaan, I have not seen you or held you in my arms," Avinash spoke aloud looking at the enlarged silver framed photograph of the polaroid that usually sat next to his bed. This longing to feel her in his arms now looked like a distant dream. Physically, he was back to his older self. The fractures had mended, stitches had healed but the wounds on his heart etched by his own insecurities were still open and fresh. Avinash had started psychotherapy sessions. These sessions had given him perspective and a little help in dealing with the guilt. He knew the truth: his previous bad experiences had marred his chances to have a happy life with his wife.

Baba and Avinash's father had returned to India, two months after his accident, giving the much-needed support to Avinash's despaired mind. Their efforts to find Sanam had doubled.

She had disappeared without any trace. He had been to every hospital, every Gurudwara he could think of in her search. Slowly his mind was giving up on seeing her again, but heart was sure that one day he would find her. With every breath, he would pray to God that she be fine. Every day, he would curse himself for not speaking out earlier...for not giving her assurance before...for not telling her how much he loved her. He had given up on alcohol and cigarettes completely in penance. His only ways of surviving were writing and exercising.

Time had passed, but with a lot of difficulty. Diwali had come and gone. When the whole world had celebrated the festival by burning diyas and candles, he sat in the darkness of his room imagining what could have been had his wife been there. Over the months, he had gathered courage and brought a few things over from his flat to his room. He had returned home with a lot of stuff that belonged to Sanam. The only saree she owned hung next to his kurtas. The other sarees that he had gifted her sat in his cupboard. The maroon colour mixer sat at the corner of his writing table. A smile came to his face when he saw the mixer again reminding him of the sweet incidents that were related to the gadget. He had also bought back the sound bar she so used to love. The sherbats and achar were almost over even though he had eaten them frugally.

Seventeenth December came and he fell more into depression. It was their wedding anniversary. That day that had bound them in 'Holy matrimony.' She had fulfilled her vows, he had failed. It was also the day his movie 'Manchali' had released to an empty first week. Seeing the empty theatres had broken Avinash. He had not charged anything for this movie. Instead, he had requested a dedication to two special women in his life! Director Sudeep Misra had gladly given it to him. That week had almost ended Avinash…in more ways than one. Despite the appreciation by his father and many industry stalwarts, he had felt it was the end of his professional career. Nothing that his parents said could shake him out of his gloom.

However, destiny willed it otherwise. The empty first week had been discouraging, but the excellent word of mouth by the few who had watched the movie had turned the tide around. It was the first movie of the new year that had achieved both critical appreciation and set the cash registers ringing. The subsequent weeks of the movie went houseful. Apart from the box office, this movie had also set fire to social media and news discussion rooms with its main theme: A woman openly embracing her sexuality. The fact that the woman openly demanded sexual pleasure from her husband and yet managed to retain her innocence alive, was a paradox that many were trying to figure out.

Although Avinash had been relieved with the acceptance of the movie by the audience, this success made no sense to him without his wife.

At the movie success party too, he felt indifferent to and stifled by the sycophantic adulation he had started receiving by the same set of people who had shunned him two years back. He attended the party for exactly half an hour before Nihar had extracted him.

Nihar had been given strict instructions by Karuna to not let Avinash get photographed with any woman at the party. Karuna has seen the crumpled newspaper at Avinash's flat with his and Nitika's picture gracing the front page. Her experienced heart had understood what poor Sanam must have gone through. She understood what must have pushed her to leave the flat in a span of a few hours, leaving everything she owned behind. After the party, Avinash had again retreated into his sanctuary till the present day ...

"Five months...twenty weeks...152 days!" Sanam told Daaku, draping the shawl closer to herself. Once Daaku was done with his business, he was kind enough to sit down at her feet as she sat on the garden bench and listened to her. It was early March, and the weather was still nippy in Pune...especially the early mornings when Daaku got the call of nature.

"Daaku tujhe pata hai....152 days have gone by when I lost everything of mine again," Sanam swallowed in pain. A pain which she could only share with Daaku because he would not tell a soul. She could not tell Doctor Sahib or Nani because they were already going through an ordeal of their own. Sanam had often seen both Nani and Doctor Sahib visit Sarah's room (when they thought the other was not looking) and sit there for a long time. Sarah had been the light of their lives. Nani and Sanam had never again had a heart to heart after the day when Nani had told her about her great escape. Neither Nani nor Sanam were willing to talk about the pain that they were going through. They had kept it light in these few months, respecting each other's privacy.

Sanam had studiously avoided everything that could have talked about Avinash Shastri. She had stopped watching news, stopped reading newspapers, blocked entertainment and film cards from her newsfeed except for one old picture of Avinash she had downloaded from the net. The old photograph was a few years old. It was of the time he had started his career when he was carefree and happy. She did not want any other reminder of the life she had lived with Avinash.

"Par is dil ka kya karen Daaku?" Sanam cried tears of loss. Sensing the gloom in her voice, Daaku came and licked her cheeks, trying to soothe her down.

"Ewww ...Daaku...bas yahi baat pasand nahi hai mujhe!" Sanam playfully scolded him bringing another whining session from him which melted Sanam in a moment.

A few hours later, she joined Doctor Sahib and Nani at the breakfast table.

"Sanam please be ready, I will return at lunch time, and we will leave for the bank," Doctor Sahib said in a terse tone. Dr. Rajeev and Sanam had managed to become sort of friends in the last few months. Although there was still formality in the relationship, they had fallen in an easy camaraderie till Dr. Rajeev had rocked the boat a week earlier.

That day...
"Sanam it is almost five months now.... you have had a chance to think about your past," Dr. Rajeev had tried to broach the forbidden topic as they sat in his study sharing an evening cup of tea.

"You are still in love with him. If you want, I can talk to your husband...try to save your relationship while you still can!" Dr. Rajeev said with a lot of thought.

However, Sanam had already seen red.

"Doctor, if this is a subtle sign to leave this job, then I will leave as soon as possible!" Sanam answered in a bitter voice, keeping the cup of tea on the table with a bang.

"You know this is not what I meant!" Dr. Rajeev swore with exasperation.

"Then Doctor, please stop interfering in my personal life!" Sanam said as she walked away leaving a shocked and hurt person behind. Since then, their relationship had been strained. Nani had noticed but not said a thing about it.

"Did I overreact Daaku?" a sullen Sanam had asked the cute dog the next morning.

"You too think I did? Then I must have done," Sanam noticed with a heavy heart. Dr. Rajeev had been nothing but nice to her since the time she had met him. He had no idea about her story, and he was trying to be a good friend by proposing a patch up between her estranged husband and me," thought Sanam with guilt.

She had found it difficult to get a chance to apologise to him especially because soon after that incident he had declared that he was going to London for a conclave and a project for ten days. He had tried very hard to avoid her and succeeded in doing so as well. But this did not go well with Sanam. In these months, Sanam had gotten used to his 'hmmm' and 'Ohhh' as she shared things that Daaku did in the entire day.

Dr. Rajeev came at the said time and took her along to the bank. Till now she had avoided taking a salary by citing hospital bills, the Macbook and the latest I-phone he had gotten her. Slowly, she had run out of excuses and had given up today when the doctor had insisted on opening her bank account.

She gave her Adhar Card, and her name was added into their household account for emergency purposes and a personal account in her name was opened.

"Let's go...the cheque book and debit card will come via courier!" the Doctor told Sanam.

"Sanam," Dr. Rajeev repeated for the second time, but Sanam paid no heed as she was busy admiring a movie poster put outside a mall across the street with Kartik Aryan on it.

"You want to watch a movie?" Dr. Rajeev asked her gently.

Sanam nodded with excitement.

Dr. Rajeev called up his secretary and cancelled all his appointments.

"Sanam, they do not have the Kartik Aryan movie soon! Do you want to watch this other movie…it just started ten minutes ago?" Dr. Rajeev called her from the Box office window.

"Haan chalega!" Sanam said. She was feeling excited and happy.

"Doctor…I am sorry," Sanam said softly as they climbed the staircase.

"Kya? Wapis bolna? The great Sanam Kaur Bedi is apologising …a rare sight!" Dr. Rajeev teased her.

"Nahin sachi…Dil se sorry!" Sanam pinched her throat.

"It's ok…chalo," Dr. said with a smile.

"Popcorn len?" Sanam asked shyly.

"Of course...come quickly...we have already missed the first five minutes!" Dr.Rajeev said.

"Movie ka naam kya hai?" Sanam asked in excitement.

"Manchali," Dr. Rajeev read from the ticket.

A few minutes later they settled in the cinema hall. The credits had already rolled. The movie showed a rich brat moving out of his parent's villa and taking a humble accommodation in the suburbs. The heroine enters and they are married by coercion. The next half an hour showed the couple adjusting to the scenario and slowly falling for each other. It was a very beautifully written movie. Sanam's eyes blurred with unshed tears when she realised the incidents of the movie were eerily similar to her own life. She got up with a start making the cola spill.

"I need to go out! I can't breathe!" Sanam tried to speak but the words were not coming out of her mouth.

"Sanam, are you ok?" Dr. Rajeev ran after her. Sanam came out of the hall with stinging tears falling down her eyes. She looked around for the movie poster in the corridor and finally found one.

She looked at the credits...it said...

Screenplay and dialogues by Avinash Shastri.
Sanam let out a wail.... And walked out of the corridor oblivious to a distraught Dr. Rajeev right behind her.

"I was just a STORY to him!" Sanam kept on repeating till she fell unconscious.

CHAPTER- 48
RENDEZVOUS

Feb 20XX

Dear Sanam,

What in the hell do you have against drinking milk?

Yours,

Avinash

Avinash's face broke into a huge smile, remembering the time post their first patch up. He had come to know that she was anaemic, and he had gone on his mission to make her healthier. He had meticulously put together a healthy diet consisting of greens, dairy products, and fibrous vegetables. But easier said than done. Sanam had put up a silent resistance every inch of the way that had exhausted him. She never spoke to him about it, but thanks to her letters he now knew what all went in her heart.

Dear Shastriji,

What is this newfound obsession of yours with milk? Mummy ban gaye ho tum meri! Gosh! I am sure she must not have nagged me so much the way you do. I still would have still taken it, but you had to go ahead and do your thing.

Shastriji, seriously have you tasted the tetra pack milk you have made us change to recently? Why did you have to throw that 'Doodh wala bhaiya' out? I strongly suspect you have done something to him. He cuts my phone, and that day ran away the moment he spotted me in the building.

Same with the local grocer's guy. He was practically shivering that day while delivering groceries.

Shastriji aap duniya bhar ko andha nahin kar sakte! I think you have a scanner in your eye! You know Iron Man types...everywhere we go, you end up scanning the whole place for potential stareres (is that even a word?...I guess no!)

Uff...Khair returning to the point, no one ever took care of me Avinash. Tumhare saath nakhre karne ka mann karta hai...kabhi kabhi lagta maybe you will put up with my tantrums, but most of the times I know I don't have any right on you. How will I survive when you leave me and go?

I stretched your patience today; I promise to be a better girl tomorrow onwards.

Yours,

Sanam

He had read her letters hundreds of times, but still could not get enough of these. Avinash smiled yet again. The way she knew him. He had indeed noticed the 'Doodhwala Bhaiya' leering at his wife. It had taken his entire energy to keep calm. The moment the milkman had left their home, he had followed, taken him to an uncrowded alley and had beaten him. The grocer's guy would have suffered the same fate had he not been a minor. Avinash had only 'browbeaten' him, he didn't need to do more.

He was now surprised that Sanam had caught him at this only twice. He had beaten up the 'Istriwala' (laundry man) and an 'over friendly neighbour' too! And not to forget the tapri wala(chaiwala) who had been looking at his wife in the most lascivious way.

"What is a husband supposed to do? Avinash asked himself, feeling his anger rising on the memory of those incidents.

"A husband is supposed to trust his wife. He is supposed to be there for her; not leave her alone in difficult time. A husband is supposed to clear all misunderstandings with his wife and not abandon her when he knows she has no one else in the world," his conscience answered back.

A wayward tear slipped his eye.

"Avinash...a few more hours bacha!" Karuna held his hand as they travelled towards Pune. From the last few months, she knew the drill. Whenever he would read a letter, he would smile and laugh initially and curse himself towards the end. Hopefully, it will all end today.

It was eight in the evening yesterday when the Shastris had received a phone call from the detective agency. Sanam had been located in Pune. Avinash had cried for a long time at the news. He had wanted to leave for Pune right away, but the agency had requested time till 11am to figure out the address at which she was staying.

Karuna did not want to send Avinash alone. Things could go from bad to worse if dealt with only emotions. Karuna thought it was prudent for her to go along to clarify things between the couple. And it was only befitting that a mother should go to bring back a lost daughter. Unknown to Avinash and her husband, she had read almost all the letters…leaving the ones she shouldn't have. She had been unable to keep away from them. She wanted to know everything she could about Sanam. And Karuna was glad she did. She had gotten to know so many things about her own son because of these letters.

"Aai…Aai?" Avinash's cry broke her train of thought.

"We have the address! She is with some lady called 'Prabhjyot Kaur Dhindsa'," he spoke amidst tears.

"Bas Pillu! The wait is over!" Karuna pacified him.

"I was just a STORY to him!" Sanam kept on repeating till she fell unconscious.

Dr. Rajeev put her down on the floor and shouted for the staff of the multiplex to get a first aid kit. He knew her blood pressure had suddenly plummeted. The first aid kit had absolutely nothing useful.

"Is this a First Aid kit? I will complain to the health ministry!" he yelled at the staff.

Seeing no other way, he picked Sanam up and asked a staff member to stop the lift. Thankfully, his car had been parked in the Mall's basement. He directly took the lift to the basement and put Sanam down on the passenger's seat. He took out his medical kit to administer a glucose injection to her. Sanam gained consciousness in the next few minutes. By that time, they had already reached home.

A little later, Sanam lay lifeless on the bed. Life had dealt her another blow. The moments they had spent as a couple came back to her with a vengeance. Those were their moments…who gave him the right to make them public? I had a right on those moments," Sanam thought and broke down again. She did not know when she had drifted to sleep. It was around midnight when she woke up again and saw that Nani was lying next to her holding her hand in hers, while Daaku rested wound up around her legs.

Sanam's movement woke Nani and Daaku up.

"Bacha…theek hai tu? Kya hua tha? Why do you have to take so much stress?" Nani had been so concerned about Sanam that she had been unable to control her tears. Daaku started whining seeing Nani crying.

Hearing the commotion, Dr. Rajeev came in and checked both the ladies' vitals that were fortunately perfect. Dr. Rajeev was being his typical moody self.

"I am leaving now. I have my flight for London in a few hours from Mumbai. In my absence, Dr. Indu will come for regular check-ups. Both of you please behave while I am in London. Nani, please control your sugar levels. Sanam, please eat something and keep on hydrating yourself," Dr. Rajeev huffed.

He joined his hands and said, "Ladies please allow me to properly present my paper at the convention. I want photographs of what you are doing every two hours. Is that fine?" Dr Rajeev gave a sermon like an irascible school principal.

"Ladoo…London jaa kar ek kaam karega?" Nani asked Dr. Rajeev.

"Haan..bolo!" Dr. Rajeev asked dutifully.

"Go and get some action there!" Nani said with a wink.

"Nani!"Dr. Rajeev exclaimed in embarrassment and almost ran out of the room.

The ladies broke into laughter the moment he went out and shut the door.

Daaku woke up Sanam at the regular time in the morning. They had not slept properly at night. Nani and she had gotten talking and for the first time in life, Sanam had told her entire life story to anyone. Right from the death of her parents to her miscarriage. They held each other and cried together. They both had been sleep deprived but miraculously it felt lighter.

Nani woke up with renewed energy as well.

"Let's go to Gurudwara," she declared right away.

It was almost eleven am when they asked the driver to drive down to the nearest Gurudwara located in Viman Nagar.

It was almost eleven in the morning when Avinash and Karuna reached the building complex Sanam was apparently putting up.

At the same time, Avinash got a call from the detective agency.

"Sir, they just left the building right now in a black Mercedes-Benz," they said.

Fortunately, the agency was able to follow the car to the Gurudwara.

Sanam and Nani got down from the car and slowly walked towards the Gurudwara. Once they had been into the inner sanctum, they sat inside the hall for a long time.

Avinash and Karuna sat outside the sanctum waiting for them. They saw them coming out, and Sanam had her back towards him.

Sanam heard someone call her out. She turned around and saw or thought she saw a pair of searing eyes and bearded face.

Just then a bearded man, who looked similar to Avinash walked past her. This was enough to send Sanam into a frenzy.

Avinash froze with shock when he saw the way Sanam responded to the bearded man who happened to be very similar to him in looks and stature.

Sanam started shaking like a leaf and gasping for air.

"Sanam...Sanam...kya hua?" Nani raised an alarm as Sanam collapsed. A lot of people came to help.

"Indu wapis anxiety attack aya hai!" Nani yelled into her phone.

"Sanam," Avinash yelped, seeing her condition but Karuna stopped him.

"We will make it worse beta!" Karuna told him blatantly.

Avinash stood there helpless as the passers-by helped the ladies into shade. Someone who was a doctor came forward to provide medical aid.

Avinash stood helpless but out of sight watching the whole scene.

"Sanam hates me so much now?" Avinash could not believe the surreal turn his life had taken. From a distance they saw Sanam, and the old lady walk out towards the car and leave.

"It's not as easy as we thought, Bacha!" Karuna said as Avinash sat in the car, shocked out of his wits.

"She hates me Aai!" Avinash said dejectedly.

"Maybe for now...but she loves you from her heart...or at least you do!" Karuna said gently.

"I do," Avinash said.

"Then do something and get her back to loving you!" Karuna replied

"But what should I do?" he asked, confused.

"You are a writer and a Shastri. You will figure it out!" Karuna said with a small smile.

CHAPTER- 49

SUFFERING

It had been five days since Sanam had got another anxiety attack. She had been shaken by the whole incident. She could swear the eyes she saw were her husband's ...ex-husband's ...she reminded herself.

"Sana...chal beta...eat something," Nani came into her room and called out to her. Sanam had taken Daaku out in the morning, returned and slept.

"Sana...chal beta!" Nani gave her a big slap on her bums. Nani had started calling Sanam 'Sana' in affection.

"Three days now and you have not stepped out at all! Today we are going to have a day out!" Nani urged her to come out and eat, which Sanam politely refused.

An hour later, Nani barged into her room with Mitali (the cook).

"Mitali beta aise daal dupatta!" Nani said looking at her phone and kept on guiding Mitali continuously to drape an ornate white dupatta on her head, leaving Sanam utterly confused.

"That's like my girl...Aankhen toh pehle se hi laal hain...that's done. Fetch daaru ki bottle now Mitali, then the look will be complete!" Nani said with relish.

"Nani kya try kar rahi ho?" Sanam asked sarcastically.

"See Sanam, you have already decided to be a Meena Kumari...I am only giving you the get up and the right props! Proper feel aayega!" Nani said.

Sanam looked at Nani with exasperation, but her mock anger could not fight the smile that just slipped.

"Ab hasi aarahi hai toh has le Sana!" Nani admonished Sanam in the cutest way.

Half an hour later, Sanam was at Nani's disposal.

"Kya hukum hai mere aaka?" Sanam said with a flourish.

"Ghar par baith kar bore ho gaye hain...meri look se bhi main bore ho gayi! Aur tu toh buddi rooh (old soul) hai...Main toh teri look se bhi bore ho gayi! What to do?" Nani said dramatically.

"What to do?"Sanam repeated.

"Chal thoda make over karwate hain...Phir FC Road par dinner!" Nani ordered.

A few hours later, Nani and Sanam left the parlour with huge smiles on their faces. They both were twinning with a blunt haircut and a fringe. They stood outside the salon and pouted for a selfie to send to Dr. Rajeev. They headed for dinner to a famous restaurant on FC Road.

"What should I order Nani?" Sanam asked.

"Yahan ki Pav Bhaji mast hoti hai! Woh order kar...ab main toh khaa nahin sakti...you must taste! Order a dosa for me!" Nani said.

However, the tables turned when the order came. Nani jumped at Pav Bhaji making Sanam laugh wholeheartedly.

"This picture shall be utilised for blackmailing purposes in future," Sanam said as she took out her phone and clicked Nani's picture gorging on Pav Bhaji.

"Haye...Hitler ki dum!" Nani grumbled.

Dr.Rajeev had been very strict with Nani this time. Along with Sanam he had ensured that Nani did not get away with rude food. The result had been astounding. Nani was now in the pink of her health. Sanam too had put on a little weight. Although the Doctor often pulled her up for ignoring herself, she managed to pacify him every time.

The Doctor had stopped Nani's kitty parties and social gatherings. A compromise had been reached where Nani invited a few of her friends over for a card party or a social do at her own place but under the strict supervision of Doctor and Sanam. In due course, Nani had given the Doctor the moniker of 'Hitler' and Sanam 'Hitler ki Dum.'

Happy and tired by the hectic activity, they reached home to find an upset Daaku. He was not used to the family members not being there. For the next two hours, Daaku made sure that Sanam ran after him in the whole house, attending to him. Nani had already retired for the night.

Sanam too after taking Daaku for a walk went to bed straight away. In the wee hours of morning, Sanam woke up to Daaku pulling her blanket away and doing a happy dance and song routine in her room.

She came out to see Dr. Rajeev had returned home; two days before he was supposed to return. Daaku was going berserk with happiness. Dr. Rajeev could not stop smiling too and that shocked Sanam! For the first time she had seen him really smile.

"Aap chai lenge?" She asked the doctor.

"Mitali?" Doctor asked the cook.

"Arre, I can make it...she is sleeping...I am awake!" Sanam told him.

"Then I am very hungry too!" he smiled.

"It's good to have you back home Doctor!" Sanam nodded with a warm smile.

An hour later, Doctor crashed into his room and Sanam in hers.

"Sita aur Geeta ka aaj ka programme kya hai?" Dr. Rajeev joked when he came out of his room in the evening. He had slept for twelve hours straight.

"Haye Sita na bula Ladoo! Old wali feeling aati hai!" Nani said dramatically.

"Nani apki personality dekho...Sita to Sanam hai...aap Geeta ho!" he pulled Nani's leg while Sanam laughed.

"Ladoo! Mera bacha missed you!" Nani hugged and kissed him. They spent the next half an hour cracking stupid jokes. Sanam had been pleasantly surprised by the change in the Doctor's personality. He was teasing Nani again when his cell rang.

In a few seconds Dr. Rajeev's smiling face morphed into an angry one.

"What the fu*k does he want from me after so many years!" he barked into the phone in anguish and went into his study.

Sanam was shocked by his anger. She had never seen him angry...irritated yes but never angry.

A while later they heard a huge crash in the study. Sanam and Nani rushed there to find the study in a disarray. The whole floor was full of broken shards of glass from a broken vase and the Doctor was sitting slumped in his chair.

"Ladoo," Nani wailed.

"He is dying! He wants me to meet him, Nani! He expects me to drop everything in my life and fly away to Chicago for him!" the Doctor said in a grave voice.

"Kaun?" Nani asked him, alarmed.

"Meri mummy ka husband," the Doctor spoke with disgust.

"I have a flight in a day from Mumbai! I might have to stay away for a month or two...till he decides...Dr. Indu will come every alternate day. Sanam, will you manage? I love Nani a lot. She is the only one I have. Will you please take care of her?" the Doctor said in an emotionally charged tone.

"Of course, Doctor!" Sanam assured him.

"Doctor, if you don't mind, may I say something?" Sanam spoke with hesitation.

The Doctor did not respond.

"I do not have parents, I always wanted to say so many things to them! If you can stop running away from this relationship, you might find something precious in this! At least, you will not regret the rest of your life that you did not try!" Sanam said.

"When will you stop running away from relationships? Stop running away from your marriage, face it. And when will you stop running away from your talent? What about the story you wrote? Why not publish it? Why not TRY to publish it? No Sanam? No, you will not do it...you know why? Because it takes guts. It takes guts to face failure...in career or in relationships! So, first practice what you preach Ms. Sanam Kaur Bedi," the doctor left after spitting these words.

Sanam spent the rest of the night tossing and turning. Although the doctor's words were scathing, they were correct. She had run away from one relationship...from the one home she ever had.

In her first month, she had taken to scribbling on paper again when one day, the doctor had picked a few stray papers, read them, and urged her to write.

The next day, he brought a laptop and a cell phone for her. Sanam being Sanam had refused to take the gift and had asked him to cut the salary for it. As a result, her next few months' salary went into paying for the gadgets. It was only last week that an exasperated Doctor had opened a bank account for her and deposited the salary amount.

Sanam took a deep breath. The doctor was right. She had indeed been running away from failure. She should do something for her story...some would call it a small novel.

"What should I do? Whom should I approach? Whom should I ask?" Sanam wondered as sleep finally claimed her.

Next morning, Sanam went to the Doctor's room to talk to him. She did not like the way things had ended between them. She was surprised to not find the Doctor in.

"Ladoo left early morning Beta! He was called in for Visa approval today in Mumbai!" Nani told a shocked Sanam a while later.

"Nani woh bahut gussa ho gaye the kal...I never seen him like that!" Sanam told Nani.

"Beta...what do I say? Poor bacha never got much in life. Life dealt him really bad cards. Come sit down...I don't tell a lot of people, but I will tell you our story today!" Nani asked her to join her on the couch.

"When I reached Pune, my daughter Sarabjeet was one year old. I sold my jewellery to buy a decent bungalow in a safe neighbourhood of the city. I started a catering business. Slowly, things became better, and we mother daughter became happy. Such amazing years we had. Sarabjeet went to Fergusson college. She was so delicate and beautiful. I always thought I would send her to my alma mater: London School of Economics, but destiny had other plans. She fell in love with a Bengali Marwari doctor. They wanted to get married as soon as she turned eighteen years old. I refused as she was so young. I had so many dreams for her. I had to give in when my Jeet made up her mind. They got married and soon left for Chicago. I was left all alone again. I took comfort in the fact that at least my darling daughter was happy. Two years later, Ladoo was born. I went to the US to visit her during her pregnancy. My heart broke to see how her husband ignored my daughter. He was busy setting up his career, and my daughter yearned for his time. I told her time and again to leave him…to return home but she refused. She loved him so much. This guy was so mean that he did not even spend time with his son. Bechara Ladoo would see his mother laugh and giggle in the daytime and secretly cry at night. Ten years later, Jeet got pregnant again. By this time, they had drifted apart as a couple. Ladoo barely knew his father. Jeet was five months pregnant when she walked onto her husband and his young female colleague getting 'comfy' in his cabin. She was so distraught that she returned to India right away with an innocent broken boy and a broken heart. Few months later divorce papers arrived with a huge settlement. She refused the settlement and took full custody of the children. Life slowly moved on, but my Jeet never remained the same. A couple of years later, we lost her to breast cancer. Ladoo never forgave his father for doing this to his mother. He vowed he would become a better and bigger doctor than his father. He did it too. For years he was so driven. He went to take coaching in Mumbai. Went to London to study medicine. Did some path breaking research and made some variant of a heart-valve. Earned ten times more money than his father did all his life. Look at all of this…it is because of him…Loaded with all the money, and with an aim to defeat his father, he lost his happiness somewhere. A few years back, he met this colleague, married her, and shifted back to Mumbai…all in a matter of two months…just like his mother. And as they say: marry in haste, repent at leisure. They got married but separated soon. They tried to get back together but it did not happen. In between, Sarah fell ill and got diagnosed with blood cancer. We all were crushed. The disease took away my Sarah last year. Ladoo was devastated and so was I, till you came into our life and brought some hope. In all these years, we never heard from their father till yesterday. So, if Ladoo lost it, I do not blame him. He has been strong all these years, but he is a human being after all," Nani was now inconsolable.

"I am not the only one suffering …Suffer we all do, one way or another," thought Sanam that night as she tried to find peace because her tumultuous thoughts centred around only one person: Avinash.

The Shastris sat in their lounge, discussing the situation at hand trying to cover all angels. Karuna had made Avinash understand that staying back in that elite building complex, even in his car, was going to look very suspicious.

So, Avinash had returned to Mumbai, leaving his soul behind in the other city.

"I think we will have to take this slowly! Sanam needs to come out of her grief!" Baba told the rest.

"But how Baba? How will Avinash do it? The moment he came in front of her, the poor girl had an anxiety attack!" Alok said.

"Alok woh tera paintara(trick) lagega idhar! Woh jo tune…woh thee na teri…woh ladki tere college main..kya naam tha uska…," Baba thought aloud not realising that Alok Shastri's face had lost its colour.

"Baba kya bol rahe ho aap?" Alok said nervously, stealing a glance at Karuna whose face had gained colour: red.

"Arre Wahi.*ek ghar banaunga..tere ghar ke samne, duniya basaunga...tere ghar ke samne!*" Baba broke into the hit retro hindi number.

"Kya Baba? Aap examples mat do! Saaf saaf bolo!" Alok said as Avinash chuckled.

"Arre tujhe kaise yaad nahin? Remember during your college, you insisted on living with your best friend at his place. We came to know later that it was because the girl that you liked lived in the opposite building," Baba could barely contain his laughter as Alok went red in embarrassment.

"Main chai le kar aayi!" Karuna walked out in a huff.

"Baba!" both Alok and Avinash exclaimed in unison; Alok got up and ran after Karuna.

"Chalta hai beta...Shadi ke itne saal baad kabhi kabhi life mein tadka lagna chaiye!" Baba chuckled and Avinash smiled after a long time.

"Montu...tu bas aise hi smile kiya kar...sab theek ho jayega!" Baba said in a voice heavy with emotion.

A few hours later, the Shastris had worked out the preliminary plan. They contacted their people in Pune and put them to work to find an empty flat in the same building complex.

The detective agency was asked to tail Sanam and photograph their residence. Avinash was adamant that the pictures should be non-intrusive...i.e., they should be of the balconies or her going out etc. He did not want anyone to be privy to her private moments.

The Pune branch manager of the Shastri industries was given simple instructions: Hunt for the flat that provides an unfettered view of the Dhindsa residence and maintain secrecy about everything.

Three days later, the Shastris received a phone call.

"Baba, they have found an ideal one. Get ready we are going to Pune tomorrow!" an excited Avinash yelled after getting off the phone.

"I am coming for you Jaan!" said Avinash, opening his favourite letter...this pair started with a letter by Sanam...

April 20XX

Shastriji,

I HATE YOU!

Sanam

The reply...

Hey,

No Sanam!

You L-O-V-E M-E

Yours,

Avinash

CHAPTER- 50

PAYAL

The Shastris had gotten themselves a huge four-bedroom apartment in the building opposite to the Dhindsa residence. It was a taller tower, and they were one level up than the Dhindsa residence. The distance between both the buildings was respectable. It was not in your face that would intensify the scope of getting caught. However, it was not that far that you could not identify the people occupying the opposite balcony.

Exactly eleven days after he had seen his wife fall unconscious, Avinash was returning to win her back. These eleven days had been meticulously spent on covering every angle.

"You need a makeover Sanam ki tarah!" Karuna teased Avinash who was busy looking at the pictures (sent by the agency) of his Jaan in the new haircut.

"Cute lag rahi hai na Aai?" Avinash said with his eyes still stuck on the picture. Sanam was in a black snug skin fit pants with an oversized lemon green T-shirt. A strap of her black sports bra was clearly visible.

"She is CUTE," Avinash said aloud.

"Bahut cute! But now you need to think of a makeover too!" Karuna said seriously.

"Main? Kyun? Yeh beard aur kurte main kya problem hai?" Avinash was baffled.

"Dekh if you want to be caught on day one and give her a panic attack then please go ahead," Karuna warned him.

"Acha Aai...what do you suggest?" he said, understanding her point.

"You need a drastic makeover. Because of the accident, your latest pictures are all over the media. High chances that someone in the building might recognise you. Throw away your kurtas...wear something that Sanam would never expect to see you in. Yeh dekh...This guy is so dashing!" Karuna said in excitement, alarming Avinash's father.

"Kaun hai dikhao," Alok took the I-pad before Avinash could even look.

"Yeh toh ganja hai? Tum isko dashing bol rahi ho Aru?" Alok said with a mix of shock and jealousy.

"Papa, he is Jason Statham, and he is dashing!" Avinash pitched in.

"Aap na bas ghar banate reh gaye aur duniya main handsome ke mayne hi change ho gaye!" Karuna huffed and walked away from there.

"Baba ne seriously phasa diya!" Alok walked after his wife who was still miffed by his four-decade old indiscretions.

Karuna had called a stylist home who had given Avinash a buzz haircut. The mark of three stitches near his right eye remained, giving his face a distinct character. His mother made him go for T-shirts and trousers. She had hidden all his shorts and given him night suits.

"Aai night suits kaun pehenta hai ghar main? Am I a five-year-old?" Avinash had whined and whined when his mother had relented and given him some full track suits for outdoor pursuits.

"Aai, she used to love my hair," Avinash said dejectedly as he saw his beautiful hair shavings strewn on the floor.

"Pillu, hair will return...your wife is your top priority. Just one last thing...change your perfume!" Karuna coaxed him.

"My perfume! Why? I love it? I have always used it and she just loves it!" Avinash asserted.

"Exactly...she will smell and recognise you from one mile away! So, if you want to be near her, make a difference! Become a different YOU!" Karuna said with a smile.

"Vaise Aai, aren't you a little criminal minded?" Avinash exclaimed, earning a whack in return.

Finally, the day or the night arrived when Baba and Avinash left for Pune. It was decided that since Alok and Karuna were famous faces they should stay away. The makeover fever had caught Baba too. He had gotten rid of the moustache that he had kept for decades. The *'clean shaven'* Shastris reached the housing society at four in the morning. Their luggage had already been sent with Baba's confidante Bansi Kaka. They did not know what would happen or how they would set things straight...but they had packed for one month at least. Their plan was- playing it by the ear!

Avinash was determined, he would not let Sanam go away from him. Avinash looked around the flat in excitement. Surveying the view from the bedrooms. The decorator had been briefed about the clients' requirements a week before. The brief was simple: comfort not opulence.

Avinash's bedroom was with the best view of the Dhindsa residence or as the photographs evidently showed Sanam's room. Most of those pictures had been clicked on the balcony. The room was huge. Avinash soon unpacked his most valuable package- a high end celestial and terrestrial viewing telescope. He quickly opened the tripod and took half an hour to set the coordinates aimed to view his wife. The other corner of the room had an acoustic drum set and a huge writing table with a comfortable chair. A cute maroon colour mixer sat at the corner of the table.

"I love this room Baba! The vibe is so good! I have not felt this good in months!" Avinash exclaimed.

"Beta vibe room ki nahin, mohabbat ki hai!" Baba laughed to himself.

"Bansi kaka chai banayo! Montu chai piyega?" Baba called out to Avinash who did not respond as he was already lost in the telescope.

"When will you stop running away from the relationship, Sanam?"

It had been ten days since the Doctor had made this scathing commentary on her personality, but the memory of it still managed to shake Sanam up. He had been harsh but hit the nail. Sanam accepted that she had run away from facing the truth. But there was another truth as well. She might not have survived had she faced the truth at that point of time. Sanam had gone into the introspective mode since that day. She realised that she had been extremely lucky to have found Nani at the time she did. She had taken care of her like a mother would. Sanam never felt like an outsider in their home. It felt like her home. For the first time she had felt she belonged somewhere, with a family. Although the Doctor and she never conversed much, whenever they did, he always guided her. He was the one who had forced her to read books. He had thrown open Sarah's collection in his study for her and kept ordering new books every month. Thankfully, Nani too was an avid reader. She always threw her opinions out in the open and then argued every step of the way with whomever dared to oppose her. Sanam broke into a smile. The Doctor had pushed her into joining a Zumba class that had started last month in the club house of the complex. She had attended a few sessions and made a couple of acquaintances. She had got friendly with a particular group of women and had started chatting with them after the class. The ladies were turning out to be fun.

"I think I need to give myself another chance…at least my parents would have wanted me to!" Sanam smiled to herself.

"5:10 a.m.? I still have a little time to catch a quick nap before Daaku…," Sanam was about to close her eyes when Daaku growled and pulled her blanket away!

"Daaku…. ladies ka blanket kabhi aise nahin kheenchte!" Sanam admonished him in a terse tone. An over enthusiastic Daaku mewled an apology and turned to flattery by licking her all over!

"Haye Daaku moya!" Sanam ran away from him towards the balcony followed by the dog.

"No more Meena Kumari mode Daaku…..ab Superwoman mode on!" Sanam told Daaku dramatically as she petted him, and in return Daaku growled at her over acting.

Avinash was rewarded half an hour later when at around 5:15 am the room's light was switched on and Sanam came out on the balcony dressed in an angelic sleeveless white frock that hardly reached her knees. Around her feet a chocolate brown Labrador danced excitedly. Sanam bent down, petted the dog and stood up laughing. She was pretty far but thanks to the telescope, she looked so close…very close. Avinash extended his arm instinctively to touch as he slowly observed her. She had lost a lot of weight since he had last seen her. Her cheek bones had gotten emphasised due to the loss. Blunts made her look younger than her twenty-five years. The fringe emphasised her almond shaped eyes. In a matter of seconds, he saw her body react to the cold breeze of the morning. Instinctively Sanam rubbed her own shoulders bringing her breasts together in a beautiful cleavage. She smiled and left the balcony.

Avinash's mind and body both reacted instantly to the image before them. It had been months since he had felt this strong need. He was now hard with desire.

"You minx...what do you do to me baby? You make me feel alive!" Avinash said overwhelmed with emotions as he rushed to the ensuite washroom.

By the time he came out, Sanam's room's lights had been put off. A deep disappointment hit him. He came out of his room and was making a cup of tea for himself when he heard a very distinct bark. He peered out of the window to see this female figure walking the society with a chocolate brown Labrador.

"Got her back!" Avinash did a small victory dance and ran back to his room taking his tea along.

After half an hour, he saw her return to her building. Avinash was already seated with his latest gadget. He saw the dog prancing in what seemed to be a huge drawing room. A few minutes later Sanam brought a dog's bowl and set it on her balcony. The dog lapped up the food happily wagging his tail vigorously. She went in and came out with a hot cup of tea and sat in the pod swing chair. The dog was dancing around so to give him more room she kept her feet on a high stool in the balcony. Unbeknownst to her, she looked alluring even in a simple white frock.

"My pretty maiden in white!" Avinash thought to himself.

"I love her legs! She has the perfect arch of the calf muscles and beautiful, dainty feet," Avinash mused when a sudden thought pained him.

"You removed the payals Jaan!" Avinash said, touching her payals that always remained with him since he had found them in the flat.

He went and brought out the circular tin cookie box with small hearts, opened and got out the letter she had written on the night he had left her.

Avinash,

You left me...My baby and I are all alone. I cannot bear this...I never thought you would do this to me. I am scared alone. What if something happens to me ...will my baby be left alone? No... no... God forbids! But what if I am no longer there? Will my baby have a miserable, lonely life like me? Will no one care for my child? Will you never be there for our baby? Will my baby be called an 'Orphan' like I was?

Payal pehni thi ki koi shayad meri zindagi ke sannate mein mujhe sun le! Tumne suna...nazdikiyan badhai...sapne dikhaye aur mera sab apne saath lekar chale gaye! Aaj yeh payal ki awaaz karkash(screeching noise) ki tarah kaan mein jaa rahi hai...Kabhi nahin socha tha tumhari di hue payal utaar doongi...par kabhi yeh bhi nahin socha tha ki duniya main iss tarah akeli reh jaungi!

These payals were for Mrs. Avinash Shastri,which I never was.

Sanam

CHAPTER- 51

BREAK THROUGH

It had been almost two weeks since Sanam had started going for Zumba regularly and she had started enjoying the company of her small gang. Almost all the women were of the same age. They let her in on the gossip of the huge residential complex. Today Sanam was a little late in joining them. The gossip had already started as Sanam came out holding her exercise mat for Zumba. They were discussing Kartik Aryan, the film star.

"Haye Kartik ka birthday hai kal! Kitna handsome hai!" Sanam launched into the discussion with excitement.

"Yaar itna handsome bhi nahin hai! Chal main use Twitter par tere liye wish kar doongi!" Sammy told Sanam.

"Best hai tu!" Sanam rewarded her with a kiss on her cheek! Samna Chowdhary a.k.a Sammy was a corporate lawyer. She was notoriously called a 'Doyen' in the courtroom, and they meant both: English and Hindi. She literally ate the opposition alive if the situation called for. The courtroom martinet was shockingly the opposite in her personal life. She was a loving mother to three kids: Two toddlers and one husband.

"Oye Dina... How was your date with your boyfriend? Tia asked Dina. Tia was a young marketing professional who worked in the city and an absolute sweetheart.

"Guys ex-boyfriend please!" Dina said in exasperation. Dina was a psychology and English literature paradox. Sanam had started calling her a paradox because one moment she would throw in the wisest one liner and the next minute she would speak some wild crap which would make your stomach churn. She was an amateur writer and poet. Dina had shown some of her works to Sanam and Sanam had loved them. Sanam had almost told her about her own novel but held back at the same time to remind herself that there was a reason she wanted anonymity.

"Dina Di…last week hi toh bana tha…ab ex bhi ho gaya!" Krissy exclaimed. Krissy was the youngest of the gang. She was all of sixteen years but exceptionally talented and wise beyond her years. She was the favourite of all.

"We were supposed to go out and then he messaged me saying that he was playing Badminton with his friends hence will get a little late! So, I broke up with him!" Dina fumed.

"Wasn't that a little too drastic Dina?"Ritika, a feisty MBA student said. Tisha, her very cute looking classmate agreed with her.

"He wrote B-A-T-M-I-N-T-O-N,' Dina spoke with derision. Dina was a logophile and a spelling error was akin to crime in her book.

"Akki Tatas (darling in Dina's vocabulary) teri blind date kaise thee that day?" Dina asked Akki. Akansha Sharma a.k.a Akki was a software professional working at the IT hub of the city. A typical Delhiwali, her razor-sharp tongue had cut down many people to their size.

"The guy was fine, but would you beat it? His ex arrived at the date! but BC blind date main uski ex aagayi. She gave me such a bad look…I thought I would tell her… 'behen dekh bande mein koi dum nahin hai..mujhe nahin chahiye!' But that woman…. I swear… she was such a bitch! She must have given me a shraap(curse)! I was down with fever for days!" said Akki making one and all crack up.

"But girls: the sad reality of life…Pune main aaj ki date mein ek bhi handsome ladka nahin!" Akki said dejectedly.

"Haan ek woh iska Doctor tha…woh bhi chala gaya US!" Sammy said dreamily.

"Oh yes Sammy Di…the doc is so dreamy!" Krissy chimed along.

"Par hamare bhagya main Nayansukh bhi nahin hai!" Akki whined.

"Guys shut up…Woh 'mera doctor' nahin hai!" Sanam huffed.

"Acha acha we were just joking Di," Tia said, hugging her.

"But itni badi housing society usme handsome ladke nahin hain?" Sanam wondered aloud.

"Nahin Sana Di, sab sad hain. Full pan-gutka khane wale cow belt ke bulls hain!" Ritika said in a bleak tone.

"Bas ek doctor sahib thee…Woh bhi America chale gaye! Acha admi tha…smile karta tha dekh kar! Miyaanji ko bhi bola tha maine…Doctor cute hai!" Sammy said, taking a deep breath.

"Yaar ab toh ek hi hope hai…. our new neighbour. The flat above mine…it is 4Bhk…two flats combined. They have just shifted a few days back. Usme koi toh roz drums bajata hai! Aur kya drum bajata hai!" Akki said enthusiastically.

"But there is an old uncle in that flat. I met him the other day!" Krissy butted in.

"Arre Krissy…I saw a lot of gym equipment going and honestly BC seventies main itna fit sirf Sean Connary hi tha! Ab woh bechara old uncle iss umar main drums thodi na bajaenge!" Akki responded.

"Chalo guys …it is getting late! Aren't you all? Whats app group main catch up karenge!" Dina shooed everyone away.

"Sana Di, come on Social media na…it will be loads of fun!" Krissy tried for the umpteenth time to convince her but in vain. They all hugged each other and bid adieu for the day.

Sanam gave a broad smile and wished them for a good day. She already was having a great one. She remembered her camaraderie with Madhu and Akriti and missed her friends with a vengeance. She had a huge smile on her face as she walked towards the building.

It was almost one week in Pune now and he was as close or as far from Sanam as he had been on day one. And Avinash was losing it.

He dutifully got up at 4:30 every morning, got ready by 5am (laced with the new cologne) in tracks and a hoodie. The first time he had tried to pass Sanam, the Labrador had almost bitten him. Thankfully, Avinash did not yelp and cry outdoors, or his voice would have exposed him.

"Daaku baby kya hua?" Sanam had pacified the dog.

"Fu*k 'Baby' is my name! She called me by this name! Kya Biwi, kutte ko itna pyaar aur pati par atyachaar!" Avinash had cursed his own destiny as he had jogged away from her.

Next day onwards, 'Daaku' his nemesis made sure that Avinash maintained 'Social Distance' from his wife.

Surprisingly, the breakthrough came when it was least expected.

Karuna had asked Baba to perform a pooja for Avinash at the nearest temple. Baba had gone there with Bansi Kaka.

The pandit performed the hour-long pooja. Karuna had wanted Avinash to be there, but he had refused.

Once the Pooja had been done, Baba sat on the marble bench in shade.

"Aru (Karuna) bitiya, Montu ko nahin laye...bahut udaas hai do-teen din se. He has not even eaten food properly. He just gyms, plays drums and listens to music. He isn't eating at all! I will tell him...you do not worry," Baba kept the phone down.

"Baba Montu bhaiya theek ho jayenge! Aap pareshan na hoon!" Bansi Kaka placated him.

"Dekho Bansi, humse jo hua, humne kar diya...ab yeh pathar ki murat shayad mere bache par taras kha le aur khushiyan de de usko!" an emotionally overwhelmed Baba broke down into silent tears.

"Uncle aap theek hain? Please paani pee lijiye!" a sweet voice broke his silence. Baba turned around and saw Sanam with her head covered offering him a bottle of water.

"Thank you, beta!" Baba could barely reply as more tears escaped looking at the compassionate nature of the girl, he had heard so much about.

"Sab theek ho jayega Uncle...aap chinta na karen! Lijiye prashad!" Sanam offered suji ka halwa to Baba and Bansi kaka.

"Hmm...beta yeh aapne banaya hai?" Baba asked Sanam. The shock in his voice was evident.

"Haanji uncle, theek nahin bana?" Sanam asked with concern.

"Bahut acha bana hai...meri late wife ka bhi exactly yahi taste hota tha!" Baba said emotionally. Baba's tears were not stopping today.

"Oh, how sweet uncle! Then please I insist that you take this halwa along!" Sanam said, handing over the tiffin box.

"Arre nahin beta...how can I?" Baba felt a little shy.

"Beta keh diya, so why stand on formality now!" Sanam said.

"Theek hai...vaise what's your name?" Baba asked her.

"Ji Sanam!" she smiled and spoke.

"I am Satyendra Kumar," Baba just stopped himself at the last minute from giving out his surname.

"I am called Satti by my friends," he added with a smile.

"I am called Sana!" Sanam smiled.

"Chaliye uncle, nice meeting you!" Sanam said standing up to take leave.

"Beta, let us drop you home. Car and driver are here," Baba said as they were walking out of the temple.

"Nahin Uncle, I will walk up. I stay near...in that housing society," Sanam said.

"Uncle Nahin ...Baba....All my children call me Baba!" Baba said.

"Ok Baba!" Sanam giggled.

"Ab Baba keh diya hai toh saath bhi chalna padega...we also stay in the same complex," Baba took her to the car.

Baba and Sanam started talking and didn't even realise that the car had been at her building gate since the last few minutes. They exchanged phone and flat numbers.

Avinash had been waiting for his Jaan to return when he saw a familiar car stop outside her building.

"Oh God, that's Baba! He dropped Sanam home!" Avinash jumped in joy.

He patiently waited for Sanam to enter her building and then called Baba.

"Baba...safe to talk?" Avinash just could not control his excitement.

Baba laughed at the other end.

"Pata chal gaya tujhe? I am coming home, then we will talk," Baba smiled.

Baba came home and offered him prasad.

"You will eat first then I will talk!" Baba admonished Avinash.

Avinash took the box and started eating.

"Sanam!" Avinash spoke aloud as he realised it had been made by her. Silent tears fell from his eyes, but he kept on relishing the halwa.

Baba hugged him and told him the whole story.

"But I couldn't understand how she was at the temple. She goes to Gurudwara na?" Baba asked Avinash. A temple was the last place where he had expected Sanam to be.

Avinash smiled and got circular tin cookie box with 'True Love' printed on it. He took out a paper and asked Baba to read it...

9th December 20XX,

Dear Avinash,

This really feels weird. This is the first letter I am writing to you when you do not even remember me. Not surprising, I am nobody...no reason for you to remember me. But I have not met anyone like you! You have often been in my thoughts from the last two years! From the last few days, I see you coming home drunk every night. I know you are troubled. Like everyone, I too have heard about the various controversies that have haunted you since the last one or two years. But I am sure you are not what they paint you to be.

I have seen you feed stray dogs every night. I have seen you being nice to the children who stay on the signal. Most importantly, I know my heart. My heart will never accept a person who is mean...and you are not. You are a really nice guy stuck in a difficult situation.

I do Jhapji Sahib every day for you. I think I should start going to the temple too! My Waheguru is working on you, your Gods would add to the strength.

As they say...The more, the merrier!

Yours,

Sanam

Baba broke down again for the nth time that day.

CHAPTER- 52
MOMENT

It was eight in the night when Sanam saw Akki's message in the Zumba girls' messaging app group.

"The drums have just stopped! Let us go to their place! Kaun kaun chalega?" Akki wrote.

As the girls had been going gaga over the Drummer, Sanam had paid attention to the music coming from the opposite building today and she had to agree with Akki...the guy indeed played very well.

"I am busy, sorry!" Sanam typed.

"Sammy, khane main kya banaya hai?" Akki asked Sammy.

"Chicken Biryani!" Sammy answered.

"Theek hai pack a good portion!" Akki wrote.

"Pagal...mere bache kya khayenge?" Sammy wrote with a shower of emoticons.

"Arre unke liye pizza order kar lena! Ghar ka khana is critical for introduction!" Akki wrote back.

"Aur agar woh log vegetarian nikle toh?" Sammy wrote back.

"Toh tere pizza ke paise bach gaye!" Akki retorted.

Ultimately, it was decided that Sammy, Dina and Akki will go to visit the new neighbours along with Chicken Biriyani.

A little later...

Baba opened the door to three eager young women.

They sat down once the introductions were done; Baba offered them tea. His wise eyes could see that the women were looking out for something or someone.

"Beta aap kya dhoond rahe ho?" Baba asked the leanest girl with spectacles (Akki).

"Nahin Uncle...nothing much! Woh drums aap bajate hain?" She asked cautiously.

Baba understood the curiosity and laughed heartily.

"Nahin beta woh mera pota(grandson) hai! Aap complain karne aaye ho?" Baba asked with a smile, handing them the hot cups of tea.

"Bansi Kaka...mera Nimbu Paani do!" someone yelled from inside.

The girls' attention was diverted by this sentence spoken by someone in a sexy voice. They were startled to see a tall, muscular, and handsome man standing in the lobby. He had six pack abs and well-made biceps. Sweat was dripping from his body suggesting that he had just come out after exercise. He was wearing just black shorts and trainers. He was rubbing his head with a towel as he came out. Although one half of his face was hidden with the towel, the other half was enough to tell the guests that face was a very handsome one.

Avinash was as shocked looking at them as they were.

"Ladies!" Avinash quickly made a perfunctory remark and literally ran away from them.

All the ladies were completely in shock.

"Yaar bahut garam hai!" Sammy spoke aloud dreamily, almost spilling the hot tea on herself.

"Kya hua beta?" Baba tried to bring sanity into the room.

"Uncle, matlab chai garam thee!" Akki tried to salvage the situation.

"Hanji uncle ji naam kya bataya aapne?" Dina tried to angle out the hunk's name from Baba.

"Beta if you do not mind, I need to rest...I am not keeping well. Thanks a lot for the Biryani!" Baba hustled them up before they could ask for the name again.

Ten minutes later, Sanam checked and was startled to see that Zumba girls' messaging app group had around four hundred unread messages. All about this handsome gifted stranger in the opposite building.

"Pagal ladkiyaan hai! Mere Avinash se zyada handsome koi ho hi nahin sakta...," Sanam spoke aloud and then gasped at her own stupidity.

"I should forget him!" Sanam reprimanded herself as cried her heart out sitting in the balcony oblivious to the fact that someone was crying along with her.

Once Avinash got to know that Sanam still visits the temple, his hope that she would still love him became a firm belief. At night, he had seen her break down sitting on the floor in the balcony. His heart had broken again for her.

"What have I done to her? I have put her through so much pain, do I really deserve her?" his heart cried.

"If you have screwed it, then set it right!" his heart told him.

"But first, I need to breathe her scent! I have been dying just breathing the same air as she does!" he told himself. Slowly an idea took shape in his mind and a smile spread over his lips.

He took out his phone and ordered a portion of 'Chicken Tangri.'

It was five in the morning and Avinash was at his telescope waiting for her. As soon as he saw her getting ready, he sprung to action.

Sanam woke up with a big headache. She was in two minds to ask Mitali to take Daaku down for the walk. She was still sleepy, but then she thought of the cute face Daaku made. He was whining and pulling her night dress.

"Daaku chal rahi hoon baby!" Sanam yawned and put on her shrug. Once down, she put him on lease.

"I need sleep!" Sanam yawned again. Last night had been spent crying, tossing and turning.

"I had so many things to do today!" Sanam thought to herself and yawned away again.

Sanam always let Daaku take the lead...after all it was his 'call'. They were lucky, the whole complex had only two parks that allowed pets. The one under their building and the one at the other end.

Avinash saw Sanam happily walking with her eyes almost closed.

"Aww...meri cute Punjaban sleepy hai?" Avinash smiled to himself. Adjusting his hoodie, he started to execute his plan.

Avinash took out last night's chicken tangri and hid it in the bushes that formed the periphery of the park. The plan was to get Daaku busy, so that he could at least come near his wife.

"Kya dhoond raha hai Daaku? Haye kisi ki billi ka peecha mat kariyo Daaku! Unki mummiyan meri jaan kha jayengi!" Sanam warned Daaku as she saw him vigorously sniffing around the bush. Cats were Daaku's nemesis and many times he would chase them away from the park. A lot of cat owners had already complained to Sanam about this. Sanam tried her school marm voice, but Daaku would know how to exploit her weakness. He was at his best behaviour only in front of the Doctor; the ladies, he knew, would get emotionally blackmailed.

Daaku chose to ignore Sanam's warnings. The moment he sniffed a Chicken tangri, he pulled on the leash with all his might, jerking a sleepy Sanam and throwing her completely off balance. Sanam closed her eyes bracing herself for the fall, but at the last moment, a sharp cologne hit her senses and two strong arms came to her rescue, swiftly putting her back to her own feet. Although the touch was momentary, it did leave a tingling sensation. Sanam opened her eyes to look around to see 'The Drummer' jog away. Sanam was left numb by the accident. Her heart and senses were screaming 'Avinash', but her mind knew Avinash could never be there. And even if he were here, he would not live in the opposite building. This did not make sense.

Daaku was still gnawing at the bone when Sanam sat down on the nearby bench and looked around for the stranger. He was nowhere to be found.

"Holy cow! I was this close to getting caught!" Avinash thought in excitement.

"Thank God, she had closed her eyes or else...Gosh I touched her! She was this close to me!" Avinash replayed and relived the same moment in his mind for the next few hours. That mere touch had melted him. He had been extremely close to her face. Had he not planned the whole incident he would have kissed her luscious lips. The recall of her beautiful face and luscious lips brought back all the lascivious thoughts he had for his wife.

Avinash sat in his chair, adjusted the telescope, and took out his favourite letter for that mood.

Dear Sanam,

You are such a M-I-N-X!

Yours,

Avinash

He remembered that Sanam had teased him with these questions the entire day. The letter went:

Dear Handsome Shastriji,

For all your erudition, you could not answer a few simple questions! And then, you have the audacity of calling me a MINX!

G-A-N-D-A   B-A-C-H-A

Let me write those questions to remind you how innocent my questions were and how naughty you are....

Q. I come in a lot of different sizes. Sometimes, I drip a little. If you blow me, it feels really good. What am I?

---Your nose.

Q. Arnold Schwarzenegger's is really long. Michael J. Fox's is short. Daffy Duck's is not human. Madonna does not have one. What am I?

---A last name.

Q. I start with a "p" and end with "o-r-n," and I am a major player in the film industry. What am I?

----Popcorn.

Q. What gets longer if pulled, fits snugly between breasts, slides neatly into a hole, chokes people when used incorrectly, and works well when jerked?

----A seatbelt.

See, common sense is so uncommon....

Yours,

Sanam

Sanam sat dumbfounded. She just could not believe that a mere touch of a stranger could electrify her. She had not experienced this since...since...Sanam did not want to go there. Sleep would have been a lost cause now, so Sanam found it prudent to attend the Zumba class to know more about this stranger. Now, she was intrigued.

"OMG girls...you should have been there! He is so hot!" said an excited Akki.

"Yaar full six pack abs, itne bade biceps! Haye...meri toh death hi ho gayi! I am in heaven!" Sammy sighed.

"Tatas you forgot the most beautiful feature...his thighs. His thighs were so sinewy, so delicious!" Dina cooed dreamily.

"Bald hai, eyes ke pass yeh scar and a stud in his ears (wearing a stud was Avinash's contribution to his own makeover), he is a BAD BOY! But.. but... kya maal hai!" Akki panted.

"Yaar, he looks like the ultimate handsome villain. Maine Miyaan ko bataya...how hot this guy is...he said 'Bandar, woh tumhari building main hai, tumhare naseeb main nahin!" Sammy sighed again, evoking a collective sigh from the group.

Sanam's mind knew he wasn't Avinash but listening to these women had confirmed her logic. The revelation that the Drummer was not Avinash had somewhere disheartened her a lot.

She longed for her husband, the proximity they had shared. Many times, she had woken up at night with sheer need that only Avinash could have fulfilled. This Drummer had fanned that need. Sanam felt hot flashes as she walked up to her building. She had not realised that 'one moment' with a stranger could turn your life upside down.

CHAPTER- 53

MISSION PADOSAN

Sanam returned home from the Zumba class with a sullen face.

"Oye kudiye! Inna jeha muh banaya hua hai? [Why such a sullen face?]" Nani called Sanam out of her misery.

Initially, the days had been miserable for both as the Doctor had left abruptly. In the following days, Sanam had tried her best to cheer up Nani, but she had been down in the dips as her dearest 'Ladoo' had been depressed. The doctor had appeared worried and upset in the long video calls that they had. His relationship with father was status quo. The strains that the proximity was putting on him was evident to everyone. Finally last night, Sanam saw the Doctor in a little better mood. It reflected on Nani right away. Today Nani had come out of her room after four-five days.

"Nani chai pee apne?" Sanam sat down next to her once she was done with her daily rituals.

"Oho tere bina thodi na!" Nani said back to her old affable self.

"So how are your Zumba classes going on?" Nani asked Sanam while drinking their tea together.

"Nice Nani...I now have a small group of friends!" Sanam told Nani about the fun these guys had, carefully not mentioning the 'handsome stranger'!

"Nani, can I ask you something...if you don't mind?" Sanam asked her.

"Of course," Nani replied.

"You didn't remarry?" Sanam broached the topic carefully.

"Nope. Why get a cow when you can buy milk easily!" Nani quipped, scandalising Sanam.

"Nani...sachi na!" Sanam rolled with laughter and spilled the tea on herself in the process.

Nani smiled looking at her.

"Tu aur Ladoo jab hanste hain toh dil mein sukoon pahuchta hai!" Nani said aloud with a sigh.

"I love you Nani!" Sanam said, hugging her.

"Chal hat Meena Kumari! Subah-subah senti kar diya. Chal meri Mills and Boon pakda!" Nani whacked Sanam's bum.

"Nani...what is with you? Kabhi 'Stephen Hawking ki A Brief History of Time' padhte ho... aur kabhi yeh thirty rupees ke purane Mills and Boon padhte ho! Matlab kya?" Sanam said, frowning at her Nani's intellectual-to-pedestrian range of reading.

"Tu bhi purane wali pdha kar...kitni romantic hoti hain...page 180 par kiss, phir page 182 par seedha shadi...shudh paravarik romance!" Nani said dramatically.

"Life aisi nahi hoti!" Sanam repeated the Doctor's dialogue.

"Oye Meena behen! Please mail the publishers! Ladoo reminded us twice last night!" Nani sarcastically reminded Sanam.

"Uff...Doctor will kill me if I do not! Nani, I am going to the study! You had your medicine? Good girl!" Sanam kissed her forehead and climbed the stairs to the huge study. She at times sat in the study in Doctor's absence. There were many reasons for it. One, she loved the decor and especially the Doctor's chair. It was most comfortable. Second, it was full of books. Third, it housed a state-of-the-art music system that was Sanam's weakness. At times when the doctor would be at home, they would share a cup of tea in the study and listen to songs together without exchanging even a word. Many times, she had written her novel sitting here for hours.

"Kuch naya karne ja rahi hoon...Babaji meher karna!" Sanam prayed aloud as she drafted her mail to the first publisher.

Sanam had mailed a few publishers and was in the process of mailing a few more when the bell rang.

Sanam ran to open the door as Mitali had already left for the market.

"Hello beta!" Baba stood at the door with a few tiffin boxes in his hand.

Avinash spotted Sanam in the huge hall that was right above her bedroom. From what he could see, it looked like a huge sunroom that had been converted into a large study with the French windows and walls lined with books.

He saw Sanam running down and lowered his telescope.

"Wow! Baba is in their territory!" Avinash yelled as he spotted Baba enter their spacious drawing room.

Since last night Avinash had been urging Baba to go to the Dhindsa residence, to return the tiffin box in which suji ka halwa had come. This he had learnt from Sanam...never to send a tiffin back empty.

He took out her letter!

Dear Sanam,

You gave all my ladoos away! WTF!

Angry,
Avinash

The reply...

Dear Avinash,

You look so hot when you are angry! Maan ja na!

There was not anything at home other than that Avi! Khaali plate thodi na bhejhti! This is what happens in middle class households...Quid pro quo!

And you know, the boy who came stays with his grandparents and Chacha-chachi. His mother passed away while giving him birth and his father now roams around in streets drunk and heartbroken. The poor child has no one to talk to! I see myself in him every time single time I see him hide in a dark corner of the building compound and cry. But he does not show his tears to others; he always smiles. Have you noticed his smile? It is beautiful. And he loves my besan ke ladoo. I know if you knew this, you would not have got this angry. But you refused to talk to me once he left.

Isliye I am really sorry! Not for giving him your share ...but for not making enough ladoos.

Loads of love mere pyaare Gappu!

Sanam

Avinash smiled and remembered how that evening had unfolded. Sanam had made the child comfortable. She had slipped a few chocolates in his pocket and made him have a few ladoos in front of her while engaging the child in a small talk.

She had emptied the small plate that had contained two barfi pieces and filled it with besan ladoos. She hugged him when he left.

Avinash had quietly watched her do all this with tears in his eyes. He had been so overwhelmed with emotion that he had snapped at her for giving away all the ladoos to hide his raw emotions from her.

Avinash smiled as he came back to reality and wondered what they must be talking about!

Sanam ran to open the door with Daaku at her heels, as Mitali had already left for the market.

"Hello beta!" Baba stood at the door with tiffin boxes in his hand.

"Arre Baba aap! Please come in!" Sanam smiled at Baba -taking a ferociously barking Daaku away from baba.

Baba came into the tastefully decorated hall of the penthouse.

"Beautiful!" Baba exclaimed looking at the decor and a certain someone sitting on the plush sofa.

"Beta ye aapke liye!" Baba handed her the tiffin boxes.

"Arre uncle take a seat! Nani, this Baba," Sanam said.

"Hmm," Nani said while openly sizing him upfront. Her blunt scrutiny was making him nervous.

"Baba, this is my Nani!" Sanam said, oblivious to the undercurrents running in the room.

"Ji Satyendra Kumar in short 'Satti'!" Baba joined his hands in greeting.

"I am Prabhjyot Kaur Dhindsa called 'Pammi' ONLY by my friends!" Nani replied in attitude. Daaku, who had by then sized up Baba was standing between the two and growling at Baba every now and then.

Sanam quickly gave Nani a recap of her meeting with Baba.

"Par Baba aap ye kya laye?" Sanam enquired.

"Beta kuch nahi...Bas thoda sa! Montu ki dadi kaha karti thi khali dabba nahin dete hain!" Baba covered his tracks.

One tiffin was the one she had given him yesterday at the temple. It was filled with exotic chocolates.

"Oh, these are my favourite! And Pakoras!" Sanam exclaimed.

The other tiffin had Paneer and Mirchi pakoras in it.

"As far as I know, beautiful women can't resist Chocolates and Pakoras!" Baba said while looking at Pammi.

"I don't like flattery!" Nani quipped; her voice dipped in sarcasm.

Baba was completely flabbergasted. Never in his decades of being a debonair, had he ever received such a response.

"Acha, toh I will take your leave!" Baba got up with the pakora tiffin and turned toward the door.

"Nani!" Sanam silently appealed to Nani.

"I said I do not like flattery. I did not say I do not like Pakoras! Sana beta let us have tea along with the pakoras! Aap please chai pe kar jayen!" Nani said, softening in her stance.

After a few false starts, the two got talking about the best type of mirchi for pakoras. The next two hours passed in a jiffy with the three talking and laughing.

"Chalo beta ab chalta hoon! Just one thing, can you tell me where I can get a printout. Our printer is not working. Bansi went but could not find a shop," Baba asked her.

"Arre Baba, our printer is working. Please come!" Sanam insisted.

Sanam took him to the study where Baba got a print out and borrowed a book.

Baba took leave with a sense of accomplishment on making inroads in the Dhindsa household.

Extremely happy with the success of the 'Mission Padosan', Avinash thought of trying the 'Chicken Tangri' again.

Next morning, Avinash was ready with the 'Chicken Tangri' resting in his track pants pocket. He saw the light in Sanam's switch on and then off. Taking his cue, Avinash excitedly went downstairs and started jogging in the park. But his excitement was short-lived.

Sanam had woken up to realise that she had started her periods and was suffering cramps as a result. She had woken up Mitali and made her take Daaku down. Consequently, both Avinash and Daaku were in a foul mood.

The moment Avinash spotted some other lady walking the dog, he was crestfallen. He immediately made a beeline for the exit. However, in his disappointment, Avinash had completely forgotten that he had a 'Chicken Tangri' resting in his track pants pocket which still remained there. In a moment Daaku picked up the scent of the meat and went out of control. Breaking his leash, he lunged towards Avinash barking his heart out. It took Avinash a few seconds to realise that Sanam's dog had gone crazy and was chasing him. Avinash ran like he had never run before. He was almost in his building gate, when Daaku caught up with him and launched his teeth into Avinash's thigh.

CHAPTER- 54
TEA TIME MANORANJAN

Sanam made her coffee and came to the balcony. She tried to convince herself that it was not for the stranger but did not succeed. She looked down, seeking the athletically built Drummer.

"Why am I looking for him?" she asked herself confused.

"He looks like Avinash!" her heart whispered.

Soon her eyes found the person they had been seeking. He was jogging in the park. The moment he spotted Daaku, he ran towards the exit.

"Why is he always so scared of Daaku?" Sanam asked herself.

The next few moments gave her the answer. The moment the Drummer turned towards the exit, Daaku ran towards him.

"Oh shit!" Sanam almost spilled her coffee as Daaku bit into the Drummer's thigh.

Thankfully, Mitali was able to pull on Daaku's leash a little later, giving the Drummer a chance to save himself from more bites. From where she was standing, she still couldn't see his face.

Sanam kept her mug down, changed her clothes and ran down as fast as she could.

Daaku had calmed down till then.

"Mitali itna bhi kya hai...sambhal leti thoda...bechare ko kitna dukha hoga!" Sanam went there and gave an earful to Mitali.

"Aur Daaku!" Sanam called him out with real anger and Daaku recognised it. He whined and hid behind Mitali trying to avoid eye-contact with Sanam.

Sanam then headed towards the Drummer's flat.

It took Avinash a few seconds to realise that Sanam's dog had gone crazy and was chasing him. Avinash ran like he had never run before. He was almost in his building gate, when Daaku caught up with him and launched his teeth into Avinash's thigh.

Avinash yelped in pain. However, he made sure that he didn't take off the hoodie and was thankful that it was a rather dark corner of the building.

"Saala kaat liya! Sanam ka bodyguard ! Biwi tumhe manate-manate dekh tere husband ki kya halat ho gayi hai!" Avinash talked to himself as he exited the lift. He woke up Baba and asked him to immediately leave with him for the hospital.

"Tu itne pange kyun leta hai Montu! Sabar nahin hai tujhme!" Baba scolded Avinash.

They had just exited the lift on the ground floor when Avinash pulled Baba back as he spotted Sanam get into another lift in their building.

"Bach gaye! Baba jaldi chalo!" Avinash urged Baba to head towards the parking lot.

Sanam remembered it was the top most floor but didn't remember the flat number. She looked around in the lobby and found there were only two flats. One looked as if it had been closed for ages, and the other one looked like it had been done up recently. Sanam rang the bell and soon the door was opened by Bansi Kaka.

"Arre bitiya aap?" Kaka smiled.

"Kaka Baba kahan hain?" Sanam asked him.

"Bitiya woh toh Montu baba ko le kar hospital gaye hain! Bas abhi nikle!" Bansi Kaka told her.

"Theek hai...jaise hi wapas aayenge, unko bolna!" Sanam left from there and headed home.

Since there was nothing that she could have done, she thought of attending the Zumba class to do a light workout, maybe that could pep up her mood.

"Kisi ko dikha kya apna Drummer?" someone asked once they were done with the exercise.

The Zumba girls were now obsessed with the Drummer.

"Oh God! I wish he would look at me!" said another.

"Guys I have been keenly observing his pattern from the last few days. He plays drums between 9 and 10 pm every day. The best thing is after that he plays a song...on high volume....without fail...everyday!" Akki told the women.

"Haye...you know iska matlab?" Sammy asked the rhetorical question. She was practically jumping in her place!

"No Di...batao na!" Krissy asked her.

"He is trying to send a message to someone!" Sammy exclaimed, happy at her own deductive skills.

"Hmmm...very possible! Because he can listen to songs at the regular volume...why play only one song at high volume?" Akki responded.

"Hayo rabba...Tum sab ladkiyaan na pagal ho gayi ho! Itna obsession? Boyfriends banao!" Sana exclaimed.

"Tatas, if I could get a guy half as sexy as him, boyfriend kya main usse apne pati-parmeshwar bana longi!" Dina said dramatically, making everyone crack up.

Sanam felt a little better and headed home. Nani had woken up and was waiting for her for their morning tea ritual.

Sanam updated Nani about Daaku's 'kaand'. Daaku, who was sitting at Nani's feet, picked up his name and looked around embarrassed. He whined, wagged his tail and started licking Sanam apologetically.

"No Daaku! Not today! Bechare ko kitna zor se kaata! Woh waise bhi tujhse darta hai! Haye bechara tujhko dekh kar door-door bhagta hai!" Sanam admonished Daaku. She had been disturbed since she had witnessed that scene. Her heart was heavy, and she could feel his pain. And the drummer's pain was melting her heart.

"You have Mr. Kumar's number? Let's call him and apologise," Nani said.

"Moye Daaku...billi ke peeche bhaga kar...teri mummy woh sambhal legi...Yeh kaya naya siyapaa daala?" Nani too admonished Daaku, who whined in return.

After receiving a scolding for an event in which he perceived himself to be innocent, Daaku looked down and went and sat in the corner.

"Hello Baba? Ab kaise hain woh?" Sanam asked Baba.

"Beta he is much better! First injection aaj laga hai...chaar baqi hain!" Baba replied.

The phone was on speaker and Avinash's heart was singing listening to the mellifluous voice of his love.

"Unse baat ho sakti hai kya? I want to apologise to him!" Sanam asked politely.

"Ummm...beta woh kisi se baat nahi karta...bahut chup ho gaya hai!" Baba repeated the already well-rehearsed dialogue.

"Mr. Kumar...we deeply apologise for this unfortunate event," Nani took over the conversation.

Baba had not expected this.

"No..no Mrs. Dhindsa, I understand!" he took the phone off the speaker and walked away talking to her.

"Yes...most welcome. I ...we will be waiting for you!" Baba concluded the call and returned with a sheepish smile.

"Baba…yeh kya? Aap toh meri setting karne gaye the na?" Avinash gave him a baffled expression.

"Arre nahin nahin...aisa kuch nahin hai badmash! Pammi is a very educated and decent lady!" Baba said with a blush.

"Launde ban gaye ho Baba!" Avinash gave him a teasing stare.

"Harami...chal dafa ho...oh ! By the way..aaj teri biwi ghar aa rahi hai...pehli baar....chai par!" Baba teased back.

Avinash had almost reached his room when he did an about turn.

"Kya?" Avinash couldn't believe his luck.

"Haan dono chai ke liye aa rahe hain...4p.m.," Baba said with a smile.

"Sach?" Avinash was unable to believe what he had heard.

"Haan bhai…ab tu raat ko 'Shayad meri shaadi ka khayal' gaana mat laga dena!" Baba chuckled.

"Aapko pata hai?" Avinash blushed and scratched the base of his head.

"Beta, mujhe lagta hai jald hi zamane ko bhi khabar ho jayegi!" Baba chuckled again.

It took ages for the clock to strike 4. For all.

"Puttar woh achaar bhi lekar chal!" Nani told Sanam.

"Nani vaise aap chai ke liye zara overdressed nahin ho?" Sanam looked at Nani who was wearing a beige anarkali suit. Nani had called a beauty personal home and gotten a hair spa and other beauty services done.

"Sanam grooming oneself is a duty not a luxury!" Nani said in a stern tone.

"Tu bhi kuch aur pehen…kya old fashioned patiala suit pehna hai!" Nani said, trying to take Sanam's mind off from herself.

Nani looked and huffed at the clock….. Sanam too looked and waited for the clock to strike 4…..it was still 3: 40 pm.

"Baba…waah! Pajame se patloon ka safar!" Avinash teased his grandfather.

"Tu kyun itna ban-than ke baitha hai? Tune toh bahar hi nahin nikalna!" Baba teased him back.

The smile on Avinash's face vanished. It was painful to be so near and not be able to touch her

"Koi baat nahin beta! Thoda aur sabar..sab theek hoga!" Baba consoled him.

Avinash went and sat at his telescope and spotted them come out of the opposite building. Sanam was wearing a simple peach coloured Patiala suit. She had worn her mother's earrings, but had removed the infinity pendant and a ring, Avinash thought with a pang.

"They are on their way!" Avinash announced. The bell rang and Avinash went back to his room to hide.

Pammi and Sanam entered.

"Welcome ji!" Baba said politely.

"Uncle this is for you guys!" Sanam said, giving him a few containers.

"Arre beta kyun takleef ki?" Baba said modestly.

"Arre nahin uncle..hardly anything. These ladoos I have made with sugar free. And this pickle is Nani's recipe ….I can guarantee you wouldn't have had a better mango pickle ever! And uncle do you like Dahi Bhalle? It is very north Indian…we made some extra for you!" Sanam said chirping away. She was feeling a little like her old self once she heard about the tea party.

She was happy. Just happy. She smiled and looked around the tastefully decorated hall.

"Bansi kuch lao bhai!" Baba called out.

"Baba main dekhti hoon!" Sanam said and walked towards the kitchen leaving two people who were having a very awkward moment.

"Where is your grandson Kumar Sa'ab?" Nani asked Baba once Sanam left for the kitchen.

"Actually, he had an accident some months back and an emotional breakdown too! He has become a recluse since then!" Baba explained

"Life is so tough for these kids. Sanam too has had a very tough time lately. She has had a spate of anxiety attacks," Nani quipped genuinely trying to share her pain.

"Ooh!" was all that Baba could manage before Nani gave him a little idea about the hardships faced by Sanam.

"Bansi kaka…kya bana rahe hain?" Sanam asked.

"Bitiya sabudana vada hai airfryer main banaya hua! Aur bas momos steam karne rakhe hain. Aap baithiye, main chai lata hoon!" Bansi Kaka told her.

"Chaliye, main banati hoon!" Sanam said with a smile.

"Jaise theek lage bitiya. Thodi zyada banana…Montu baba full flask lete hain!" Bansi Kaka replied.

"Bansi Kaka...yeh aapke Montu baba bahar nahin aate kya?" Sanam asked him carefully.

"Nahin bitiya...Kuch mahine pehle accident hua tha...tab se kisi se jyada baat nahi karte! Theek se khana nahin khate! Kabhi kuch bolte hain...kabhi kuch! Abhi kal hi kehte, Kaddu ki sabzi banao kaka...aloo ki sabzi jaise honi chahiye! Kurkuri! Humne bola toh aloo ki subzi hi khaa lo na! Bahut gussa hue!" Bansi Kaka said, exasperated and that made Sanam giggle. She poured the tea in the flask and arranged the plate beautifully with snacks and handed it over to Kaka and took the rest over to the dining table.

They had an enjoyable tea time with wisecracks made by Baba and Bansi Kaka. Towards the end Nani too contributed with her witty one liners. For the first time in many months, all these people had a happy evening.

Sanam and Nani left for their house with a big smile on their lips. Sanam felt an affinity towards Baba and his grandson 'Montu Babu'.

"Montu Babu!" Sanam giggled to herself at the choice of the sobriquet. She waited for the clock to strike at 9p.m. Sanam came out with a cup of steaming hot coffee and sat in her swing.

A few minutes past nine , the Drummer played a happy beat for longer than usual. A few minutes later, a Bollywood retro song 'Kitne bhi tu karle sitam' was played at a high volume The song left Sanam utterly confused because it was from the movie 'Sanam teri kasam'

CHAPTER- 55
NEWS

Sanam had asked Baba to get a freshly worn hoodie of his grandson 'Montu' so that she could get Daaku comfortable with his scent. Daaku had barked ferociously when Sanam had taken the dark maroon coloured hoodie near him. Sanam went to her room and took off her top to wear the hoodie over her bra and denim shorts. It was almost ten in the night; she hadn't bothered to pull the window curtains completely. She didn't normally bother about it as the residence being a penthouse, was quite high and the pod swing covered most of the glass window. So, there was no chance of flashing herself to others.

"It wasn't like someone would actually sit there watching me!Hah!"
Sanam mused to herself.

Sanam stopped for a few minutes in the mirror to admire her own figure. She felt sexy today after a long time. She remembered the wild night that they had on...what was supposed to be their...honeymoon.

Sanam took a deep breath, and her hands instinctively went to her full breasts, squeezing them gently, remembering her husband's touch. Today, she was full of want for the first time in the last few months.

"Why is this stranger awakening dormant desires in me?" Sanam thought with a mix of guilt and confusion.

"I am turning out to be just like the Zumba girls," Sanam huffed and pulled the hoodie on. Notes of plum green, grapefruit, and vanilla wood engulfed her. The scent was sharp and fresh but also deep and exotic.

"I am going crazy!" Sanam hugged herself smelling the stranger's aroma and threw herself on the bed trying to catch a breath.

Avinash was at his voyeuristic vocation when he saw Sanam come in with his hoodie in her hands. She took off her top and started looking at herself. Avinash couldn't believe his luck. His body tensed with desire. He couldn't control it now. He closed his eyes.

The main door of Dhindsa residence was open. Avinash tiptoed towards Sanam's room. Sanam was still lost in her own world in front of the mirror, hugging herself, clutching the hoodie and smelling it. Avinash hugged her from behind giving her a massive shock. But he didn't allow her time to get out of the shock. He quickly claimed her lips. She initially resisted but a few moments later she responded with equal fervour. In quick swift moments Avinash opened her denim shorts and pushed them down.

"Fu*k, you are so hot baby! I missed you!" Avinash said as he pulled her shorts and lace panties off her legs. He pushed her on the bed and took off his t-Shirt in a jiffy. He came back to kiss her swollen red lips, eating away her moans, making her delirious with pleasure. Avinash pulled off the hoodie from her body and unclasped the hook of the bra. He was very rough with her today, but his baby was completely ready for him.

"You like it rough baby?" Avinash asked her, biting her luscious bottom.

In a few seconds Sanam lay there moaning, naked and inviting.

"I love you Biwi!" Avinash groaned as he pushed off his own clothes and entered her cave of pleasure. In no time they were moaning loudly.

"Aviiinash!" Sanam screamed his name.

"I am almost there baby! Just a moment more," Avinash screamed, whacking her bum. But the pleasure changed instantly to fear when he heard a sinister growl. He turned around and felt the dog's jaw going for his posterior.

"Aaaaaahhhhh," Avinash howled as he fell down from the chair and came back to reality.

"Shit..I was almost there!" Avinash groaned as he pulled himself up and headed for the washroom. The pain of UNFULFILLED dreams poked him to no end.

Wearing the Drummer's hoodie, Sanam went out.

As she headed out, Daaku barked loudly first, then smelled her and his bark reduced to a growl and finally a whimper. Daaku looked at her with accusing eyes knowing she had changed the party.

"Come here Baby!" Sanam cuddled Daaku and showered love on him.

The next few days went away in a jiffy. Sanam cooked something or the other every day for the men. Baba now became a regular for the four p.m. tea time manoranjan. The tea party would happen alternatively at the Dhindsa or the Kumar residence. They would talk shop, have fun and pull each other's leg.

Sanam would now eagerly wait for the Drummer in the balcony and a new song every day. Sometimes she would smile, sometimes cry.

"Baba ab toh Sanam khush rehne lag gayi hai...should I meet her? Apologise to her now?" Avinash asked Baba.

It was a week later that Baba and Avinash had sat down to take stock of the situation.

"Pammi bol rahi thee...that Sanam has been under a lot of mental duress and has been getting a lot of panic attacks in the past months," Baba said what he had inferred from Pammi.

Fortunately, Baba had gotten to know from Nani that Sanam was not open to talking about her personal life and if someone could get her to do something...it was only the Doctor.

"The doctor will return in another few weeks...till then I don't think so we should make a move! Vaise bhi she won't leave Pammi till then!" Baba said and Avinash agreed half-heartedly. He knew Baba was right but looking at his heart living a couple of feet away was slowly eating him up.

Sanam woke up to a letter of rejection from another well-known publishing house. Till now, two leading publishing houses had rejected her novel. Sanam's morale took a nosedive. She took Daaku out with a sullen face. She didn't look around and sat with drooped shoulders on the bench in the park leaving Daaku to do his business.

She didn't even notice that the Drummer had passed by twice. Since the day Sanam had worn Avinash's hoodie, Daaku had become a little benevolent towards Avinash. Now, he would occasionally growl and watch him keenly whenever Avinash would come near Sanam but not charge.

Zumba did take her mind off (for some time) the setback she had suffered. They sat outside in the garden where they used to generally sit after Zumba class.

"Maine apne Miyan se bola thodi friendship karlo drummer se!" Sammy told the girls.

"Phir kya hua Di?" Krissy asked, completely intrigued.

"Miyan bole 'Karunga aur usse ghar bhi invite karunga! Thode months main rakhi jo aa rahi hai!" Sammy cried in despair.

"So many days have gone, we haven't seen him at all! He plays a song everyday...whom is he trying to get the message across to? Who all can listen to the volume? I think 4-5 buildings!" Akki started putting all the strewn clues together.

"Kuch investigation karni padegi!" Akki said.

"Tum logon ki SNIT se toh main dukhi ho gayi hoon! Har baal ki khaal nikalna zaroori hai?" Sanam huffed.

" What is SNIT dude?" Tia, Ritika and Dina asked.

" Arre Sneaky Neighbourhood Investigation Team-SNIT!" Sanam replied.

"Oooooh that sounds groovy Tatas!" Dina said.

"Theek hai ….toh I am the chairperson of the team!" Akki declared and the whole group started talking excitedly again.

After listening to Dina's recently written sonnet on the stranger and exchanging a few recipes with Tia, Sanam headed home a little happier than what she had been in the morning.

It was two days later and three in the afternoon when Sanam screamed in disbelief. Her novel had been accepted by a leading publishing house.

She ran to Nani's room with her laptop to show her the mail. Nani started reading…

Dear Sir/ Madam,

We are glad to inform you that it will be our pleasure to publish your Novel in the romance section of our publication. You will have to sit with the editor to make your story more suited to our readers. Currently, your story has a sad ending, we would like to work around it and make it palatable for our genre.

We would also like to inform you that you will be required to make media appearances across the spectrum to introduce the novel.

You will find the remuneration offer up to the market standards. However, it is negotiable.

Waiting for your response ,

Ostrich Publishers.

"I will have to appear in the media?" Sanam read again and registered. Earlier she had been too excited to understand properly.

"Yeh mere sath hi kyun hota hai Nani? I don't want to face the Media! They will get to know my story. Mazak ban jaungi main sabke samne! They will talk nonsense about him too! I can't do it! I can't do this to him! Kasam di the usne mujhe!" Sanam cried and started shivering. She felt her pulse drumming in her ears. Her breathing became laboured.

"Mitali, Dr. Indu ko phone kar jaldi! Sana beta saans le...kuch nahi hua!" Nani rubbed her back.

Avinash was shocked to see her like this. One moment she had been dancing and screaming in excitement, and the other moment she had a panic attack.

" Baba...Baba..Sanam ko panic attack aaya hai....please jaa kar dekho!" Avinash was almost in tears.

Sanam had fainted by the time Baba reached their house. Nani was very upset. She was glad to have Baba by her side.

"Mrs. Dhindsa, she has been better since the last one month. Did something happen today that triggered her? Has she been eating properly? I will draw some blood to check her haemoglobin levels. Just keep her happy! I have given her sedatives, so that she can relax," Dr. Indu told Nani.

"Aur kitna dukh likha hai bachi ke naseeb main?" Baba wondered as he kept on looking at Sanam as she lay quietly on the bed. He had tears in his eyes. He clicked a picture and sent it to Avinash.

Nani was devastated as well. She told him what had happened in the morning. She swore him to secrecy and told him about the book and showed him the mail.

"Sab theek ho jayega Pammi. Hum dono mil kar bachi ka khayaal rakhenge!" Baba consoled her.

"Satti Ji, Ladoo hota toh use sambhal leta. Woh samjhata hai toh yeh aur Daaku jhat samajh jate hain. Mujhe halke main lete hain!" Nani whined.

"Main kabhi nahi loonga!" Baba didn't realise that he had actually spoken this loudly. They both blushed.

Baba quickly reassured Nani and took leave. The moment he came out of the building, Baba took out his phone and made a spate of calls. By the time he reached home there was a big smile on his face.

Next day…
"Baba, Sanam is feeling very low today! Kuch acha banwao kar lekar jao…vaise bhi Sunday hai..it will be a good excuse!" Avinash told Baba. He himself was feeling blue because his wife was sad. He sat on the drums and drummed away his sadness.

Sanam heard the drums while having her customary tea with nani. Nani heard those too!

"Vaise drums bahut ache bajata hai Mr. Kumar ka pota! But poor guy, he had a nervous breakdown some months back. That's the reason he is completely off people," Nani told Sanam.

"That explains a lot!" Sanam said. She was glad that she had followed her instinct and not told the Zumba girls that the Drummer jogged in the wee hours of morning.

Sanam had recovered from her panic attack. She randomly checked the mail and then heaved a sigh of relief. It was an acceptance letter from another reputed publication.

Dear Sir/ Madam,

We are glad to inform you that it will be our pleasure to publish your Novel in the fiction section of our publication. Our editorial board finds your story a little short of a proper novel. We would like you to work with a mentor who will guide you with the nuances.

Hope to hear from you soon. The remuneration offer will be discussed in the next mail once we receive your reply.

Editor,

Saraswati Publications.

This time Sanam didn't jump in excitement, she just smiled. After all, it isn't every day that your book gets published. She picked up the phone and called Dr. Rajeev.

Dr. Rajeev gave her the number of their lawyer who not only ran the background check on the publication but also handled the whole thing efficiently. It was a small but reputed publication. The offer wasn't as generous as the previous one, but they were willing to offer a small percent royalty on the book after the sale of a stipulated number of copies. The best thing was they were willing to keep her anonymity intact. The only downside was that she had to edit the book in one month as they were running on a tight schedule.

Two days later, Sanam received a letter from her 'mentor'.

Dear Mr/ Ms. Anonymous Butterfly,

Congratulations on the contract. I have gone through your book...it's good. However, I feel there is a lot of potential to make it great. Please allow me to help you on your journey. Since you want anonymity, this shall be our only mode of communication.

Waiting for your reply.

Sincerely,

Rajeev Khanna.

CHAPTER- 56
DARLINGS

It had been a week since Rajeev and Sanam had started working on the novel 'The last woman standing'. The story was about an old lady who lived in a building and refused to sell her flat to the evil builder. There were a few subplots running parallelly in the book. An unfulfilled romance that the Old Punjabi lady had with a neighbour played in flashbacks. Two love birds that were brought together by the old lady formed the sub plot. This love story unfolded on the background of Builder -politician nexus that consumed the love nests...figuratively and literally.

Sanam sat down and looked back at her conversations with her mentor Rajeev. She felt exhilarated. It was a wonderful feeling to imagine that one's words would float on the paper, weaving a magical tapestry for the readers. To imagine that her book will become a place where people would lose themselves to her words to escape from the cruel realities of life, just as she did in the books that she loved.

She remembered the first day they had a conversation. The day that she almost gave up on her dream.

It had been the first day of their conversation and they started talking on the chat available on their mail ….

AnonymousButterfly: Hi Sir, from where should we begin?

Rajeev: Hmm...from the end.

AnonymousButterfly: end?

Rajeev: I wasn't convinced with the ending

AnonymousButterfly: Hmm…ok? What wasn't convincing?

Rajeev: Well….the old lady took the decision going by logic and not by her heart. That goes against her characterisation.

AnonymousButterfly: I disagree…

AnonymousButterfly: Women can think by mind too! Why can't men like you understand this?

Sanam had put her points forward and Rajeev had slashed them one by one with his logical rebuttal. He had gone ahead and slaughtered her characterisation layer by layer. Not once was he rude. He sounded stoic, calm and logical. His logic had driven Sanam to the brink of pulling her hair.

She ended up leaving the meeting mid-way in tears. These were her characters…her babies…and Rajeev had torn apart her characters from the core. These were not mere words for her…she had lived and breathed with her characters.

Sanam couldn't take it. She howled and howled at leaving her own protagonists without defence. She had felt like a mother who again couldn't take care of her own child. She had left the study, gone to sit in the pod chair swing and broken down. Daaku had consistently barked looking at her emotional state. Finally, he had brought Nani out to the balcony to console her.

"Arre kya hua bache?" Nani came out.

Sanam told her the story between the hiccups and the tears.

"Uffo! Itni si baat?" Nani almost laughed at the incident.

" Teri toh na PTM ho gayi!" Nani said.

" PTM matlab?" Sanam quizzed.

" PTM matlab 'Parent-Teachers meeting'. Tu kabhi parent teachers meeting main jati…hamare zamane ki toh pata chalta!" Nani asked.

"Wahan pehle bache ki dhulai karte thee..phir kuch acha bolte thee! Samjhi?" Nani told her, leaving Sanam confused.

"See better it comes from your mentor than the critics! Dekho beta, apni weakness sune ki himmat honi chaiye! He could have sweet talked to you too! He didn't mince his words. He was a gentleman all through. In fact, you threw a tantrum. He was trying to help you beta. I think he is a nice guy. Koi aur hota toh kaafi rude ho sakta tha! This guy sounds sweet! Ja maafi maang apne sir se!" Nani said.

Sanam sat on the balcony and introspected a lot. She realised that she had indeed gone overboard. The beat of drums reminded her that she had been sitting in the balcony for almost two hours. That night the Drummer played 'Jugni' from the movie 'Queen'.

Sanam just closed her eyes and felt as if the song had been written exclusively for her. It just rejuvenated her. She felt some karmic connection with the Drummer. He always played songs that she needed to hear. At times, she thought that Akki wasn't wrong: he was indeed trying to send someone a message. "Who could that girl be?" Sanam thought and felt a pang of envy tear her heart somewhere leaving her baffled.

"Concentrate on your book ...," she had scolded herself as Sanam went inside and opened her laptop. She had apologised to Rajeev Sir, and he had accepted it humbly.

AnonymousButterfly: Hi Sir, I am really sorry. I overreacted.

AnonymousButterfly: I really got emotional.

AnonymousButterfly: I cried and cried.

AnonymousButterfly: I couldn't listen against my characters.

AnonymousButterfly: I am sorry.

After Half An Hour.
Rajeev: It is ok Butterfly. I can empathise with you. I felt the same way when it happened to me.

AnonymousButterfly: So, you are a writer too?

Rajeev: No..no ...I meant otherwise in life. Now are you ready to 'Kill your darlings'?

AnonymousButterfly: matlab?

Rajeev: Sometimes, a writer has to sacrifice his favourite scene or characters for the greater good of the book. It is a very difficult and painful lesson. Let's see if you have learnt it or not. Let's get going.

Since that day, Rajeev and she had become good friends. She had a lot of respect for him. He had become a true mentor for her and showed her the ways she could cut out the flab in her writing. He had gradually become a person whom she had started trusting. After long, she felt she had got a friend who inspired her to trust herself. Though she had gotten friends- the Doctor, Nani...they were just amazing people. They were important to her, but the kind of pull she felt for mentor Rajeev had startled her. She wanted to talk to him. They jammed at an intellectual level. It was just surprising. She would want to talk to him about everything and absolutely nothing. Sanam wanted to sit down in a cosy corner and share a cup of tea with the stranger cum friend and tell him everything. He was filling a void in her that she never knew existed.

Her stomach growled loudly to remind her that she had skipped her lunch.

That evening, Sanam found herself yet again in the balcony, sitting in the pod swing, waiting for the stranger to play the drums. As always, Nani had retired for the day around eight. Sanam took her laptop to the balcony to work on her book. Sanam realised she had been sitting there since eight because she didn't want anyone to get an idea that she was waiting for something. The Zumba girls had really become very observant.

"You never know when SNIT would catch me coming out, especially for the Drummer! Better play safe! It should look natural ! Organic!" Sanam thought.

Akki's flat was a few floors below the Drummers flat. She too had started standing in the balcony to guess whom the Drummer wanted to impress. Sanam felt a squeeze in her heart. Her mind wanted to know whom he was after that is if he was...but her heart had a mind of its own. She felt this deep attraction to this stranger. She had for the moment stopped feeling guilty about getting attracted to this stranger. She had explained herself that...

1. The Drummer has a body like Avinash.
2. The Drummer has a great body. Period.
3. The Zumba girls tell he has a hot face too.
4. He is an awesome drummer.
5. He plays some fantastic songs.

"You are only human Sanam! Does he know that you are attracted to him...or look forward to his performance! No? Then chill! Enjoy till it lasts!" Sanam cooled herself down and feigned typing something.

But of course, Shastriji had been watching every move of hers. Avinash's song selection depended on Sanam's mood. Even though he couldn't talk to Sanam, he could still understand all the non-verbal cues. If she would be happy, she wouldn't sit down for a moment while walking daaku; If listless, she would keep her hands in the pocket of her jacket and not lift her head and walk briskly. Sometimes she hummed happily while feeding Daaku his breakfast, and sometimes she would look so lost and unsettled. With the Zumba girls, she would tilt her head when she would get zoned out. If she would sit in the pod for longer and move her feet to the music, he would know she loved the song. If she would rush back into the room, he knew she felt overwhelmed. That day when he had spotted her crying, he had wanted to tell her that she was stronger than she thought herself to be and had played "Jugni".

He had looked at one of her letters then.

January 20XX.

Dear Sanam,

You are stronger than you think!

Love,

Avinash

Reply...

January 20XX.

Dear Avinash,

It means a lot to hear this from you. It has been killing me to not be able to share my problems with someone. I don't have a lot of money. I need to find PG accommodation soon. I don't know what or how I will do it. I am tired of acting strong all the time. But thanks for just being there. I find solace in just looking at you!

Loads of love,

Sanam

Avinash thanked his lucky stars that he had brought his DSLR camera with a tripod. Had he not placed it adjusting it to the telescope, he would have never come to know that she came out specially to listen to him drumming. Instantly, he felt a gamut of emotions. He felt happy that he was being heard by her and felt a pang of jealousy that his wife was getting attracted towards another male...who of course happened to be he, himself. At the end, he didn't know what to feel.

"Kill your darlings Avi," he scolded himself.

CHAPTER- 57

BANI

Avinash had been waiting for Sanam to come out. He put the camera on and took his place at the drums. The Drummer played two songs that night, back-to-back, that sent Sanam into a musically induced coma.

The first song he played was 'Neele neele ambar par' from 'Kalakar' followed by 'Khairiyat' from 'Chichore'.

"Guys...tumne suna? He played TWO songs! TWO fucking songs!" Akki screamed in their ears the moment the Zumba instructor let them off the hook. Sammy, Akki and Sanam were the only ones from the gang today! The rest were absent for one or the other reason.

"Haan kya? My kids were on the TV, and we were busy in the shower...I mean I was busy!" Sammy said, blushing away. Married for almost ten years, the couple were still completely into each other. Their chemistry was envied by many in the complex and their social circle.

"Haan samajh gaye(Understood!)!" Sanam and Akki laughed as Sammy turned beet red.

"Guys back to the Drummer! I need to tell you so many things! Chalo na aaj coffee par chalte hain ya fir drinks?(Let's go for coffee or drinks)" Akki asked.

"I don't drink!" both women said in unison.

"Uff! Sati Savitiris!" Akki said.

"Sun...sati savitri mat bol! I will tell you guys some other time!" Sanam said as she cracked up remembering the actual 'Sati Savitri'.

"Chalo boring women...coffee par today evening? Jo cancel kare usse bhootni chipak jaaye!" Akki said, not waiting for a response from them.

They laughed and went away to their houses to meet again in the evening.

Sanam asked Nani and Pammi was absolutely thrilled.

"Nani, I will be back in two hours!" Sanam told her for the umpteenth time.

"Arre, I am a big girl! Aur waise bhi tere Baba aarahe hain! We will have our sugarless tea here. He has challenged me to a game of chess! Huhh!" Nani replied.

"Best of luck!" Sanam giggled.

"Best of luck rakh tere Baba ke liye...He doesn't know what he is getting into!" Nani said with an attitude.

As she got out of the building, Sanam called up Baba to inform him about her plan and ask him to make sure Nani avoids eating anything adventurous like Pakoras etc.

"Arre bitiya main toh Chicken tikka la raha tha...air fried not oil fried," Baba exclaimed.

"Baba leave some for me then! Bye!" Sanam kept the phone down and got into the car with the girls.

"Kahan gayi woh?" Avinash asked Baba.

"Friends ke saath gayi hai!" Baba told him.

"Sab ladkiyan hain...don't worry!" Baba laughed at Avinash's love-stricken expression.

"I will follow them!" Avinash said.

"Arre kabhi space de use!" Baba made him understand.

"Baba ab nahin hota...I can't be like this...it's already been one month. Ab nahin hota!" Avinash sat down with his head in his hands, overwhelmed with emotions.

"Bas beta, I think in two weeks the doctor should be back. Then definitely, we will talk. Chal ab kuch kaha lo...aaj teri biwi ne kuch nahin bheja tere liye but that doesn't mean that you don't eat anything at all!"

Sanam had nowadays started bringing in or sending something or for them. Avinash laughed when he remembered how they had almost been exposed.

A few days before, the ringing of the doorbell pealed through the noise of the Shastri household. Baba was on the phone and Bansi kaka had been on the mixer along with listening to Vividh Bharti. Avinash was fed up with the constant ringing, he went and without looking through the keyhole opened the door to find a beautiful girl in blunts talking on the phone and fortunately she had her back to the door.

Avinash instantly knew it was his wife. He shut the door in nervousness.

"Bach gaye!" Avinash ran to the kitchen to bring up Bansi kaka and ran to his room.

There she was in his home again, just a little away from him. He just wanted to go and hug her, but...life.

"Ok...shoot now!" Sammy said impatiently once they settled in the cafe.

"Haan toh yesterday he played two songs...but most important are the songs!" Akki said and opened her bag and took out a piece of paper.

"Just this week he played...look at the list...Please pay attention to the lyrics!" Akki put the paper out for inspection.

Sunday- *Jaadugar tere naina...*

Monday- *Meri Bheegi Bheegi Si Palkon Pe Rah Gaye*

Tuesday- *Dilbar mere kab tak mujhe ...Aise hi tadapaoge*

Wednesday- *Main phir bhi tumko chahunga*

Thursday- Sorry by Justin Beiber

Friday - *Zaroorat Hai Zaroorat Hai*

Saturday- *Neele neele ambar par chaand jab aaye*

And *'Khairiyat' from 'Chichore'*.

And pay attention to the lyrics...

Sunday ko... *'Ruk Jaau...Tera Mukhada Main Dekhu Jahan'*

Matlab, he is watching her!

Monday ko..*Anaamikaa Tuu Bhi Tarse*

Anamika means 'Anonymous'! Means he doesn't want to tell others...but there is someone!

Tuesday ko...

Main aag dil mein laga doonga woh ki pal mein pighal jaaoge

Matlab khula challenge!

Phir....

Is it too late to say I'm sorry now?

BC he is apologising!

And yesterday two songs...Dono ultra romantic.

"Oh my Gosh! I never thought about this!" Sammy exclaimed.

"Me neither!" Sanam said all the while hoping Akki hadn't caught her listening to the Drummer.

"And I have more news!" Akki said, extremely happy with her SNIT snooping.

"I took their rental agreement details from the Secretary's office. Chachu is the Secretary by the way! The flat has been leased on the name of a company 'Nextrix Inc'.Its a shell company and has no digital footprints," Akki said dramatically letting the fresh information sink in.

Sanam and Sammy were shocked and completely intrigued.

"Akki tujhe kaise pata?" Sanam asked her.

"I tried hacking into their system! But hua nahin," Akki said goofily.

"Durr Phite muh Akki! Police pakad ke le jayegi tujhe hacking karegi toh! Computer engineer is liye bani thee?" Sanam huffed.

"Arre, I think this Drummer is running away from the Police!" Akki replied.

"What?" Sanam and Sammy said in unison.

"Dekho...he hides himself...wears a hoodie! Jogs when no one is watching him! Aur saali kamini Sana you know woh subah run karta hai aur tune hume bataya nahin!" Akki said.

"Fu*k!" Sanam thought to herself.

"Arre, woh Baba ne mana kiya tha! Sorry!" Sanam said apologetically.

"Oho...theek hai...forget it Sana! Akki you are accusing the Drummer of very serious charges! Do you understand the gravity of your accusations?" Sammy asked Akki in her typical professional lawyer tone.

"Oye! yeh tera court nahin hai!" Akki said in her patented sarcastic tone.

The girls laughed at this.

"Mujhe lagta hai usse restraining order mila hoga! He must have walked in on his girlfriend cheating on him and must have lost it! Isliye chupta hai!" Sammy said.

"Yaar bahut creative ho tum log...bas karo! Let's have coffee! And then let's go shopping! Mujhe Zumba karne ke liye appropriate wear lena hai!" Sanam said, trying to change the topic.

They left the cafe to shop. Sammy and Akki made Sanam buy a lot of adventurous clothes...hot but decent.

"Let's have dinner!" Akki insisted.

"I need to ask Nani!" Sanam said, taking out her phone.

"Mujhe bhi Miyaan ko phone karna hai!" Sammy said.

"Nani is fine! Vaise bhi Nani and Baba were planning to go out for dinner! They were planning to pick me up!"Sanam said.

"Chalo this is better...why be a 'kabab main haddi!" Akki said.

"Shut up Akki...kuch bhi bolti hai!" Sanam reprimanded Akki.

"Abey aise hi nahin bolti! Society ka sabse handsome budha tumahari Nani ke peeche hai! Unka toh hashtag bhi ban gaya hai #BaNi!" Akki said.

"Haye Akki...Shak toh mujhe kabka thaa! Once or twice, I have seen Baba setting his hair in the lift with a huge smile on his face!" Sammy giggled.

"Sachi?" Sanam asked them genuinely.

"Haan...sabse pehle meri Dadi ka patta kata....She had specially coloured her hair for him, but he addressed her 'Behenji'! My Dadi came home and cried and cursed Pammi aunty's beauty!" Akki said dramatically leaving everyone in splits.

"So, he is the judge tomorrow at the cooking contest?" Sammy asked.

Sunday was the Society's annual day. The managing committee had organised a cooking contest for the society members and a cultural show. Baba and one other person was chosen as judges for the cooking competition. The Zumba girls had a dance performance in the cultural show.

"It's going to be so much fun!" The girls squealed in unison.

Avinash was sitting at home idle. He didn't even feel like playing drums.

"What is the use? She isn't here!" he thought aloud.

"Let me do some work! Let's see if the butterfly is online or not!" Avinash spoke aloud once again.

Saraswati printing press had been named after Baba's mother. Baba had bought the printing press when he had gotten to know that Alok Shastri was going from one press to the other to publish his novel anonymously. Alok had refused help from Baba. Baba had got Alok's novel evaluated. Once Baba was sure that it had a lot of potential, he had taken over a loss-making printing press. He had offered to publish it with anonymity without letting Alok know about the owner of the press. He had turned loss-making printing press around with his son's subsequent novels. Over the course of years, Baba had finally spilled the beans to Alok, sending him into a shock.

Many years later Alok also did the same to his son. Alok had read the novels that Avinash had shown him after their misunderstandings got cleared during Ganpati. Both the novels held a lot of potential. So, Alok took to editing both Avinash's novels. He had been convinced that his son's books had a lot of potential and he was proven right too. Avinash's first novel had been anonymously released by Saraswati Publications two days before Baba had been taken ill. It had been their plan to release it before his movie to surprise him. The novel had not been a resounding success but had garnered good reviews from the critics. However, a critically acclaimed novel and movie later Avinash was none the happier. Nothing made sense without his wife.

A few days back Baba had asked him to involve himself in business. Baba had asked Avinash to take over the work of one of their oldest editors, Rajeev Khanna, who had gone on leave suddenly. Over the last two weeks, Avinash had gone through a volley of manuscripts and shortlisted a few. A few of them needed mentoring. He had taken over Khanna Uncle's email ID and started mentoring the three writers. Two were non-fiction writers and one was a romance writer who would rather stay anonymous. She was an interesting character. Maybe because her reactions always reminded him of his wife.

Avinash went to the telescope once again to see if she had returned or not. It was then that he spotted two young men in their late 20s following Sanam and her friends. Avinash followed them from his telescope and saw them entering the next building. Sanam and her friends were now safely home. Before he could play the song, loud party songs could be heard from the adjacent building, 24th floor. Those were the same guys.

As the clock struck eleven, Avinash went down and inquired about the men from the watchman. The watchman opened up with Avinash after accepting a pauwa(a small Rum bottle) from him.

"Arre sahib yeh ladke...MBA college ke hain...bahut chichore! Ek bitiya rehti hain samne ki building main...Sana Madam...kuch mahine pehle inhone unko cheda tha!" the watchman told him.

"Phir kya kua?" Avinash asked him calmly. His eyes betrayed the calmness of his voice.

"Agle din, chupke se unka Doctor gaya ladkon ke flat mein! Teeno ladke, jo sharab main dhut thee, unko doctor sahib akele peet kar aya! Mujhe 2000/- ke panch(five) note diye..aur bola bhaiya sab bhool jao! Ab bolo......poore mahine ki pagaar hamare haath main...aur badmash ladke bhi bhag gaye...hum kyun yaad rakhen?" the watchman had now completely spilled the beans.

"That bloody Doctor! Who in the fuck is he? Why don't I have any information on him?" Avinash screamed into his phone once he reached his flat.

Somehow, the Doctor's information hadn't been provided by the agency. His mind appealed that he should be happy that the Doctor stood up for his wife. His heart somehow couldn't take someone else fighting for his wife without having an ulterior motive.

A few hours later, Avinash received an email from the agency about the information on the Doctor.

Avinash opened the file and downloaded the picture.

"You betrayed me, Dr. Rajeev Kedia a.k.a. BITTU!" was all that Avinash said before picking up the table lamp and smashing it on the adjoining wall.

CHAPTER- 58

HEER-RANJHA

"You take care of yourself Dr. Rajeev!" Sanam said.

"You too, guys! Sanam, have fun at the performance! Nani, please don't kill people with your food! Daaku... love you!" the Doctor said in the parting shot of his regular video call with his ladies.

"My ladies?" Rajeev thought with a smile. "I wish it were true!" his heart sighed.

Dr. Rajeev Kedia kept the phone down and walked up to the French window of his father's apartment overlooking the beautiful Belmont harbour in Chicago. He opened his phone again and admired the pictures Sanam had sent. 'His ladies' with the cool dude 'Daaku'! For the umpteenth time Rajeev wondered what was with these ladies and names. Who names a dog 'Daaku'? Forget the dog, he himself had been given many nicknames by the women in his life. His mother had always called him 'Bittu'; his Nani still called him 'Ladoo' in front of everybody. And Sanam? She had surpassed all and called him 'Doctor'. No one called him by his real name. Ever.

Nani never liked his name 'Rajeev' because he had been named by his father in the remembrance of his own grandfather. To think of it, she hadn't liked anything to do with his father. Her prejudice ran deep. Nani was least concerned about getting her facts right about his father. His father hailed from a Marwari family settled in Calcutta for generations, but Nani always saw it as Bengali and took his father as a Bengali. Her prejudice hadn't helped his marriage to Debanjana at all. The fact that Debanjana was actually a Bengali had become a bone of contention between Nani and him. The fact that Debanjana and he were completely incompatible had added insult to injury.

However, Nani wasn't completely wrong as well. After all, his father had done the unthinkable...taken her only precious daughter away from her and then abandoned her and her kids.

He sat down with a hot cup of ginger tea and remembered the day he had been coaxed to drink this wonderful concoction by the girl, who a few years back had come into his life like a breath of fresh air.

It was his second day at the cardio health camp that they were holding at the Gurudwara. He had been working for six hours straight. It had been hectic.

"Next!" he had called loudly.

"Ten minutes break sir!" Sanam had come in with a cup of ginger tea and pakoras.

"I don't take breaks. I don't take tea," Rajeev had informed her curtly.

"Haww...Robots bhi break lete hain...aap toh insaan hain! You have been working since morning. Now I have made tea especially for you. The rest of the nurses also have taken a tea break. Chaloji apne aap ko paap na lagao meri chai reject karke," Sanam had spoken animatedly.

"I am Sanam Kaur Bedi," Sanam had offered candidly.

"Dr. Rajeev Kedia," Rajeev had replied while drinking the hot flavoured concoction for the first time.

"Ki-di-a?" Sanam tried to pronounce it correctly many times, but it was obvious that she was having a little trouble in pronouncing his surname.

"It's ok...you can just call me Rajeev... that will do," Rajeev offered.

"Nahin...I will call you Doctor!" Sanam said giggling.

"Yes, I am a doctor, but I have a name too!" Rajeev exclaimed.

"Arre Doctor Sahab, your name is so boring!" Sanam giggled.

For the first time in days, Rajeev had smiled. He had been going through the separation phase of his marriage. It had been taxing...very taxing.

"By the way Doctor, the unmarried nurse in this dispensary, has a huge crush on you! And woh Mrs. Kapoor jo aayi thi na...ekdum old...woh bhi flat ho kar gayi hain aap par. Are you aware how many women you have slaughtered in the span of two days?" Sanam spoke non-stop giggling at the shocked-out-of-his-wits and blushing pink Rajeev!

"Meri friend ka bhi crush aap ho! Aaj ke liye itna jhatka kaafi hai! Bye! Next Sunday aap aayenge? Chai-Pakore saath main? Bye!" Sanam had left the ever-serious Rajeev smiling from ear to ear.

There are some people who are God's children. They spread happiness and positivity wherever they went. Sanam was one of those.

Dr. Rajeev had started looking forward to the weekends of volunteering at Gurudwara. It used to be his actual day-off. A day off from his so-called 'wife's' indifference. A day where someone cared enough to share a cup of tea with him. A day where Sanam, even if as a matter of courtesy, asked why he looked so tired? Those ten minutes spent with her would give him energy to work for another cruel week.

Rajeev hadn't realised when he had fallen in love with Sanam.

'It shouldn't have happened! I am not right for her!' he would think again and again.

"I am almost ten years older than her and going through a divorce! Why would I want to destroy her chance of young love?" Rajeev often questioned himself.

One year had gone by quickly. Rajeev's love for her had slowly grown stronger. It wasn't the lustful love; Rajeev couldn't even think about Sanam that way. His was more towards respect, companionship and a little attraction. The pain was that Sanam hadn't even realised that he felt attracted towards her. For her, Rajeev was a mere 'nice acquaintance', for him she slowly became 'everything'.

It was his misfortune that he got entangled with his divorce and his sister's illness. The day he returned to Mumbai to propose to her, destiny gave him a rude shock. By the twist of fate, he met his old friend Avinash and realised that the girl he wanted to get married had already got married to his friend.

That night, it had taken him all his might to keep his hands to himself and not bash Avinash up for doing what he did to her; although, he did look remorseful. Rajeev wanted to burn the world when he saw her at Avinash's home. Sanam, whose smile had lit up his world, had been lying in the pool of blood. Rajeev knew that Avinash was a good man, he didn't want to judge his old friend without talking to Sanam.

"She is anaemic and mal-nourished" he had told Avinash. "And I know it's your personal life, but I didn't know you were a brute Avi ! She is delicate…please deal with her humanly," he had said with a hint of derision . Rajeev had given Avinash a list of medicines and left; promising himself to check on her again.

Rajeev had returned to check on Sanam. This time he had decided to meet her at her office. He had just parked his car when he saw Sanam smile and run towards him. Rajeev couldn't believe his good luck. However, it lasted for an instant when he spotted Avinash standing a few metres away from him.

Avinash had broken into a big smile watching Sanam drop everything and run towards him, with a big smile on her face. Avinash had smiled as she reached him. The couple was oblivious to everything around them.

Rajeev had seen real love in both their eyes. He knew Sanam would never look like this at anyone again in her life. He knew he stood no chance.

That's why, it had been all the more shocking when Rajeev had met Sanam alone at Nanded. Her subsequent emotional breakdown had perplexed him. In the next few days, he had left many messages for Avinash but had not been able to contact him. One day, he had come across a newspaper clipping of Nitika sitting in Avinash's lap at a party. He had understood everything. Avinash and Nitika's on-off relationship wasn't a secret.

Every time he tried talking to Sanam about her marital life, she shrugged him off.

"I will have to do something now! She can't keep on running away from her relationships. I need to meet Avinash once I return to India!" Rajeev spoke aloud to himself as he took a firm resolve.

AnonymousButterfly: Hi Sir, how are you doing?

Rajeev: Let's start Butterfly!

AnonymousButterfly: You don't sound so good Rajeev Sir!

Rajeev: Hmm...how did you know?

AnonymousButterfly: You are never so cryptic Rajeev!

Rajeev: I am in a bad mood Butterfly.

AnonymousButterfly: Oh...how can I help?

Rajeev: You can help by not making it worse. Did you complete what we discussed?

AnonymousButterfly: I did, Sir. Why do you always reduce me to a school girl?

Rajeev: Apologies Butterfly if this is what you felt. I am in a rotten mood today.

AnonymousButterfly: I sensed it when you asked me to have a chat this late.

Rajeev: Hmm…let's work now!

AnonymousButterfly: No…I don't feel like working.

Rajeev: Well, then I think we can connect tomorrow .

AnonymousButterfly: Can't we just talk? I need a friend right now.

Rajeev: Hmm…I am not a good friend Butterfly.

AnonymousButterfly: Why would you say that?

Rajeev: Well because my friends often end up betraying me! Hence, I must not be a great friend. Definitely not the one who can hold on to his friends.

AnonymousButterfly: I think for an erudite, your logic here is really skewed. If they can't hold on to you, it's their fault not yours Rajeev.

Rajeev: Ok…first of all…My name is not Rajeev. I don't like this name.

AnonymousButterfly: Oh! Why may I ask? I know someone by the same name, and he is an absolute darling. He is a very dear friend. He has been my strength during my difficult time.

Rajeev: Rajeev Khanna is a random guy in the Saraswati Publications. His account was given to me to mentor the upcoming writers.

AnonymousButterfly: Oh! So, what is your name?

Rajeev: I like my anonymity Butterfly!

AnonymousButterfly: Hmmm…Whatever your name might be…but I think you are a writer!

Rajeev: Hmm

AnonymousButterfly: What hmm? Tell me am I wrong or right?

Rajeev: Maybe!

AnonymousButterfly: Hmm...May I ask one thing?

Rajeev: Please go ahead.

AnonymousButterfly: How does it feel to get one's work published on paper?

Rajeev: I guess it feels good...That's the reason people want to get their stories published.

AnonymousButterfly: hmmm

Rajeev: What hmmm?

AnonymousButterfly: Why can't you give a proper answer? You promised!

Rajeev: When did I promise? You said you wanted to ask a question...I never promised to answer it!

AnonymousButterfly: You are a writer for sure! Editors are...for the lack of better words...unimaginative!

Rajeev: Woohoo FLY! You are very observant! So, tell me who are your favourite authors?

AnonymousButterfly: R.K. Narayanan, Khushwant Singh, Jane Austen and Shiv Kumar Batalvi. Batalvi is a Punjabi author. I am not sure if you know him...but he is just brilliant.

Rajeev: I have read about Batalvi! Any favourite works of his?

AnonymousButterfly: I love that song *'Ki puchde o haal fakiran da'*

Rajeev: Why?

AnonymousButterfly: I don't know why, but the lyrics resonate with me like no other...especially these...

Takdeer ta apni sounkan si

Tadbeera satho na hoiyaa

Na jhang chutiya na kann paate

Jhundh langh gya injh heera da....

It means, "Unlike Ranjha, I wasn't able to escape the circumstances of my birth…or the confines of my destiny…I wasn't able to rebel against what society expected of me, even though opportunities(like Heer) passed me by."

These sentiments resonate with me. I have always been bound by my destiny. Even when love came into my life, my destiny played foul and took it away.

Avinash had been having meaningless conversations with the anonymous writer on the other side. She had momentarily taken off his mind over the pain of betrayal he felt from his friend. But the moment he read *"Na jhang chutiya na kann paate; Jhundh langh gya injh heera da…. "* he stopped dead in his tracks. A film of moisture hit his eyes! He quickly got up and picked up the old cookie tin box. After looking for what seemed to him a long time, he finally found what he was looking for !

August 20XX

Dear Sanam,

One writes one's own destiny!

Love,

Avinash

The reply

August 20XX

Dear Avinash,

Takdeer ta apni sounkan si…Jhundh langh gya injh heera da….

These lines written by a famous Punjabi poet Shiv Kumar Batalvi are the crux of my life. Like the poet, I feel I won't be able to escape the circumstances of my birth. I won't be able to keep you in my life. Destiny will take you away from me just like it took away my parents and brother.

My Ranhja will leave me one day!

Dying to call you mine,

Sanam

CHAPTER- 59
TWENTY QUESTIONS

Takdeer ta apni sounkan si

Tadbeera satho na hoiyaa…

These lines were exactly what Sanam had written in her letter…in fact he had come to know about Batalvi through her letter. Did that mean that this anonymous writer was his wife? Tears somehow found a way from his eyes. Avinash got up and went to Baba's room. It was post mid-night and Baba had already slept.

"Baba! Baba!" Avinash was silently crying as he shook Baba from sleep.

"Montu! Montu! Kya hua? Tu theek hai?" Baba woke up with a start.

"Baba…woh romance writer Sanam hai na? Sach bolna…aapko meri kasam!" Avinash cried openly now.

"Haan beta! Tujhe das(10) din lag gaye samjhne main? Budha ho raha hai tu !" Baba teased him.

"She doesn't know, right ?" Avinash confirmed.

"No, she has no idea!" Baba replied.

"She actually wrote that novel? She is good!" Avinash said, still struggling to absorb the shock!

"Bahu kiski hai?" Baba laughed and went back to sleep.

On the other hand, now that Sanam had vented out her emotions she was now scared that she had overwhelmed or offended the writer in some way or the other. She didn't know who he was, but she had come to respect him a lot in the last few days and the thought of offending him was now troubling her.

AnonymousButterfly: Sir? Are you there? I didn't mean to overwhelm you with my emotions!

Avi(the mentor):

AnonymousButterfly: I am so sorry...I got carried away.

Avi(the mentor):

After A Few Minutes...
Avi (the mentor): Hey Fly...No need to apologise. Actually, I should...I was spaced out for a little while. By the way, has someone told you that you are very cute?

AnonymousButterfly: Hmmm...that's fine. And cute? Are you trying to flirt with me Mr. Writer?*Wink*

Avi(the mentor): Hmmm...maybe! Is it working? *chewing-my-nails-in-anticipation*

AnonymousButterfly: Maybe! *smiling*

Avi(the mentor):*smiling-a-lot*

AnonymousButterfly: Ok...quite late, I need to go!

Avi(the mentor): Please don't go Fly! I am in a bad state! I need you!

AnonymousButterfly: Hmm...ok...what do you want to talk about?

Avi(the mentor): Tell me something, Fly...anything!

AnonymousButterfly: Hmm...ask me questions, I will answer!

Avi(the mentor): What do you find interesting?

AnonymousButterfly: The regular...I love my dog; I love to cook and I love to talk! Haan, I also love observing people..maaza aata hai!

Avi(the mentor): Anyone interesting you have met recently?

AnonymousButterfly: Many!

Avi(the mentor): Tell me one!

AnonymousButterfly: Hmm...you know there is this guy who has just shifted in the opposite building!

Avi(the mentor): [*oh..so biwi has been keeping tabs on me!*] Oh...interesting!

AnonymousButterfly: Abhi to start hua hai!

Avi(the mentor): [*damn fucking interesting Biwi*] Arre wah!

AnonymousButterfly: You know what SNIT has discovered?

Avi(the mentor): What is SNIT?

AnonymousButterfly: Sneaky Neighbourhood Investigation Team-SNIT... Acha if you want to listen to this then let me type...

Avi(the mentor): Ok done..

AnonymousButterfly: You know my friends have been keeping a tab on this guy because he is so handsome!

Avi(the mentor): Wait...what do you think? Is he handsome enough for you?

AnonymousButterfly: Arre let me type...ab no disturbance...otherwise I will leave!

Avi(the mentor): No...No...I promise!

AnonymousButterfly: So, you know this guy plays drums and he is awesome at those. I haven't seen his face, but I see him from far jogging in the morning. He is actually quite delicious.

Avi(the mentor): Oh!

AnonymousButterfly: So, he plays drums every night at a particular time followed by a song on loud. Just one song! The song choice is amazing by the way! So, SNIT says that he is after a girl he is trying to impress! They also think that he is a stalker and has a criminal bent of mind.

Avi(the mentor): What? Why?

AnonymousButterfly: Because he doesn't interact with others...hides his face! The girls saw his face quite by chance. And my dog bit him too...in the thigh!

Avi(the mentor): So that makes him a criminal???

AnonymousButterfly: No...but my dog knows people! Vaise I know his grandfather...he says he is asocial. Bechara!

Avi(the mentor): What do you feel for him?

AnonymousButterfly: What will I feel? Nothing! I just enjoy the songs!

Avi(the mentor): Hmm

AnonymousButterfly: Chalo I need to sleep now!

Avi(the mentor): Fly...don't go!

AnonymousButterfly: Ek toh...why are you calling me fly? It means 'Makkhi'! Main kya 'Makkhi' hoon?

Avi(the mentor): Nahin tum cute ho!

AnonymousButterfly: ok. We have a cultural evening tomorrow in the building and I am really tired.

Avi(the mentor): Ah...ok...I will go back to work...maybe try if some other friend is online! Or else I will dip my worries in smoke. Good night!

AnonymousButterfly: Arre nahin. Thodi der aur...I always keep on asking questions...today is your turn, ask me a question!

Avi(the mentor): Ok...so after whom has your protagonist been based? Any person in real life?

AnonymousButterfly: Hmm...the old lady is a mixture of a few characters I have seen while growing up, but the core character is me: me in my old age! LOL!

Avi(the mentor): And the lover? Is he your husband or boyfriend?

AnonymousButterfly:

Avi(the mentor): Fly? Did I get too personal? I am sorry, I just wanted to know. He sounded interesting.

AnonymousButterfly: He is my ex.

Avi(the mentor): Well very handsome ex I must say!

AnonymousButterfly: Yes he is extremely handsome! And a gem of a person!

Avi(the mentor): Why did you guys break up?

After a long silence...

AnonymousButterfly: He left me. I wasn't good enough for him.

Avinash stared at the laptop and broke down. "You don't know what happened Jaan! I love you so much! You don't DESERVE an idiot like me!" he cried.

Avi(the mentor): He must have been a moron.

AnonymousButterfly: I am very sleepy Sir. I need to go. Bye.

Avi(the mentor): Bye Fly...I am very thankful to you for today. I apologise if I overstepped. But I really needed you today.

AnonymousButterfly: Goodnight Sir.

Avi(the mentor): One last thing Fly...I don't know why you have kept your pseudonym 'AnonymousButterfly'...I have always felt that you were a PHOENIX!

Sanam read this and smiled between her tears, suddenly feeling lighter than she had felt in the recent weeks.

CHAPTER- 60

PUNGI

Next day...
Avi(the mentor): Good morning FLY!

FLY FLY FLY

Sanam: *NO RESPONSE*

Avi(the mentor): FLY FLY FLY

FLY FLY FLY

FLY FLY FLY

FLY FLY FLY

FLY FLY FLY

FLY FLY FLY

FLY FLY FLY

FLY FLY FLY

FLY FLY FLY

FLY FLY FLY

FLY FLY FLY

Sanam: *NO RESPONSE*

Avi(the mentor): FLY FLY FLY

FLY FLY FLY

FLY FLY FLY

FLY FLY FLY

FLY FLY FLY

FLY FLY FLY

FLY FLY FLY

FLY FLY FLY

FLY FLY FLY

FLY FLY FLY

FLY FLY FLY

FLY FLY FLY

FLY FLY FLY

FLY FLY FLY

FLY FLY FLY

FLY FLY FLY

FLY FLY FLY

FLY FLY FLY

FLY FLY FLY

FLY FLY FLY

Sanam: Yes Sir!

Avi(the mentor): Kahaan thee yaar?

Sanam: Sir I was doing household chores! Are you well? What happened?

Avi(the mentor): Nothing happened...I just wanted to talk to you!

Sanam: why?

Avi(the mentor): Woh..woh..I was feeling very creative in the morning! I thought let's discuss the next chapter.

Sanam: Sir, I am really caught up with a few existential questions! *exhausted emoji*

Avi(the mentor): Ooh! Anything that I can help you with?

Sanam: I am contemplating what to cook for lunch! I have a busy day ahead and need a quick fix!

Avi(the mentor): Well...I am being confronted with the same question!

Sanam: Well, what is your wife suggesting?

Avi(the mentor): Fly...I am as single as I can be .

Sanam: Ooh!

Avi(the mentor): Yes...so please decide something and tell me...I will also **order the same.**

Sanam: Hmm...what do you feel like eating? I will cook the same!

Avi(the mentor): Aloo-puri?

Sanam: Hmm...fried!

Avi(the mentor): Egg bhurji and paratha?

Sanam: Kal hi khaya

Avi(the mentor): Mutter Pulao? I just love spicy pulao with koshimbir (vegetable raita in marathi cuisine)

Sanam: Wow! Thanks sir...sun kar hi bhook lag gayi!

Avi(the mentor): So, when can we work next? There is not much left, but some crucial chapters need revision.

Sanam: Tonight sir? I have a Zumba performance in the evening but before that we have a war to win!

Avi(the mentor): War! Holy hell FLY! Jhansi ki rani ban gayi ho tum!

Sanam: Sir, the cooking competition is like a bloody war here...it's the question of our prestige. My Nani is pretty worked up about it. Will let you know how it went. We must talk tonight and start the next chapter!

Avi(the mentor): Looking forward to it! Best of luck for your competition.

Sanam: Thanks Sir! But sir, just one question.

Avi(the mentor): Ask away!

Sanam: Sir....Why still FLY? I am Phoenix na?

Avi(the mentor): You might become a Phoenix or a nightingale tomorrow for the world….for me you will always be my FLY!

Sanam: Ok Sir…bye!

"'MY FLY'…did Sir actually realise he had called her 'My FLY'?" Sanam felt a bolt of current pass her body making her shudder at the mere thought of being claimed by someone.

"I am sure he meant in a 'mentor-mentee relationship' way. I am overthinking!" Sanam reprimanded herself. She smiled and hummed as she went towards the kitchen.

"Chal bechare Drummer ke liye kuch banati hoon! Who knows if he has eaten or not? Poor thing, I feel guilty when I don't feed him!" Sanam sighed.

In an hour's time, Sanam had delivered steaming hot vegetable Pulao with koshimbir to the drummer's place.

As soon as Sanam had left, Avinash attacked the dish and finished it off with relish while Baba chuckled at his child-like actions.

An hour later, Avinash mailed Sanam a picture of veg Biryani take away from a famous Pune eatery.

"Oh teri…Baba aaj toh bade dude ban kar jaa rahe ho!" Avinash whistled, making Baba blush.

"Oye badmash!" Baba chukled.

"Saj dhaj ke kahan ja rahe ho?" Avinash teased Baba despite knowing fully that Baba was going to judge the cooking competition.

"Aapke wali kya cook kar rahi hai?" he teased further.

"Pata nahin!" Baba quipped.

"Kuch bhi banaye….first toh wahi aayengi na jab aap judge ho!" Avinash said.

The effect was exactly what he had envisaged. Baba had gone pink and was smiling ear to ear.

"Lagta hai meri mummy ko package deal milegi! Bahu ke sath saas free…free…free!" Avinash broke into throaty laughter after receiving a smack on his backside from Baba.

Avinash tilted his telescope towards the park, where the events were going to be organised. Thankfully, it wasn't covered, so Avinash could enjoy watching his wife jump here and there to encourage her Nani and her Zumba gang.

The cooking competition was in full swing. This competition had a milieu of internal rivalries that had been running in the society complex from the last many years. Due to a few new and enthusiastic members in the society committee, the rules had been changed this year. This year the participants were given a choice of different ingredients and they had to create from the ingredients. The ingredients were: Yam, Jackfruit, eggs, green peas, milk and a few staples like eggs, flour etc.

The cooking time was one hour, and they were allowed to take on a helper only in the last half an hour.

The judging panel comprised Mr. Paranjape, a retired reputed civil servant and Mr. Satyendra Kumar, since both these gentlemen were new to the society and the organising committee's assumption was that they will play fair. Another factor that tilted the selection in their favour was that both the senior citizens were in the pink of their health(tasting a variety of dishes doesn't come without its risks) and single(almost all entries in the competition were women). And that was exactly what went wrong in the evening.

"Doctor, I am so happy you came on Facetime! You know it is a real test of skill and talent. The ingredients are so bizarre!" Sanam was happily chatting away with Rajeev who had joined via facetime to encourage Nani . It was four in the afternoon in Pune but four thirty in the morning in Chicago. Poor Doctor was struggling to keep awake but wouldn't dare to disappoint his ladies.

"Kaisi ho Sana?" Rajeev asked her softly.

"Main theek hoon...aap kaise hain? You know you have lost weight! Aap theek toh hain na?" Sanam couldn't keep the concern out of her voice. It had been three weeks since the Doctor had lost his father to Cancer. Rajeev hadn't been himself since then. He was experiencing a strange mixture of relief and guilt.

"Aap kab aa rahe ho? Nani kitna miss kar rahi hai aapko!" Sanam whined.

"Soon...I will return soon!" Rajeev said with a smile.

"Hi Doctor!" the Zumba girls screamed as they came near Nani's table to encourage her. Tia and Dina were participating in the competition.

"Hi Doctor, how are you doing?" Akki said, trying her seductive tone just to tease him while the other women cringed and laughed.

"Hi girls!" Rajeev blushed in plenty and looked away from the camera.

"Doctor women are crazy about you here!" Sanam laughed.

"Sana woh wahan Anita aunty hai na….keep Nani away from her!" Rajeev cautioned Sanam.

Ms Anita Daruwala had been a page three socialite in her hay days. These days she was relegated to the 'ex-wannabe' kitty party group. She had earned the moniker 'man-eater' in her youth when she had encroached upon her best friend's handsome husband, tagged him along for a few months and had ultimately left him for greener pastures. In the last decade she had settled to a quiet life in and around the society, but her Queen Bee instincts never grew old. She wanted to be the centre of attention in the society too but there was only one thing standing as an obstruction….her nemesis...Pammi. That the new men were relatively handsome than the rest in their age group and one of them was really interested in Pammi had not escaped her notice. She had taken part in the competition merely to spite Pammi and try her luck with the new dishy dude 'Satti'. She had already almost kissed Satti in front of Pammi to gauge her reaction. Anita had laughed a silent laughter when the arrow had hit the mark.

Meanwhile, the judges had been locked away to keep the judgement as unbiased as possible.

"What a dynamic lady she is!" exclaimed Paranjape as they sat in the Society office, banished from the festival.

Baba was lost in his own thoughts. He had caught Pammi's murderous gaze as the other lady had tried to get comfortable with him.

"Which lady?" Baba asked absentmindedly.

"Pammi! Mrs. Dhindsa for you!" Paranjape quipped good naturedly, unaware of the storm he had started in the tea cup.

"Do you know her?" Baba asked him cautiously, trying not to expose his own curiosity.

"Arre haan...I know her very well. We are 'good friends'. Just yesterday we dined together! Such a beautiful lady! I wish I had met her in my youth, I would have married her right away!" Paranjape yapped, fortunately not aware of the looks Baba was giving him. The fact that he had exaggerated the cup of tea he had at the Dhindsa household, didn't bother Paranjape. A mild exaggeration here or there was pretty acceptable for him.

"Sir, we are getting the dishes!" someone came and broke his train of thoughts.

After a lot of discussion…more bickering and wrangling the two judges reached a decision. Mr. Paranjape till the end couldn't understand why he was being butchered for no reason at all. If only he knew.

As soon as the judging got over, Baba spotted Paranjape head over to Pammi and take her hand in his. Blinded by insane jealousy, Baba did exactly what a Shastri would do…retaliate by offence. He went towards the lady Ms. Anita and gave her his full attention. Soon everyone headed towards the cultural performances for the evening. After an hour of a variety of performances, the most awaited dance performance of the evening came: The Zumba girls.

The performance started with Sammy's cute as a button 'little ones: Radia and Rifa' dressed in cute red kimonos dancing on 'Mera Naam Chin Chin Chu'. The first piece was met with a thunderous applause. The dance number gave way to the older women who did BollyZumba on peppy tracks.

Avinash had come down to watch the dance up close. He had kept himself to the last row where the passers-by were standing. As the dance was going on, he heard three boys from the twenty fourth floor of the adjoining building talk and pass lewd comments on the Zumba gang.

"Saali bahut hot hai yaar! Look at her moves! Her hot lips! Yummy!" the short man said.

"Baaki bhi kam nahin!" the taller one said.

"Yaar mat bol Sana ke baare main…Doctor ne kitna maara tha…yaad hai na?" the youngest one uttered in fear.

"Hai kya Doctor Pune main? Nahin na? Aur yaad rakho hum badla lene aaye hain Doctor se…Sana ke saath ab koi nahin hai!" the short guy spoke again.

"Pakka na? Maza aayega phir!" the youngest added as they left for their building.

Avinash had never felt such a furry. His nostrils flared and eyes became bloodshot. The steel bottle that had been in his hand had been reduced to a twisted mess.

"Beating them up has not taught them anything. They need a good lesson. Band bajana padega inka! Bastards!" Avinash muttered a mute oath.

Meanwhile, the evening ended with Tia winning the competition with her innovative 'Jackfruit gnocchi' and Nani came a close second with her 'Mutter ki kheer'. The function came to an end around seven in the evening leaving a lot of people with a rainbow of feelings. Sana was ecstatic, Nani was miffed, Avinash was furious, and Baba was well...scared. He knew he had already dug his own grave.

Baba's shoulders hung as he walked home.

"Baba congratulations! Aapke wali toh jeet gayi phir aap udaas kyun ho?" Avinash asked Baba.

Baba told him the entire episode.

"Khandani problem hain humko Baba!" Avinash chuckled. He was suddenly in a better mood. An evil plan of setting those rowdy men right had already formed in his mind.

"Tu Sana ke liye roz gaane play karta hai...aaj meri wali ke liye bhi laga!" Baba told him.

"Ok!" Avinash said.

"I will just message her!" Baba said enthusiastically.

Pammi...this song is dedicated to you

-Satti-

XOXO

A few minutes later Baba received this message on his phone from Avinash

Baba sorry...I couldn't resist!

-Avinash

Two minutes later, the PUNGI song from Agent Vinod played in the Drummer's apartment.

CHAPTER- 61

NUTELLA AND JAM

Two minutes later, the PUNGI song from Agent Vinod played in the Drummer's apartment.

Kahan Chal Di, Pyaar Ki Pungi Baja Kar!

"Montu harami hai tu!" Baba screamed at the top of his voice, but Avinash had already left with car keys to shop for the revenge party he had planned.

Almost two hours later, around nine p.m. Avinash returned home to a pensive Baba.

"Baba sorry!" Avinash touched his ears and bent down.

"Yaar woh phone nahin utha rahi hai!" Baba picked two glasses of whisky and offered one to Avinash.

"Montu tune galat kiya!" Baba looked at him.

"Sorry Baba...apne unke sath galat kiya...I was just punishing you on her behalf! Chalta hoon...mere wali wait kar rahi hogi!" Avinash chuckled to earn a tight slap on his back.

"Baba don't worry...love story main thoda tadka lagna chahiye!" Avinash ran away before Baba could respond because his wife had been indeed waiting for him.

Earlier in the morning, Avinash had mailed Sanam a picture of veg Biryani take away from a famous Pune eatery.

Sanam: Hello Sir! OMG...apne bhi veg biryani khayi? That's so sweet!

Sanam: Oh wait...You reside in Pune?

Avi(the mentor): Hi Fly! Sorry to have kept you waiting. Yes I reside in Pune.

Sanam: Wow...me too!

Avi(the mentor): Sweetheart, may I remind you that you wanted to remain anonymous!

Sanam: Haan..toh I am not telling everyone...just you!

Avi (the mentor): Why? Am I special?

Sanam: I feel safe with you.

Avi (the mentor): You haven't even met me Fly!

Sanam: Still, I feel safe with you.

Avi (the mentor): Thankyou for the vote of trust but for all you know I could be a psycho killer who enjoys the flesh of beautiful young maidens.

Sanam: Uff...the writer speaks. I still think I will be safe with you.

Avi (the mentor): But the question is why would you want to meet a person like me?

Sanam: Did I say I wanted to meet you?

Avi (the mentor): Oh! So, you don't want to meet me, Fly?

Sanam: Nahi...I didn't mean that Sir!

Avi (the mentor): Ok...so prove me wrong...have coffee with me.

Sanam: Sir I think we should start with the book!

Avi (the mentor): It's ok Fly...I understand. People like me are loners. We are left alone on our birthdays too! Never mind.

Sanam: When is your birthday?

Avi (the mentor): In a few days...three days actually!

Sanam: Ok...where do we meet?

Avi (the mentor): Fly...it's ok...you don't have to take pity on me!

Sanam: No sir...Tell me where do we meet?

Avi (the mentor): Take your pick! Your choice of place and time!

Sanam: Ok...so eleven in the morning and Starluck cafe in Viman Nagar?

Avi (the mentor): Sounds good!

Sanam: How will I recognise you?

Avi (the mentor): I will send my picture five minutes before eleven! Vaise even I wanted to meet you! You sound so sweet and beautiful!

Sanam: Sir kitna flirt karte hain aap! Uffo!

Avi (the mentor): Masti nahin karenge toh life main kya reh jayega Fly?

Sanam: Done...chalo let's talk now!

Avi (the mentor): Let's talk about sex baby! Let's talk about you and me!

Sanam: WHAT??????

Avi (the mentor): Let's talk about sex, baby; let us talk about you and me SALT n PEPA ka Gana hai FLY! CHILL!

I meant let's talk about the love making chapter!

Sanam: OOh...sorry!

Avi (the mentor): Tumhe kya laga?

Sanam: Nothing at all ...let's get back to the story!

Avi (the mentor): Oh! Why so prude, Sweetheart? Oh God! Please tell me **you are not a virgin!**

Sanam: No...I was married once upon a time!

Avi (the mentor): Oh...sorry! Then why are you so uptight in the description of sex? Oh...I think your sex life must have been sad! Bad sex can do such things to people!

Sanam: On the contrary, sex was terrific. It was the best thing I had ever experienced. In fact, it was the only thing in our relationship. We had nothing else between us. Now can we NOT talk about my failed relationship please?

Avi (the mentor): I am really sorry Fly!

Sanam: Sir, let's move on.

Avi (the mentor): So, if you have experienced great sex, why has the description been so insipid. Go into the recesses of your memory and put some soul into it!

Sanam: Ok...I will get back to you tomorrow!

Avi (the mentor): Fly...don't break my heart...ok?

Sanam: I won't. Good night sir.

"There we go...there is no looking back now!" Avinash thought aloud. He had run out of patience waiting for the Doctor to return. Now that the novel was almost over, he wanted to take his chance.

"You are still in love with me baby! I know you won't be able to resist me!" Avinash spoke aloud, peeping into the telescope.

Meanwhile, Sanam was in deep thoughts. Sir had caught her today. He had been right. She had indeed tried to rush through the sex description. In the past months she had suppressed her sexual urges. She had feared her memories because if she went into her memories, she would crave more for her husband.

"Oh Avinash! You have spoiled me for everyone! My body craves only for you!" Sanam moaned as she kept her laptop aside and went to the kitchen and returned with a spoon and a jar of Nutella. She moaned again as she took out a spoonful of Nutella and licked it with the tip of her tongue.

"Holy fuck!" Avinash gulped as he saw her licking the spoonful of Nutella with fervour! He experienced an instant hardening of his member. He went and looked up the old cookie tin box.

April, 20XX

Dear Sanam,

Bedsheet or NUTELLA?

Yours,

Avinash

April, 20XX

Dear Sexy and hot Shastriji,

BOTH!

Want to lick Nutella off you but I want to keep my favourite bed sheets too! I love them! Samjhe buddhu?

Waiting for you like a bitch in heat!

Gosh you are so gone Sanam!

F@@k you soon!

XOXO

A little while later, feeling relieved and completely rejuvenated, he played a Yeshudas song 'Maanaa ho tum behad haseen' that gave shivers to Sanam.

A few hours after he had face-timed Nani and Sana, Doctor Rajeev finally sat down in his cabin to watch the recording again. Nani had sent him more videos of Sana's performance. The videos were shot badly; Nani was not good with cameras at all. The phone would often slip from her hands; she also ended up sending a lot of dummy videos where no action was happening. Rajeev was about to shut down the I-pad when in one of the dummy videos, a face caught his attention. It was a short man of about twenty-five. His heart skipped a beat when he spotted that man in the crowd. His face broke into fury. In rage, his hands pulled into a fist.

There is no mistaking that face.

"Bastards have returned! One beating wasn't enough for them! This time I will finish them," Rajeev muttered furiously.

He picked up his phone and made a few calls. The first call went to his long-trusted driver Mushtaq Bhai to confirm the presence of the three troublemakers.

"Mushtaq Bhai aaj aap Sana ko bahar nahin jaane dena," he told the aged driver.

He called the security agency next and arranged for a security personnel to act as a driver from the next day. His last call was to his secretary.

"Mrs. Martha, please book me a ticket to India at the earliest!" he barked into the phone, startling the lady who had never seen the Doctor lose his cool in the last two months.

It was three in the morning and the lights in the twenty fourth floor flat had gone off half an hour ago. It was time to put Phase two of the plan into action. Phase one had already taken place. Avinash had discreetly given whisky bottles to the watchmen at the security counter and the ones who manned his and the adjoining building. He had also manipulated them into asking him for Mutton Biryani!

"Kya bhaiya...itna sab khana pina hua building main..aap logon ko kisi ne khilaya pilaya ki nahin?" Avinash had asked the security gate watchmen in jest.

"Arre babu hamare kaun dekhta hai! Aap bade log ki diwali hoti hai...Hum toh bas dal bhat kha kar so jate hain!" the watchman had said.

Avinash had taken out a whiskey bottle and ordered for one kg mutton biryani on the phone.

"Enjoy karo bhaiya...bas mera naam mat lena...building wale problem karenge!"Avinash had let the dialogue slip by.

At two in the morning, he had come down to check if the watchmen had consumed liquor or not. The watchmen were eating, drinking and wasting away. He realised that they all would pass out in another half an hour max. Taking advantage of their merriment, he had taken exactly two minutes to turn off all the CCTV cameras.

It was three in the morning now and Avinash picked his huge duffle bag that had all the required paraphernalia and a shovel. He wore his black track pants, hoodie and kept a mask handy.

It was four in the morning when Avinash rang the bell of the twenty fourth floor. After ringing the doorbell for ten minutes, the door was opened by a sleepy man in shorts. The moment the door opened, Avinash pushed him inside the flat and closed the door behind him.

"Be##@c**d kaun hai tu?" the short guy screamed.

Avinash slapped him once, looked around, found a discarded pair of socks and gagged the short guy.

"Saale baki ladke kahan hain?"Avinash asked him, taking a plastic tie fastener from his pocket and tying the guy's wrists together.

The short guy took Avinash to the bedroom where his other two friends were sleeping.

Avinash took pink fur handcuffs and tied him with the window grill. Fortunately for him, it was a wrought iron bed . It was convenient to tie the other two sleeping guys to the bed. Avinash gagged their mouths with their own socks. He opened his huge Duffle bag and took out an actual leather horse whip and started whipping the men.

The men who must have been drunk while going off to sleep were now wide awake. Deep fear reflected in their eyes.

"Tum log ladkiyon par buri nazar dalte ho? Bada shauq hai na mard banane ka? Chalo aaj mardangi dekhte hain tumhari!" Avinash whipped them again.

"Yaar maza nahi aa raha, thoda explore karte hain!" Avinash locked the door and took out a big sharp blade cutter and went near the short guy who had been tied to the window grill. Looking at the blade, the man started shivering in fear.

"Zayada fudakna nahin...cut kar raha hoon!" Avinash cut his plastic tie and the short guy tried to run.

Avinash caught him with ease and punched him.

"Bola tha na...jyada shana nahin ban! Now do what I say or else I won't spare you!" Avinash pulled his hair.

He stood with the whip and hit the short guy.

"Yeh le scissors....cut their clothes and then yours! Chal!" Avinash shouted at them.

In a span of a few minutes, all the men were buck naked.

Avinash took out a big bottle of jam and gave it to the short guy.

"Put this on you friends and yourself...especially on the balls!" Avinash said.

In the next few minutes, both guys were smeared with jam. Avinash then sprinkled sugar granules on their bodies.

"Make them wear this ...," Avinash gave him neon orange and black mouth gaggers.

"You lechers!" Avinash gave them a kick in their behind.

The men had nothing, but fear written all over their faces.

Avinash took out another pair of fur-coated pink handcuffs and handcuffed the short guy to the bed.

"Wow the scene is set!" Avinash said as he took out his phone and clicked a lot of pictures. Avinash was correct. The setting looked like a page out of a BDSM movie. He got the cutter out and brought out a huge plastic bag. The plastic bag contained big pieces of mud structures. These mud structures were ant colonies. Avinash had recently read on the society bulletin board that the building was suffering the ant menace. Finding them here and there hadn't been an issue. The park was full of them. However, digging them out with a shovel and not getting bitten by them was a task.

Avinash cut out the upper half of the plastic bag and emptied it on the bed where hundreds of ants rushed out. The processed sugar was a great way of attracting ants.

The men shivered at their impending fate.

"By tomorrow, you should have left the city to never return! If I spot you near a girl...You can't even imagine what would happen. I have my eyes on you!" Avinash growled.

Avinash turned back and saw with satisfaction the red ants climbing the naked men who were whimpering due to the intense pain of ants biting their naked Jam smeared flesh sprinkled with sugar granules.

Avinash left a few more BDSM toys for them and left their house a little ajar. He was happy that his hard work had borne fruit. He picked up his shovel and headed for the lift.

Once he reached his own building, he looked around for the audience. He was glad he had managed to leave and return unseen.

The moment he pressed the lift button, it opened with a person standing in the corner.

"Wait a minute, this is Sanam's friend!" Avinash smiled while recalling that this was the same girl who had a doubt in him.

Akki had left for someone's birthday party right after the cultural function had ended. There had been drinks and Akki might have downed more than she had bargained for. So, she had somehow reached the lift but was facing difficulty in pressing the required button.

The lift refused to do anything and then suddenly the Drummer made an appearance. He had been covered head to toe. He had a huge duffle bag and a black mask on his face. Suddenly she saw the shovel in his gloved hand and traces of mud on him. Her mouth turned into a big ooh! Her fears about the Drummer being a criminal were coming true. He looked like a murderer.

Avinash could read her mind. He had to give it to her for a very creative imagination. He thought of taking advantage of the situation and giving her more fodder for thought. He went ahead and pressed the required floor buttons. And kept staring back at her.

Akki stayed on the 23rd floor and Avinash on the 26th floor. In between the 14th and the 15th floor, Avinash pressed the STOP button in the lift.

Akki's heart was now beating a crazy tattoo…one-this guy was really hot, and two-he looked a murderer straight out of a murder scene.

"I just wanted to tell you that I am watching you! If you go to the Police etc…then I know where you stay!" Avinash said menacingly.

"Never…I swear never," Akki ran towards her apartment, the moment the lift doors opened leaving a laughing Avinash behind.

CHAPTER- 62
THE SECRET

Next morning at seven, a shrill scream pealed the silence of the society.

Kanta Ben had come to work in the adjoining flat when she saw the boys' flat door opened. She entered and saw that the bolt was up, but it had missed the mark, classic case of a drunkard. The boys had done this once or twice before.

"Wapis pee lee hogi…bewde log!" Kanta Ben muttered. The boys had employed her to cook for them, but the timing was eleven in the morning.

Kanta Ben, a gentle soul, just wanted to make sure the men were ok. However, what she saw shocked her to the core. Two guys were sprawled on the bed, tied to the bed. The third guy, with one hand cuffed to the other person, was bent on one of the boy's member. It looked like the third guy was sexually exploring the other two. One open pink handcuff was hanging on the bedpost. All three boys were naked. Their bodies were weird pink in colour. Kanta Ben couldn't suppress her nausea. She pressed the pallu of her saree, went out and started screaming at the top of her lungs.

In five minutes, the whole flat was swarming with watchmen, maids and society members. The boys were now awake and trying to get out of the handcuffs. People were making videos and clicking selfies with the three men in the background. The news soon spread like a wildfire. The secretary and other committee members were called. Two empty whiskey bottles, a few marijuana joints and a few used injections were found by the committee members. It was a police case now. The committee members were happy because the boys had been a nuisance for a major part of the year. The boys had been hurling abuses at one and all by the time the Police came. They were taken in by the Local Police. They were making bizarre claims about a tall guy setting this up. No one including their families believed it. A lot of green bundles were swapped under the table and the boys were left with a warning against entering the city.

The videos however had reached social media and became viral instantly. '50 shades of Pune', 'India's answer to 50 shades' headlines rocked the media.

Avinash had mutely watched the whole scene unfold. He had spotted a Police Van and had hoped that the boys would be thrown out.

"Huh...I can sleep now!" Avinash sighed as he lay down.

"Hold on...one more thing!" Avinash got up and took out a foolscap paper and a marker.

Avi (the mentor): Good Afternoon FLY!

FLY FLY FLY

Sanam: *NO RESPONSE*

Avi (the mentor): FLY FLY FLY

FLY FLY FLY

FLY FLY FLY

FLY FLY FLY

FLY FLY FLY

FLY FLY FLY

FLY FLY FLY

FLY FLY FLY

FLY FLY FLY

FLY FLY FLY

FLY FLY FLY

FLY FLY FLY

FLY FLY FLY

FLY FLY FLY

FLY FLY FLY

FLY FLY FLY

FLY FLY FLY

FLY FLY FLY

FLY FLY FLY

Sanam: *NO RESPONSE*

Avi (the mentor): FLY FLY FLY

FLY FLY FLY

FLY FLY FLY

FLY FLY FLY

FLY FLY FLY

FLY FLY FLY

FLY FLY FLY

FLY FLY FLY

FLY FLY FLY

FLY FLY FLY

FLY FLY FLY

FLY FLY FLY

FLY FLY FLY

FLY FLY FLY

FLY FLY FLY

FLY FLY FLY

FLY FLY FLY

FLY FLY FLY

FLY FLY FLY

Sanam: Haazir Janaab!

Avi (the mentor): Did you see what happened in Pune today morning?

Sanam: I did! Shocking na?

Avi (the mentor): Absolutely...poor boys!

Sanam: Why Poor boys? They were assholes!

Avi (the mentor): LANGUAGE FLY!

Sanam: Sorry Sir!

Avi (the mentor): How do you know they were assholes?

Sanam: No particular reason...just a feeling.

Avi (the mentor): They were poor men who got carried away with their BDSM orgies!

Sanam: Haan...I don't know why people do BDSM!

Avi (the mentor): People get a kick sweetheart! Have you ever been in control?

Sanam: Umm...no!

Avi (the mentor): Liar!

Sanam: How do you know I am lying?

Avi (the mentor): I just do...just a feeling.

Sanam: Ooh! But I don't like all of this!

Avi (the mentor): All of this means what? SEX?

Sanam: No..I mean BDSM

Avi (the mentor): So, you like SEX?

Sanam: Sir...

Avi (the mentor): What? Why a prude again?

Sanam: Tell me one person who doesn't like SEX!

Avi (the mentor): Hmm...you got me there Fly!

Sanam: Men like different aspect of sex...women like different!

Avi (the mentor): Interesting ..please continue!

Sanam: So, men are typical you know ....wham, bham, thankyou ma'am. Women like more...you know foreplay...before and later. A girl wants to be held and cuddled all night.

Avi (the mentor): Trust me Fly...there is nothing better than cuddling the whole night after a stormy session of lovemaking! I don't prefer the word 'sex', I prefer 'love making'.

Sanam: Sir...I need to go. Bye.

Avi (the mentor): Wait...when will the last piece get done?

Sanam: Mostly by tomorrow afternoon.

Avi (the mentor): Acha suno

Sanam: Ji

Avi (the mentor): what have you made for lunch today?

Sanam: Palak paneer

Avi (the mentor): exactly what I feel like eating today...thank you!

Sanam: welcome sir!

Avi (the mentor): Just one last thing ....you will meet me the day after tomorrow?

Sanam: Yes I will.

Avi (the mentor): What if you don't like me then?

Sanam: Then, I will not meet you again!

Avi (the mentor): You break my heart FLY!

Sanam: I need to Fly away!Bye

Avi (the mentor): Haha...Bye

"Girls, coffee today? Apni society main itna bada kand hua hai! Let's gossip about it!" Akki had put on their private whatsapp group which had only Sammy, Sanam and her. After a little cajoling from Akki, the women decided to meet up.

"OMG! Subah subah yeh kya ho gaya!" Sammy screamed the moment the girls met at the cafe in the evening.

"What really happened?" Sanam asked them.

"Arre you do not even know half of it...Chachu is the secretary ...sab pata laga liya maine! But you guys have to hear what happened with me last night!" Akki said. She narrated the whole story of meeting the Drummer, his clothes and his threat.

"Akki, is he a criminal?" Sanam couldn't believe her ears. Her eyes were filled with unexplained moisture.

"Sana, why are you crying?" Sammy spoke. Surprise was evident in her voice. "Do you have a crush on him?" Sammy asked gently.

"Nahi yaar crush-vrush nahin hai...bas ek ajeeb tarah ki emotional attachment ho gayi hai usse jo nahi honi chahiye thi!" Sanam spoke. The quiver in her voice was discernible.

"Arre why not? Why do you have to feel guilty? Are you still married?" Sammy asked Sanam.

"Haan..matlab Nahi...matlab pata nahin!" Sanam replied.

"Arre either it is a 'yes' or a 'no'! What is this 'Pata nahin'? Akki quipped.

Sanam took a deep breath and gave them her story in brief without particulars.

"So, you don't know if your divorce is final or not? And you haven't met your asshole-husband again?" Akki spoke in realisation.

"Woh asshole nahi hai....bas thoda woh hai!" Sana retroted.

"Kya?" Sammy asked with amusement.

"Gadha hai!" Sanam said in a tender voice.

"You still love him!" Sammy said softly. It was a statement.

"I think so!" Sanam finally accepted what she had pushed to the deepest recess of her heart.

"That is why I feel guilty when I think about the Drummer against my own wishes!" Sanam bared her heart.

"Arre you are a human. Woh banda hai hi itna hot ki hum sab fisal gaye! He is the ultimate Bad boy!"Sammy laughed, making the others crack up too.

"That means because of this 'Kasam' you haven't tried to contact him?" Akki asked Sanam.

"No. Uske baare main search bhi nahin kiya!" Sanam said.

"Search? Celebrity hai kya?" Akki questioned back.

Sanam lost her nerve for a moment. " Nahin, I mean on Social Media!" Sanam handled the situation.

"Do you know his lawyer?" Samnah asked.

"I think I remember his name!" Sanam replied.

"So, all you need to do is get your lawyer to send notice to his lawyer asking about the status of the proceedings and asking for the copy if the Divorce has been sanctioned. It's a half an hour job. They will draft this notice and send via fax and send the physical copy by registered post! I would have done it but since I am a corporate lawyer, I can't do it. Our company doesn't allow it. Ask Nani and Doctor, they might have someone known and reliable," Sammy explained it to Sanam.

"If I am already divorced Sammy? Then what will happen?" Sanam almost broke down.

"Then you can lead your life guilt free! And if it has not been filled then it means that there are things to be cleared!" Sammy explained patiently.

"I think it's better to have your heart broken than to live under a wrong impression!" Akki gave her pearls of wisdom.

"Acha pata hai...I never told the whole story because you cried before!" Akki said dramatically to change the topic.

The other women chuckled good naturedly.

"So last night, I returned home sloshed. And Drummer ne poora nasha utar diya. Then in the morning Chachu woke me up. He said come quickly; you need to check the CCTV tapes. I asked him to tell me what I am looking for. Chachu refused to tell. He didn't tell me. When I went to the control room, one of the maids showed me the video. Meri toh hasi rukki nahin. Those bastards were a pain. Those three guys were evil. So, whoever did that...was awesome. So, I watched and rewatched the video. There was something that just wasn't right. Kuch toh jhol tha...And then I figured out...there was a mound of hardened mud that seemed like a part of an ant's colony. Everyone had missed it. The question is how an ant's colony would come on the 24th floor and in the bedroom. It was too much of a coincidence. I went back to the last recording and before the camera went blank, the Drummer was standing a metres away from it. I erased that portion too! Well, my analysis says, it was the Drummer who did it! But this remains between us! Promise? Cross your hearts!" Akki took a deep breath after the monologue.

Sammy and Sanam pinched their throats to show their devotion.

"Apart from being a good person, he has an awesome sense of humour! In the morning when I returned, I found a note on my main door saying…

I Know Where You Stay.

By that time, I knew that Drummer was a good dude! I also went and reversed the paper and wrote…

I Am Not Scared. I Know What You Did Last Night!

I went, rang the bell and gave it to his grandfather telling him to whom to give it. I was about to leave when I heard a deep, throaty laughter. Tab toh confirm ho gaya!" Akki said dramatically.

"Yaar, tu toh kainth(awesome) nikli!" Sanam said as they both looked at Akki with sheer admiration.

The rest of the evening went in a jiffy.

They were about to leave when Sanam went to the ladies room.

"Akki tune bataya kyun nahin Sana ko that we think that the Drummer is after her?" Sammy asked Akki.

"You saw how sad and guilty she felt? Let her figure it out! If not, then it wasn't meant to be!" Akki replied.

CHAPTER- 63
NOTICE

Sanam opened the door with her set of keys to find Baba and Nani in a deep discussion. Actually, Nani was venting out and Baba was just trying to keep his side. Mitali had gone down with Daaku.

"Baba toh gaye! Must be getting pulled for yesterday's flirting session with Anita aunty!" Sanam told herself and laughed. They both were so engrossed into each other that they didn't even realise Sanam's presence. Sanam stood in the background and enjoyed the session. Nani was in her Prima Donna avtaar! Nani finished off her monologue with a steady stream of tears that brought Baba to his knees.

Since the time Akki and Sammy had told her, she had started paying attention to the relationship that was unfolding right under her nose. She noticed a deep affection growing between them.

"Both are as involved in their….ahem…relationship! Lo bol diya! The doctor will return and kill me when he notices this! Maybe or maybe not." Sanam hoped that both the Doctor and the Drummer both would understand Baba and Nani….#BaNi.

Sanam turned back to the main door and walked out of the house. This time she rang the bell and loudly put the keys in the lock and then walked in. The scene had changed now: they were sitting far apart, and Nani had wiped her tears away.

"Hi Nani…Hi Baba! Kaise ho aap? Chai pee apne?" Sanam asked them.

"Bas bitiya tumhara hi wait kar rahe the!" Baba replied.

"Sana bacha baith…main banati hun!"Nani said, much to the chagrin of Baba.

"Arre nahin, main banati hoon na!" Sanam insisted but Nani refused point blank and went to the kitchen, which was a good thing as Sanam got a few moments with Baba.

"Aapse kal se naraz hain...Anita aunty ko muh kyun lagaya?" Sanam asked.

"Muh nahin lagaya...bas zara baat ki," Baba got a little defensive.

"Baba full flirting kar rahe thee aap!" Sanam accused Baba.

"Woh bhi toh Paranjape ke saath baat kar rahi thee!" Baba said sullenly.

"OOOh…toh yeh baat hai...isliye aapne woh kal Pungi wala gaana lagaya?" Sanam almost accused Baba.

"Nahin woh maine nahin, Montu kamine ne bajaya thaa….panga daalne ke liye! Ab faila diya raita!" Baba said with a stricken voice that made Sanam laugh.

"Baba...vaise I approve! You have my blessings!" Sanam cracked up more when Baba blushed at her dialogue.

In the next hour Sanam did her best to get Nani to give up on her anger. By the time Baba left Nani had almost worked the anger out of her system.

As Baba left after dinner, Sana and Nani sat down for their post dinner gossip.

"Cute hai na Baba...vaise I approve!" Sanam pulled Nani's cheeks that had turned pink with blush. Sanam then told her about what had actually happened in the society, discreetly leaving the Drummer's part unmentioned.

As she lay in Nani's lap, Sanam came to the point right away and discussed her divorce with Nani.

Nani too agreed with Sammy's advice that knowing the truth would emancipate her. Nani had also suggested their family lawyer who had previously helped them with the book contract. Nani told her to consult the Doctor too. However, they couldn't get in touch with the doctor and that worried the ladies a lot.

Sanam did a little research online and finally got hold of his secretary. From her she got to know that he had already left for India.

"I am happy that the Doc is returning, but in such a hurry?" Sanam sighed and hoped everything was well.

Sanam requested Nani to call the lawyer right away as she didn't want to chicken out and change her mind later. The lawyer assured them that it will be done by the earliest.

After talking her heart out to Nani and putting her to sleep, Sanam headed towards the balcony. She had mixed feelings about this. Her mind told her to accept that Avinash had divorced her, but her heart still held onto the hope that he cared for her. A feeling of despondency was taking over her.

Sanam sat in the swing and Daaku jumped in too. He had grown into a full-fledged dog and was quite heavy now.

"Haye Daaku Moya….kitna heavy ho gaya hai…Doctor ki treadmill par bhaga kar! Koi kuttiya tujhe bhav nahi degi aisa raha toh!" Sanam mock reprimanded him.

Daaku sensing a scolding, got up and sat in the balcony corner, making Sanam feel guilty right away.

"Oh, sorry mera shona shona bacha!" Sanam got up from the swing and lay down to hug him. Both got comfortable with each other.

Avinash had been watching this entire scene unfold. He put on "Main aur meri tanhai aksar yeh baatein karte hain…" followed by the song 'Yeh kahan aa gaye hum!'

"Daaku…aaj toh yeh jaanab bade gaane baja rahe hain!" Sanam talked to Daaku about the Drummer. Daaku being Daaku was deeply offended by the Drummer's mention. He stood up barking furiously at the mention and left for Nani's bedroom for the rest of the night leaving an embarrassed Sanam behind. She quickly looked around and sat on the swing. She hoped he would play another song. She loved the surprise upliftment of her mood that his songs had brought.

Avinash hoped she would be looking forward to a few more songs. Today he felt like taking her in his arms and kissing her for eternity.

He chose "Inteha ho Gayi Intezaar ki' from the film 'Sharabi'. He had always been an avid Bachchan fan.

Sanam smiled as he started the song. He knew he was on the right track.

The last song he played was his favourite Shashi Kapoor romantic song, 'Aaj ham ishq ka izahaar karein to kya ho?' from Trishul(1978). This song seemed to have been made for his Sanam.

Sanam had been lulled to sleep in the swing by the beautiful songs.

"Baby thand lag jayegi...andar jaa!" Avinash spoke aloud when he saw her hugging herself in the swing.

A few minutes later, Sanam got up and retreated into the bedroom, leaving a sleepless Avinash behind on his telescope.

Avinash finally slept in the wee hours of the morning, missing his daily run and the entry of Doctor Rajeev into his own home.

It was seven-thirty in the morning when Sanam returned from Zumba to be greeted by an over enthusiastic Daaku barking and prancing around.

"Daaku aaj pagal ho gaya hai? Itna pagal toh tu sirf Doctor ke aane par hota hai!" Sanam reprimanded Daaku when Daaku danced around her, almost toppling her.

Her dialogue was followed by laughter. Sanam turned around to see the Doctor and Nani laughing at Daaku and her exchange.

"Oh God Doctor! So good to have you back!" Sanam squealed and hugged him in excitement. Even if they didn't talk much, she had missed him a lot in the past weeks. The hug was not expected by the doctor who clearly was a little awkward by the unexpected display of affection. The awkward moment passed.

"Kaisi hai?" Doctor asked tenderly.

"I am good. Chai banaun? Sab saath main piyenge!" Sanam said excitedly.

"Sana ...kuch khane ko bhi please…I am hungry!" Doctor Rajeev pleaded.

"Of course, Doctor!" Sanam smiled and left.

After a quick breakfast, the doctor left for his bedroom. He had been hit badly by jet lag.

The day went like every other day. It was four in the evening when Sanam, sitting in the swing with her laptop, was preparing the final draft of her novel that she received a phone call from the lawyer.

The lawyer said that the notice had been served to her husband's lawyer. According to the records, no divorce case had been filed till now. The lawyers were waiting for the other party's reply.

The news that the divorce had not happened came as a shock to Sanam. Her mobile phone slipped out of her hand and unabashed tears started flowing down. Avinash had been watching her from his window. He grew worried at her reaction. He was wondering what had happened. Before he could do anything, Doctor Rajeev came out on the balcony and his Sanam flew into the Doctor's arms right away.

At the same time, Avinash received a call from Lawyer Mehta's son Shashank that Sanam had sent a Notice. Avinash was furious.

"That bastard! Mera divorce karwaya? Meri biwi hai….kisi aur ki nahin ho sakti! I will kill you Doctor Rajeev Kedia!" Avinash picked up the vase from the table and threw it across the wall and ran outside his home, down the stairs and towards the opposite building.

CHAPTER- 64

CONFRONTATION

It was four in the evening when Sanam, sitting in the swing with her laptop, was preparing the final draft of her novel when she received a phone call from the lawyer.

The lawyer told her that the notice had been served to her husband's lawyer. According to the records, no divorce case had been filed till now. The lawyers were waiting for the other party's reply.

"So, he hasn't divorced me? Why? Does he want me back? No...don't give yourself false hopes. False hopes die a painful death! Oh Fu*k!" Sanam's vision got clouded with tears. Her hands started trembling and the phone fell from her hands. She tried to put the laptop aside and stand but the laptop charger and the extension cord fell with a big thud. Her feet got entangled in the wires so carefully arranged earlier and now a mess that she couldn't get out of.

Rajeev had just gotten up and wanted to drink the 'Sanam special tea'. He had been knocking on the door for quite some time when he heard a big thud and opened her door without permission. The sound had come from the balcony. He reached the balcony to find Sanam entangled in a mess of wires and almost losing her balance, which she did eventually. It was fortunate,(or rather unfortunate...retrospectively) that he had been there to catch her.

"Sana what happened?" Rajeev asked, baffled by her lack of composure.

"Doctor...why is love so difficult and painful?" Sanam stood there in his arms and cried. There were times in life when every human being needed a shoulder to cry on...needed to be held. Sanam just wanted someone's support today.

"Sana what happened? Will you please tell me?" Rajeev just couldn't understand what had happened to make her cry so bitterly.

He took her inside and made her sit on her bed. She was trying to blabber something when he calmed her down. Rajeev had just about offered her water when the incessant door bell ringing pushed everyone over a precipice.

Avinash had been watching her from his window. He grew worried at Sanam's reaction to a phone call. He was wondering what had happened. Before he could do anything, Doctor Rajeev came out on the balcony and his Sanam flew into the Doctor's arms right away.

At the same time, Avinash received a call from Lawyer Mehta's son Shashank, that Sanam had sent a Notice. Avinash was furious.

"That bastard! Mera divorce karwayega? Meri biwi hai...kisi aur ki nahin ho sakti! I will kill you Doctor Rajeev Kedia!" Avinash picked up the vase from the table and threw it across the wall and ran outside his home, down the stairs and towards the opposite building.

He was furious like he had never been.

"I shouldn't have paid heed to what everyone said. I should have put her on my shoulders and taken off. Kuch din naaraz hoti, par mana leta. Yeh toh nahi dekhna padta!" Avinash was cursing himself as he ran towards her building.

Fortune favoured him as the lift door opened the moment he entered the foyer. The two or three minutes that the lift took to take him to the Dhindsa residence felt like eternity to him. Finally, he reached the floor and started ringing the bell.

The door was opened by the cook.

"Bittu kahan hai?" Avinash pushed the door to get inside.

"Aap kaun ho?" Mitali looked at him, startled.

"Avi?" Rajeev who had just come outside Sanam's bedroom spoke the rhetorical question.

"Nahin…teri maut!" Avinash growled and threw a punch at Rajeev's face…almost breaking his nose. Rajeev, though taken aback initially, dodged the second one and gave back a powerful punch which made Avinash lose his body balance and fall.

Daaku, who had just been brought back from his walk, still had his leash tied to the door, started barking ferociously. Mitali started screaming and Sanam came to the hall to see the two men at each other's throats.

"You betrayed me!" Avinash screamed at the top of his voice.

"No, I did not!" Rajeev screamed back, offended and angered.

"Avinash stop it!" Sanam tried to get into their fisticuffs.

"Doctor stop it!" Sanam tried to separate them only to push back. She banged into a cushioned stool, toppled over it and fell with a big thud losing her consciousness .

Both the men were so involved with each other that they hadn't realised Sanam had come near till she fell down.

"Saaaana….," Nani screamed. She had woken up with the commotion.

"Sana!" Rajeev screamed leaving Avinash.

"Sanam!" Avinash rushed towards her fallen figure.

Daaku, who had gone crazy barking, broke away his leash and charged towards Avinash.

"Daaku stay!" Rajeev commanded, making Daaku halt just in time.

"Daaku Sit!" Rajeev commanded again. Daaku, though in a rebellious mood, wasn't going to overrun Rajeev's command.

Rajeev and Avinash both bent down at the same time to pick Sanam.

"Meri Biwi hai!" Avinash growled at Rajeev.

"I know! But I am the doctor!" Rajeev answered back in a measured tone. Daaku growled again in the background.

"Sana…Montu kya hua?"Baba asked as he appeared at the door. The way Avinash had run out of the apartment, Bansi Kaka had woken up Baba, who was in the middle of his siesta.

"Take her inside!" Rajeev instructed Avinash.

"Mitali mera medicine bag lao!" Rajeev screamed at Mitali.

"Nani sit down before you fall. Sir...you too!" Rajeev addressed Baba.

"I am so sorry baby!" Avinash had put Sanam down and was still holding her hand.

"Avinash, I need to check her...move!" Rajeev told Avinash sternly.

Avinash had the good sense to move out and let Rajeev do his job.

"I think it's more of a shock than a physical injury! She should regain her consciousness in ten fifteen minutes!" Rajeev declared to everyone who was in the room.

"Mitali get ice-packs from the freezer!" Rajeev instructed as he moved towards Avinash.

"Sit down. Let me check you!" Rajeev told Avinash. Avinash stared back at him in shock.

"Hippocrates!" Rajeev said aloud. "It is my profession, let me do it!" he added.

Ten minutes later, everyone sat in silence in the hall. Rajeev and Avinash both were busy putting ice packs to different parts of their anatomy. Nani was busy giving bad looks to Avinash and Baba, respectively. Baba was trying to find a place to hide himself somewhere!

After a few minutes, they heard a murmur from Sanam's room. Sanam had gained consciousness.

Avinash was the first one to reach her.

"Baby!" Avinash cupped Sanam's face gently.

"Avinash?" Sanam looked into his eyes, taking a finger to trace the mark left from the accident.

"Are you real? You will leave me again when I wake up!" Sanam said in a dreamy voice. She was still in a daze. It was the after effect of the injection. She felt as if she had just woken up from a deep slumber.

"Sana are you in pain?" Rajeev asked her from afar. As Sanam looked at the Doctor's bleeding nose and Avinash's swollen-soon-turning-black-eye, she gasped in horror. The events of the evening came flooding back to her along with the realisation that it wasn't a dream. Avinash was indeed in front of her.

"Is it paining Sana?" Rajeev gestured to Avinash to move. Rajeev checked her pulse and pupils.

"Doctor, is it painful?" Sanam asked the Doctor softly.

"That you will tell me...touch where it hurts!" Rajeev replied.

"No, is your nose hurting?" Sanam asked Rajeev, making him break into a smile.

"Yes...but hopefully it will subside soon!" Rajeev said in a matter-of-fact manner.

Sensing the awkwardness around, Rajeev told everyone, "She needs to rest. Nani everyone needs tea. Please get Mitali to make some. Sir let's move out and talk." They all moved out of the room to give the couple some privacy.

"Avinash, make sure she doesn't get up from the bed!" Rajeev instructed Avinash as he shut the bedroom door.

"Baby," Avinash held her hand and kissed it. Sanam tried to take her hand back, but Avinash was persistent.

"Avinash please leave me alone!" Sanam said in anger.

"Baby, please I am sorry!" Avinash came near her to hug her.

"Avinash we need to talk first please!" Sanam told him.

"Theek hai! Bolo!" Avinash told her in a resigned tone.

"Leave my hand first!" Sanam said.

"Woh nahin hoga!" Avinash told her.

"MY HAND...and I want IT back!" Sanam said tersely.

"YOUR HAND...and you won't get it back," Avinash said, flashing his million-dollar smile. He feather kissed her hand again.

Sanam felt the familiar tingles in her body. She knew that a little more of Avinash's touch and she would melt away. But almost a year of suffering can't be forgotten in a weak moment.

"You can't let him walk all over you Sanam," she told herself.

"Ok...so we are done here!" Sanam said in a bitter tone remembering the way they had parted, his dalliance and her own subsequent loss of their child.

Avinash had observed the small smile that had played on her lips when he had refused to let go. Her mercurial change in mood caught him off-guard. He still held on as his body refused to let go of even one finger.

"Avinash, I am serious. Let go of my hand or I will call the Doctor! Don't think I am alone in this world!" Sanam said.

"There you go...happy?" Avinash hissed at the loss of contact.

"Can't she understand I am dying here for her!" Avinash asked himself.

"What was this all about?" Sanam asked.

"What? I love holding your hand baby...always have!" Avinash said sheepishly.

"Oh God Avinash...why did you hit the Doctor?" Sanam asked in an irritated tone.

"Biwi, we have met after almost a year, and you are asking me about the Doctor?" Avinash couldn't believe his ears that this was the most important question his wife had asked him after a year.

Sanam looked back at him in anger.

"I gave him what a guy should give a person who touches his wife!" Avinash said in an attitude.

"Are you mad?" Sanam asked in rage, getting up from the bed.

"Haan...I had become mad when I saw you run into his arms!" Avinash almost screamed.

"Avinash tum na...vaise ke vaise hi rahoge...arrogant and gadhe! Out now!" Sanam screamed at him.

"Acha Baby sorry! You didn't run into his arms...he hugged you!" Avinash tried to pacify her.

"Avinash, you are now a bigger asshole than ever before. I don't even feel like talking to you! Disgusting!" Sanam was now in tears. She went to the door and opened it.

"Out Mr. Avinash Shastri. I have no wish to talk to you," Sanam said, trying to hold back her tears.

In the hall, Rajeev, Baba and Nani were completely shocked at how quickly Avinash had managed to enrage Sanam to get thrown out of the room.

"Vaise for your kind information Mr. Avinash Shastri, I would have fallen had the Doctor not held me! You are a hypocrite of the nth degree...You keep Nitika, try to keep me on the side-lines and you have the audacity to ask me about a person who helped me out in my difficult time," Sanam screamed at Avinash.

"Baby… Nitika was never anything to me. I was going to confess to you then...but destiny didn't let that happen," Avinash tried to grasp her by shoulders, but Sanam had gone into the pain zone. The painful memories of her had started haunting her. Tears were falling unabashedly.

"Biwi, I went crazy after the Doctor sent me the Divorce notice. On top of it you fell into...yes you fell...I couldn't control my anger! I am sorry, meri Jaan!" Avinash almost pleaded in front of her.

"DIVORCE?" Rajeev asked, shocked at Avinash's accusation.

"Avinash please go now!" Sanam was now openly crying. She was finding it difficult to breathe.

"Sanam!" Avinash screamed as she fell down unconscious.

CHAPTER- 65

D.N.D

"Oh God... concussion!" Rajeev cursed under his breath and reached out for his medicine kit.

"When she got up...was she walking straight? Was she losing her balance?" Rajeev asked Avinash.

"She lost her balance a little!" Avinash replied.

"Did she appear dazed?" Rajeev asked him urgently.

"Yes!" Avinash replied.

Rajeev pulled out an injection and gave it to Sanam.

"She has a mild concussion! Don't worry by morning she will be fit and fine. Nani please don't worry," Rajeev told Nani who was about to cry.

"I don't want to take any risk...although I am sure it is a mild concussion, I still want to do a CT Scan to be sure," Rajeev addressed Avinash who nodded in return.

"We should take her to my hospital," Rajeev told them.

Nani looked pale and Baba made her sit down.

"She will be fine ...don't worry!" Rajeev told him as saw a fear in Avinash's eyes.

Driver had been asked to come near the lift. Avinash picked up his wife and they proceeded towards the lift.

"Dr. Indu we are coming through the back gate. Post someone there with a stretcher. Sana has a mild concussion possibly with an episode of Panic attack. Call Dr. Palash too...ok?" Rajeev instructed.

In some time, Sana had been taken for a CT scan.

Dr. Indu had taken a look at Rajeev and Avinash and declared both lucky to have escaped major injuries.

"Dr. Rajeev, the whole thing will take time. We will call you once she regains consciousness. And when Dr. Palash comes!" Dr. Indu told him.

"Come!" Rajeev took Avinash to his luxuriously minimalistic office.

"You work here?" Avinash asked him.

"Haan…from the last one and a half years! I am an investor in this hospital. I needed something to do in Pune while Sarah was undergoing treatment! My M.D. batchmate Dr. Indu and her husband Dr. Dheeraj- the ones we just met were looking for collaboration…this happened," Rajeev said.

"These files are Sana's…Sorry Sanam's. Nani started calling her Sana and we all followed," Rajeev said with a smile.

"What files are these?" Avinash asked him, puzzled.

"I have known Sana since the past three-four years. I used to volunteer at the Gurudwara, where Sana was a regular. Sana had a physical and mental breakdown soon after Nani collapsed in Nanded. She was a little suicidal too. Nani told me that she was contemplating jumping off the running train. Fortunately, Nani understood and pulled her back just in time," Rajeev told a shocked Avinash who had already had tears falling from his eyes.

"When I met her, she told me that you guys had mutually ended your marriage. I offered to intervene, she threatened to leave. I decided to wait for a few days before doing anything. I tried getting in touch with you, your phone was unavailable. In the following days she would often roam listlessly , not sleep properly, sit quietly and cry endlessly. She resisted the idea of therapy. When we shifted to Pune, I consulted Dr. Palash, a psychiatrist. We started giving her medicines to increase her dopamine levels. Daaku helped her a lot to come off the medicines," Rajeev said in a matter-of-fact tone. He halted for a few moments to give Avinash a little time to soak in the revelations.

"Avinash, I came to know about your accident pretty late. Almost after two months. Nani had been battling death. Neither Sana nor I had anything else on our minds. Once things were fine, I visited Mumbai to talk to you!

I was about to enter your home when I met Nitika on her way out. She was talking to someone telling how you valued her in your life. And how you were going to get engaged soon. I left from there. I was angry at you....furious. Maybe I should have met you that day. I would have saved you a lot of heartache. I am so sorry," Rajeev said apologetically.

"Nitika! How I had misjudged her! We came to know pretty late that she was trying to get mileage out of me . She plotted the pictures in the film teaser release too. I was too devastated to bother. She came near me just at the right time, got clicked by the media and made everyone believe her lies. By the time we could do something, she had spread the rumour of us being engaged. My mother had to threaten to expose her to make her stop," Avinash said in a voice that was full of remorse.

Rajeev then told Avinash about the panic attack at the movie theatre, the subsequent attacks and his own absence from the country.

"Did you guys not wait till credits? I had dedicated the film to her. Oh no! Bittu, I was the reason for her panic attack again. My one wrong decision wrecked both our lives," Avinash said distraught.

"Things are not so bad Avi! Sana is a fighter. She is slowly coming out of the whole thing. Will you believe it...she has even written a novel...it's soon going to be published!" Rajeev said with pride. His eyes shone in appreciation.

It was then that Avinash realised that his dear friend had fallen in love with his own wife. He suspected it wasn't a recent one.

"Bittu, remember when we met in Mumbai last year, you had come down to propose to a girl you had secretly loved for a long time. What happened to that?" Avinash asked casually.

"That did not happen! I have forgotten it. Love is not in my destiny!" Rajeev tried to answer calmly, putting his game face on. He tried to avert Avinash's gaze. However, Avinash with razor sharp observation caught the flexing of Rajeev's muscles.

" But what happened exactly?" Avinash harped on.

"Kuch nahi hua yaar...uski shadi ho chuki thee! Bas the end!" Rajeev said in a resigned tone.

"Toh...divorce bhi toh ho sakta hai? You could have done something!" Avinash went on sadistically, knowing he was hurting himself and Rajeev too, but he still wanted to push and twist the dagger in the wound.

"Uski shadi ho chuki hai...she is in love with her husband, not me and her husband loves her back. Why would I take away her happiness? How can someone else's wife be my lover? I can only wish that she stays happy forever with her husband!" Rajeev stared into his eyes, meaning every word he said.

The tension in the room was palpable. Slowly, Avinash's eyes grew heavy with moisture. Completely contrary to his personality, he felt sadness for his dear friend. From what he had seen in the past few hours, Rajeev had gone out of his way to keep his wife out of danger. He had done everything knowing that Sanam would never be his. He had been selfless. He always was. Rajeev had always been the deep one, selflessly helping everyone he could ...even when they were in their teens.

Avinash remembered one of Sanam's letters that she had written dated right after Dhruv had brought a cyclone in their lives...

Sanam,

Tumne haan kaise boli Dhruv ko? Kaise boli shaadi karti usse?

Avinash.

Her reply....

Dear Avinash,

Kisi se pyaar karna kya bura hai?

You didn't see the pain in Dhruv's eyes. His heart was breaking. He knew I would never be his...but my few words could have saved him from feeling worthless! Maybe his love was not love, but mere infatuation...still it amounted to something. I couldn't have forgiven myself if he did something to himself because of me.

I have never been loved. I have always craved love. I too am in a one-sided love with you Avinash. I know you will never love me back. I would give my life to hear from you that...

"I would have loved you Sanam had Nitika not come in my life first!"

Maybe not worthy of your love,

Sanam.

Today, Avinash truly understood what Sanam meant.

He had misunderstood a very nice person: Rajeev. His Sanam was so lovable that no one could resist falling for her. She had touched so many lives.

"Bittu...I am so sorry for today ! I misunderstood you! Please forgive me!" Avinash stood up and walked towards Rajeev. Both knew the apology wasn't only for the punch. Rajeev saw a genuine apology when he heard one. They hugged like they used to in college. With warmth and trust.

"May I come in Dr. Rajeev?" Dr. Palash came in.

Dr. Palash primarily reiterated what Rajeev had already told Avinash. However, he added something both Avinash and Rajeev had not considered.

"The event of a miscarriage in the first trimester is very common but there is no standard or uniform reaction. Every woman reacts differently to it. In Ms. Bedi's case, the mourning got prolonged because she had postponed her grieving for many years. She had been a small kid of ten years when her family passed away. The next moment she was thrown in the hands of cruel relatives and left to fend for herself. She never stopped and mourned for her loved ones. When she lost her child, in the unfortunate circumstances that we all are aware of, her loss got magnified. Her grief manifested in various ways. Now there is a theory that at times people going through a panic attack find it easier(unknowingly....subconsciously) to fall unconscious than actually facing the problem. I suspect that's the case here also. It is a very common way of our subconscious to save the person from inflicting more harm on oneself," Dr. Palash said.

"How can I help her?" Avinash asked Dr. Palash.

"Make her share her experiences...talk to her. Share your experiences ...that heals too. I hope Ms. Bedi recovers soon!" Dr. Palash said as he took leave.

"Ab jitna bhi gussa kare Sana, please tu usse mana lena! Don't break her trust now!" Rajeev advised Avinash.

"Yaar...ek aur panga hai...usse sambhalna hai!" Avinash said in a sullen tone.

"Kya?" Rajeev asked him.

"You know her novel? We are publishing it and I am her mentor! I have been talking to her from the last three weeks! Woh pakka maar dalegi!" Avinash said despondently.

"Tu kya?" Rajeev couldn't believe what he had heard. He just couldn't stop laughing.

"Oh fu*k! I want to laugh so much but it fu*king hurts! Dude…best of luck!" Rajeev howled in pain as he laughed.

"Waise, tum Shastris full planning ke saath aate ho hain?" Rajeev teased Avinash.

"Sir, your patient is awake!" the nurse knocked and announced.

"Chalo peshi lagne wali hai hamari! Best of luck to us! Sana ka 'Jhansi ki Rani' mode bahut khatarnak hai!" Rajeev said laughing.

"Tum log ne experience kiya?" Avinash asked good naturedly.

"Arre phir kisi aur din story sunaunga!" Rajeev laughed.

This was how Sanam saw the men enter…talking and laughing together. They had fallen into the same years old camaraderie. No one could have said they had been at each other's throat a few hours earlier.

"Sanam, dono ne ullu banaya tera…thoda attitude banta hai! Attitude de! Sanam told herself.

"Haye vaise Avinash kitna hot lag raha hai tracksuit main!" Sanam almost moaned. " Oye, stop drooling over him…stay strict!" Sanam scolded herself.

"Doctor, why is he here?" Sanam asked Rajeev.

Avinash stiffened at the question. "Biwi is not going to make it easy!" Avinash thought.

"Because I am the husband!" Avinash said.

"Isn't it too late to play husband?" Sanam was in no mood to let go.

"No… It's better late than never!" Avinash too put his foot down. They were back to their old selves. He was back to what he absolutely loved…teasing her…irritating her…riling her.

"Doctor, tell him to get out!" Sanam said, almost on the verge of tears.

"Avi, give us a few minutes please!" Rajeev said sternly to Avinash.

Avinash weighed his options and went out.

"Khush?" Rajeev asked Sanam.

"No Doctor. I am angry with you as well!" Sanam told him honestly.

Rajeev took a deep breath.

"Sana, had I told you that I know whose wife you are, would you have stayed back?" Rajeev asked her.

"No!" Sanam had the guts to face the harsh truth.

"I tried talking to you, you refused…shut me out!" Rajeev said.

"I am sorry Doctor. I truly am. I have never thanked you for what you did for me," Sanam told him.

"None required Sana. Just stay happy. That's the only thing that will keep Nani and me happy!" Rajeev told her.

"I don't know Doctor…I am so confused. So much has happened. I am feeling too many feelings at the same time. I am angry…confused…a little happy too!" Sanam bared her soul.

"That's it Sana…hold on to this feeling of happiness. Nothing else matters. You both are a few lucky ones who have found love! Why fight it?" Rajeev asked her.

"Love? I don't know if he loves me or not?" Sanam was still confused.

"Sana, this guy almost got crushed looking for you and you still question his love?" Rajeev said quietly.

"What? When?" Sanam started crying.

"It's ok…he is ok! Please don't cry!" Rajeev said.

"Should I send him in?" Rajeev asked her gently.

"Haan…" Sanam nodded.

Rajeev went out to see a pensive Avinash. "These guys will serve you both dinner and medicines in half an hour. Last call is at 10 p.m. The premium rooms have their own locks. In between the staff generally doesn't disturb the patients. Breakfast is at 6 a.m., make sure you open up by then," Rajeev teased Avinash who blushed and started scratching his head.

As Avinash entered the room, Rajeev shut the door and put a D.N.D sign outside. It said-

D.N.D - Do Not Disturb.

CHAPTER- 66
YOU'VE GOT MAIL

Avinash entered the room expecting an angry Sanam, but he was startled to see wife distraught and crying bitterly. His anger melted into concern.

"Baby what happened? Bittu ne gussa kiya?" Avinash asked her.

However, Sanam was too distraught to register anything.

"Baby...you are killing me..plea...," Before he could complete Sanam put her hand on his mouth.

"Marne ..ki...baat... mat... karna..." Sanam could barely manage to speak in between her tears.

"Hua kya hai? Meri Kasam ...say something...my heart is breaking watching you cry!" Avinash felt so helpless. They both had spent enough months apart crying, he didn't want to spend another moment in misery.

"Tumhari kasam ki wajah se hi I didn't even look you up for so long! Didn't even search you in Google! Kasam jo de ke gaye the tum! I just got to know that you had an accident!" Sanam said.

"Bittu told you? He shouldn't have... look at me...I am all right! See bacha!" Avinash gently cupped her face and came pretty close.

Sanam closed her eyes to feel the heaviness of his breath against hers.

"Open your eyes Jaan! Look at me!" Avinash commanded gently.

Sanam found herself doing exactly as Avinash instructed. She was again falling under his magical spell.

Avinash kissed her tear-stricken face gently.

"Dekh sweetheart, I am absolutely ok...Kuch jyada nahi hua tha" Avinash told her in between the feather kisses.

"Par hua kya tha?" Sanam demanded to know.

"Nothing much…It happened, It's over! Don't stress!" Avinash pacified her.

"Matlab tum nahi bataoge? Ok…I will search on the internet!" Sanam said, extending her hand for his phone kept on the side trolley.

"Nahin…Don't search it…don't ever search it. Kasam hai tumhe…I will tell you!" Avinash said in a resigned tone. He had wanted to save her from the pain. He had taken a promise from his mother too. The images online were pretty graphic in nature. Someone had taken the video off the CCTV camera of him getting hit by the garbage truck. The photographs of him on the hospital stretcher drenched in blood were very pretty horrific. Thankfully, his Uncle and cousins had made sure that those videos and photographs didn't reach his mother. But his father hadn't been so lucky. His father had seen the video and had been devastated for days.

Before Avinash could say anything further, a ward boy brought the food plates.

"Chalo first you eat something then I will tell you everything!" Avinash picked up one of the two beautifully cling film wrapped thalis that the ward boy had left.

Sanam giggled as she saw Avinash making a face at the contents of the thali.

"Itni sundar packing aur andar 'Lauki' and khichdi!" Avinash complained.

"Haan toh room premium hai….par phir bhi hai toh hospital…resort thodi na hai! Khana wahi aayega jo non-serious patients ko jata hai!" Sanam said.

"Chalo, let's eat!" Avinash kept the thali in front of her on the bed table.

"No…" Sanam nodded a no.

"Baby khana khaa varna ek din aur yahan rehna padega!" Avinash requested her.

"Nahin mere haath dard ho rahe hain…Can you feed me?" Sanam said dramatically.

Avinash's smile knew no end.

"Of course, Biwi!" Avinash said sitting along with her on the bed.

In the next half an hour Avinash fed her food just like he used to feed her at times when they were together. The doctor came in just when they were done with food.

Once they were done, Avinash locked the room.

"Room lock kar sakte hain?" Sanam gasped.

"Haan Bittu ne bola subah 6 a.m. tak kar sakte hain," Avinash told her as he climbed into her blanket. After so many months of separation, finally they were together...in one bed.

Avinash adjusted himself in the bed and collected her in his arms.

"Hmmm....you smell so good Biwi! Avinash moaned as pulled her more into himself, dipping his head into the deep valley of her breasts. He felt her body respond to his touch. She moaned and her skin broke into goosebumps. Then he lifted his head, and his lips found their way to her lips. They broke a while later for the lack of breath.

"You need to listen up first Baby! If I start, I won't be able to stop," Avinash told her.

"Who will ask you to stop?" Sanam smiled with a deep blush.

"Itna bhi kamina nahin hoon...ki biwi hospital main padi ho aur main uska fayda uthaun!" Avinash replied.

"Biwi hi keh rahi hai...fayda utha lo!" Sanam said with a smile.

"Not today Biwi! We need to talk. I need to tell you so many things," Avinash said as he pecked her lips quickly before he lost his control.

They lay with their legs entwined and she was resting her head on his shoulder like always. They both were just staring at each other, trying to take their fill after almost half a year of longing.

Avinash started with the sordid affair he had with Nitika Trehan and Rashi Patel, the bad press and the sexual misconduct charge framing incident. He gave her a quick recap of how the events had unfolded with him. The Saurabh-Meena frame-up and their confrontation. His New York visit and his meeting with Madhu and Rohan! Sanam had a lot of questions, but he wanted to offload everything. He briefly told her about the accident and his recovery. Sanam, who had been silently crying all along, broke down at the mention of his accident and surgeries.

For a long time, he just held her and kissed her tears. He knew what she was going through. Once, the tears subsided, he brought his lips down to her and kissed her till they both got breathless.

"And the biggest mistake I made was to wait for the right moment to tell you that 'I love you'! I wanted to make it really special for you baby...what I didn't realise was that the moment you say it, makes it special. Sorry Jaan! I could have saved both of us so much pain and suffering!" Avinash told her, leaving her shocked.

"Matlab, you love me?" Sanam asked to confirm what she had just heard.

Avinash banged his palm on his head. "Arre pagal aurat...itna sab ho gaya..itna sab bol liya..kyun? Because I love you baby! Apne dimag mein daal lo yeh baat! I-L-O-V-E-Y-O-U," Avinash said, pinning her down.

"Do you love me?" Avinash asked Sanam, facing her, pulling her more into himself.

"Hmmm.....soch ke bataungi!" Sanam said with a smile that went till her eyes.

"Mujhe tadpa rahi ho meri hot Punjaban! Bolo jo dil main hai!" Avinash cupped her head and mock threatened her, making her giggle more.

"Shastriji thoda toh sabar kijiye!" Sanam teased him.

"Biwi...I have waited my whole life to hear these words. I have yearned for someone, apart from my family, to tell me that she loves me selflessly. I don't want to die unlov...," Avinash's mouth was quietened by Sanam's lips.

"I love you Avinash! More than I have ever loved anyone. I love you so much that it hurts...it scares the life out of me. I have lost so much in life...I lost my...our baby Avinash! I don't think I can bear to lose you too!" Sanam broke down again.

"You won't Jaan! I love you and I am never going to leave you. I am sorry about our baby... can you forgive me for it?" Avinash lifted her chin and peeped into her moist eyes.

"It is not your fault Avinash...It was our destiny!" Sanam said.

"I swear, I won't let anything happen to us now baby! We will have loads of kids! Full football team!" Avinash said earnestly.

"Hai...full team? Matlab isi main hi mujhe busy rakhna hai?" Sanam asked innocently, making Avinash laugh.

"Jitne tu chahe baby! At least two...right?" Avinash said, making her smile.

"I love you Avinash!" Sanam said cupping his face and kissing his scar.

"I love you Baby!" Avinash said back. They kept pecking each other till they drifted into a content sleep.

By eight in the morning, Sanam was released. Rajeev's driver collected both of them from the hospital.

"Tum mayke aa rahi ho ya sasural?" Avinash smiled, not letting her hand go.

"I need to talk to Nani...she will be worried," Sanam told him.

"Woh meri 'Saas' hain yaa 'Hone wali Dadi' ? Just thinking!" Avinash teased her.

"Aviiinash!" Sanam cried, giving him NOT-in-the front-of-the driver looks.

"Aaj date kya hai? Oh! I had to go somewhere. Avinash I will meet you around 12 in the afternoon?" Sanam said while getting down from the car.

"Kahan jaa rahe ho?" Avinash asked her. He remembered that they hadn't talked about the novel.

"Nothing much. I will return and tell! Chalo bye!" Sanam said while entering the lift.

"Pakka, are you meeting me at lunch?" Avinash held her back and Sanam nodded.

"Where are you coming?" Sanam asked him as he entered the lift.

"Dropping you home Biwi!" Avinash said as he held her hand.

Sanam blushed and Avinash smiled.

"So, are you coming in?" Sanam gestured while exiting the lift.

"No...later!" Avinash said.

As Sanam turned to leave, he pulled her back and kissed her lips.

"Bye! See you soon!" Avinash said and jumped back in the lift as they heard the door being opened.

Sanam had a big smile when she entered her home. Nani was relieved to see her smile and blush.

"Kaisa hai tera husband! Did you guys sort it out?" Nani asked her and Sanam launched into the whole Saurabh-Meena set up and Avinash's accident. By that time Rajeev too had joined them at the breakfast table. They had breakfast together like a family.

"I need to meet my mentor Nani! For the novel. Is it ok if I go to Avinash's place after that?" Sanam asked shyly.

"Of course...husband hai woh tera pagal ladki!" Nani said laughing but her tone changed the very next minute.

"Ab tu bhi chali jayegi Sana?" Nani's eyes became moist.

"Zyada door nahin jayegi Nani...Rona nahin!" Rajeev scolded Nani.

"Sana, do you know this mentor?" Rajeev asked her tentatively.

"Actually, I am meeting him for the first time. It's in Starluck cafe! So, I guess it is safe in the crowd!" Sanam told him. Frankly, she was a little nervous now.

"It should be safe but still take Mushtaq Bhai along...I am at home. Just call me if anything goes wrong. And be careful!" Rajeev said, trying to maintain a straight face. He knew it was Avinash or else he would have never let Sana go alone.

Avi (the mentor): Fly, I hope you aren't breaking my heart today.

Sanam: Happy Birthday Sir! We will meet at 11a.m. Starluck cafe. Vimaan Nagar.

Sanam was ready in sky blue and pink patiala suit looking every bit of a cute Punjaban. She had tied her hair in a high ponytail . The infinity earrings and chain were back. She kept the mangalsutra in her bag. She wanted Avinash to tie it for her. After a long time Sanam felt happy and cheerful. She kissed Nani and left with the driver.

It was sharp eleven and Sanam reached the Cafe.

Sanam: Sir, I have reached the cafe. I am in a skyblue and pink punjabi suit.

Avi (the mentor): *No response*

Sanam had been waiting for the mentor to show himself when she saw something, and her heart skipped a beat.

Avinash entered the cafe dressed in his signature white kurta and blue acid washed jeans. He had his aviators on. He entered the cafe and approached her.

"Avinash, what are you doing here? You followed me? I told you I will come to you at 12 p.m. I am here for professional reasons! Please don't create a scene," Sanam said in a miffed tone.

"Biwi, whom are you meeting? I am not following you...I am here for a professional meeting too!" Avinash replied and took the table behind her, where his back would meet hers.

"Vaise abhi tak aya nahin tumhara 11 o'clock?" Avinash asked, teasing her. He knew he was playing with fire, but he was having fun irritating her.

"Aa jayega," Sanam said.

"Matlab ladka hai? Hot hai?" Avinash jumped in his seat.

"Respected hain!" Sanam replied.

"Naam kya hai?" Avinash asked her.

"Woh pata nahin...," Sanam replied.

"Toh tum blind date par aayi ho Biwi?" Avinash jumped from his seat and sat opposite to her.

"Avinash...irritate kar raha hai tu mujhe!" Sanam whined.

Sanam was at the edge of her patience. She mailed the mentor.

Sanam: Sir I have been waiting in the cafe for the last fifteen minutes and I am going to leave in five minutes if you don't arrive.

Avi (the mentor): Hi FLY! I am there but there is a 'Himalaya' type of person sitting at your table.

Sanam: Sir just come. It's ok. Please send me your picture so that I can recognise you!

Sanam received the chat on mail and looked around. There were a lot of people outside. She couldn't figure out who the mentor was. She got up and changed her table.

"Baby you've got mail!" Avinash tapped her shoulder.

Sanam opened her phone lock and saw that there was indeed a new mail in her inbox. It was from the mentor.

This is me FLY!

"How did you know Avinash that I had new mail?" Sanam asked Avinash.

Sanam's eyes widened in shock as the photograph of the mentor started downloading. It was her husband's.

"Tumne Sir ka phone churaya?" Sanam turned towards her husband.

"Avinash, please tell me you didn't hurt him. He was a nice guy! Hai kahin murder toh nahin kar diya tumne?" Sanam said in shock.

Of all the things he expected from his wife, this wasn't it.

"Abey Gadhi! Mentor main hi hoon!" Avinash stood up and told her.

"Matlab, I have been talking to you all this while?" Sanam asked him seriously.

"Haan Biwi! Surprised?" Avinash asked sheepishly.

Sanam looked at him keenly at first and then slapped him across the cheek and walked away, leaving pin-drop silence in the cafe and a shell-shocked Avinash behind.

CHAPTER- 67
SLAPGATE

It took a minute for Avinash to realise that she had slapped him and walked off.

"She is my wife!" Avinash spoke aloud for the benefit of the crowd.

"Biwi! Sanam!" he ran behind her.

By this time Sanam had already taken off in her car. Avinash quickly sat in his car and followed her. He tried ringing her phone, but Sanam didn't respond.

"Sana what happened?" Rajeev and Nani were alarmed when Sanam walked in crying.

"Nani, Avinash ne mujhe dhoka diya!" Sanam howled in Nani's lap.

"Kya? Uska affair hai? I will kill him!" Nani, who was already angry with Shastri bandhus, claimed in anger.

"Nahin….affair nahin…woh hi mentor hai! Baba and Avinash cheated me!" Sanam spoke between hiccups.

Rajeev heaved a sigh of relief. For an instant he had forgotten to breathe thinking something untowardly had happened with Sana.

"Avinash should have handled it! God knows what went wrong between them again!" Rajeev thought.

A while later the incessant door bell ringing announced Avinash's entry. Daaku, as always, went crazy barking. Rajeev went to the door after tying Daaku.

"Yaar Sanam kahan hai? Bahut gussa hai?" Avinash asked Rajeev who chuckled in a yes.

"Mar gaya yaar!" Avinash swore.

"Sanam...You completely misunderstood the whole thing...please give me a chance to explain!" Avinash rushed in.

"Jo baat hogi sabke samne hogi! What have the Shastris been up to?" Nani said in anger.

"Avinash this was my one achievement of my life or so I thought...It was sacrosanct. Baba and you violated it!" Sanam said tersely, trying hard to stop her tears.

"Sanam, how have we violated it?" Avinash was unable to understand.

"Avinash, full chu@@ya kata hai mera! That's why you were laughing at me today in the cafe today!" Sanam replied in anger.

"Language Sanam! And is this what you think of me? Main aisa karunga tere saath?" Avinash was now completely irritated.

"I don't want to talk about it!" Sanam stood away from him.

Avinash tried to catch her arm but Sanam, who was clearly pissed, evaded it.

"Why don't you want to talk to me? Tujhe laga toh ho gaya kya? Tere lagne par duniya chalti hai kya?" Avinash said in an irritated tone.

Nani had been standing there observing how Avinash was getting louder and louder in his tone and actions. At last, her control snapped and she turned towards Avinash. Suddenly a stinging slap came and landed on Avinash's cheeks.

"Nani Please!" Rajeev, who till now was enjoying the show, suddenly got into action. Sanam and Avinash looked shocked.

"Dadi yeh kis liye tha?" Avinash asked softly once he came out of the shock. Although he didn't know what had brought this on, he had the decency to look remorseful.

"Nani! This was for screaming at my daughter, making her cry and playing the Pungi song!" Nani said succinctly.

"Avinash tu chal abhi...I will talk to Sanam!" Rajeev again had to unwittingly play the role of referee between the couple.

"Sorry Nani! Sorry Sanam!" Avinash apologised to the women.

"Sorry Sanam, tere Avinash ko thappad laga diya! Kitni badtameezi se baat kar raha tha!" Nani told Sanam, who giggled in return.

"Maine bhi laga diya aaj cafe main!"Sanam told chirpily to Nani who giggled in return.

"Is ghar ki auraten pagal ho gayi hai! Mitali chai le kar aayo! Now you women need to cool down!" Rajeev scolded the women.

"Doctor Sahib garam chai se dimag thanda kaise hoga?" Sanam chirped in and both the women giggled again.

Rajeev banged his palm on the forehead. "Mitali lassi le kar aao!" Rajeev called out.

"Nani, why did you have to slap Avi?" Rajeev asked Nani.

"No one talks to my daughter like this!" Nani jumped to her own defence.

"Nani...woh Avinash hai...ek sur upar main baat karta hai! Aadat hai...he doesn't mean to offend!" Rajeev explained.

"That said and done...I will still ask him to control himself!" Rajeev said.

"Now Sana what happened?" Rajeev asked her who launched into her version.

"But did you ask him why? Wait, did you give him a chance to explain himself?" Rajeev asked pointedly.

"No...he was laughing at me!" Sanam said.

"Sana, was he laughing at you or was he just laughing? Tumhare aas paas hote hi he starts smiling ear to ear without any reason! Daaku se khud ko katwa bhi liya...now at least spare that idiot!" Rajeev said smiling.

Sanam broke into a deep blush.

Suddenly, they all heard a song playing on full blast...

Anna mere pyar ko na tum jhootha samjho jaana...

Everyone looked at each other and burst into laughter.

"Yeh tumhara Romeo gaana baja raha hai?" Rajeev asked Sana in a serious tone.

Sanam nodded and blushed again. Rajeev broke into laughter again.

"Cartoons ho tum dono!"Rajeev said. Meanwhile, Avinash played another song...

Dard-E-Dil.. Dard-E-Jigar Dil Mein Jagaya Aapne,

"Ab mood theek karo and chalo let me drop you at his place! Varna tum logon ki love story breaking News ban jayegi!"Rajeev teased Sanam, whose blush intensified.

"Aur Nani yeh 'Pungi song' ki story kya thee...we will talk when I return!" Rajeev told Nani, catching her blush in time.

Avinash was at his telescope trying to figure out what was happening in the Dhindsa household, when in time he caught Rajeev and Sanam walking towards his building.

"Love you Bittu!" Avinash exclaimed.

"Baba...Baba...woh aa rahi hai...chalo aap jao abhi!" Avinash came to request his Baba to leave the house to give them some privacy.

"Arre Montu main kahaan jaunga?" Baba teased him.

"Hilton main suite book karwa diya hai ! Maine Dadi ka thappad khaya na aap ke liye?" Avinash also knew how to get things done from his beloved grandfather.

"Chal hat Badmash!" Baba slapped him deeply, blushing at the word 'Dadi'.

On cue, the doorbell rang, and Avinash took only a moment to open the door.

"Hi...welcome!" Avinash said enthusiastically, which was so funny and goofy that even Sanam, who had vowed to give him an attitude, started laughing!

"Bitiya, I am sorry!" Baba apologised to Sanam as she came inside.

"Baba please! Main naraz toh hoon but it's ok!" Sanam hugged Baba.

"Bitiya, woh tumhari Nani?" Baba gathered enough courage to ask her.

"Bahut guesse main hai...thappad wale mood main! Doctor abhi hospital jayenge, app jaa kar mana lena!" Sanam whispered in his ears.

Meanwhile, Rajeev was advising Avinash,"Bhai ab suspense bas kar...sab kuch clearly bol dena! Badi mushkil se maani hai!" Rajeev told Avinash.

"You are the best Bhai!" Avinash told Rajeev.

"Beta, I will come along with you to apologise to Pammi...i.e., Mrs. Dhindsa!" Baba told Rajeev and took him out of the flat followed by Bansi Kaka.

Finally, they were alone in the house.

"Ghar nahin dikhaoge?" Sanam said sarcastically.

"Haan...of course!" Avinash took her towards his room and bolted the door once they entered.

"Wow!" Sanam said as she entered his room. She was astounded by the sheer size of it. It had been made by joining two bedrooms. In the middle was a huge bed. In one corner lay the Drums and the other corner a huge writing table and next to the table stood a huge telescope.

"Avinash tumnen sab kuch kal kyun nahi bataya?" Sanam asked.

"Woh kal tum alag zone main thee...I knew you would get angry once I told you and I wanted to hug you and sleep!" Avinash whined away.

He looked so amazingly cute that Sanam struggled to keep a smile off her face but there was no denying the fact that his actions had hurt her.

"So, you guys had this entire elaborate plan to trap me from all sides....You must have been laughing na...bechari Sanam so stupid! Hum is ki Chut#$a bana rahe hain..usko pata bhi nahin!" Sanam said. Sanam words dipped in sarcasm had hit the mark.

"Kya karta...mujhe dekh kar toh tu behosh ho gayi! Not once, but twice! What should I have done? You know what ? You are right! I should have picked you up and put across my shoulders and taken you away. I thought I have always behaved like an asshole with you, let me behave sensibly! But look at you...tum husband ka thodi na sochogi...tumhe toh Drummer ki kitni chinta hai...making food for him...roz naya...naya...pyaar se...uske gaane ka wait ho raha hai! On the other hand, you are crying away for that Mentor! Avinash...kahin murder toh nahin kar diya tumne?" Avinash mimicked the last line.

"Aur tum...anjaan auraton ka mentor ban ke sara din sex..sex..sex ki baaten karte ho! You knew my type...you knew my weakness...you exploited it!" Sanam counter attacked. She was now angry.

"You have a type?" Avinash exclaimed.

"Apparently! My type is tall, handsome and one who exploits others' emotions! It's my birthday FLY...don't leave me alone!" Sanam mimicked Avinash now.

"Sanam hurt sirf tu hi nahin hui hai...main bhi hua hoon! Kaise tumne bola...our relationship was purely physical?" Avinash asked in anger.

"So, it wasn't only physical? Did you share your emotions with me? Then too you would always be stuck between my legs , today also your eyes are somewhere else.....you are talking to me, but your eyes are resting on my breasts!" Sanam huffed in fury.

"So, what do you expect? Itne mahine ke sookhe ke baad if you get magnificent melons what will a person do? Insaan ho main...I am a human Biwi! You can lust after the Drummer, but I can't lust after my own wife?" Avinash replied in sheer frustration.

Sanam lost her temper and brought a stinging slap again on her husband's cheeks. They both stared at each other, but their eyes were full of passion instead of anger. Their verbal battle had in a perverse way acted as foreplay. Both were highly aroused. The next moment Avinash covered the physical distance between them and brought his lips to hers for a searing kiss. Sanam kissed him back with equal passion.

His hands cupped her ample breasts and Sanam moaned in satisfaction. Avinash pulled the chords of her salwar and brought it down with her panties. He picked her and took her to the huge table.

"Avinaash...I need you! NOW! "Sanam said in between her moans. Avinash didn't have the patience to take his and her lowers completely, so he just lowered them and spread her legs. He pushed her kameez up to knead her supple and perky breasts.

"Gosh you are so wet Baby!" Avinash said in a raspy voice as he thrust deep inside her. Sanam screamed in ecstasy as he drove her harder.

"We are fu*king good together Baby!" Avinash said as they came over the edge together and fulfilled each other in more ways than one.

CHAPTER -68
PREM PUJARI

A lot later, Sanam and Avinash lay naked under the fluffy duvet, in each other's arms grinning and smiling away...just being there with each other was exhilarating.

"Biwi...bhook lagi hai!" Avinash spoke when his stomach growled breaking the blissful silence

"Mujhe bhi! Kya banaun?" Sanam tried to get up to go to the kitchen, but Avinash was not ready to leave her.

"Mat jao mujhe chod kar Baby!" Avinash said in a baby tone.

"Par tumhe hi toh bhook lagi hai!" Sanam tried to reason out with him.

"Chalo...tum bhi chalo! Akele bore hoga mujhe!" Sanam said as she got up.

"Avinash mujhe apna T-shirt de na...mera favourite suit toh gaya!" Sanam said looking at the fabric of her kameez that lay torn to shreds by her over-enthusiastic husband.

"Chalo...we both need a bath," Avinash lifted his wife and took her to the bathroom. Sanam had been so thoroughly loved that she was in no condition to stand straight. Sanam purred like a lazy cat when Avinash soaped her under the shower.

"Biwi, you are sore...don't excite me with your moans now! I am running low on control," Avinash warned his wife who was making the most erotic sounds while being bathed. Finally, Avinash wrapped her in a fluffy navy-blue towel and brought her out and placed her in his favourite chair.

"You look like a wet cat Sanam!" Avinash whispered in her ears and pecked her lips.

"You look like a wet...wet...wet...Lion!" Sanam whispered back.

"By the way Biwi you need to do lunges and kegels to strengthen your core!" Avinash said.

"Now you look like a wet...wet...wet...khadoos Shastri!" Sanam pouted, cracking up Avinash.

Avinash brought something out and kneeled down and stretched her leg on his knees. Avinash brought out the anklets he had bought for her before destiny had torn them apart. Sanam felt something cold touching her ankles.

"These were always for you Sanam! Mrs. Sanam Avinash Shastri! You have no idea how you complete me! Please don't ever leave me! I am not staying another moment without you Baby!" Avinash said kissing her payals.

Sanam didn't have any words to express the overwhelming love she was feeling for him. She threw herself into his arms and cried.

They would have been at it had Avinash's stomach not growled again loudly.

"Ab toh kuch khilana padega!" Sanam kissed him and got up to take out his T-shirt. As she opened his huge wardrobe, she was pleasantly surprised.

The only saree she had owned hung next to his kurtas and T-shirts. Her kurtis and other stuff lay neatly stacked next to his clothes.

"I told you I can't survive without you!" Avinash said as he hugged her from behind. Sanam shed silent tears as she realised just how much loneliness and pain Avinash must have undergone in her absence. For the first time since had entered his room, she actually turned around and observed carefully. The maroon colour mixer that she loved, sat at the corner of his bedside table. A smile came to her face when she saw the mixer again reminding her of the sweet incidents that were related to the gadget. The sound bar she so used to love sat mounted on the opposite wall.

"Biwi chalo, wear this and let's eat!" Avinash put a T-shirt on her and took her to the kitchen. He himself had settled for grey colour shorts sans the T-shirt.

Bansi Kaka had been disturbed in the process of making an elaborate lunch. He had been able to boil the dal, boil potatoes, cut bhindi and soak rice. Fortunately, Sanam was able to find a loaf of bread and a big chunk of paneer.

Creativity struck and she quickly made aloo-paneer sandwiches with hot elaichi tea.

"Gosh I missed your tea so much!" Avinash exclaimed as he washed the sandwiches down with tea. They both ate from one plate just like the old times. Once done, Avinash refused to give her even a minute to clean up and put things in the refrigerator.

"Avinash sab khana kharab ho jayega!" Sanam whined as Avinash lifted her and carried her to the bedroom. He threw her on the bed and climbed in, putting his leg across her body.

"Hmmm....Avinash neend aa rahi hai! Thak gayi hoon main!" Sanam said when he started tracing the curve of her bottoms with his fingers. She purred loudly and turned her back to him and let him spoon her.

Suddenly, something caught Sanam's attention, and she gasped. Sitting on the bedside table, there was an old familiar cookie tin box

"You read my letters?" Sanam asked him in shock. She got up and sat at the edge of the bed. Her eyes got moist as she picked up the box and gently traced its outline.

Avinash got up from the bed and walked up to the other side. He kneeled in front of her and offered his cheek, confusing Sanam.

"Kya?" Sanam asked him, baffled.

"Ab tum thappad marogi, toh tum utho nahin...here is my cheek!" Avinash surrendered.

Sanam grinned amidst her tears and kissed him on his cheeks several times till he growled and took to her lips. They broke the kiss a while later to breathe. She placed the box back on the table and hugged him as they stretched again.

"Baby...I am sorry!" Sanam said.

"Huh...kyun?" Avinash asked her in a surprised tone.

"Woh I slapped you na...that too In front of everyone!" Sanam said remorsefully.

"Forget it! I also was teasing you! Don't think about it baby!" Avinash said softly.

"Nani ne bhi laga diya..Sorry about that too! Tumhe bura laga hoga na?" Sanam asked.

"Bura...laga but thodi der ke liye! Then, I thought from her point of view. She loves you so much Sanam, that I have seen it with my own eyes. And honestly, I was irritable and aggressive. A person who witnesses my temper for the first time, will definitely think the worst about me. I mean if someone were to talk to my daughter like that, in front of me I would have definitely slapped him...maybe more than that. Also, the 'Pungi' song was kind of demeaning...at such an age, to hear this shit! I was in a mastivala mood, so I played it but still. In the past few days, I have insulted her with an offensive song, entered her house and beaten up her grandson, and screamed at her daughter. Toh ek thappad toh banta hai!" Avinash said, emotionally overwhelmed. He vowed that he would profusely apologise to Nani and set things right.

"You know Avi, Nani is not bad," Sanam then told Avinash about Nani's story: right from the beginning to their co-incidental meeting in the train. She also told him about the days that followed her own departure from Mumbai. They talked and talked, telling each other anecdotes from the past, their hopes and dreams.

"Arre wait, I forgot one thing!" Avinash said with a start and went towards his writing table to pull out a blue circular box with 'Cookies' written on it.

"Avinash abhi toh khana khaya...I can't eat cookies now!" Sanam said amidst her yawns.

"Abey cookies nahin hain...dekh toh sahi!" Avinash said shyly.

Sanam opened the blue circular box to find letters neatly stacked inside, addressed to Sanam by her Avinash.

"Mere samne mat padhna, main jab jaunga tab padho!" Avinash said.

"You will leave me?" Sanam was distraught.

"Absolutely not...I meant when I am not around...example when I go to take a bath!" Avinash said grinning.

"Acha toh bol kar batao na...please...You are in front of me, please tell me what you have written in these letters!" an emotionally overwhelmed Sanam urged Avinash.

Avinash went quiet for a few moments, pulled her closer and then started humming a song from the movie 'Prem Pujari'…

Phoolon Ke Rang Se,

Dil Ki Kalam Se,

Likhi Roz Paati…

CHAPTER- 69
CONVERSATIONS

The love birds were woken up by the sharp shrill of the mobile phone.

"Haan Baba...everything is fine, please don't worry! How was your date?" Avinash chuckled good naturedly.

"Ok..bye!" Avinash hung up.

They had gone off to sleep sometime in the evening after talking for hours. It was almost eleven in the night. Sanam too had freshened up while Avinash was on the call.

"Baba the? Kya keh rahe the?" Sanam asked Avinash as they again snuggled up into each other in the duvet.

"Nothing much..he just wanted to enquire if we were fine! If things were sorted! I said all was well! In fact, very well!" Avinash said.

"Avinash!" Sanam said in a serious tone.

"Bol baby!" Avinash replied.

"Ab hamara kya hoga?" Sanam asked tentatively.

"Kya hoga? Matlab? We are already married, and married couples stay together. Baby, I can't live without you!" Avinash sat up with a start. His heart was almost in his mouth.

"Avinash...Nani, Doctor and Daaku are my family now! I can't leave them!" Sanam told Avinash upfront.

"Toh baby I am not asking you to leave them. We will work out something. We can stay here. I will shift my work here. Then you can visit Nani whenever you want. I swear baby I will not take you away from her! Just be with me," Avinash said all in one go. The fear of losing her was apparent on his face.

"And you can't beat the Doctor again!"Sanam told him sternly.

"Arre sirf maine hi nahin mara, tere Doctor ne bhi kitne zor se mara hai! It is still hurting Baby!" Avinash said dramatically.

"Aww...mera bacha!" Sanam kissed his blackened eye and was soon pulled into a deeper kiss by her husband.

Their kiss was broken by the doorbell.

"Kaun hoga?" Sanam held the duvet closer.

"Pizza sweetheart!" Avinash jumped into action.

Once they were done with the Pizza, Sanam got up to throw the box into the dustbin and tidy up the room.

Avinash was checking his phone when he heard a sharp gasp.

Sanam was bent over the telescope.

"Fuck!" Avinash muttered waiting for her to explode in anger but instead he was surprised by her naughty giggle.

"Hwww....Avinash!" Sanam gasped and giggled again as she bent and saw the view of her own balcony.

"Matlab tune sab dekha?" Sanam asked him shyly.

"Haan baby! Sab dekha!" Avinash pulled her to him on the bed and switched his position to be on top of her.

"Amma! Main toh curtain bahut baar band nahin karti thee!"Sanam said softly.

"Uske liye thanks baby...that just made my life borderline bearable!" Avinash kissed her softly.

"Nani chai!" Rajeev entered with a tray with two cups of tea. Daaku had tagged along too, wagging his tail.

"Arre Ladoo...tu kyun laya? Sana abhi uthi nahin? Is she fine?" Nani said ruefully before she remembered that Sana was no longer there. Silent tears slipped down her eyes.

"Don't cry Nani! We both knew she was going back to her husband someday!" Rajeev said gently.

"I know Ladoo…but it's so damn difficult to let go!" Nani cried.

"Bas kal se under-eye circle aagaye hain aapke…Anita aunty will spread this news far and wide!" Rajeev told her.

Not able to control herself, Nani laughed.

"Sit down Ladoo…I need to talk to you!," Nani said. They both sat down and had their tea.

"How are you feeling beta?" Nani asked Rajeev.

"A lot better Nani! The swelling is completely gone. The tenderness will go away in one or two days!" Rajeev touched his nose while talking.

"Good. And your heart?" Nani enquired gently.

"What about my heart Nani? I am a Cardiologist for heaven's sake! I am fit and fine!" Rajeev replied, clearly avoiding eye contact with Nani.

"Nani hoon teri! Woh dil kaisa hai jo Sanam ke liye…," Nani could barely manage to say.

"Nani…what are you saying? She is married!" Rajeev interrupted his grandmother before Nani could complete her sentence.

"I know Ladoo, and you have never crossed your limits, I know that too!" Nani said with a sigh.

"You think I didn't know that when Sana would howl in her room at night, you would pace the corridor outside. I know why you brought Daaku in this house, just the same way I knew when you beat up those disgusting boys who made a pass at her. I have known this all along…just didn't interfere. Unfortunately, I also knew that Sana was so into her husband that she wouldn't even look at someone else ever again. I could see you fighting with yourself every day, pining for love that will never be yours. You were doing a good job pretending you didn't care for her. I didn't say anything because I didn't want to embarrass you," Nani said.

"Then why today?" Rajeev asked. His eyes were of unshed tears.

"Today because I am going to ask you something which I know you will give, but it will put you through a lot of pain!"Nani told him with a lot of anguish in her voice.

"Ask away Nani!" Rajeev said.

"Sana and Avinash were married in a ceremony which was nothing but an obligation. I want to get them married again...properly this time. Your mother and father had a court marriage. I kept on requesting him for a Gurudwara wedding, but he didn't pay heed. When Sarah got engaged, I had thought I would get her married with traditions...sangeet, mehendi...par meri bachi...aise hi chali gayi!"Nani broke down.

Rajeev got up and sat in bed right beside her.

"Ladoo, watching Sana getting married is going to be painful for you!" Nani said.

"Nahin Nani...I will be happy if she is...and she actually is. What pains me is that why doesn't someone love me? I am not worthy of love? Will I never be loved?" Rajeev broke down in his Nani's lap. He had addressed his feelings after a long, long time. He clung to Nani for a long time.

Once Rajeev recovered, he sat up and said, "Go ahead Nani...We will get Sana and Avi married with aplomb this time!"

"Ladoo vaise ek baat bolun?" Nani called him as he got up to leave.

"Bolo!" Rajeev said, trying to read his grandmother.

"Ek tarfa pyaar ki taqat hi kuch aur hoti hai ... Auron ke rishton ki tarah yeh do logon mein nahi batti ... Sirf aapka haq hai ispe Rajeev Babu!" Nani delivered the dialogue from the famous movie with required emotions.

"Yucks Nani.....hahaha! Kitna cheesy tha!" Rajeev exclaimed and laughed till his jaws ached.

It was ten in the morning when the doorbell of the Dhindsa residence rang making Daaku dance ecstatically.

Rajeev had called a few minutes back to invite the couple to breakfast but didn't have to because as Avinash informed him...they were already on their way to their place.

"Daaku sit down!" Rajeev called sternly and Daaku, who completely adored Rajeev, had to oblige.

"Daaku...mera Shona Baby!" Sanam exclaimed the moment Rajeev opened the door. Daaku, still in compliance, sat there, wagging his tail vigorously and sticking out his tongue expectantly. He continued to look at Rajeev trying to get out of the stern order his master had just passed.

"Ook..Daaku!" Rajeev said, exasperated at being manipulated by a mere pooch.

That was all that Daaku needed. He jumped on Sana, licking her face and dancing excitedly around her. A while later everyone burst into laughter when they found Daaku giving a low-key growl to Avinash when Avinash tried pulling Sanam towards himself.

The breakfast, although had started awkwardly, went smoothly after a few false starts.

Avinash and Rajeev kept the conversation flowing, though Nani was still a little frosty towards Avinash.

Nani asked Sana to go into her room.

"Sana, I need to talk to you husband. Send him to the study!" Nani said sternly once done with the breakfast.

Sanam got a little nervous as Avinash followed Nani in the study.

"Doctor kya hoga?" Sanam asked Rajeev nervously.

"Kuch nahi hoga...dono dramebaaz hai!" Rajeev smiled and Sanam relaxed. Although they were already married, Sana still felt like Nani's nod meant a lot to her. She desperately wanted her husband and Nani to have a good rapport.

Avinash entered the huge study where Nani sat in an imposing chair.

"Hi Nani!" Avinash said nervously.

After the conversation with Sanam and his Baba yesterday, Avinash had understood that Nani had become extremely important to his family. Baba had been heartbroken after Nani had given him a cold shoulder. Avinash had vowed that he would do anything to get into Nani's good books. He was so nervous that he had bitten the finger along with the nail.

"Are you still hungry?" Nani asked Avinash.

"What? No..I am full thankyou!" Avinash replied.

"Toh nails kyun khaa rahe ho!" Nani asked cryptically.

"Shit...Oops sorry! I am feeling very nervous! I do this when I am nervous!"Avinash said apologetically.

"Pata hai!" Nani said.

"Kaise?" Avinash asked, surprised.

"You have taken after someone I know very well!" Nani said with a warm smile. The moment she realised she was smiling; she dropped it and took on a stern expression.

"If you know that then you would also know that he is miserable now!" Avinash silently implored.

"I don't like liars!"Nani said brusquely.

"He never lied. He only omitted to mention a few uncomfortable truths. Kumar is indeed his middle name. My nickname is Montu. And I indeed had a nervous breakdown when Sanam left me. I had literally stopped eating in that period. It was all true,"Avinash said.

"Hmm...you make a compelling case!" Nani said in a contemplative mode.

"His love for me has always made him do highly inappropriate things!" Avinash said.

"Like what?" Nani sat up in her chair.

"Like lying to you! Trust me he has felt guilty every single day!"Avinash told Nani.

"And flirting is the expression of guilt?"Nani asked him pointedly.

"Hmmm...you make a compelling case here!" Avinash said.

A small smile played on Nani's face.

"I need to tell you something...Sana was completely broken when you guys separated. I don't want that to ever happen again. Please don't think she is alone in this world. This house is always open for her. I am warning you if you ever hurt her again, I will murder you!" Nani said in a threatening tone, opened a drawer, took out a shining handgun and kept it on the table.

Of all the things Avinash had expected, this hadn't been one of them. For a moment, his face lost colour. His vision went from Nani to the handgun and back to Nani when he finally caught the mirth in Nani's eyes. And all of a sudden, Nani broke into a fit of laughter.

"Got you...Khaali hai!" Nani was shaking with laughter. Rajeev and Sanam were waiting in the drawing room when they heard peals of laughter coming from the study. They both rushed to the study to find Nani in a fit of laughter and Avinash standing lost...still trying to come to terms with what had happened.

"Don't tell me Nani!" Rajeev picked up the gun and burst into laughter. Sanam too joined them hugging Avinash who was trying to laugh and get over the embarrassment. The expression on his face was....priceless!

"Nani had got this gun from Punjab when she had left with my mother! Since then, she has been threatening people with this empty gun. At that time, she used to threaten leering men who would approach her with indecent proposals. In recent years, she has brandished it at the Sabziwala, the laundry wala and the latest victim 'Sana ka Gharwala!'" Rajeev said laughing.

"Nani darr gaya mera bechara husband!" Sanam complained.

"Sorry Avinash beta...Is prank ke liye bhi aur kal ke thappad ke liye bhi!" Nani got up and hugged Avinash.

"I know you will keep my daughter happy! I have seen her happiest with you! Mitali mirchi laa..nazar utarni hai dono ki!" Nani pulled Avinash's cheeks and kissed Sanam.

"Hamesha khush raho tum dono! God bless you!" Nani blessed them when the couple touched her feet.

"Aur tu aise kyun hai? Chal parlour jaa...tere sasural wale aa rahe hain aaj..tera rishta le kar!" Nani chuckled.

"Hai sachi?" Sanam asked Nani astounded. The moment had come for Sanam to meet her in-laws and she, like every other girl, got extremely nervous.

"Avinash's mother just called up before you came! We are going to have a wedding!"Nani clapped in excitement.

"Ammma" was all Sanam could utter.

CHAPTER- 70

CHEATING

It was four in the afternoon when the Shastris reached the Dhindsa residence.

Avinash accompanied the entire Shastri entourage along with Bansi Kaka to the Dhindsa residence. Avinash's mother and father were the only ones who hadn't met Sanam, and they were very eager to meet her.

Rajeev opened the door and greeted them by touching their feet.

"Arre Rajeev, how are you beta?" Karuna asked Rajeev.

The two years Rajeev had been in Mumbai to prepare for his medical, Avinash had been preparing for his engineering. During this time, Rajeev and Avinash had become thick friends co-studying and hanging around. Most of their group used to hang at Rajeev's rental bachelor pad but Rajeev remembered the few times he had gone to Avinash's home for food and was given a warm welcome by Karuna. She had taken care of him like a surrogate mother. She often used to send food for Avinash and the boys at the bachelor pad.

"It's so nice to see you again aunty!" Rajeev bent down to take blessings.

Alok didn't let him touch his feet, he hugged Rajeev. The tall, lanky and shy boy that he had seen almost two decades earlier had grown to be a handsome man.

"Kamaal hai! Rajeev humare Avinash ka friend tha mujhe kabhi pata hi nahi chala! Kismet bhi kya cheez hai...jise milana hota hai, mila deti hai!" Baba said, turning towards Nani, who had just arrived. His heart fell when Nani gave him a cold shoulder again, but his heart sang when he noticed a small smile play on her lips a moment later.

"Yeh meri Nani hain! Mrs. Paramjeet Kaur Dhindsa!" Rajeev introduced as Nani entered the drawing room.

Avinash's parents bent to take her blessing.

"Thank You so much for taking care of our daughter!" Karuna joined her hands together in front of Nani. Nani just smiled and hugged her.

"Sanam kahan hai?" Karuna looked around expectantly. Her eyes searched for the girl who had already made a place for herself in Karuna's heart.

"She must be getting ready. Thodi nervous hai! Avinash jaa apni heroine ko lekar aaja uske room se!" Nani chuckled and looked at Avinash who was looking around for Sanam too.

Avinash jumped as if he was waiting for someone to mention this and went towards her room.

Sanam had heard the doorbell and was waiting for someone to call her out. Suddenly, Avinash barged in with a bang and scared Sanam.

"Amma...you scared me! " Sanam whined.

Avinash froze as he laid his eyes on her. He had asked her to wear the mint green floral printed chiffon saree that he had bought for her a few months back. How he had fallen in love with that saree then. It had a delicate print of pastel-coloured flowers and tapering of gold beaded lace. The breezy chiffon was enhancing Sanam's rosy complexion. Her hair had grown out of their blunts and fell straight on her shoulders. The sleeveless blouse complimented her saari. The delicate blouse set off the infinity chain set. Just a hint of lipstick and a small red bindi made her look ethereal. Avinash felt himself getting enamoured by his beautiful wife again.

"Avinash...I am so nervous! What happened to you? Hum statue statue nahi khel rahe hain," Sana whined.

Avinash snapped out of the trance and took her hands in his.

"Baby don't be nervous; they already love you! You are meant for me, my Sohni Punjaban! Look at you looking so pretty in this saree! I am getting more of these for you!" Avinash said as he gently kissed her cheeks.

The genuine praise from her had warmed Sanam. She felt a little less nervous.

Avinash took her hand and led her outside.

As Sanam came out of the room, both Karuna and Nani gasped in appreciation at the classic Indian beauty that was standing there in a saree.

"Aai majhi bayko![Mummy, my wife!]," Avinash took his wife to where his mother was sitting.

Sanam bent down to touch her feet, but Karuna stopped her mid-way and pulled her into a hug.

"Papa, my Sanam!" Avinash introduced his wife with pride in his eyes.

"Beta, daughters don't touch feet! God bless you!" Alok put his hand on her head.

"So, Rajeev, how is the hospital going?" Baba said to divert the attention as sudden silence had fallen in the palatial drawing room.

"Sana, just check on Mitali...let's have tea!" Nani said.

"She is a little nervous!" Nani told Karuna who smiled back knowingly.

The conversation was put to a stop as Sanam and Mitali wheeled in the trolley with tea and snacks. Earlier in the day, Sanam had refused to go to the parlour and had joined Nani and Mitali in the kitchen. They had together made small bite sized aloo-palak tikki, spring rolls, mutton kebabs, sponge cake and gajar ka halwa.

"Oh wow...itna sab! We put you guys through so much trouble!" Karuna said apologetically.

"Arre nahin nahin...I am glad aapne yeh sab banaya Naniji! It's so tasty! Aise nahin Baba yahan aane ka bahana dhoondte the!" Alok chuckled.

Baba, who was about to sip on the tea, coughed and almost spilled the tea on himself.

"Mujhe toh maa ki yaad aa gayi!" Alok said again, munching on the food enthusiastically.

"Aaho...thodi sharam karo..bete ke sasural aaye ho...kitna khaoge!" Karuna said embarrassed.

"Arre I am giving a compliment by eating. Itna tasty khaana khila ke Naniji phas gayi hai...ab toh har weekend main yahin aaunga!" Alok chuckled yet again.

"Waise Shastris ka ek hi funda hai...jisne ki sharam...."Alok laughed at the embarrassed Karuna, and this made everyone in the room laugh along.

Alok was signalling Karuna about something, but she shut him up with a stare. Once the food was over, Karuna made Sanam sit next to her and brought a jewellery box.

"These are Montu's Dadi's bangles! She will have wanted you to have it! And these earrings are my mother's. They both will be at peace today. Your husband was their favourite,"Karuna said with a wistful smile.

"Thank You aunty!"Sanam said.

"Arre aunty nahin, mummy bol,"Nani reprimanded.

"Sorry Mummy...woh galti se nikal gaya!"Sanam tried to hide her nervousness.

"Mrs. Shastri I was hoping...I mean if you don't mind...if the wedding could be a Sikh wedding?"Nani requested.

"Of course, Naniji...we have no objections. Anyways they have already taken agni-pheras. And we will love to witness the Sikh traditional ceremony!" Karuna said with folded hands. Karuna had already had a discussion with her husband and her father-in-law about this.

This was all that was needed, and everyone started discussing the wedding. A little later, Karuna's phone buzzed, and she started looking for someplace private to take the call. Sanam took her to her own room and left.

"Hello Vahini! Yes we have reached. Oh! She is so beautiful and sweet. The photographs don't do justice to her. Yes, I gave her the jewellery. She looked so pretty. No...I didn't give that to her. I felt so embarrassed. You know they had cooked 'Gajar ka halwa' so well...I felt embarrassed to ask her to taste mine. I will have to learn from her. Their way and ours is so different,"Karuna turned as she was talking to see Sanam with a teary face. Tears were falling unhindered from her eyes.

Sanam had come again to switch on the AC for Karuna when she heard her Mother-in-law's conversation. The fact that her Mother-in-law had thought so much about her to cook something for her made Sanam throw her inhibitions away.

"Vahini, let me call you back. Beta what happened?"Karuna asked, alarmed.

"Maa!"Sanam cried and hugged Karuna.

Karuna couldn't understand much but pulled her into her arms. It felt as if the missing part of her family had been put together. Her family now felt complete.

For a long time, Karuna and Sanam sat together like long lost friends. Sanam told Karuna about the death of her parents. They cried and held each other, when Karuna told her about Avinash's accident. This is how Avinash found them when he came to call both the women. The door had been left ajar and he heard them talking and crying together. He walked away from there, shutting the door properly and leaving the mother-daughter duo behind.

After almost an hour since Sanam and Karuna had gone MIA, Nani knocked at Sanam's room.

"May I join you ladies? The gentlemen are so boring!" Nani chuckled to be hugged by Sanam.

"Maa..acha batao aapne jo halwa banaya woh kahan hai?" Sanam asked in excitement.

"Haan na..mere bag main hai...jaa le kar aa!" Karuna said.

Sanam took the Tupperware box of halwa and started devouring it. In a few minutes, the box was snatched from her hands by Avinash.

"Maaaaa,"Sanam whined when he took away her halwa.

"Arre mujhe bhi khana hai moti!"Avinash whined.

"Haww.....Avinash tune mujhe moti bola? I am not talking to you now!"Sanam pouted.

"Nahin baby! It was a joke! Yeh le tera halwa!"a scared Avinash promptly returned the box to her.

"Bas...asanch? [Just like that you returned the box?]" Karuna teased Avinash knowing that Avinash normally wouldn't give in so easily but of course this was none other than his wife.

"Ho...asanch!" Avinash silently pleaded with his mother to drop the topic. Karuna was enjoying this scared-of-his-wife facet of Avinash's personality.

Soon the women threw Avinash out and started talking about the wedding and the wedding dress.

"Yaar aap log bahar aao na...we are getting bored," Avinash came inside their room for the nth time leaving a blushing Sanam and giggling Nani and Karuna.

By the time the women emerged from the bedroom, the men had helped themselves with alcohol.

"Itna maza aa raha hai..ghar jaane ka dil nahin kar raha!" Karuna said. It was already nine in the night.

"Toh aap ko jaane kaun de raha hai aunty! I have ordered a special Mutton biryani for dinner. Aap log abhi nahi jaa rahe," Rajeev said.

Once the dinner was over, the actual conversation started. It was decided that they will be married on the next weekend, giving both the families at least seven eight days for preparation for the three-day wedding ceremony.

It was almost twelve when the Shastris got ready to leave.

"I just can't wait to take you home!" Karuna said while kissing Sanam.

"Chal ghar!" Avinash pulled Sanam when all the byes were done.

"Arre! Avinash!" Sanam blushed, taking her hand away.

"Arre you guys are getting married!" Karuna gave Avinash a stare.

"Haan of course we are!" Avinash responded, still not letting Sanam go.

"That means you let her stay here...in her mayka!" Karuna spelled it out for Avinash, much to the amusement of everyone.

"Kya? Aisi koi baat nahin hui thee! That's not fair Aai! That's cheating!" Avinash blew up like a petulant child. Sanam turned red with embarrassment as others chuckled.

"Avinash, Tu kitihi ghoda tari mi tula chabkane fodun kadhu shakte [Tu kitn bada ghoda ho jaye, tujhe chabuk laga kar sidha karna mujhe aata hai!]," Karuna said in a terse tone.

"Sorry!" Avinash had to shut up in front of his mother's warning.

"Kimaan shabdat kamal apman![Maximum insult in minimum words]," Alok chuckled displaying his savage wit and those who understood it chuckled too.

"Tomorrow morning, I will meet you at your Zumba class!" Avinash scowled like a child who had been cheated out of his favourite candy.

CHAPTER- 71

WAGERS

"You were involved in this Biwi?"Avinash complained to Sanam.

"Avinash, common sense! Shaadi se pehle kaunsi biwi apne husband ke ghar rehti hai? I am surprised you didn't catch it!"Sanam replied defensively as she spoke to her husband just half an hour later.

"But you are already my wife! I didn't expect this from Aai. How am I supposed to stay without you for eight days? How am I supposed to sleep? Kisi ko mera khayal hi nahin!" Avinash whined.

"Baby...ab jo hai so hai! I want to become a traditional bride! I am feeling excited!"Sanam said in excitement.

"Aai aur Papa ko bhi samajhna chahiye tha na!"Avinash said, still disgruntled with his parents.

"Avinash please...bas kar ab! Hai Rabba kitna drama kiya aaj sab ke samne!"Sanam giggled. Avinash melted listening to her giggles.

"Biwi tere bina kaise rahunga main itne din? Acha, has everyone gone off to sleep there?"Avinash asked her casually.

"Haan!" Sanam replied.

"Ok...then you sleep..aaram se! Good night sweetheart! LOVE YOU...MUAH!"Avinash told her and ended the video call

"Ammma...yeh toh itni jaldi maan gaya!Call bhi band kar di!" Sanam thought. She was sad because she still wanted to talk to him.

Ten minutes later, Sanam's mobile phone pinged with a message from Avinash-

Avinash-Baby open the door. I am outside.

Sanam-Are you mad? Gadhe ho tum?

Avinash-Baby open the door before Daaku smells me.

Sanam-Ok...wait...I am not wearing a bra!

Avinash- Super Awesome.....mood ban gaya...ab darwaza khol!

Sanam- Arre bra toh pehne do!

Avinash- Take a dupatta and come

Sanam- Oh yes..that can be done!

Avinash- Sanam stop wasting time typing....open the door!

Sanam- Ok...Ok

Avinash- Sanam...don't waste time messaging...OPEN-THE-BLOODY-DOOR!

Sanam- Ok

Avinash would have pulled his hair out had Sanam sent another message instead of opening the door.

She took him inside and closed the door.

"Ouch!" Sanam uttered in her nervousness as she banged into the sofa.

"Ikhata kar le sabko...chila chila ke!" Avinash hissed.

Not able to take his sarcasm, Sanam started whimpering softly.

Avinash had just about had enough for the day...or night. He kept his palm over her mouth and signalled her to move to her bedroom. Avinash heaved a sigh of relief when they reached Sanam's bedroom and shut the door. He removed his palm and put his mouth drawing in a long and passionate kiss.

"Aviiinash," Sanam whined when they broke up the kiss.

"Haan baby!" Avinash whispered.

"This looks really bad!" Sanam said.

"Kya...you want me to go?" Avinash said. The disappointment in his tone was very noticeable.

"Maine aisa toh nahi kaha!" Sanam said sharply.

Avinash tried to pep her mood by taking her into his arms

After the initial resistance, she settled down in his arms.

"Avinash...hamare honge na?" Sanam asked him in a disbelieving tone.

"Kya baby?" Avinash replied, cupping her face gently.

"Kids? Grandkids?" Sanam asked wistfully.

"Sab honge baby! Bahut dukh dekh liya, ab sab theek hoga! And you will make an awesome mother!" Avinash assured her.

"Acha sun! Will I be a good father?" Avinash asked her.

"Just the best!" Sanam beamed back, pecking him on his lips.

They didn't realise when they both fell asleep talking and weaving dreams of their future together.

Sanam was woken up by a series of deep growls. It took her a few moments to make sense of her surroundings and remember what had happened last night. When she came to her senses, Sanam found herself naked in the arms of her husband and Daaku growling right outside her bedroom door. She struggled to get out of his arms, but her husband's grip was so tight that she could barely move.

"Daaku I am coming!" Sanam screamed as she didn't know what to do. She heard a few more growls when to her relief heard the Doctor whistle to Daaku.

"Sana I am taking Daaku, you sleep!" Rajeev called out from the other side of the door.

"Thanks Doc! You are such a sweetheart!" Sanam smiled while replying softly. She was sure the Doctor would not have stopped to hear her reply.

"Avinash utho...it's morning!" Sanam said softly to wake him up.

"Baby! I love you!" Avinash pulled her into his arms again.

"Nahin Avinash utho! Ghar J-a-o!" Sanam literally pushed him off herself.

"Kaisi biwi ho yaar? Husband mohabbat ke mood main hai aur tum dhakka de rahi ho?" Avinash tried to romance his wife, but she refused to melt.

"Avinash get dressed now and out you go! Or else.." Sanam said in a menacing tone. The tone was scary enough to shake Avinash up! He instinctively knew he had pushed his wife to the brim of her patience. Avinash sprang up to his feet and in five minutes he was ready to leave.

"Apni fans se miloge aaj?" Sanam teased him.

"I will come at the end of the zumba class…saalion se milne!"Avinash smiled and pecked his wife.

They both tiptoed out of her bedroom. They were near the main door when Nani called out for Mitali. Sanam freaked out and literally pushed Avinash out of the house.

"Apni biwi se hi chup chup kar milna pad raha hai! Kya zindagi ho gayi hai!"Avinash muttered under his breath as he got into the lift. He was still in his thoughts when a familiar voice called him out. Avinash realised that the lift had already reached the ground floor and Rajeev was standing in the foyer!

"Avinash?" Rajeev was surprised initially but then broke into laughter.

"Abey main usko Zumba ke liye lene aaya tha..then realised it's too early so I was returning!" Avinash rubbed the back of his neck trying to hide his embarrassment.

"Of course…ofcourse! That was why Daaku was growling!" Rajeev laughed and laughed.

"But Thank you!" Rajeev said, taking a breath in between his bouts of laughter.

"Thank-you kis liye?"Avinash asked as they both walked out of the building.

"Nani and I had bet that you will show-up in the night! Nani had bet that you would wait at home at least one night and I had bet that you would show up last night which you did! So, I won!" Rajeev said, smiling ear to ear.

"Abey tu yaar hai mera, mat bol na!"Avinash put his arm around Rajeev's shoulder.

"I will lose the bet! That will be really devastating!" Rajeev said wistfully.

"Abey kitne ki bet hai?" Avinash asked him.

"Arre yaar paise ki nahi hai! Nani is doing some matchmaking! If I win, she will stop! That's why 'Thank You'! " Rajeev replied.

"Tujhe lagta hai bet haarne ke baad Nani will let go of her matchmaking?" Avinash reasoned with Rajeev.

"Dekh, I have a deal for you! Haar ja bet...if you don't like the girl, tell me I will help you get rid of her!" Avinash offered.

Rajeev thought for a while about Avinash's proposition. It seemed like a win-win scenario. Anyways he wasn't going to rat them out and embarrass Sana.

"Chal Deal!" Rajeev said as they shook hands and sealed the deal.

"Oh my God ...Oh my God! Look, there is the Drummer!" Sammy literally screamed into their ears. The Zumba girls were standing outside the club house after a gruelling hour of Zumba!

"Haye...he is not wearing his hoodie either! So handsome!" Dina said dreamily.

"Aaj bada bahadur ban raha hai...kuch toh jhol hai!" Akki said thoughtfully.

The entire Zumba gang looked at him while Avinash jogged from his building towards the Club house

"The drummer is coming this way…." Sammy said, jumping in excitement.

The others too struggled to keep their calm as Sanam giggled away imagining their reactions for the impending shock that the women were going to receive.

Avinash looked at his wife with her friends. She was wearing a neon-pink short t-shirt over a fancy cut sports bra. Her skin was glistening after the workout. Her fair complexion was now healthy pink matching the shade of her sexy garment.

"Ladies!" Avinash bobbed his head in courtesy.

"Hiiii" the women almost sang in unison.

"Baby!" Avinash turned towards Sanam and kissed her cheeks.

"Hain!!!!!!!" most of the women gasped in unison again.

"OH-MY-GOD" Akki and Sammy were the first to recover as they hit a Hi-five in excitement.

" See I told you...I bloody well told you!" Akki said, punching in the air.

Sammy screamed and hugged Akki.

Now it was Avinash and Sanam turn to wonder what had just happened.

"Ok girls! This is Avinash and we are getting married next Sunday!" Sanam said.

"Yay! OMG!" The Zumba girls, now a little out of shock, screamed in joy and hugged Sanam.

Once the excitement had settled down...Sanam introduced all of them to Avinash.

"This is Krissy...Ritu..Tia..Tia khana bahut acha banati hai!" Sanam added as Avinash shook hands with all of them.

"Aur yeh Dina hai….isko thighs bahut pasand hai!" Sanam being Sanam said with her usual flair. Sammy, who was drinking water, almost spit it out.

"Chicken thighs...Chicken thighs!" Akki added to handle things better.

"Why were guys saying, 'I told you'?" Sanam asked Akki and Sammy once the introductions were done.

"Actually, Akki had figured out some days back that the Drummer was playing the songs for you!"Sammy declared with pride.

"L-O-V-E-L-Y….HOW INTERESTING!" Avinash wondered aloud, encouraging Akki to come out with her logic.

"See your songs can be heard only in these three buildings. Only ten women fit the age criteria. I listed them on a paper and kept on removing the names when the time of you playing the song wouldn't match their appearance. There was only one girl who was always there when you played the song. And the day we went for coffee...you didn't play the song. Phir your jogging time coinciding with Sana's walk was a dead giveaway! And the ANT-gate!"Akki said in excitement.

Avinash smiled and gestured to her to hold her info on the ANT-gate!

"Baby have you invited my saalis to our wedding or not?" Avinash turned towards Sanam and kissed her cheeks again. Their hands were entwined, and the glow of love was visible on their faces.

"Awwww!" most of the Zumba gang gasped in unison.

"Girls, you have to attend our wedding next weekend! Formal invitation will reach you shortly!"

"Of course, we will come!" The Zumba gang sang again.

Karuna had called up Pammi and extended the invitation to Sanam and her family for tea and dinner. The leading wedding planners had been called invited as well.

It was almost four when Sanam reached the Kulkarni residence along with Rajeev and Nani. Avinash had wanted to take her but he along with Baba had gotten stuck in a meeting. He had been angry with himself, but he couldn't help.

"Kab pahunchenge hum Baba? Mamu ko bhi heart of the city main ghar lena tha? It's so congested!" Avinash exclaimed for the nth time. He wanted to fly off to his wife. He was dying to see her in her new anarkali suit. She had indeed sent a picture but LIVE was LIVE.

"Montu please don't embarrass us again like you did last night!" Baba warned Avinash, making Avinash blush at the memory of his mother roasting him in front of his in-laws.

Finally, they reached the Kulkarni residence. He practically ran inside, but he had been duly warned by Baba and didn't want to give unnecessary ammunition to his cousins. Before he saw her, he heard her giggles. A huge smile came on his face. Sanam looked the epitome of beauty and grace in the pink Anarkali. The outfit, although brought in a rush, was beautiful. It was a fuschia 'U' neck, quarter sleeves silk highlighted with resham thread, dori and embroidered work. The dress looked like a golden constellation drawn on a pink sky. Avinash lost himself in her. He stood there frozen, admiring his beautiful wife. He observed that her cheeks were growing redder by each passing moment. Slowly, he realised that she was blushing because he was staring at her like a love-sick puppy and everyone in the room was watching their dynamics.

"Sayli, Avinash Dada is here!" Sagar, his cousin, called out to Sayli, his wife giving him the much-needed diversion.

Everyone literally jumped on Avinash. It was evident that Avinash had been missed in the Kulkarni household all these years. Sanam was all smiles when he saw Avinash's cousins pounce on him with love.

"You are loved so much Avinash....more than you know!" Sanam mused to herself.

The evening had gone fabulously well. Sanam and her family had been very well received by her in-laws. The family had met and rejected quite a few Wedding Planners before zeroing down on a young newlywed couple.

By the time dinner was over, Karuna had forged a deep attachment with Sanam and Pammi. Pammi was the new darling of Mrs. Kulkarni, who was completely impressed with the elderly lady.

The men as always had been drawn away by hot snacks and alcohol. The local seven-star hotel had been finalised as the wedding venue along with the Gurudwara. Finer details had yet to be worked out.

Finally, Sanam left with Rajeev and Nani. Avinash had insisted that he would drop her home, but Sanam had been scared that he had consumed alcohol and given him her kasam.

"She looks a little off!" Avinash realised as Sanam got into the car. "Maybe it is because she is chumming. Let me ask her tomorrow," Avinash said. He hadn't been interested in sleeping without his wife, but his cousins had insisted and he had given up after asking Sanam.

It was almost twelve, when Sanam sat in her pod chair on the balcony staring in the space for almost half an hour when she heard a knock at her door.

"Sanam…" Rajeev peeped in.

"Doctor please come in!" Sanam stood up.

"Coffee?" Rajeev extended one of the two steaming cups of coffee to her.

"Aapne kyun banayi? Mujhe bolte!" Sanam said.

"Ab itna bhi gaya guzra nahi hoon! Now drink coffee...it will help!" Rajeev said.

Sanam blushed profusely.

"Sana, I am a doctor! And I guess a good one at that!" Rajeev said with a smile.

Both smiled and sipped on the steaming coffee.

"Ab bataogi what's bothering you?" Rajeev asked.

"Nahin kuch nahin!" Sanam avoided eye contact.

"Sana please…" Rajeev said earnestly.

"Doctor all this…you know…so much opulence! It's very difficult to take in! I mean I know you all have a status in the society…but…lakhs of rupees for a lehenga? I mean what to say? I can't afford this! I don't want to hurt anyone's sentiment, but it's overwhelming!" Sanam said almost on the verge of crying but relieved of taking it off her chest.

"Sana, you know I started my career with an elite New York hospital. One of my batch mates was in plastic surgery. He used to sew up patients when they had serious accidents…skin grafting surgeries etc. One day, he met us in the cafeteria and told us about this accident case that had been coming to his department for years. The patient was a young son of a very rich Congressman. This boy had been hardly twenty-five when he had had a serious accident. However, he was extremely lucky to have gotten away with superficial injuries except a torn cheek. Numerous skin grafting surgeries later, he was still left with a long scar on his right cheek. That scar became his nemesis. His relationships with his family members became strained. He would imagine that everyone would look at his scar, get repelled and make fun of him behind his back. By the time my friend came onboard, the guy had had sixteen skin grafting surgeries on his cheek. He was never satisfied" Rajeev said.

"Umm…toh?" Sanam asked, unable to comprehend what Rajeev was trying to drive home.

"Matlab…the guy only focussed on the scar! The scar became the focus of his life and excluded everything worthwhile from his peripheral vision. Sana don't let money become the scar on your soul. Understand how much happiness you are giving to us….and that's priceless! Imagine how many people you will now be able to help with the right contacts and not worry about money!" Rajeev said, walking away, giving her time to think.

Sanam was pretty taken back by the new perspective. She was in deep thought when she walked in her room and spotted the tin box that contained Avinash's letter.

Dear Sanam,

For the first time in life, I am indulging plagiarism. I am copying your idea and writing a letter to you…But honestly, I am at a loss for words. I swear, I am a writer but have no idea what to write now. You are too good; your letters are too good. I am just hanging in there because of them. My left hand has just started flexing. I have started taking therapy too. My psychiatrist, says I am in depression. The clinical diagnosis is 'major depressive disorder'. They have put on meds to correct the Endorphins levels. The meds are numbing me out. I want to feel. I want to feel you. I should suffer because I made you suffer so much. I deserve the pain. It was because of me, that you lost our baby. I tried telling everyone this...no one is willing to listen. Aai mujhe teri kasam de kar dawa khilati hai. They don't know that these meds are not going to help. I need you. My salvation is you. I am willing to die if in return I could get five minutes with you. It has been two months without you. I don't know if I can hang in any more. Save me Baby!

Yours Forever,
Avinash.

"I was only looking at my scars Avinash!" Sanam spoke aloud as she broke down after reading his letter.

CHAPTER- 72
TWINKLE TWINKLE

Rajeev who had given her space to think, had instantly regretted his actions when loud sobs came from her room sometime later. He immediately called up Avinash and asked him to drop everything and return.

"I shouldn't have left her alone!" Rajeev reprimanded himself when he saw Sana sitting on the floor crying, while clutching the letter to her heart. It had taken Rajeev almost half an hour to calm her down and coax her to sleep.

"Aviii...Avii," Sanam whimpered softly in her sleep a few hours later.

"Shh...I am here sweetheart!" Avinash gently patted her head and kissed away the tears that rolled down even in her sleep.

"Wake up Baby! Sanam I am here!" Avinash shook her up when her cries became louder.

Sanam woke up with a start.

"Baby I am here! You were having a nightmare!" Avinash gently patted her cheeks. Sanam took a few moments to recollect herself and remember the letter that had broken her down.

"I am ok sweetheart! Why are you crying meri Jaan?" Avinash asked her.

Sanam looked at him with her child like innocence. She just kept on looking at her husband in daze.

"Baby meri letter padhi kya? Sorry!" Avinash took the lead.

"Tum bhi kitne dukh main tha na?" Sanam almost whispered.

"Tere bina dukh dukh hi thaa Baby!" Avinash sighed remembering the melancholic times.

"But now we are together!" Avinash tightened his grip over his wife who was still crying.

"Pushpa…I hate tears!" Avinash imitated a famous actor's dialogue. Sanam couldn't control her laughter.

"Vaise biwi maine sirf sad letters hi nahin…thode romantic-comedy…rom-com bhi likhe the!" Avinash said.

"Rom-Com….batao zara!" Sanam demanded.

"Arre biwi…it's almost early morning! Phir kabhi!" Avinash tried to make his wife understand.

"Baby please!" Sanam urged.

Avinash got up and picked up the cookie box. He rummaged through the letters and picked up some pages. "Yeh suno..poem likhi hai!" Avinash said dramatically. Sanam looked up at him expectantly.

Meri pyaari Sanam,

Tumhe jab jab dekhta hoon…to dil se yeh nikhta hai….

Twinkle Twinkle little star,

One day I will do you in the car,

Up above on you I will make you sigh,

Will squish your twins and make you fly!

Before he could proceed, he received a tight slap under his ears from his wife.

"Disgusting…yeh Rom-Com hai? Tharki letter hai! You spoiled a wonderful rhyme for me! Che..che!" Sanam spoke in one go aghast at what she had heard.

She pulled the letter he was reading and was surprised to see a blank page.

"Kamina!" Sanam put the letter aside to kiss her husband who had a goofy smile pasted on his face. Sanam had understood that her husband was putting up an impromptu show for his wife. Avinash actually hadn't written any such letter. He had just claimed it to make the mood lighter. He definitely hadn't expected his wife to make such demands in the middle of the night.

"Pakda gaya tu Kamine!" Sanam pulled his cheeks with love again. They talked about random things for the next hour till they both drifted off to sleep.

Nani shrieked in excitement when Avinash walked out of Sanam's bedroom in the morning. She was literally dancing thinking how she had won the bet.

"Good morning Nani!" Avinash bent to touch her feet.

"A very good morning bachon, especially Ladoo!" Nani said dramatically, pulling Rajeev's cheeks.

"Naaaani please!" Rajeev groaned as Nani smiled ear to ear mentally marrying off her grandson to a 'SarvaGun sampan Bahu' in her head.

Avinash couldn't control his smile at his friend's discomfort as well. Sanam was completely confused witnessing the non-verbal communication at the table. However, she was least concerned today as she was still suffering from menstruation cramps.

"Aaj ka kya plan hai?" Rajeev asked to take the attention away from him.

"I need to rest today! I can't move much! I am exhausted. Sana beta you must take some rest as well. You look so pale!" Nani looked at Sana with concern.

"Nani, if it is ok with you, I need to take Sanam to our flat. We need to finish the last chapter of the novel and she needs to look at a few layouts for the covers too! The deadline for the book is very near. We need to work fast!" Avinash said and Nani readily gave her consent.

"Avinash...we need to talk!" Sanam said the moment they reached his flat in the opposite building a few hours later.

"I don't want to be a product of Nepotism!" Sanam told Avinash in a terse tone.

"Good, because you are not!" Avinash replied calmly.

"Avinash I mean it!" Sanam reiterated.

"Baby sun...was ours the only offer you received? No na? I clarified with Baba and then checked with a friend at Ostrich Publishers too. They were very interested in your book. It was Baba who warned them off and made you sign up with us. See, Baba is family but a very shrewd businessman. He knows the worth of his investments. And our Publication has given a lot of opportunities to new authors. That's the reason, we haven't declared our identity. With your romance, we want to venture into the romance genre. We want to attract that audience who likes meaningful romance. We had an author scheduled for release but at the last moment we found her work plagiarised. You have in fact saved us. Ultimately, it's your call. I am happy either way. And I am happy and immensely proud that I was your mentor," Avinash said earnestly, bringing a smile to her face.

"Sachi, you liked my novel?" Sanam asked. A light tinge of pink had crept on her cheeks. She was basking in her husband's unabashed praise of her story.

Sanam didn't even realise it when Avinash set up her laptop on his table and brought a steaming cup of coffee for her.

"Baby tere liye ek surprise hai! But be quiet for some time ok?" Avinash told Sanam as he brought out his I-pad for facetime.

The call connected and she could see Rohan excitedly waving his hand to Sanam but gesturing for them to be quiet.

"Madhu darling...dekh kaun hai! It passed eleven at night in New Jersey. By the look of it, Madhu was wrapping the kitchen.

"Kaun hai?" Madhu turned to see Avinash in the frame.

"Rohan, I told you I don't want to talk to him!"Madhu shot daggers at Rohan.

Once Avinash had gotten out of the hospital, he had gone to meet Madhu's family in search of Sanam. He had called up Rohan and told him the entire story. Maybe being a husband, Rohan had empathised with Avinash, but Avinash had to bear the brunt of Madhu's anger. She had stopped talking to him after blasting him a few times. Rohan had remained his loyal friend. After giving Avinash a harsh reality check on how he had treated his wife, he had been a pillar of support to him.

"Aye Madhu...baat nahi karegi?" Avinash teased Madhu.

"Did you find my friend?" Madhu asked in anger.

"Chal baat mat kar...date par toh chal!" Avinash said, teasing her.

"Avinash dimag mat kharab kar mera!" Madhu, who coincidentally had a knife in hand, ended up threatening him.

The scene looked so funny that Sanam ended up giggling between her tears.

"Is that Sanam?" Madhu asked in shock.

"Hi Madhu!" Sanam came on the screen. What followed was a teary and emotional scene of the meeting of two long lost friends. Avinash and Sanam invited their friends to the wedding. Avinash offered them tickets, but Rohan and Madhu unanimously refused to take them but promised to arrive at the earliest for the wedding.

"Naveen and Akriti se bhi baat ho gayi aaj. I am going to make Sanam talk to them tonight. Please come asap!" Avinash told them.

"Madhu ab toh nahin maregi na?" Avinash joined his hands and asked Madhu in a fearful style.

"Marega toh tu mere haath se….chaaku se nahi toh frying pan se!" Madhu laughed, making Avinash and Sanam grin along.

"I want to call Editor Banerjee too. Deepu hota toh…." Sanam thoughtfully said once their call ended.

"Biwi…your Uncle-Aunty have been untraceable for many months. Nihar has gone to Punjab to get Deepu here for the wedding. Deepu's phone number has been unreachable for weeks," Avinash said.

"Oh, so this is what you were doing yesterday!" Sanam said with a grateful smile.

Avinash just smiled at his beautiful wife.

"I love you Baby! Thank you for everything!" Sanam said and hugged her husband.

CHAPTER- 73

MAA DA LAADLA

"Good morning Baba, kaise hain aap!" Sanam welcomed Baba the next day. Sanam had called up Baba and invited him over for breakfast. It had been almost a week since the great Shastri expose had happened, but Baba and Nani were still behaving like strangers. Nani was completely ignoring Baba; Baba was looking lost like a Devdas.

"Yaar #BaNi ka kuch karna padega!"Sanam had told her husband. Avinash and she had then gotten together and hatched a plan to create opportunities for #BaNi to come together.

"Bitiya, yeh Bansi ne pakore banaye the!"Baba gave Sanam a huge box of assorted pakoras.

"Wow thank you Baba!"Sanam said.

"Aap baithiye, maine breakfast bas bana hi liya! Aaj Mitali chutti par hai...toh mere haath ka khana khana padega." Sanam called out from the kitchen.

"Baby bhookh lagi hai...jaldi laa!"Avinash said, rolling the sleeves of his pristine white kurta.

"Wow pakore!"Rajeev joined them at the table, picking up a handful.

Soon, Sanam served a stack of Aloo-Gobhi parathas and curd at the breakfast table.

"Baba Daliya and fruit aapke aur Nani ke liye," Sanam said as she set the porridge down on the table.

Sanam stifled a giggle when both their faces fell.

"Baba, till two days back your sugar was high. And please don't forget , Doctor is sitting with us!"Sanam said with a smile.

"Arre bhulenge kaise...tum bhulne nahin deti ho...Jab dekho Doctor..Doctor..kabhi naam se bhi bula liya karo! Itna acha naam hai bechare ka!" Baba said and sneakily took half a paratha from Avinash's plate.

Sanam looked at Rajeev guiltily. "Woh Doc...nahin Rajeev...matlab" Sanam made a I-am-a-confused-cute-baby-face making everyone smile.

"It's ok Sana...jo marzi bolo but parathe idhar de do!" Rajeev chuckled.

"Bahut din ho gaye hain bitiya chai nahin pilai! Aaj do cup piunga!" Baba said endearingly.

"Sana tera Dada Sasur bahut adventurous hai!" Nani said in a tone that was sweet but laced with sarcasm.

"Sana jo khud second cup par hote hain...woh doosron ko gyan dete hue acche nahin lagte!"Baba said with a pronounced smirk.

"Atleast I can call a spade a spade! I don't have an axe to grind!"Nani replied sarcastically yet again.

"Nani please!" Rajeev tried to reign in peace but both of them were determined not to back off.

"Rajeev beta Anitaji is right...."Baba had just started speaking when Sanam, Avinash and Rajeev collectively gasped. Talking about Ms. Anita was akin to poking a dagger in Nani's heart.

"Anita ka pata nahin...Mr. Paranjape sahi bolte hain!" Nani pushed her plate and got up.

"Kya bolta hai woh bewakoof?"Baba asked in a terse tone.

"Yahi ki ….Chahe jo marzi surname laga len...Gadhe Gadhe hi rehte hain!" Nani huffed and left the table in anger.

Baba too realised his mistake when Nani left.

"Baba seriously?" Avinash banged his hand on his head while Rajeev watched the drama unfold with amused curiosity.

Baba took a deep sigh and walked out of the Dhindsa household to their flat in the opposite building. Avinash followed suit.

"Baba thoda control kar liya hota!" Avinash chided Baba.

"Yaar she has not been talking to me for almost a week….and today she did but with so much of attitude…Dimag kharab ho gaya!" Baba said in a pained voice.

"Haan Baba…ladies na…you have to handle it with care! You had called for something..a parcel. It has come" Avinash said.

Sanam went to Nani's room.

"Nani are you fine?"Sanam asked Nani gently.

"Haan bacha…Out there I lost my cool for some time. Sorry, tera dada-sasur hai but just pushes all the wrong buttons. Anita ke naam ki mala japta rehta hai!" Nani said in a sullen tone.

"To Pammi ki mala jape?"Sanam giggled.

"Besharam…Ladoo sun lega toh kya sochega? Uski shaadi ke dino main uski Nani romance lada rahi hai!"Nani whispered and giggled too.

"Matlab romance hai?"Sanam caught Nani blushing.

"Acha next time miloge toh thoda gently….Avinash bol rahe the…Baba ne bahut dino se dhng se khana nahin khaya. He hasn't been sleeping properly either" Sanam threw an emotional bait for Nani.

"Hai sachi?" Nani looked at her, guilt written clearly on her face.

"Muchi!"Sanam smiled.

"Vaise …Avinash bol rahe the? Jyada nahin ho gaya?" Nani chuckled.

"Maybe..but acha lagta hai!" Sanam blushed and ran to the kitchen to pack a lunch box for the Doctor with Nani's laughter still ringing in her ears.

"Baby Bittu hospital gaya?"Avinash called up a few hours later.

"Yes..bring Baba!" Sanam said. She had set up the table for lunch for Baba and Nani.

"Nani, let's sit for lunch!"Sanam called out to Nani before opening the door for Baba and stepping out herself.

She giggled conspiringly as she sat in the car with her husband.

"Do you think they will kill each other?"Sanam asked Avinash seriously.

"Mad or what? Woh sab hume dikhane ke liye hai! I think they will be making out now that they are finally alone!" Avinash said with nonchalance that earned him a punch in his solar plexus from his wife.

"Ouch Biwi….it hurts. Where is your sense of humour Baby?"Avinash said dramatically.

"Aise disgusting baatein kyun karte ho?" Sanam asked, clearly irritated.

"Arre mazzak tha…Waise tum violent hoti ho bahut hot lagti ho…will you like to do it a little rough?"Avinash asked her earnestly.

Sanam slapped him playfully on his cheeks, squished them into a pout and kissed the pout.

"Maybe!" She said as she let go of his face and quickly looked out of the window blushing profusely.

"To hell with the lunch and shopping. Chal upar ghar par!" Avinash told her.

"Avi mujhe jaana hai…I want to eat chinese today. And I want to shop too with you!"Sanam whined cutely, and Avinash melted away in a moment.

The rest of the day was spent in Avinash and Sanam shopping and catching a movie together.

By the time they returned home, all peace and calm had been restored between Baba and Nani.

Mrs. Karuna and Mr. Alok Shastri had left for Mumbai the day next to the dinner for two days. They returned to Pune with a battalion of designers. A seven-star hotel had been booked for the Avi and Sanam Wedding for the four days of celebration. Sanam's schedule had been booked completely by Karuna.

"The power of money!" Sanam observed when one by one leading designers came down to the Dhindsa residence for her bridal dresses and trousseau.

"Thank you Waheguru for this benevolence. I swear I will use all this to help others!" Sanam swore to herself.

"Yeh kaisa hai? I think you will rock in this one! I will choose this one for you! " Karuna brought a bright blue and orange lehenga to Sanam. Sanam looked at the lehenga and contemplated how to tell her dear mother-in-law that she found the piece a little too loud for her taste. At the end she gave up and said yes.

Karuna's expectant face fell. This reaction was contradictory to what Sanam had expected. She had thought that Karuna would be happy that she had picked up that lehenga.

"Maa...kya hua?" Sanam asked with concern as she saw a wayward tear slip by Karuna's eyes.

Nani and Mrs. Kulkarni sat up in an alert mode.

"Bas naam se hi maa hoon...tu samajhti nahi maa mujhe Sana!"Karuna cried bitterly.

"Nahin maa...sachi Waheguru di saun!"Sanam said. She was bewildered at the turn of events.

"Maa samajhti toh khul kar apni pasand bolti. You don't like that colour combination, yet you said yes because I told you . I was testing you. Maybe you will still take time. I have been dying to hear you make demands. I want to pamper you! I want everything in this wedding to be of your choice....from a flower arrangement to the dessert! And definitely your wedding dress till the last bead,"Karuna spoke in one go.

"I love you maa..."Sanam hugged her mother-in-law and cried.

"Maa...Mujhe blue and orange nahi pasand. Mujhe pastels pasand hai "Sanam said, making all the crying women break into a big smile.

"Bittu Sanam kahan hai? I have been trying her number," Avinash asked as Rajeev opened the door. It was almost ten at night when Avinash entered Dhindsa residence.

"Her phone I guess is in her room...chal I will show you where she is!"Rajeev led Avinash towards Nani's room.

Nani and Sanam were in deep sleep with Daaku sleeping on a rug next to the bed. Rajeev had returned home to find Sanam sleeping next to Nani.

"Sanam must have been massaging Nani's legs," Rajeev thought as he gently put the blanket over both the women.

Avinash and Rajeev both stood at the door looking at what both called 'Family'. They both felt a pull towards the women. It was not the blood ties, but love that made a family.

"Did you have dinner?"Avinash asked Rajeev.

"Nahin...Dinner is ready. Sana ne fried fish banayi hai, but I didn't feel like eating alone" Rajeev replied.

"That's great. Yeh dekh!"Avinash showed him the paper bags that had brought along with him.

"Abey Desi Tharra?" Rajeev eyed Avinash with amusement remembering their days of youth when they had tasted Desi for the first time together.

"Chalen terrace par? Just like the old times?" Avinash said.

"Fish utha le....mutton and chicken kebabs hain mere pass. Chakhna bhi hai!" Avinash told Rajeev.

"But Desi? Mere pass 'Glenfiddich' ki do bottles padi hain!" Rajeev said.

"Abey Dr. Rajeev ko chod kar aja. Apna yeh Armani suit bhi uttar. Mere friend Bittu ko bhej!" Avinash chided Rajeev.

Sometime later, Avinash and Rajeev were sitting on the water tank of the building terrace drinking 'Desi' and munching kebabs.

"Both must have been tired after spending the full day in dress trials with designers" Avinash said, and Rajeev agreed.

"Sana se zyaada Nani excited thee aaj. She called me twice in between the trials. You know I had seen her this happy with my sister. You never happened to meet my family na? Sarah was a darling! She was in grade two I guess when I came to Mumbai," Rajeev sighed.

"Amazing days were those! That fierce passion you had Bittu! And you did all of that whatever you vowed and even more! I never said it...I am so proud of you!" Avinash said, hugging Rajeev.

"But what was the use, Avi? The guy I wanted to bring down bit dust even before I could throw money I had earned on his face. The person I had earned the money for left this world in her youth. Instead of running after money and glory, I wish I had spent those precious years with my sister, at least I would have had more memories. For all the money I have now can't give me memories with my sister" Rajeev broke down for the second time after the death of his sister. He had never given himself time to grieve. He cried his heart out and Avinash was there to support him.

A little later, Avinash looked at Rajeev who had been sitting quietly for quite some time now.

"You know Avi why I liked you?" Rajeev asked.

Avinash looked at him confused.

"You never took pity on me...unlike others. So don't pity me now!" Rajeev said a bit tersely.

"Hmmm...I am not taking pity on you...I am concerned for you. Sanam and I take you as a family....so I am well within my rights to worry for you! Chal ek aur peg marte hain! Waise mere paas tere liye ek news hai!" Avinash said.

"Ab bhav khana band kar aur bata kya?" Rajeev said with a smile. Avinash's naughty expressions had given him a hint.

"I met Rajni today!" Avinash said.

"Rajni?" Rajeev tried remembering.

"Arre saale wahi 'Rajeev ki Rajni'... jiske saath you had popped your cherry!" Avinash chuckled.

"Fu*k!" Rajeev said, startled.

"Haan..wahi!" Avinash said smugly.

"She is Aunty's new neighbour's niece who is visiting Pune these days. And guess what my Aunty and Nani have already put the plans to bring you two together" Avinash almost laughed at Rajeev's agony.

"Yaar Rajni?" Rajeev tried to remember the thin, willowy nerdy girl with whom he had made love one drunken evening. His friends had teased him with 'Rajeev ki Rajni and Rajni ka Rajeev' for the rest of the year.

"Vaise bahut hot dikhti hai! She is now...like...hmm... well-endowed maal!" Avinash told Rajeev to get glared at by Rajeev.

"Teri biwi ko batoun?"Rajeev threatened him.

"Abey saale...mera yaar hai tu...Biwi se bhi pehle tu aaya tha meri life main!"Avinash hit him playfully and Rajeev grinned in return.

"Tujhe pata hai Promod kahan hai? Pata hai woh bhi ladki dhoond raha hai…" Avinash said, and they got talking like the earlier days.

"Yaar you Shastri men...why are you after the women in my family? Pehle tu...phir Baba," Rajeev asked Avinash after downing a few more pegs.

"You know?" Avinash asked, almost spitting out the drink.

"You have to be blind to not see! Aur teri Biwi ko bol...it's painfully obvious when she watches both of them with that expression...woh girls ka expression hota hai na…Awwww" Rajeev slurred.

"'Awwww'...aise Sana does!" Rajeev acted out Sanam.

Avinash couldn't help but laugh. But Rajeev wasn't done.

"Aaj mujhe dhake de de kar hospital bheja...zabardasti. Date planning ki hogi tum logon ne! Saale sab mujhe andha samajhte ho! But don't tell Sana!" Rajeev slurred again.

"I will not but you don't tell Sana!" Avinash said in a sing-song way.

"I love you yaar Avi...but don't tell Sana!" Rajeev rhymed in.

It was three in the morning, and both came down completely sloshed.

"Arre Avi...don't make noise! And don't tell Sana!" slurred a drunken Rajeev as they entered the flat.

"No...I never make noise. I make Jam party! But don't tell Sana!" Avinash said laughing loudly. Rajeev tried to control but burst into laughter. An hour back Avinash had told Rajeev what he had done to the guys who had misbehaved with Sanam. They had not stopped laughing since then.

"I love you bhai…But don't tell Sana!" Rajeev kissed Avinash on the cheek.

"I love you too…But don't tell Sana!" Avinash kissed Rajeev back on both the cheeks.

Both were unaware that the main door had not miraculously opened, someone had opened it after getting frustrated with their failed attempts. Poor men were not even aware that their drunken show of affection was being recorded.

" Nahiiiii!!!!!!!!!!" Rajeev and Avinash woke up to a shrill scream.

" Nahiiiii!!!!!!" Nani screamed again for effect.

"Naaaani bas!" Rajeev shut his ears.

"Yeh dekhne se pehle main mar kyun nahin gayi!" Nani said dramatically. Sanam couldn't stop giggling.

Rajeev forced himself to open his eyes to understand the cause of Nani's dramatics. His legs felt heavier than usual.

Sprawled on the rest of the bed was Avinash with his legs on Rajeev's. He had removed his kurta sometime during the night and was now only in his jeans.

"Avi!" Rajeev said in exasperation.

"I love you Baby! Ab sone de!" Avinash said in a sleepy voice.

"Abey kamine uth! Kapde pehen!" Rajeev told Avinash as Nani and Sanam rolled in laughter.

Rajeev too sheepishly smiled till he realised that he too wasn't wearing his Shirt.

"Oh shit!" Rajeev screamed and the ladies went into another laughing fit.

It was after a few minutes that men walked 'the walk of shame!' thankfully fully clothed this time.

"Sorry Baby!" Avinash went to hug his wife who successfully dodged him.

"Sorry Nani! Kal raat zyada ho gayi thee!" Avinash said as he sat down holding his head in his hands.

"Avi yeh le!"Rajeev handed him a couple of asprins which they washed with nimbu-pani that Sanam had made.

"Bachon chalo ab kuch khaa lo!" Nani offered them toasted buttered bread, eggs and loads of coffee to wash it down supposedly good for a hangover.

"Avi just call on my phone na…I don't know where my phone is."Rajeev asked Avi.

Suddenly the whole dining hall echoed with….

Maa da laadla bigad gaya…

"Again," Rajeev said, shocked. In the background Nani and Sanam almost fell off their respective chairs laughing as the new caller tone of Rajeev's phone echoed in the dining hall. Avinash too was trying to hide his huge grin.

"Naaaani" Rajeev screamed as he took his phone and went inside his room trying to stifle his own laughter.

CHAPTER- 74
THE WEDDING DAY

The last day of Sanam-Avinash three days wedding came quickly for everyone. The previous two days had gone in a jiffy with the Cocktail Party and Sangeet. Madhu -Rohan, Akriti-Naveen had arrived a day before the wedding. The women had an emotional reunion.

The day had started pretty early at the Dhindsa residence. The Anand Karaj Ceremony was slated for eleven a.m. at the Gurudwara. Accordingly, the 'Chura Charai' ceremony was kept at seven a.m.

Sanam, Madhu and Akriti had barely slept a few hours last night but were up by the first light. Deepu was proudly sitting on behalf of the 'Uncle of the bride' for the Chura ceremony. Deepu had been brought to Mumbai from Punjab as his parents were absconding after pocketing money from various people. The money lenders had then targeted Deepu, who had been rescued by Nihar. His spirit and body had recovered quickly from the ordeal he had gone through recently. Avinash had made sure that he had not been left behind. Deepu and Nihar had now become 'Chuddi-Buddies'! Everyone was getting extremely excited, except Rajeev-who was borderline anxious.

Rajeev was getting worried looking at the two over-enthusiastic septuagenarians hopping here and there: his own Nani and Madhu's Aji. They both had been singing 'Folk songs' since the Chura ceremony had started and had even done kikali[Phugadi] in their excitement.

Rajeev had lost it then. The first thing he had done was made them sit and checked their Blood Pressure and Pulse. The women had responded with a giddy laughter.

"Rajeev Bhai…come quickly…Akriti has fainted!" Madhu called out when Rajeev was checking Nani.

"Akriti had been puking since morning and then fainted suddenly!" Madhu said.

"What did you girls eat last night?" Rajeev asked Sanam and Madhu.

"Ice-cream!" Madhu said.

"She will gain consciousness in a few minutes. I doubt there is a need to worry! Exertion!" Rajeev declared and the family members heaved a sigh of relief. They left the girls alone to rest before the battery of make-up and designers arrived. .

"Call Naveen here. Ask him to get a pregnancy test along with him!" Rajeev discreetly told Madhu whose eyes dilated in excitement.

Naveen landed at the Dhindsa residence exactly half an hour later with Rohan and six different pregnancy tests. He and Rohan were still in their night suits.

"Baby, try this one first...Pareena ne bhi yahi brand se apni pregnancy declare kiya tha!" Naveen said.

"Tumhe Pareena ki padhi hai abhi? You A&&hole!"Akriti cried.

"Naveen chal, let's wait outside!" Rajeev tried to handle the situation.

"Abhi delivery nahin hui Naveen!" Rajeev chuckled and teased Naveen who had been pacing the lobby waiting for Akriti to come out. In a few minutes, the house was filled with shrill screams of the women.

"Fu*k, why are they screaming?" Naveen asked the rhetorical question.

"Congratulations Naveen…tu pregnant hai!" Rohan announced and hugged him as Madhu opened the door and gesticulated.

"Hain?" Naveen almost passed out in excitement.

"See I told you Pareena is my lucky mascot!" Naveen said in his over-enthusiasm.

"Rohan yeh pitega! Jaa pehle apni biwi se mil" Rajeev mocked him. Thankfully, better sense prevailed, and Naveen rushed to his wife.

"OH MY GOD! Look at the time!"Kenneth Joseph, the famous stylist who had already arrived with his team, screamed in anxiety. It was eight-thirty already and eleven o'clock was the wedding. In the next few minutes, the

Dhindsa residence resembled a local train station of Mumbai, where the trains were coming and going, and passengers were just being carried with the flow.

The scene wasn't different back at the Hotel where the Shastris and the Kulkarnis were getting ready. At least a dozen make-up artists and hairdressers had come first thing in the morning. All the men had been walking on eggshells.

"I am looking fat?" was the question everyone wanted to avoid.

"Papa, where are you going? Help me, I can't find the socks!" Avinash called his father out.

"Beta...aur zor se bol...teri maa subah se do baar class laga chuki hai! I am going to Baba's room to change!" Alok quickly got out of the corridor.

When he reached Baba's room, at least three more husbands had taken shelter there.

The wedding planner had been hustling up the Shastris and Kulkarnis and was able to get them ready almost in the nick of time. After the 'Sehra Bandhi rasam' the Barat was ready to roll.

"Girls jaldi karo!" Rajeev was getting anxious. It was a rare occurrence. Rajeev couldn't remember when he had felt this level of anxiety...maybe the time he was expecting his medical school result.

"Anything that can go wrong, will go wrong in a wedding!" Rajeev told himself. He had been getting this intuition since morning and till now it had been on point.

Nani and Aji had gone delirious singing, laughing and dancing during the Chura ceremony and then almost collapsed. Akriti had fainted. Nani had later cried because her make-up was not up to her standards.

Madhu had burnt her fingers while ironing her dress. Mitali had spilled a glass of water and the iced water had landed on Daaku. Daaku had gone bonkers barking and howling in the entire house. Rajeev had to come out of his shower in a towel to control the situation. Daaku's prancing had freaked out Madhu's mother, who was borderline cynophobic. To top it all Sanam, who Rajeev thought had a placid disposition, had almost turned into a Bridezella.

She had a meltdown when she realised that her nail paint shade was darker than the colour of her lehenga.

"Yes we are leaving Rekha(the wedding planner)!" Rajeev barked in the phone.

"I think we should head out to the Gurudwara...I will take care of the visitors there till the time you guys reach!" Madhu's father said, much to Rajeev's relief.

He then sent Deepu and Madhu's family, who were all ready, ahead in the car to the Gurudwara.

"Sana Barat nikal gayi hai hotel se!" Rajeev called out to hear the girls screams in return.

Fifteen minutes later, Sanam came out of the room.

"Main kaisi lag rahi hoon?" Sanam asked Rajeev and Nani.

"Hai ni...kinni sohni! Mitali la mirchan laya! Nazar uttarni hai!" Nani screamed.

"Girls chalo, muhurat nikal jayega!" Rajeev hustled the girls.

When they settled Sanam in the back seat, they realised no one else could fit in because of the expanse of her lehenga.

Madhu, Akriti, Nani and Mitali were put in one car and Rajeev and Sanam went in the other car.

The Gurudwara was not very far away but with the impending elections, a major Political party had chosen that day to plan a Rally.

"Bloody Murphy's law! Mushtaq Bhai, let's move faster!" Rajeev screamed at the Driver.

"Doctor sab theek ho jayega!" Sanam tried to pacify the Doctor. The last she had seen Rajeev this hyper had been in Nanded when Nani had become unconscious .

"Sana you don't understand...tum logon ko time par pahunchane ki responsibility meri hai! Aur subah se tum sab ladies mujhe kitne heart attacks de chuki ho!" Rajeev said exasperated.

"Sorry Doc!" Sanam giggled and Rajeev visibly relaxed when the Rally took the opposite direction, but his peace was short-lived.

Only a kilometre away from the Gurudwara, the BMW jerked and broke down.

"What the bloody F**K!" Rajeev screamed in agony.

"Rekha send a car; our BMW has broken down!" Rajeev barked in the phone.

"Doctor, I am getting nervous…What if I don't reach in time!" Sanam was on the precipice of another meltdown.

"HOLY shit!" Rajeev spoke aloud.

"What happened? Sanam looked in the direction Rajeev was looking. .

On the opposite road was a fleet of fifteen-twenty motorbikes with women riders in Nauvari sari. This fleet of motorcycles was followed by a huge convoy of cars.

"Haaye ek aur rally!" Sanam exclaimed.

"Sana yeh rally nahin tumhari Baarat hai!" Rajeev exclaimed.

"FU*K!" Sanam exclaimed as she identified Avinash pillion riding on his thunderbird that was being ridden by her own mother-in-law!

The Kulkarni women had been completely enamoured by the show of Punjabi culture in the form of Gidda and Bhangra at the Mehendi function. They too wanted to showcase their own culture in this wedding. An urgent meeting had been called and it had been decided that they would make a grand cultural entry.

"Another ten minutes and they will take a U-Turn Sana and reach here! You will be the first bride who will take a lift from her own baarat!" Rajeev said aloud.

"Doctor, do something! Jab tak car aayegi, Barat will have surpassed us!" Sanam almost cried.

"Sana, you trust me right?" Rajeev said as he got her down from the car. With no taxi in sight, Rajeev whistled for an autorickshaw.

After somehow squeezing Sanam and her lehenga in the passenger's seat, Rajeev sat on the side of the Auto driver. However, Murphy's law was still operating. The auto-driver was a highly principled person. He refused to break rules and let a passenger sit in front.

"Hum leke jayenge Dulhania ko barabar se!" the rickshaw driver said.

"Pagal hai kya...she is my responsibility!" Rajeev shouted at him.

Ultimately, Rajeev paid him a two-thousand rupee note and asked him to catch another auto and trail them.

"Doctor, you know how to drive an auto?" Sanam asked, shocked.

"I know how to ride a bike...how difficult can this be?" Rajeev exclaimed.

After a few wrong starts Rajeev started the auto.

"Woohoo! Let's get the party rolling! " Rajeev exclaimed.

In flat seven minutes Rajeev stopped the Auto at the Gurudwara where Madhu, Akriti and Nani were waiting, tied in knots with worry.

"Thank God!" Nani exclaimed as Sanam got down from the auto.

"Doctor, you are such a blessing!" Sanam told Rajeev.

"I need a favour from you Sana!" Rajeev stopped Sanam.

"Haan...anything!" Sanam responded.

"Please don't let Avinash use this in his movie!" Rajeev pleaded.

CHAPTER- 75

#TRUE LOVE

The Kulkarni women had been completely enamoured by the show of Punjabi culture in the form of Gidda and Bhangra at the Mehendi function. They too wanted to showcase their own culture in this wedding. An urgent meeting had been called, and it had been decided that they would make a grand cultural entry.

For decades, the Kulkarni clan women had been a part of Women's Dhol Tasha pathaks(groups) that performed at various pandals during the Ganesh Utsav. This practice had started as an effort to break gender stereotypes as these percussion instruments were traditionally played by men and the pathaks (band in Marathi) did not enrol women. Off late the women had started riding bikes too.

Karuna and Mrs.Kulkarni had actively participated in these groups, as had their daughters-in-law. So, it had been decided by the women that the sisters-in-law will lead the baraat of their favourite 'Devar'(brother-in-law).

"Aru you what? Kya? It has been years now!" Alok spoke shocked when his wife announced that she would ride the bike and play the dhol-tasha.

"Your back pain will flare up! And it has been ages since you rode a bike!" Alok said in a distraught tone.

"Aai, Papa has a valid point! But if I ride with you then I can handle in case anything goes wrong...and Dhol Tasha only ten minutes for you ok?" Avinash suggested a mid-way.

"We are doing it!" Karuna had come out and yelled to the ladies.

The young Kulkarni women had contacted their friends. Avinash's cousin, the local MLA, had brought out his cavalry. The fact that the opposition had tried to organise a Political rally in his Shakha had pissed him off greatly. He quickly approached the Magistrate and municipality to get required permits. Of course, the Shastri name did carry a lot of weight. Weight that the MLA threw here and there to close down many roads in the heart of the city and put a secure Police bandobast in order. He also (of course...discreetly)spread the news about the unique gesture of the sisters-in-law ,ensuring that the Shastri wedding became the talk of the nation and not the political rally.

The next morning saw the Kulkarni women dressed in the traditional Marathi avatar: Nauvari, nathni (nose ring), necklace, bangles, jhumkas, a chandrakor tikali (half-moon-shaped bindi) turban and aviators.

After the Shehra Bandhi , Avinash asked everyone to stop for a moment , joined his hands and addressed the women battalion…

"My dear Aai, Aatya, sisters and sisters-in-law,

I am deeply indebted to you all for this beautiful gesture. To be loved so much is indeed a true honour. Thank you so much for loving me even when a few of you know me very little and I am sure whatever little you know is pretty bad. I am not God...absolutely not…but I can now understand how proud Ganpati Bappa would feel to be led by women... I think the hand that feeds the future of the country with love is the greatest and it also has the strength to beat the hell out of patriarchal warlords.

Thankyou my dear Aai, Aatya, sisters and sisters-in-law for being such BAD-ASS women! I bow down to you!"

With this Avinash bowed down amidst thunderous applause. Unknown to Avinash, an over-enthusiastic TV reporter had already entered the hotel foyer had recorded the whole scene. By the time, the baraat reached the Gurudwara, National TV channels had picked up the story and were heading towards the wedding venue.

Rajeev, Nani , Madhu's parents and the Zumba Gang were already there at the entrance to welcome the Baraat.

The Granthiji had recommended that the bride and her friends could get a proper look at the baraat from the first-floor room meant for his meetings. Sanam , Madhu and Akriti had rushed to the first floor as soon as they could.

As the Baraat reached the Gurudwara road, a battery of valets appeared to take over the bikes from the women. A tempo loaded with Dhols had already been waiting for them. In a span of a few minutes, a couple of nagada player appeared and announced the arrival of the baraat.

The women took over the dhols and took their positions.

"Ganpati Bappa…. Moriya!" Karuna shouted in the microphone and the whole crowd cheered along.

With this, Karuna started the Dhol followed by the rest of the women. The whole ten minutes that the dhol-tashe resounded, were exhilarating for the everyone in the crowd.

The best thing was that the women were thoroughly enjoying the moment. The happiness on their faces was genuine and that feeling was mirrored in the audience.

A short while later, a now emotional Karuna hugged Avinash and whispered, "I am proud of you Pillu(dear one)!"

The baraat was soon welcomed by the Bride's family. Nani did Avinash's arti and the Zumba Gang teased Avinash.

"Congratulations Dulhe miyaan!" Rajeev hugged Avinash but his eyes were looking for his 'Jaan'.

"Where is she?" Avinash gestured Rajeev to which Rajeev had looked up towards a small window on the first floor.

And what Avinash saw there, froze him for a moment. He hadn't seen his Sanam look more beautiful. The moment their eyes locked, her breath quickened, and she blushed.

Sanam blushed at the intense appraising look her husband gave her. She was suddenly feeling coy like a typical bride. Although they had been married for over one year, this felt new. She had been feasting her eyes on her extremely handsome husband. Avinash was clad in a cream Sherwani with embroidery matching her Lehenga. He was wearing a turban and carrying a talwaar (sword). His face was covered with a Sehra made of flowers. True to his word he had kept his bearded look for the wedding. The whole environment was giving her goosebumps.

"Chal meri jaan...they are calling!" Madhu said.

The mood inside the Gurudwara was serene and sombre, the exact opposite of what had been outside. Soon the Granthiji asked the bride to be called. When Sanam did come, there was a collective gasp.

She looked ethereal in a peach-pink embroidered lehenga. She had opted for an emerald choker set. The highlight of her look was a big hoop of a nose ring which made her look like a princess.

All settled down for the 'Anand Karaj' ceremony. After four Lavaan(phere) the Garanthiji announced Sanam and Avinash a couple and called the couple's parents to step forward and bless the newlyweds.

"On the behalf of Mrs. Rupinder Kaur and Tejinder Singh Bedi, I take the honour of giving the responsibility of their dearest daughter 'Sanam' to Avinash, the man who I know will love and cherish her more than anything in this world. Take care of each other!" Nani spoke her heart and there was not one eye that didn't get moist.

Sometime later, the newlywed couple exited the Gurudwara amidst applause.

"Ouch," Sanam screamed as her foot got stuck in her Lehenga while climbing down the steps. She would have fallen down badly had her Hulk of a husband not caught her in time.

"Avinash!" Sanam exclaimed again but now in delight when Avinash scooped her in his arms for the rest of the stairs.

"Haan baby!" Avinash whispered back as he carried her down the stairs.

"I love you!" Sanam gave him a look full of adoration.

"I love you too baby!" Avinash replied, scooping her closer. And this moment went on to be hailed as one of the most romantic moments in the history of Indian Social Media. #TrueLove broke the social media.

Dear Avinash,

I know this is a dream but mujhe na tere saath FOREVER FEELING aati hai! Ek dum filmy…Charan Dohar types…#ForeverwalaISHQ! #TrueLove

Sachi kasam se….kabhi kabhi aisa lagta hai ki shaayad yeh sach ho jaye!

But then reality knocks. Khair, mujhe toh mera FOREVER moment nahin milega…Waheguru ke roz ardaas karti hoon ki tumhe woh mil jaye jisko tum TRUE LOVE kar sako….I will be happy in your happiness!

Loads of love,

Sanam

Dear Sanam,

I was fifteen years old when one day I went to Papa's library to impress him. I picked up what I thought till now to be a very 'hyped' novel 'The Alchemist'. I read it and was disappointed by its vision. However, years later I read it again and shamelessly used one of its very popular quotes as a dialogue in one of my movies...you know this one ...

"And, when you want something, all the universe conspires in helping you to achieve it."

'The Alchemist' tells the story of a young shepherd named 'Santiago' who is able to find a treasure beyond his wildest dreams. In his travels, he meets a series of characters who either directly help him or teach him a valuable lesson by example.

Its true meaning, I have understood only today. It feels as if everything that happened in my life...every mistake I ever made...every decision I took...every person I met along the path was destined to bring me to you!

Thank You so much for asking for my happiness....your Waheguru twisted the entire world and brought you to me...

Tomorrow is our wedding...and I promise our TRUE LOVE is going to be forever!

Trust me on that!

Only Yours,

Avinash

THE END

EPILOGUE

Thirteen years later….

"Sweetheart jaldi kar...people will start arriving anytime!" Avinash called out.

"Bas ho gaya!" Sanam said and walked out the adjoining room which they had converted into a walk-in closet cum dressing room.

Sanam was clad in a beautiful multicolour floral sundress with a thin belt securing her waist.

"Moti lag rahi hoon?" Sanam looked at herself making the cute pout that always succeeded to make Avinash crazier about her.

"Absolutely not...cute and hot…dono lag rahi hai ! How do you manage to look so sexy even after giving me two gorgeous kids almost a decade back!" Avinash said earnestly and hugged her from behind.

"Chodo na Avinash bache aa jayenge!" Sanam blushed.

"Toh aane do...main darta hoon kya? Unko bhi dekhne do how much I love their mother!" Avinash told her back, almost throwing a challenge.

And the very next minute, fate laughed back at him. The door was pushed back as Sarah and Agastaya(Ty; pronounced as 'Tie') barged in, making Avinash step away as a reaction.

"Maa...see he is not returning my phone!" Sarah complained.

"I was just playing the last level...can't my own sister be generous enough to let me complete the game!" Agastya Avinash Shastri addressed the audience.

"No...I need to check on Aradhya for the party!" Sarah almost screamed back.

"Di ...It's my birthday party that you have invited her to!" Ty replied impatiently.

"I will make sure my gang troubles all you Didis out there! And specially that Kabeer whom you stare at again and again and then giggle like a lunatic," Ty threw the phone on the bed and ran away.

"I will kill you Ty!" Sarah ran after her brother.

"Yeh kya Tsunami aayi aur chali gayi?" Avinash rubbed his stubble in deep thought.

"Let's go down and check!" Sanam huffed.

"Yeh Kabeer kaun hai? Woh Kabeer Sharma? Nursery main jiski nose behti the? Woh?" Avinash enquired from his wife.

"Avinash, Sarah is twelve...almost thirteen ...crushes toh honge na!" Sanam tried explaining to him, but his expressions warned her of the debate that was going on in his head.

Thankfully, the phone rang.

"Romance baad main karna...Avi...chal na! Waiting for you to start the beer... Rohan and Madhu aagaye hain!" Rajeev yelled on the other side of the phone.

"Coming yaar!" Avinash said now cheerful at the thought of chilled beer with his best friends. It was Ty's birthday. At the age of four, Agastya had gained clarity that he wanted to be called 'Ty' and not Chintu, Pintu, Gugu, Bugghu etc his wife had a habit of calling their kids.

"Biwi let's roll…It's our baby's ninth birthday" Avinash pulled her along.

Soon, they were enveloped with cheer and happiness: their FAMILY.

Akriti and Naveen had been able to make it with their two daughters aged Rhea(twelve) and Piya(seven). Rohan and Madhu had two daughters as well….Kiara(twelve) and Sitara(two). The younger daughter was a lucky 'accident' as Rohan always said.

Deepu had become an engineer and had recently gotten married. He had been posted on site in Germany. He had never heard from his parents again. He and his wife, Simran had especially come down for them. Nihar too had gotten married and had shifted to Nagpur permanently with his mother and wife. He was here today with wife and new-born son.

Only Nani and Baba were not there. Pammi had passed away three months after Sanam and Avinash's wedding. Baba had passed away a year after Ty had been born. As they said...they will live on in their family's hearts. They were being sorely missed.

Actually, everyone had come down especially...not only for Ty's birthday but also for the release party the next day of the new OTT series : '#TrueLove' that Avinash had written, produced ,and directed. It was nothing but their own story, but of course the disclaimer went along to declare otherwise. Avinash had taken inspiration of the title from the lid of the old cookie tin box.

The idea had been brewing in Avinash's mind since ages. After 'Manchali' he had tasted both success and failure in his career. With his family behind him, he had been able to be stoic about the highs as well as the lows. He had dabbled in documentary writing and produced two documentaries. One had sunk without trace and the second had won him a few awards. Some of his movies had done well and some of them had bombed.

Avinash had wanted to try his hand at comedy for a long time till the idea of his own love-story struck him. It had taken him a long time to convince his own wife and Rajeev. Once they were on board, the rest needed almost no convincing at all.

"Avinash...just don't put the love triangle in!" Sanam had said before agreeing.

Avinash gasped. He had shock written on his face.

"You know about it?" Avinash said.

"Haan...." Sanam said softly.

"Kabse?" Avinash asked.

"Since the time we went to Chicago to meet Vidya. Her eyes had the same emotion that I had when I had seen you with that Nitika!" Sanam sighed and kept her head on husband's shoulder.

"So, then what did you feel?" Avinash asked curiously.

"Shocked at first, then honoured and cherished!" Sanam said.

"I was honoured that someone so nice and genuine like the Doctor could think about me and kisi ko pyaar karna galat nahin hai..usse dosre par force karna galat hai. Doctor never did that, and he never made me feel uncomfortable. He went out of his way to bring us together. Our relationship doesn't have a name, but it doesn't even need one. He honoured *his word and he really cared for me! I am happy he found Vidya. They are made for each other!" Sanam said with a smile.*

She was correct. Rajeev and Vidya were indeed made for each other.

It had been almost thirteen years since his own marriage...re-marriage. A lot of things had happened but the best thing that had happened was that his best friend had struck a gold-mine of luck and found love.

Dr. Vidya Iyenger had been the only woman who had been successful in unlocking his friend's heart and healing him. Their story had been nothing short of a Bollywood masala film. Ten years back, after a lot of twists and turns, they had finally gotten married in Chennai according to Hindu rituals.

They complimented each other and their daughter and six-year-old 'Anaya' was a blessing from God. The happy couple was now expecting their second baby. After Rajeev's wedding, Rajeev and Avinash had decided to have at least one holiday every year together as a family. Sarah was especially fond of her Doctor 'Chacha' and 'Chachi'. She had long discussions with them on some or the other medical practice or concept. Once or twice, Rajeev had even taken her to his hospital in Mumbai where he would be consulting on his trips to Mumbai. Sarah had returned ecstatic and dewy eyed from her visit. Vidya had taken her a step further. She had got her a Blood pressure machine, stethoscope, pulse machine and a few things. She had taught her to take basic readings. Since then, Sarah had gone bonkers, and every second day would check everyone. The excitement had ebbed down a little over the last year...now she would check them weekly.

"Avi kya soch raha hai aaj? Release Party is all planned...right? Nervous?" Rajeev came and patted his back. Avinash was sitting in the lawn keeping an eye on all the kids.

"Guys beer ke bina baat karna gunah hai!" Naveen came with Rohan in tow with chilled beers.

"Cheers! To Ty and hamare bhai! Rhyme par dhyan dijiye!" Naveen said enthusiastically.

"Tu nahin badlega Naveen!" Avinash said laughing.

"Par aaj tu bahut different lag raha hai Avi!" Rohan said.

"Nahin yaar! Just realised how quickly the time passed. Look at our kids- all so grown up!"Avinash looked at the other side of the huge seaside lawn of their bungalow. In one corner, all their daughters were huddled as a group. Nearby, Ty was playing with his friends. Their wives too had become the thickest friends. Vidya had been an effortless addition.

"Hmm," the men agreed, understanding what Avinash was feeling.

"Khair, please tell me mere character ke liye koi handsome hunk ko liya na?" Naveen said nonchalantly, instantly drawing abuses from the rest.

Their camaraderie was broken by the girls' screams.

Avinash looked behind and saw Ty and a hefty boy involved in a scuffle. Both the guys were punching each other. Ty had caught the other guy's shirt. Soon Avinash and Rajeev held Ty and the other guy back.

"What happened Ty?" Avinash raised his voice to silence the babble that had started.

"He pulled Anaya's pig tails!" Ty said growling at the other guy.

It was then that everyone saw poor Anaya crying in one corner. By this time, the women had also come out. Vidya quickly scooped up Anaya and pacified her.

Avinash looked at the boys and saw the damage his son had done. Both the boys had punched each other. A few scratches and things would have been fine, but Ty had refused to leave the other guy while they were separating them. As a consequence, he had torn out the buttons on the other boy's shirt.

"We need to talk! But before that, apologise to the young man!" Avinash told Ty tersely.

Ty remained silent and stood there brooding.

"Ty beta...it's ok...say sorry! Let's forget this!" Rajeev intervened.

"No sir, I will not. If he does it again, I will punch him yet another time!" Ty growled at the boy who by now was close to tears.

"Bittu, ask Sanam to get this child another shirt! I will drop him home myself! Till then I need to talk to my son! Ty to study!" Avinash said in a serious tone, enough to give Sanam goosebumps.

"Avi baccha hai...aisa ho jata hai!" Sanam ran after him.

"Montu dhyaan se!" Alok told Avinash as a worried Karuna looked on.

Avinash kept on walking with Ty almost dragging along.

Avinash took Ty to his study and locked the door. He made him sit on the chair and took the one behind the desk.

"Ty, why didn't you apologise?" Avinash asked a while later when he had brought his own anger under control.

"Papa, he was wrong. I was right. Why should I say sorry?" Ty said hurt by his father's illogical demands.

Avinash observed his child and asked, "Acha now tell me what happened?"

"He pulled Anaya's pony tails!" Ty said.

"With force?" Avinash asked.

"No...gently!" Ty said honestly.

"Then what happened?" Avinash prodded his son, a small smile playing on his own lips.

"He called her cute!" Ty growled.

"Ok...so he didn't hurt her right?" Avinash said.

"He asked her to become his best friend! Anaya will be my friend! ONLY MINE! I will hit him more if he does that again!" Ty yelled.

"It's ok...Chill. Sorry I didn't know that" Avinash thought a diplomatic approach suited better here.

That pacified Ty greatly.

"I am sorry Papa...I yelled at you!" Ty said, looking sullen.

Avinash got out of his chair, went to his son. He kneeled down and hugged his son.

"It's ok baby...I love you!" Avinash said tousling his hair after kissing his cheeks.

"Eww.... Papa, why are you behaving like Mummy?" Ty made a face.

"Acha ek baat bata....why have you started calling Rajeev chahu 'Sir'? Avinash asked, trying to stifle his laughter because he already knew the answer.

"Because Anaya is not my sister...never will be. Sisters can never be girlfriends! My friend told me," Ty said logically.

"Acha yeh logic na kisi ko bolna nahin..ok? It's our secret! Ok?" he said and both father and son hi-fived on that.

By the time Avinash returned home after dropping the kid to his home and profusely apologising to the boy's parents it was dinner time. All were together in the family room. The adults had been waiting for him for dinner and the kids were currently being fed.

Dinner was a wonderful fare.

"I am thinking of coming out of the closet!" Avinash declared at the table.

Vidya gasped and silence fell at the table.

"Arre no...matlab not that wala...I mean I am thinking of planning to come out of my anonymity and claim my novels! I want Papa and Sanam also to do the same! For years I have wanted to interact with my readers face to face. I think it's time we claim our work...say what?" Avinash looked at his father and Sanam.

"We can think about it! I would like to retire now. I am done now. Maybe it's time to let the readers know who has been behind the words!" Alok said. He hadn't written a movie in around fifteen years but had concentrated on writing books. His two novels and a poem compilation had been nominated for various awards and won a few.

"I don't know...maybe!" Sanam too had many Romance novels under her belt.

"Cheers to the writers at the table!" Rajeev raised a toast, and all followed.

Almost an hour later...

"Anna, baby let's go! Way past your bedtime!" Rajeev told his daughter.

"Should I go Gusty?" Anaya turned towards Ty and asked his permission. She had shortened his name to 'Gusty'. No one else could call him that.

"Ok...tomorrow get up early...Baba will take us to the beach! Then we will eat ice-cream!" Ty said enthusiastically.

"No ice-cream sweetheart, you will fall ill!" Rajeev intervened.

"I will take care of her Sir!" Ty replied leaving Rajeev shocked.

Ty kissed Anaya's cheeks and wished them goodnight giving Rajeev a stinker look.

"Rajeev, surely you are overreacting! They are just kids!" Vidya tried to reason with her husband.

"Saale Shastri men….always after the women of my family!" Rajeev ground his teeth.

Vidya bit her lips to avoid a smile.

"That ittu sa boy, jisko maine apne haath mein khilaya hai…gave me a stinker!" Rajeev paced their room.

"Shhh…Anaya is sleeping in the next room; she will get up!" Vidya said. The Shastris had gotten a full suite ready for Rajeev after Avinash's wedding. It was a two-bedroom complete with an ensuite and a study.

"Appadi solli pona avanukum awa pudichi irukku" Vidya said laughing.

"Translation?" Rajeev huffed

"Anaya also cares for him! She changed her frock twice because he didn't like it!" Vidya giggled.

Rajeev scowled.

"They look so cute together!" She added and Rajeev grimaced.

"Yaar please!" Rajeev told her.

"Look here sweetheart, they are kids. We still have six seven more years! Uske baad dekhenge! Now bring your sexy ass here and kiss me!" Vidya pulled her husband towards herself and brought her lips to his.

"Aaj kya hua study main?" Sanam asked as she entered their bedroom.

Avinash was writing something in his letter pad.

"Avi, I am bored!" Sanam whined.

"Aa raha hoon mere do bacho ki maa! Just let me complete this!" Avinash said.

Almost twenty minutes later, Avinash got up...folded the piece of paper and opened the locked door of the wardrobe. There were two huge tin boxes sitting there...one named 'Sarah' the other named 'Ty'.

Avinash put the letter in Ty's box. They had decided to write letters to their kids and gift them this goldmine of memories for their future.

"Ty ne kyun kiya yeh sab?" Sanam asked her husband as he lay down next to her.

Avinash told her and at the end both laughed their hearts out.

"Mujhe lagta hai tumko bahu dhoondni nahin padegi!" Avinash teased Sanam.

"Pata hai!" Sanam giggled.

"Bittu apni kismat ko ro raha hoga! Sab Shastris laundon ko Dhindsa lau.." Avinash was about complete when a light smack stopped him.

"Chee...kitne bad words..." Sanam complained.

"Abey kya bad words? Tum hamesha over-react karti ho!" Avinash snapped.

By that time, his wife had already taken offence. Avinash spent the next half an hour fighting her tears.

"Avinash...sab theek rahega na?" Sanam asked him a while later.

"Haan sweetheart ...sab theek hoga..aur nahin hua toh sab sambhaal lenge!" Avinash knew she was worried about it. Along with his fame, Avinash had also invited a lot of senseless vituperative criticism. One section of the fans were almost barbaric with the abusive and hateful comments on him and his family. She didn't want him to go into that space again.

"I can take when they abuse me...call me a gold digger and what not...but I can't listen to people abusing you! It hurts me so much!" Sanam said, crying.

"Baby we can change ourselves, not others. There have been testing times, and there will be more. We can't live under the rock! Since the time you have come in my life, you have given me so much-you gave me strength and courage to fight back. You gave me my family back! I know that no matter whatever the world says about me, my family is there for me. My family is here to embrace me...to cocoon me in unconditional love. You know how I realised I loved you? You have asked me millions of times and I have never clearly answered" Avinash told her.

Sanam lay there mesmerised by her husband.

"You know how Papa is a keen gardener. So, one day I was bored, and I wanted to play with him. I found him in the garden planting 'The Curtain creeper' plant.

"Papa, why do you like the creeper variety of plants? They are weak!" I asked him. We had a string of Bougainvillaea and a variety of Climbing Vines all across our house.

"True! It is a creeper which finds it difficult to climb without support," Papa told me.

"But aren't they parasitic? They can't stand on their own and take support of a wall or a railing! Wouldn't it be suffocating for the Walls?" I asked him.

"You have a point there Avinash! But I don't know why I have always felt otherwise. Why do we always assume that the wall would hate it if the vines cling to it? It could be feeling fulfilled too. Some walls like to be clung on to! To be loved by someone so dearly that their life depends on you...that's sheer love. True love never suffocates you...it grows on you...Lucky are those who get to see such a pure form of love!" Papa explained.

The thirteen-year-old 'me' had not understood much then, but the recently married Avinash understood what his father meant that day. Somewhere in the dark wilderness, Sanam you had creeped in like a Climbing Vine and entwined yourself around my heart taking my loneliness, angst and heartache away. That was the moment I knew I was so deeply in love with you Baby. But that was the time I thought I was the wall, and you were the creeper. I realise today: You are the wall...keeping me steady and I am the creeper just wound around you for my existence. Don't ever leave me...no matter whatever the world says...They don't know a thing! You are...hence I am," Avinash told her.

Avinash wiped Sanam's silent tears and kissed her. There they lay entwined like a couple of climbing vines...entangled souls...complimenting each other in every way possible. Such was their love...such was their destiny.

BOOK II- #TRUE LOVE AND A CHANGE OF HEART

Dr. Rajeev Kedia, a famous Cardiologist, shifts to Chicago to take over his late but estranged father's hospital. Heartbroken by the recent death of his grandmother, he seeks refuge in the city of his birth. He crosses paths with a fellow Cardiologist, Dr. Vidya Iyengar and sparks fly. Mislead by the circumstances, Dr. Rajeev is forced to believe the worst about Vidya. At the same time, he is unable to deny that he feels this insane attraction towards her. Will the maze of misunderstandings untangle and will the truth reveal itself? Will the handsome Cardiologist finally find #True Love and have a change of heart?

BOOK III- #TRUE LOVE AND NO ONE ELSE

"He loves me....he loves me not!"

Agastya Avinash Shastri and Anaya Rajeev Kedia were childhood sweethearts. It was an open secret and everyone in the family expected them to get together when they grew up. But is finding #True Love so easy? Contrary to the expectations, Anaya and Agastya grew apart with the passing years. Agastya is now a part of the Indian Cricket team and Anaya is studying Performing Arts. After years, Anaya has returned to India for her classical dance training. Will she be able to rekindle the love she thought she once saw in Agastya's eyes? Will Agastya get back with Anaya?

ACKNOWLEDGEMENTS

A big thanks to my husband, who is the driving force behind this book.
The following have been mentioned in the book:
Roi na album- composed and penned by Nirmaan
Laava - SikhiWiki, free Sikh encyclopedia.
Kashta Saree Draping with Regular Shot Saree - Style Video | Aarmus
Ganesh Festivals - Siddhivinayak Temple, Mumbai
https://www.riddlesandanswers.com/v/229688
'Jugni' from the movie 'Queen'.
'Neele neele ambar par' from movie 'Kalakar'-1983
Jaadugar tere naina-Man Mandir- 1971
Anamika -1972
Satte Pe Satta | R. D. Burman | Asha Bhosle -1981
Phir Bhi Tumko Chaahunga Song | Mithoon | Half Girlfriend-2017
Sorry by Justin Beiber
Zaroorat Hai Zaroorat Hai
Zaroorat Hai Zaroorat Hai Song | Kishore Kumar | Manmauji- 1962
Pungi - Agent Vinod 2012
'Let's talk about sex, baby' by SALT n PEPA
Mana Ho Tum Behad Haseen Song | K J Yesudas | Toote Khilone
"Aaj ham ishq ka izahaar karein to kya ho?- Trishul 1978
Aana Mere Pyar Ko - Kabhi Haan Kabhi Naa|-1994
Dard-E-Dil.. Dard-E-Jigar - Karz- 1980
Phoolon Ke Rang Se- movie Prem Pujari-1970

Munda sada doli chad gaya- Dostana 2008

www.ingramcontent.com/pod-product-compliance
Lightning Source LLC
LaVergne TN
LVHW091611070526
838199LV00044B/762